THE UNITED STATES AIR FORCE
IN SOUTHEAST ASIA

The War in South Vietnam
The Years of the Offensive
1965–1968

John Schlight

OFFICE OF AIR FORCE HISTORY
UNITED STATES AIR FORCE
WASHINGTON, D.C., 1988

Library of Congress Cataloging in Publication Data

Schlight, John
   The war in South Vietnam: the years of the offensive, 1965–1968
   (The United States Air Force in Southeast Asia)
   Bibliography: p. 385
   Includes Index
   1. Vietnamese conflict, 1961–1975—Aerial operations, American. 2. United
States. Air Force—History—Vietnamese Conflict, 1961–1975. I. Title. II. Series.
DS558.8.S34 1988   959.704'348—dc19   88–14030
ISBN 0–912799–51–X

Foreword

This volume, the latest published by the Office of Air Force History in the *United States Air Force in Southeast Asia* series, looks at the Air Force's support of the ground war in South Vietnam between 1965 and early 1968. The book covers the period from the time when the United States began moving from an advisory role into one of active involvement to just before the time when the United States gradually began disengaging from the war. The final scene is the successful air campaign conducted during the Communists' siege of the Marine camp at Khe Sanh. While the actual siege lasted from late January to the middle of March 1968, enemy preparations for the encirclement—greatly increased truck traffic and enemy troop movements—were seen as early as October 1967. A subsequent volume in the Southeast Asia series will take up the story with the Communists' concurrent Tet offensive during January and February 1968.

Air Force assistance in South Vietnam during the war was principally of two kinds: close air support of troops on the battlefield, by both tactical fighters and B–52s, and the airlift of supplies and personnel. In addition to close air support and airlift, the Air Force performed many other important missions ancillary to the ground war, including reconnaissance, intelligence, psychological warfare, defoliation, destruction of enemy reinforcements and supplies, medical evacuation, and pacification and civic action.

Historically, close air support has occupied a lower priority in the hierarchy of Air Force missions than strategic bombing and interdiction. In theory since the 1930s, and in actuality since World War II, the Air Force has seen itself primarily as the strategic deliverer of destructive force on the industrial and economic heartland of an enemy. Preventing the flow of enemy reinforcements by interdicting them far from the battlefield was also considered an inherently important and effective function of air power. Close air support, for a variety of historical and doctrinal reasons, had been deemed a less fruitful use of air resources. As a consequence, more attention has been paid by historians of the conflict in Southeast Asia to the bombing campaigns against North Vietnam and the interdiction efforts against the Ho Chi Minh Trail in Laos than to the less dramatic but no less important air efforts within South Vietnam. In this volume Col. John Schlight, formerly Deputy Chief of the Office of Air Force History, describes the many issues that were awakened when the Air Force was forced to adapt some of its resources and doctrine to a jungle war in South Vietnam.

Among these issues was the question of who would command and who would control the air instrument. The Southeast Asia war was the second major test of America's unified command structure for theater warfare since its formal adoption in the National Security Act of 1947. The earlier test in Korea had shown the command structure to be effective but cumbersome and had resulted in some serious disagreements between the services. It was hoped that the unified command system could be improved in Vietnam and that American air resources could be kept intact for more effective use. As this volume shows, several major obstacles rendered this search for unity and centralization extremely difficult.

The use of airlift was a less contentious issue, but it shared somewhat in the command and control tension. The creation since Korea by the U.S. Army of an airmobile division with its own helicopters presented a serious challenge to the Air Force's airlift mission. Colonel Schlight traces the stages by which accommodation was reached on this issue as the war progressed.

The Air Force adapted to the realities of Vietnam on many levels. In some cases, long-abandoned production facilities had to be resurrected. Aircraft, weapon systems, and munitions were modified to meet the demands of the alien environment. Personnel and training practices, geared for nuclear warfare, were revamped for a war that harked back to an earlier age. Jet fighter pilots, trained for nuclear war, flew observation planes at 100 miles an hour; fighter-bombers and B–52s, designed for nuclear strikes, dropped iron bombs on enemy troops; training planes served as fighter-bombers; transport planes were employed as gunships, dropped flares, and defoliated the thick jungle underbrush; and radar for scoring practice bombing from the ground was used in reverse to direct fighters and bombers to their targets. These and other anomalies form the basis of the jet-age Air Force conducting a limited war against an enemy fighting an insurgency in a jungle environment. The study of this war, particularly that portion fought in the skies over South Vietnam in the years 1965 to 1968, has much to teach those who will apply air power into the twenty-first century.

RICHARD H. KOHN
Chief, Office of Air Force History

Preface

In times of war, air power contributes to a nation's objectives in a variety of ways. It is used to disrupt the enemy's psychological equanimity at home, observe his military preparations and activities from above, impede his movement of military resources to the battlefield, strike his ground forces as they close with friendly troops, ward off his attacks from the skies, and transport friendly troops and supplies to and from the battlefield. During four air wars in Southeast Asia between 1961 and 1973, American aircraft, at different times and in different arenas, performed the functions of strategic bombing, reconnaissance, and interdiction over North Vietnam; reconnaissance and interdiction of the trails in southern Laos; reconnaissance, interdiction, and close air support in the war waged by Laotian tribesmen against the Communists in northern Laos; and close air support, airlift, reconnaissance, air defense, and attacks against enemy supply lines and reinforcements in support of American and South Vietnamese ground forces in South Vietnam. This volume describes the U.S. Air Force's roles in the latter of these four air wars during the period of greatest intensity, between 1965 and early 1968. Other volumes in this series round out the story.

Before the war, close air support, because it ceded much control of aircraft to ground commanders, was not a favored mission of the Air Force. Anchored for decades in the strategic nuclear mission, many airmen viewed direct support of ground forces as the least efficient use of the air weapon. Despite their conviction that enemy resources were more effectively dealt with before they arrived at the battlefield, it became necessary from time to time and for a variety of reasons to use aircraft for close air support. The conflict in South Vietnam was one of those occasions. This study examines not only the results of employing air power this way, but also the tactics and techniques that evolved in an unfamiliar jungle environment, the relationship of the close air support mission to other types of missions being flown, and the interplay between the Air Force's activities and those of the other air forces that were fighting the Communists.

A special word of thanks is due to John Huston and Dick Kohn, who, as directors of the Air Force's history program, provided a sufficiently contemplative atmosphere for research and writing. David Chenoweth labored mightily in making the text publicly presentable. A special tribute is

PREFACE

in order here for Ken Sams, without whose imaginative historical work in Southeast Asia the story of the Air Force in South Vietnam would be incomplete.

John Schlight

The Author

From the early 1950s, when he flew aircraft in support of the French in Indochina, through his final assignment as Deputy Chief of the Office of Air Force History, Col. John Schlight's 31-year Air Force career bracketed America's involvement in the Southeast Asia conflict. In Southeast Asia again in 1969 and 1970, he was in Vietnam as Deputy Director of Project CHECO (Contemporary Historical Evaluation of Combat Operations), one of the Air Force's historical efforts in the war. Possessing the MA and PhD degrees from Princeton University, he has taught military history at the United States Air Force Academy, the National War College in Washington, D.C., and at several universities in the United States and overseas. From 1977 to 1981 he directed the Vietnam War section at the Air Force History Office. In addition to articles in both medieval European and modern American military history, he is the author of *Monarchs and Mercenaries* (1968) and *Henry II Plantagenet* (1973) and the editor of *The Second Indochina War* (1985). He is currently Chief of the Southeast Asia Branch at the U.S. Army's Center of Military History.

United States Air Force
Historical Advisory Committee
(As of December 1, 1987)

Contents

CONTENTS

CONTENTS

CONTENTS

Page

Page

Tables

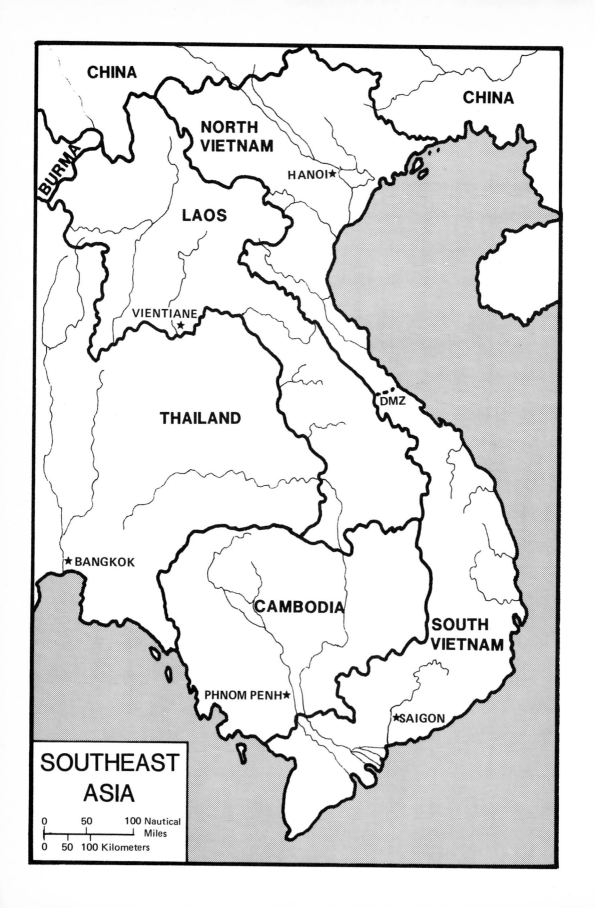

CHINA

NORTH
VIETNAM

CHINA

BURMA

HANOI★

LAOS

VIENTIANE
★

THAILAND

DMZ

★ BANGKOK

CAMBODIA

SOUTH
VIETNAM

PHNOM PENH★

★SAIGON

SOUTHEAST
ASIA

0   50   100 Nautical
                        Miles
0   50 100 Kilometers

Introduction

The Advisory Years
1955–1964

America's direct entanglement with the travails of South Vietnam began shortly after the Geneva accords of 1954 divided Vietnam in half. This agreement ended the conflict between the French and the insurgent Viet Minh and required the withdrawal of French forces to below the 17th parallel, the line dividing the two Vietnams. Before this time, the U.S. policy for Southeast Asia had been ambivalent: on the one hand, the United States had opposed the reestablishment of French colonial rule there after World War II; on the other, it needed French support for its proposed European Defense Community. As a compromise, between 1946 and 1954 the United States provided economic and military aid to the French in their fight against the Viet Minh in Vietnam, but stopped short of assuming a direct combat role. This military and economic assistance was predicated on the French eventually granting independence to Vietnam, Laos, and Cambodia.

With the defeat of the French at Dien Bien Phu early in 1954, which led to their subsequent retreat from Indochina, the United States took over as patron and benefactor of the fledgling southern nation. Involvement in so distant a region reflected America's global determination to forestall the spread of communism. This policy of containment, originally a response to Soviet expansion in eastern Europe during the late 1940s, was reinforced in Asia by the Communist victory in China in 1949 and the North Korean invasion of South Korea the following year. By 1955, U.S. policymakers were depicting the newly created South Vietnamese republic as the leading Southeast Asian domino, with its capitulation to communism leading to the similar submergence of its neighbors.

1

THE WAR IN SOUTH VIETNAM

In Saigon, the capital of South Vietnam, the principal instrument of U.S. aid was the Military Assistance Advisory Group (MAAG), one of twenty-three such groups the United States maintained in Third World countries around the globe. After 1955, the efforts of the MAAG, Vietnam, were guided by three politico-military policies. In line with the containment strategy, the United States sought to resist Communist advances by relying on the armed forces of the threatened nations without direct U.S. combat participation. Accordingly, the group's activities were limited to giving counsel and advice and to providing equipment and training under the Military Assistance Program. Second, despite a warning by the Joint Chiefs of Staff to Secretary of State John Foster Dulles that President Ngo Dinh Diem's government was weak and had to be strengthened before an effective army could be built, American policy emphasized creating a strong military force in hopes that it, in turn, would lead to the development of a viable government. As a result, the advisory group was thrust into the forefront and, at times, into conflict with the U.S. ambassador and his country team, of which the MAAG was a part. The third policy, stemming from the United States' recent experience in Korea, called for shaping South Vietnam's armed forces primarily to meet a large-scale invasion from the north, rather than to deal with subversion in the south. Memories of the Chinese inundation of Korea were still vivid, leading to the American view that monolithic communism, spearheaded by the Chinese, represented the chief threat to the area. These three policies determined for the next decade the type of organization, equipment, training, and counsel that the advisory group provided for the ground, air, and naval components of the Republic of Vietnam's armed forces.

Although the United States was not signatory to the Geneva accords, it at first abided by that agreement's provision limiting the size of the advisory group to 342 officers and enlisted personnel. This number doubled early in 1956, however, with the addition of Army logistic personnel needed to recover and ship back to the United States the surplus military equipment left after the French departure. The MAAG chief, as well as 535 of its 740 personnel, were members of the U.S. Army,[1] while the Air Force had 68 representatives. Overwhelming emphasis was placed on developing the South Vietnamese Army, while the Vietnamese Air Force was assigned minor support roles of airlift, paradrop, reconnaissance, and medical evacuation. It was envisioned that any tactical air support that might be needed against an invasion from the north would be obtained from members of the Southeast Asia Treaty Organization outside Vietnam.[2]

Diem's government at first proved unexpectedly strong in overcoming internal opposition and in preparing an agenda for internal reform. As a result, in 1959 the leaders in Hanoi decided to resort to force to overthrow the southern regime and began gradually to infiltrate men and equipment to bolster the southern revolutionaries, the Viet Cong. Although aware of the increasing tempo of attacks throughout South Vietnam, Diem's secretiveness and suspicions led him to keep this intelligence to himself; and the United States continued to prepare the South Vietnamese against overt attack from the north.

By the time of President John F. Kennedy's inauguration in January 1961, the South Vietnamese Army of 150,000 had been organized into 7 conventional infantry divisions, an airborne group, and 19 separate battalions. In contrast, the Vietnamese Air Force had but 4,000 personnel in 6 squadrons: 2 C–47 transport squadrons, 2 L–19 (O–1) liaison squadrons, an H–19 helicopter squadron, and an AD–6 (A–1H) fighter squadron. Most of these aircraft were obsolescent, and the service was short of trained pilots and technically proficient support personnel.

The containment policy suffered several sharp reverses during the first months of Kennedy's administration in 1961. An unsuccessful invasion of Cuba in April, a humiliating summit conference in Vienna in June with Soviet Premier Nikita S. Khrushchev, and the Communist construction in August of the wall separating East Berlin from West Berlin threw into question the adequacy of America's total reliance on nuclear weapons to discourage adventurism at lower levels of violence. Most serious for Asia was a string of military successes by the North Vietnamese-sponsored Pathet Lao Communists in their attempt to overrun the government of Laos.

In light of these setbacks, Kennedy, strongly influenced by his military advisor, Maxwell Taylor, began to modify the country's policy of nuclear deterrence. Taylor, a highly successful World War II commander of the 101st Airborne Division in Europe and later Chief of Staff of the Army, had long doubted the ability of the threat of nuclear weapons by itself to prevent smaller conflicts. Motivated in part by his desire to restore to the U.S. Army a role in national strategy that it had not enjoyed since World War II, Taylor advocated, and Kennedy initiated, a strategy of flexible response in which the United States would have forces that could react to aggression at any level, from nuclear attack to local insurgencies.[3] The most immediate effect of this shift in policy was an increased American presence in South Vietnam beginning late in 1961.

Although the Laotian situation eased with the signing of the Declaration and Protocol on the Neutrality of Laos in Geneva on July 23, 1962, the implications of the crisis for its neighbors led to an increased U.S. commitment to South Vietnam to a level just short of combat. Between the end of 1961 and the opening months of 1965, the size of the Air Force contingent multiplied almost a hundredfold, from 68 to 6,600 (table 1) personnel and from a handful of liaison planes to 84 aircraft of various types. Many of these men were members of irregular units employing aircraft and tactics improvised for the counterinsurgency environment.

3

Farm Gate aircraft in Vietnam in 1962: in the right foreground, a T–28; next to it, a B–26, and in the background, a row of T–6s.

By the end of 1964, the tactical cutting edge inside the country was the Farm Gate operation at Bien Hoa Air Base near Saigon, an outgrowth of the original air commando detachment that had introduced an assortment of propeller-driven C–47s, B–26s, and T–28s into Vietnam during the late 1961 buildup. Farm Gate at first trained Vietnamese pilots in counterinsurgency air operations, principally to support the Vietnamese ground troops; but as the war heated up, combat missions began to outnumber those devoted to training. At the outset, these planes had been flown by pilots on six-month assignments from the Tactical Air Command. By May 1964, however, the flyers were on one-year tours. The aircraft bore Vietnamese insignia, and an indigenous observer was supposed to be aboard each combat training flight. At the beginning of 1965, there were two air commando squadrons (the 1st and the 602d) flying fifty A–1Es, also propeller-driven, that had gradually replaced the worn-out World War II craft.* [4]

Other fighter aircraft were positioned within striking distance of Vietnam at bases in the Philippines, Okinawa, Taiwan, and Japan. In 1962 the Air Force had begun rotating several jet fighter squadrons between the United States and these stations close to Vietnam. Aircraft and members of these squadrons moved in and out of forward bases in South Vietnam and

---

*See Appendix 1, Major USAF Units and Aircraft in South Vietnam, 1962–1968.

Thailand. Following the Gulf of Tonkin incident in early August 1964, two squadrons of eighteen B–57s* each quickly moved from Clark AB to Bien Hoa; and the Air Force, in a deployment codenamed One Buck, rushed into the area a composite air strike force of one F–105 squadron, two F–100 squadrons, three squadrons of C–130 transports, and six RF–101 reconnaissance aircraft.[5]

Table 1

U.S. Military Personnel in Southeast Asia
1960–1968

Year	Army	Navy	USAF	USMC	USCG	Total
South Vietnam						
1960	790	15	68	2		875
1961	2,050	103	1,006	5		3,164
1962	7,890	455	2,429	552		11,326
1963	10,119	757	4,630	757		16,263
1964	14,697	1,109	6,604	900		23,310
1965	116,755	8,446	20,620	38,190	303	184,314
1966	239,422	23,260	52,913	69,235	448	385,278
1967	319,521	31,669	55,908	78,013	476	485,587
1968	359,794	36,088	58,434	81,377	441	536,134
Thailand						
1960	218	38	44	19		319
1961	424	39	57	22		542
1962	2,755	372	1,212	14		4,353
1963	2,730	285	1,086	25		4,126
1964	3,374	153	2,943	35		6,505
1965	4,765	185	9,117	40		14,107
1966	7,995	241	26,113	38	102	34,489
1967	10,330	656	33,395	42	94	44,517
1968	11,330	365	35,791	51	94	47,631

Source: MACV and MACTHAI

American forward air controllers (FACs) during these advisory years had been performing a combined training and combat operation, both in their own squadron (the 19th Tactical Air Support Squadron) at Bien Hoa with the

---

*Half of the thirty-six B–57s rotated back to Clark on October 22, only days before a mortar attack at Bien Hoa destroyed five and damaged many of the remaining Canberras.

Vietnamese Air Force (VNAF) and at province and major ground force headquarters throughout the country. Since the squadron's arrival in the middle of 1963 with twenty-three O–1 Bird Dogs and forty-four pilots, it had been attempting to teach the Vietnamese to perform visual reconnaissance and to direct air strikes against the Viet Cong. Air Force planners thought originally that the training could be done in one year. However, unforeseen problems, such as the Vietnamese practice of siphoning off pilots into fighter cockpits and their penchant for standing back and letting the energetic Americans fly many of the combat missions, slowed the VNAF's progress toward self-sufficiency. When the squadron was turned over to the Vietnamese after one year, they were unable to assume the controller role; and by January 1965, the squadron was back in American hands. By then the Air Force had seventy-six controllers stationed throughout the country.[6]

As with other facets of operations in South Vietnam during these early years, the aerial reconnaissance effort supporting the Army of the Republic of Vietnam (ARVN) was shaped by the climate and geography of the country, the insurgent nature of the war, and the existing command structure. The most effective way to locate the enemy from the air was through visual reconnaissance by forward air controllers in O–1s or by other pilots flying over the dense jungle. In addition to the Air Force's Bird Dogs, the Vietnamese had three C–47s in the southern Mekong Delta region; and the U.S. Army was flying several OV–1 Mohawks on reconnaissance missions. However, the visual reporting method was far from perfect. Learning from experience that firing at aircraft gave away their positions, the Viet Cong discontinued this practice and, instead, hid or camouflaged themselves when a plane approached. They became masters of concealment. Often an enemy soldier would carry a piece of green khaki tied around his waist and, when alerted, would climb high in a palm tree, tie the khaki to two palms, and use it as a hammock. His weight would bend the palms over his body, shielding him from observation.[7] The appearance of low-flying aircraft signaled the coming of an air strike, and the slow reaction of most attack planes in arriving at the scene gave the enemy ample time to move out of the area before the strike took place. At the beginning of 1965, there still was no systematic visual reconnaissance program that could keep the entire country under surveillance from above.

With all its shortcomings, however, visual reporting was still more widespread than photographic reconnaissance. By late 1961 the Air Force had set up two photo processing units, one at Tan Son Nhut Air Base in

Saigon and the other at Don Muang Airport outside Bangkok in Thailand. The forty-five men who manned each of these units processed and interpreted the film brought in by reconnaissance jets, briefed the pilots on targets, and prepared reports on enemy activity. For the first month, there were four RF–101s at each location; but in November, the Voodoos in South Vietnam returned to Okinawa, leaving the four aircraft at Don Muang as the only jet reconnaissance force in all of Southeast Asia. A year later these planes moved to Tan Son Nhut; and in May 1963, they were joined there by two RB–57s on temporary assignment. By early the following year, the Vietnamese had a reconnaissance squadron of their own that flew T–28s from the Saigon base.

A turning point for both the American and Vietnamese programs came in May of 1964. The beginning of reconnaissance flights over Laos subdivided the Air Force's already meager jet assets. Due to a shortage of fighter pilots, the Vietnamese reconnaissance squadron was disbanded that same month and the pilots retrained to form a new fighter squadron. At the same time, when the U.S. Army added to its fleet of Mohawks, the Air Force command, the 2d Air Division, wanted these aircraft placed under its operation at Tan Son Nhut to form a joint reconnaissance task force. The Military Assistance Command, Vietnam (MACV), 2d Air Division's parent, thought differently and in December 1964 set up its own targeting branch, the Target Research and Analysis Center, at its Saigon headquarters. This further diluted the Air Force reconnaissance effort because the Mohawks were left independent and because many Air Force photo reconnaissance sorties were diverted to support the MACV function.[8] Equally debilitating for the Air Force, it ensured that MACV rather than the 2d Air Division would determine when, where, how, and how frequently reconnaissance missions would be flown.

Traditional photographic reconnaissance was hampered in Vietnam by the triple-tiered jungle canopy that covered much of the country, the frequent poor weather, and the Viet Cong proclivity to move and operate at night. Throughout the early years, both the Air Force and the Army searched for better techniques. They had some success with infrared cameras, which photographed heat radiating from human bodies and campfires. However, photography could not keep up with the mobile enemy; and early in 1965, the Air Force was experimenting with improved airborne detection equipment that could plot the location of Viet Cong radio transmitters on the ground.[9]

One-third of the Air Force's planes in Vietnam at the beginning of 1965 were transports. Two squadrons of C–123 Providers had arrived in 1962 expecting to fly such combat missions as dropping troops and supplies and carrying out assault landings. These aspirations conflicted with the Army's concept of air mobility that emphasized the use of Army transports and helicopters for these functions.[10] Although the issue was still alive early in 1965, the Air Force's airlift contingent, now grown to three squadrons at Tan Son Nhut and one at Da Nang,* had to content itself with flying resupply missions, principally to the fifty outposts strung out along South Vietnam's western border.

When the first Providers arrived in 1962, under the name Mule Train, there was no centralized arrangement for using them. Within a year, MACV had organized the C–123s into a system for South Vietnam and Thailand (the Southeast Asia Airlift System), which it operated through a troop carrier group, the 315th, at Tan Son Nhut. Keeping with its doctrine, however, Army fixed-wing and helicopter airlift planes remained outside this system, attached to the individual ground units.[11] Besides hundreds of airlift helicopters, the Army by early 1965 was operating six companies of CV–2 Caribous, a plane about half the size and with half the load capacity of the C–123. Normally these planes operated at MACV, division, and corps levels, but were pressed into service at lower combat command levels when needed.

By January 1965, the United States Air Force had a sprinkling of jet aircraft in South Vietnam and neighboring Thailand, the remnants of the force that had arrived the preceding August. Besides the reconnaissance RF–101s and RB–57s at Tan Son Nhut, a squadron of air defense F–102s was divided between Tan Son Nhut and Don Muang, and a squadron of F–100s was stationed temporarily at Da Nang. Another squadron of F–100s was located temporarily at Takhli, as was a squadron of F–105s at Korat. Ten B–57s at Bien Hoa were manned by rotating crews from the 8th and 13th Tactical Bomb Squadrons of Clark AB, Philippine Islands.[12] Despite repeated requests from the field to rescind the ban, none of these jets in either country was allowed to fly combat missions in South Vietnam.

The command structure that had evolved for American forces in the conflict mirrored the peculiarities of the theater. For Air Force commanders, this structure posed two problems. One concerned the relationship between the resources they needed for South Vietnam and those they had to use elsewhere in Southeast Asia and the Pacific. The other dealt with the interface between Air Force and non-Air Force planes inside South Vietnam.

The command arrangements that had developed during the advisory period accommodated the first of these issues better than it did the second.

---

*The 309th and 310th Troop Carrier Squadrons and the 19th Air Commando Squadron were at Tan Son Nhut; the 311th Troop Carrier Squadron was at Da Nang. See Appendix 1, Major USAF Units and Aircraft in South Vietnam, 1962–1968.

Left to right: Gen. Hunter Harris, Jr., USAF, Commander in Chief, Pacific Air Forces; Gen. William C. Westmoreland, USA, Commander, Military Assistance Command, Vietnam; and Lt. Gen. Joseph H. Moore, Commander, 2d Air Division.

The MACV, which had replaced the earlier MAAG during the escalation in early 1962, was a subordinate unified command reporting directly to the Commander in Chief, Pacific Command (CINCPAC) in Hawaii. The MACV Commander, Gen. William C. Westmoreland, a combat veteran of World War II and Korea, had commanded both the 82d and 101st Airborne Divisions and subsequently served as Superintendent of the U.S. Military Academy at West Point. As Secretary of Maxwell Taylor's Army General Staff in the mid-1950s, he had played a major part in the Army's drive to augment its role by increasing the ground force component of America's deterrent force.

Relations between the Army and the Air Force within MACV were somewhat unorthodox and at times strained, stemming from the different responsibilities held by the two services. While it was acknowledged that the conflict within the borders of South Vietnam was primarily a ground war in which air power would support the ground troops, CINCPAC's air chief in Hawaii, Gen. Hunter Harris, Jr., Commander of the Pacific Air Forces (PACAF), was also looking at contingencies beyond those borders that could affect the military situation inside them. He opposed both extremes: too wide a dispersal of control over its air assets on the one hand and too narrow a concentration of air power within South Vietnam on the other. Westmoreland was given operational control of the Vietnam-based planes he needed to carry on the war against the Viet Cong, but he lacked control of the carrier-

9

based naval aircraft. The seeds of a future problem for the Air Force were sown when Westmoreland delegated his control of Marine planes in I Corps to the Marine commander in that area. The other aircraft in Southeast Asia were controlled by General Harris, acting through the Thirteenth Air Force in the Philippines. The Air Force's focal point within Vietnam for these arrangements was the Commander of the 2d Air Division in Saigon, Lt. Gen. Joseph H. Moore.

Like Westmoreland, Moore had seen extensive combat experience in World War II, having flown numerous tactical missions in the Philippines and Australia and in Europe during the Normandy invasion and the subsequent campaigns across northern France and the Rhineland. He remained in tactical fighters after the war, commanding several wings and, by 1958, the Ninth Air Force. The following year, he received the Bendix Trophy for setting a new world speed record—1,216 mph—in an F–105 Thunderchief. In January 1964, he moved from his position as operations director of the Tactical Air Command to take over the 2d Air Division in Vietnam. Moore, a boyhood friend of Westmoreland, was now serving both as MACV air component commander for South Vietnam and as the Thirteenth Air Force's forward commander for missions in the rest of Southeast Asia.

For the war inside South Vietnam, the overall MACV arrangements satisfied neither the Air Force nor the Army. As a subordinate unified command, MACV should have had proportional representation from each of the services fighting the war. General Westmoreland, however, did not create a separate Army component commander comparable to his Air Force and Navy component commanders. Without a separate Army staff to handle Army matters, he used the MACV staff for both Army and unified functions. Eighty percent of the staff's efforts were devoted to Army matters, the remainder to joint affairs. Since the small number of Air Force people on the MACV staff were unfamiliar with Army military requirements and operations, these functions were handled for the most part by Army representatives. For example, the chief of MACV plans, the only Air Force general on the staff, was excluded from day-to-day planning and concentrated on long-range matters, such as planning for the Southeast Asia Treaty Organization. He had little to do with the war itself, which was handled by the J–3 Army general. The Air Force was severely underrepresented on the staff. Despite repeated proposals to place more Air Force generals in key MACV positions, Westmoreland had no intention of doing so unless the Air Force were willing to place all its air resources under his command, including the fighters in Thailand and the C–130s delivering material into Vietnam from Pacific bases. PACAF, keeping an eye on the possibility of a larger war, was loathe to tie down all these assets in South Vietnam. As a result, the Air Force lost a good deal of stature with the Army for not "joining the team."[13] MACV remained a unified command in name only, and Air Force leaders were concerned that their ideas about how best to use air power would not be reflected in MACV's plans and operations.[14]

Foremost among these ideas was the need for a centralized focus to plan and operate all American and allied air activity within Vietnam. Issues arose from doctrinal differences between the Army and the Air Force, as well as from different perceptions each service held of its roles and missions, not only in Vietnam, but in the broader arena of national security as well. Each service applied the principle of unity of command differently. For the Army, air power was seen as most responsive to ground needs when there was unity at the operating level, which in Vietnam meant the Vietnamese Army corps area.* Air Force leaders were equally convinced that, both tactically and economically, air power was most efficient, especially in this type of war, when it was centrally controlled at MACV and concentrated at vital flash points. To bring enough of the right kinds of aircraft to bear on these points, the MACV air commander needed the flexibility to call on any or all his assets when he needed them. None should be withheld for "peripheral" engagements. Air power was best employed, and with a minimum of costly duplication, when it was controlled centrally at the MACV level.

Out of these differing views, two separate systems for controlling aircraft were growing up: a tactical air control system (TACS), which directed Air Force and VNAF operations, and an air-ground system, which controlled Army and Marine[†] aviation from each of the four corps tactical zone headquarters. Although recognition of the shortcomings of this arrangement had led in mid–1964 to some closer coordination between the two controlling agencies, a unified tactical control system was not in place at the beginning of 1965.

The goal of the United States Air Force during the advisory years had been to build the Vietnamese Air Force into a balanced air arm capable of supporting Vietnamese ground forces and opposing the threat from the north. Until the escalation in 1962, American support for the Vietnamese had been low key. The small air section of the MAAG had succeeded in converting the Vietnamese way of doing things from French to American. Some new bases and units were activated, aircraft and personnel came to mirror the Air

---

*For military purposes, South Vietnam was at first divided into three and later (November 1962) into four corps tactical zones (CTZs).

†The Marines had a medium helicopter squadron at Da Nang that had moved there from the Mekong Delta in 1962.

Air Vice Marshal
Nguyen Cao Ky, VNAF

Force's system, and American training methods were introduced. Between 1962 and the beginning of 1965, the VNAF created the basic force it was to use for the next 4 years, increasing the number of personnel from 4,000 to over 10,000. The 6 squadrons and 97 aircraft of 1962 had grown to 14 squadrons with 285 planes 3 years later.* The Air Force had shepherded the creation of a command structure in which control flowed, in theory, from VNAF headquarters in Saigon down to 4 tactical wings, an air training center, and a logistics wing.

This expansion was too rapid and left some heavy problems in its wake. The Vietnamese Air Force suffered from a lack of strong direction from the top—a microcosm of the larger national problem. As members of a young service, emerging leaders possessed insufficient flying and managerial experience. Many of those who had such talent, such as Air Vice Marshal Nguyen Cao Ky, VNAF Commander, preferred to invest it in the political market.[15] Ky's decisive support of the government during a coup attempt in September 1964 proved to be a mixed blessing for his air force. While it marked the rise of the service to political prominence, it also drained the VNAF of many of its experienced people. The effects were becoming apparent by early 1965, particularly in the ever-widening chasm that separated the VNAF's headquarters from the squadrons.

This lack of direction hampered the solution of other problems. The combat sortie rate suffered as some key units were diverted from tactical operations and placed on "coup alert" during the seemingly endless political eruptions in Saigon. Air base construction had not kept pace with the influx of people and aircraft, both American and Vietnamese, and there was serious overcrowding of facilities. Still missing were some of the basic elements of an effective combat force. Communication facilities were inadequate. The

---

*Of these squadrons, four were fighter, four were helicopter, four were liaison, and two were air transport.

Vietnamese had a rudimentary reporting system and, consequently, no way to measure the results of their missions.

Absence of centralized control meant that it was impossible for the VNAF to be fully integrated into the tactical air control system the Air Force advisors had installed. Both the central air operations center at Tan Son Nhut and its field tentacles, the local air support operation centers, while technically performing their primary functions of scheduling and coordinating Vietnamese sorties, were actually "after the fact" agencies that did little more than schedule missions demanded by the wings. About seventy-five percent of all Vietnamese fighter attack sorties were being flown against "free strike" targets, which meant they were outside the control of a forward air controller and used little or no intelligence support.[16] The Vietnamese Air Force was still being run largely at the local level and, as a result, was seldom able to respond quickly to calls for assistance from the South Vietnamese ground forces.[17] In the eyes of most American advisors, the VNAF was not yet ready to fly on its own.

Brink Hotel in Saigon after the bombing on December 24, 1964.

Chapter I

End of the Advisory Period
November 1964–April 1965

Indications were plentiful late in 1964 that time was running out on the South Vietnamese and, no less, on the American advisory policy. In the year since the assassinations of Presidents Diem and Kennedy, South Vietnam had been buffeted by a series of changes in governments. At the same time, the growing enemy infiltration from the north now included increasing numbers of regular North Vietnamese soldiers.[1] The United States recognized the gravity of the situation but was having difficulty devising a formula for political success in this feudal, decentralized country. Until November, President Lyndon B. Johnson, occupied with the national election, continued to hope for the emergence of a leader in South Vietnam who could inject a sense of purpose into the struggle against the insurgency. He resisted repeated pressures from many of his counselors to bomb North Vietnam[2] on the grounds that the Saigon government was still too weak to withstand the reaction that was certain to follow such a course of action.

The introduction of a large number of American soldiers into Vietnam was not seriously considered at this time. What few discussions that did take place about sending ground forces to the south centered less on the military than on the psychological benefit of such a move. American decisionmakers were unable to predict whether the presence of American combat forces would strengthen the Vietnamese will to fight or, as Maxwell Taylor, now Ambassador to Vietnam, believed, cause the Vietnamese to "shuck off greater responsibility onto the United States" and "encourage an attitude of let the United States do it."[3]

A series of military and political reverses that began in November 1964 forced the United States to reexamine its priorities for South Vietnam. The Viet Cong, bolstered by North Vietnamese regulars, were displaying new aggressiveness and new tactics. The November mortar attack on Bien Hoa Air Base that destroyed five B–57s and their Christmas Eve bombing of the Brink Hotel American barracks in Saigon showed that they could strike with impunity. When they destroyed a Vietnamese Marine battalion and two ARVN ranger companies at Binh Gia at year's end, it was clear that they were as adept at set piece battles as they had earlier proven themselves at hit-and-run tactics.[4] In the Bien Gia battle, an initial ARVN attempt to rely solely on armed helicopters for close air support against an attacking VC battalion proved inadequate. The South Vietnamese ground commander's subsequent request for VNAF A–1s was turned down at ARVN headquarters, which deemed it unnecessary. The ensuing blood bath changed many official attitudes about tactical air power in Vietnam. General Westmoreland decided, in the aftermath of this defeat, to rely heavily on air power to turn the tide against the mounting enemy offensive.[5] This was to involve not only greater employment of American and Vietnamese A–1s, but eventually also the use of jet aircraft and carrier-based planes.

Concurrent with this decision to use U.S. tactical aircraft against the enemy in South Vietnam were decisions to employ air power directly against the north and against the infiltration routes in Laos. Before the Bien Hoa attack, the Joint Chiefs of Staff were split over the question of which should come first in American policy—governmental stability in Saigon or military pressure against North Vietnam. Gen. Curtis E. LeMay, the Air Force Chief, and Gen. Wallace M. Greene, Jr., the Commandant of the Marine Corps, advocated, in military councils, bombing the north as a means of strengthening the Saigon regime. At first the other chiefs agreed with Ambassador Taylor that political stability must precede escalated military action against Hanoi. The loss of American lives and the destruction of the B–57s, however, united the chiefs; and on the 1st of November, they recommended sending American aircraft to bomb infiltration trails in Laos and to attack targets in North Vietnam. However, the Secretaries of State and Defense counseled patience; and President Johnson, concerned not only for the safety of American dependents in Vietnam but also about the outcome of the coming presidential election, heeded their advice. No reprisals were undertaken. On the first of December, however, Johnson reluctantly approved the first step of a two-phase program against the north. Covert naval attacks by the South Vietnamese on the north and American aerial raids against the supply trails in Laos were increased. On the 14th, the latter became a formal interdiction program called Barrel Roll. President Johnson also agreed in principle to the idea of reprisal bombing of the north for any "unusual actions." Although the United States did not retaliate for the Brink Hotel bombing, that incident, along with the Vietnamese Army's display of ineptitude at Binh Gia the following week, won over Ambassador Taylor to the side of those who favored reprisals against the north.

This stepped-up Viet Cong activity threatened to swamp American air assets. The United States had enough airplanes in the country and at bases in nearby countries to handle the situation, but self-imposed restrictions limited their value. The 1954 Geneva accords had banned the introduction of jets into South Vietnam; and the United States, while not a signer of the accords, had tried over the years to abide by its spirit.

Until the Tonkin Gulf incident the preceding August, the civilian leadership had rejected recommendations to use jets in the country. In the wake of that attack on the American destroyer *Maddox,* the thirty-six B–57 Canberra bombers flew to Bien Hoa and several squadrons of F–100 Super Sabres began staging in and out of Da Nang. These tactical fighter squadrons deployed temporarily with personnel rotating after ninety days and aircraft rotating every six months. However, the ban on their use in combat inside South Vietnam continued. The Canberras flew visual reconnaissance missions along the roads leading into Saigon, and the F–100s flew in Barrel Roll.

After the defeat at Binh Gia, General Westmoreland, anticipating an acceleration of enemy raids in II Corps during the coming Tet holidays in early February and skeptical of the ability of the politically oriented VNAF to contain them, asked again to be allowed to use the jets in South Vietnam. On the 27th of January he received permission to do so, but only in emergencies and only after receiving mission-by-mission approval from the Joint Chiefs and the concurrence of Ambassador Taylor and the Vietnamese high command.[6]

No occasion arose to use the jets in South Vietnam during the holidays; but a Viet Cong mortar attack near Pleiku on the 7th of February set in motion a series of American responses that, taken together, added up to a new strategy of primary reliance on air strikes against the north (along with bolstering defenses around the southern bases from which the attack planes were launched). The Pleiku raid brought a change of heart to most members of the National Security Council in Washington. Those who had formerly insisted that political reform of the Saigon government must precede attacks on the north now agreed to immediate reprisal. U.S. Navy jets from the carriers *Coral Sea, Hancock,* and *Ranger* bombed the Dong Hoi barracks just north of the Demilitarized Zone on the 7th; and the next day, VNAF planes struck at Vinh, while Farm Gate aircraft hit barracks at Chap Le. These raids, called Flaming Dart, were followed on the 11th by another attack against Dong Hoi.

While this second series of strikes was taking place, fifteen B–52 Stratofortresses took off from Mather Air Force Base in California and another fifteen left Barksdale Air Force Base in Louisiana. Within hours, thirty-two KC–135 refueling aircraft had departed the same bases. The bombers arrived at Andersen Air Force Base, Guam, on the 12th; and by the next day, all the tankers had landed at Kadena Air Base on Okinawa. This

Marines landing at Da Nang, March 1965.

contingency task force was prepared, if needed, to join in the raids against North Vietnam.[7] After a three-week lull the bombing attacks resumed, but without the B–52s, in what soon became a systematic program called Rolling Thunder. Although the Stratofortresses were ready to hit twenty targets in the north, it was decided to keep them in reserve. Eyes now turned toward air power as the principal instrument for bringing Hanoi to the negotiating table.

At the same time, defenses in South Vietnam were shored up against expected Viet Cong reaction to the bombing. On the 8th of March, a U.S. Marine battalion landed at Da Nang from waiting ships, while the Air Force flew in a second battalion from Okinawa using 76 C–130s. The 3,500 Marines took up defensive positions around Da Nang Air Base, the main base in South Vietnam from which Air Force jets launched their strikes against the north.[8]

General Westmoreland had first exercised his emergency power to use jets on the 19th of February when B–57s from Bien Hoa attacked enemy troops east of Saigon, the first use of American jets in the south. For several weeks the Canberras continued to hit the areas around Saigon, joined by F–100s from Da Nang that struck the enemy farther north in II Corps. On March 9, most of the remaining restrictions on jets were removed, essentially giving Westmoreland carte blanche to use the jets at his discretion.

This was a new environment for jets and the crews began developing tactics and procedures to cope with it. The key to success of the attack missions, whether they were in close support of troops in contact, direct support against enemy troops who were not engaged in battle, or interdiction against enemy supplies, lay in striking a balance between hitting the target accurately and avoiding ground fire. Since the enemy was using only small arms against the planes, the flyers remained above 1,500 feet as much as possible. They devised attack patterns to confuse the enemy and keep him from anticipating the direction from which the strikes would come.

Ordinarily, a flight of four jets linked up with the forward air control plane; and while all the aircraft were en route to the target, the FAC and flight leader carried on a vital and often lively dialogue. The FAC first gave the flight leader a rundown on the mission, pointing out the peculiarities of the target, any restrictions to tactics, the directions of attack and breakaway to be used by the fighters, and the location of friendly troops, if any. The flight leader could, and often did, suggest changes that, if agreeable to the FAC, were adopted. When they reached the target, the FAC marked it with a smoke rocket. Then the fighters, still under FAC control, struck.

A favorite tactic used by the F–100s to throw the enemy off guard was the "wheel" pattern. The general flow of aircraft around the target was circular, corresponding to the rim of a wheel, with the hub representing the target and the spokes the attack paths. While the leader made his initial run along one of the spokes, the second plane continued on around the rim and flew at the target along a spoke roughly a quarter of the way around the wheel. Continuing around, the third aircraft attacked from a heading approximately reciprocal to that of the leader, while the fourth plane came in on a heading about 180 degrees opposite that of the second craft. This called for close radio contact between all the planes. Aircraft spacing was critical. Before a pilot could strike, he had to make sure that the preceding aircraft was off the target and that he had the FAC in sight. The aim was to have continuous bombardment of the target. When the planes carried different types of ordnance, they alternated between high and low angles of attack to confuse the enemy further.[9]

It was often impossible to get a clear picture from the air of what these raids accomplished, since the target area was usually obscured by trees, smoke, or darkness.[10] Ground followups were rare, particularly in the enemy areas of War Zones C and D north of Saigon. This absence of quantifiable bomb damage assessment allowed for differences of opinion between advocates of propeller aircraft and those who favored jets.

This "prop versus jet" controversy was to continue in one form or another throughout the war. The direct beneficiaries of the jet strikes, the American Army senior corps advisors in the field and the Vietnamese chiefs of the districts where the attacks took place, praised them as sorely needed morale boosters for the Vietnamese Army.[11] Some American diplomatic officials in Saigon, however, who had opposed the introduction of jets in the first place, questioned the wisdom of using them, pointing not only to the

19

Geneva accords but also to the potential for jets to alienate the Vietnamese and to hit friendly troops and civilians in areas under Viet Cong control.[12] Many Air Force personnel, particularly those flying the A–1Es, believed the propeller planes were more suitable in South Vietnam than were the jets. General Moore's appraisal from Saigon early in March was cautious and based on tactical considerations. He warned that jet aircraft should not be viewed as substitutes for ground action and exhorted his staff not to rely too heavily on them. Further, he said, there was a danger that Vietnamese ground commanders, knowing that they would get American rather than Vietnamese pilots, might call in jets against targets that would be better attacked by the slower conventional A–1 planes.[13] In addition, both he and General Westmoreland had been disturbed by the number of jet missions that had been canceled since the 19th of February because final approval from the Vietnamese Joint General Staff was not obtained in time. The situation improved when, on the 9th of March, the MACV Commander was permitted to use his own discretion in launching jets for missions in the south that the Vietnamese could not handle.[14]

A simultaneous slackening of the reins on nonjets moved the United States further from advice to open combat. From the beginning of the American involvement in Vietnam, the advisory and training nature of the U.S. mission had required that a trained Vietnamese pilot be aboard all fighter aircraft and armed helicopter missions. This rule had been relaxed slightly late in 1964 when a critical shortage of qualified Vietnamese pilots made it unworkable and the Joint Chiefs agreed that the flights could take place with Vietnamese student pilots or observers rather than experienced pilots. With the rise of military activity early in 1965, even this became difficult; and scrambles were frequently delayed and even aborted due to the lack of Vietnamese observers. For example, Col. William E. Bethea, Commander of the 34th Tactical Group at Bien Hoa, seldom found enough observers to keep all his planes in the air. He estimated that he could double his daily sortie rate if the Vietnamese assigned him the forty-four observers they promised, rather than the twenty-two or so he usually had on hand. On one desperate occasion he took an observer out of jail, fed him, sent him aloft, and then returned him to confinement after the mission.[15] However, although occasionally useful in identifying targets when flying with a FAC in a liaison plane, an observer rendered little assistance on fighter or armed helicopter missions. His primary function was to lend legitimacy to the employment of U.S. firepower.[16]

General Moore relayed these difficulties to Washington late in February, emphasizing that the observer rule was not only cutting down the sortie rate, but was at least partially responsible for the slow reaction time of strike aircraft. Washington agreed on the 9th of March to drop the requirement for a Vietnamese companion on air commando flights. On the same day,

Secretary of Defense Robert S. McNamara approved putting USAF markings on Farm Gate planes to replace the Vietnamese insignia they had borne over the years.[17] In his request for this change, General Westmoreland pointed out that, due to the gravity of the Viet Cong threat, the mission of air commando squadrons had shifted strongly toward combat and they were flying eighty percent of their sorties in support of the Vietnamese Army.[18] With the removal of these restrictions on both jet and prop aircraft, the Air Force became the first of the services officially to play an overt combat role in South Vietnam.

Throughout March, contingency military planning was running ahead of an American decision on an overall strategy for Vietnam. The Pacific Command had developed several plans for the use, if need be, of American forces either to take a direct part in combatting the insurgency, to counter a North Vietnamese invasion of the south, or to defend against a sweep through Southeast Asia by either the Chinese alone or in concert with the army of Hanoi. This last possibility hung like a shadow over the military planners, causing a rift between the Air Force Chief, Gen. John P. McConnell,* and the other members of the Joint Chiefs of Staff.

The issue centered on whether the United States, while waiting for the Vietnamese Army to rebuild itself, should place the weight of its effort on the ground in Vietnam (Plan 32) or in the air and seas around the periphery of China (Plan 39). General McConnell, strongly supported by his field commander at PACAF, General Harris, opted for the latter strategy, warning that Southeast Asia must not be viewed in isolation from the rest of the western Pacific. The plan the Air Force favored called for a holding action in the south, assisted by more direct support and reconnaissance aircraft, while deploying, initially, fifteen strike squadrons around the edges of China. These aircraft, located in Taiwan, Okinawa, Japan, and Korea, would back up the operations in South Vietnam; deter (or defeat if they did not deter) the Chinese from adventures in Laos, South Vietnam, Cambodia, or Thailand; and oppose any diversionary military actions the Communists might undertake in the northern Pacific.[19] McConnell stressed the advantages of this approach over a ground strategy. It was the most flexible of the plans being considered, adaptable to any potential development—enabling the United States to call the shots by engaging or disengaging the enemy at times and places of its own choosing. Since it relied more on technology than on

---

*General LeMay had retired on February 8, 1965.

manpower and since a large part of the forces were already in place or on alert, it did not require extensive logistic preparations and could be turned on and off more quickly. In short, it avoided getting the United States bogged down in a land war in Asia.

The political and military climate in neither Washington nor Saigon favored such a strategy. Intelligence sources in Washington played down the Chinese threat.[20] In Saigon, Westmoreland was convinced that the battle of Binh Gia had signaled the beginning by Hanoi of what it considered the final phase of the war. In his judgment, the enemy was close to cutting South Vietnam in two at a line running from Qui Nhon on the coast westward through Pleiku. The South Vietnamese were proving ineffective and the MACV commander pressed for American ground reinforcements.

Westmoreland's conviction that the enemy must be met on the ground in South Vietnam was conveyed back to Washington early in March by Gen. Harold K. Johnson, the Army Chief of Staff, after he visited Saigon. Johnson painted a somber picture of South Vietnamese disintegration and recommended twenty-one military steps to halt the Communist tide. He also carried a request from Westmoreland for an American Army division for the Pleiku area in the central highlands. These American troops would hold the line by providing a favorable force ratio between the South Vietnamese and the enemy during the next few months while the former were bringing themselves to full strength.[21] As the South Vietnamese Army became healthy, the Americans would gradually take over the job of guarding the enclaves in the south, releasing the Vietnamese soldiers for combat. The final proposal was to stop the infiltration from the north by sealing off the Demilitarized Zone and its extension into Laos with four divisions of American and SEATO troops.[22]

The twenty-one steps included little that was new, calling for accelerating programs already under way. However, they did reflect MACV's conviction that the most immediate step in stopping the enemy would have to be taken by air power (or, as General Johnson labeled it, "heavy firepower"). More than half of the recommendations called for increased air activity, including sending three more Air Force squadrons and three Army companies of O-1s for surveillance, three more Army companies of helicopters for mobility, removing restrictions on Rolling Thunder, increasing air reconnaissance against Viet Cong-infested coastal areas, improving aerial interdiction of the Ho Chi Minh Trail by separating it operationally from the rest of Laos, and speeding up the construction of jet airfields.

Only on the question of sending additional jet fighter-bombers to South Vietnam did General Johnson hesitate, recommending that the decision be deferred until the results of their new unrestricted use could be weighed.[23] In this matter, he was probably influenced by the divided opinion in Saigon over the value of jets in the country. President Johnson, feeling increasingly frustrated and cornered by persistent National Security Council recommendations to increase the bombing of the north, approved these measures on the 15th of March, in part to defuse his advisors' insistence. Their implementation was soon under way.

The proposal to send an Army division to Vietnam and to seal off the Demilitarized Zone with SEATO troops was another matter. When he heard of it, General McConnell's immediate reaction was that it was a bad idea. In his view, the suggestion contradicted what the Joint Chiefs had earlier agreed upon; and he felt it was the wrong way to go. He opposed introducing American ground forces, at least until the infiltration had been stopped; and there was no way to stop it with ground forces. His staff estimated that it would take more than five divisions to seal off the north at the 17th parallel; and even if such a move succeeded, the Viet Cong, as indicated by prisoner reports, would get supplies elsewhere and continue to fight. Before any ground units were put in, the chief said, the land routes from the north should be closed by air power and the sea routes by the Navy. It would take about sixty days to learn if such an operation was working, and the United States could not get the divisions ready to go in that time. If it did succeed, there might be some rationale for introducing some ground forces later.[24]

McConnell aired these views to the other chiefs when they discussed Johnson's recommendations between March 17–19. He argued that Rolling Thunder had been hobbled and had not been given enough time to produce results. Furthermore, he said, setting an Army division down near Pleiku, an area surrounded and controlled by the Viet Cong, would plunge the United States directly into the ground war. He proposed instead taking the wraps off Rolling Thunder, deploying four fighter squadrons to the south, and limiting the Army division, should it be sent, to the mission of "developing and expanding additional coastal enclaves south of Da Nang to provide security for important installations."[25] Over the Air Force Chief's objections, the Joint Chiefs recommended to the Secretary sending the equivalent of three divisions (one Marine, one Army, and one Korean), increasing air attacks against the north, and dispatching four fighter squadrons to Southeast Asia.[26] Although the recommendation to dispatch three ground divisions was not approved at the time, it focused the attention of the presidential advisors on the use of ground forces, a focus that was to sharpen in the succeeding weeks.

Developments in South Vietnam, however, were pushing the United States almost by default into a ground strategy akin to that envisioned in Plan 32—direct American participation in the counterinsurgency. The forces called for in the second phase of that plan had been on alert since the beginning of the year. During March and April many pieces of the plan were falling into place, even though the plan had not been officially adopted.

The rapid pace of events during these months placed a particularly heavy strain on the 2d Air Division. The proliferation of air programs not only stretched General Moore's resources, but wrenched them into a new configuration. "We got caught in a whirlwind of change in our operations here," he explained later. "We jumped suddenly from very restricted in-country operations utilizing air commando assets to a full-scale jet operation both in and out of country."[27] The air war in South Vietnam had to adjust to the need to share its aircraft with operations over North Vietnam and Laos, both north and south. Thus from its birth, the American air war in Southeast Asia was circumscribed by the requirement to apportion sorties between four competing operational areas. This, in turn, made it even more imperative that air resources be managed from one central hub.

Although the March call for more Bird Dogs had been approved, it would be summer before the planes were ready. Except for the 23 O–1s belonging to the 19th Tactical Air Support Squadron (TASS), the Air Force had owned none of these Cessna planes since the Korean war. The Army gave the Air Force 106 of them and made them ready for combat. The planes were fitted with communication and navigation equipment, bomb shackles, adapters for launching rockets, and antigroundloop gear. The Air Force had asked the Army to fit the planes with constant-speed propellers, but the engines to handle these propellers were not available and the propellers could not be installed on the existing engines. The Army estimated that the first planes would be ready late in May and the entire lot by mid-August.

While the Army prepared the planes, the Tactical Air Command expanded its existing school to train jet pilots in visual reconnaissance and strike control. The new course began in May, lasting thirty rather than the standard forty-five days. The three new squadrons of O–1s were scheduled to be in place by August, and twenty pilots were scheduled to graduate every two weeks until the newly authorized FACs were in place. In the meantime, MACV was preparing a visual reconnaissance plan for these planes and the three Army companies of O–1s that were also on the way.[28]

Of the four tactical fighter squadrons that arrived in April as the first part of a deployment called "Two Buck,"[29] three went to Thailand and the fourth to Da Nang. By an understanding with the Bangkok government, the Thai-based F–105s and F–4Cs would not be used in South Vietnam. The squadron of F–104s that went to Da Nang joined the two F–100 squadrons already there in attacks over the north and in Laos. Although the number of B–57 Canberras at Bien Hoa was boosted to eighteen early in March, this provided little additional firepower for the southern campaign. Since the 19th of February, when these planes were first used in combat, they had been

Two F–105s from Thailand refuel on their way
to a target in North Vietnam, October 1965.

flying interdiction missions against Viet Cong concentrations not far from
Saigon. Starting early in March, more than half of the daily sorties were being
diverted to either Rolling Thunder or to attacks against targets in Laos.[30]

The Vietnamese Air Force showed great interest in striking targets in the
north at the expense of operations in the south. Westmoreland and Taylor
agreed to let the Vietnamese join Rolling Thunder to demonstrate solidarity
of American and Vietnamese purpose. General Ky's forces devoted 119
sorties in March and 97 in April—about 10 percent of their total attack
effort—to the area north of the demilitarized zone.[31]

One difficulty created by the new situation was that of maintaining the
level of sorties in the south in the face of the northward migration of aircraft.
While the loss to the southern air war was offset somewhat by the arrival of a
Marine squadron of F–4Bs at Da Nang on April 12 and the use of
carrier–based Navy jets against the Viet Cong, the 2d Air Division's
commander had to rely principally on squeezing more from the resources on
hand to bridge the crucial months until more forces arrived. This he did
through persuasion and diplomacy, convincing the Vietnamese to tie their
helicopter, transport, and strike sorties more directly into the air operations
center, compensating somewhat for decreased assets with increased efficiency.[32] Fortunately, the number of Viet Cong attacks fell off sharply during
March and April, allowing American aircraft to concentrate on interdiction

missions against the enemy, who was building up for an offensive during the coming monsoon season.

The airlift system was also showing the strain. Air Force C–123s and Vietnamese C–47s could not keep up with logistic demands, and a backlog of cargo clogged the aerial ports. The 315th Air Commando Group* called for help from the intratheater airlift C–130s which, until then, had operated in and out of, but not within, Vietnam. In April, four of these Hercules transports were dispatched to Vietnam in what was intended as a temporary measure to eliminate the bottlenecks. Once in the country, however, the C–130s stayed; and as the tempo of operations continued to expand in the next few months, their number grew first to thirteen and later to thirty as they gradually became a permanent part of the airlift force within the country.[33]

The new turn of events highlighted the scarcity of operating space at South Vietnam's air bases. The three jet airfields at Tan Son Nhut, Bien Hoa, and Da Nang, where the Air Force was a tenant, were seriously overcrowded. As late as the summer of 1964, when the United States was still thinking in terms of withdrawing from the country, the Air Force had been willing to put up with the tight and barely adequate conditions on these bases. However, as the Air Force responded to the new enemy strategy early in 1965, the situations at the bases worsened, with promise of even greater density in the future.

At Tan Son Nhut, which also served as the Saigon International Airport, the Air Force's headquarters and squadrons coexisted with elements of the Vietnamese Air Force, the Vietnamese Army, and the U.S. Army. In April, five EC–121D airborne control and warning planes began staging into the field from Taiwan. When added to the existing airlift, reconnaissance, and strike forces at the base, this placed a further burden on the overtaxed facilities.

Conditions at Bien Hoa were no better, and real estate was at a premium. The destruction of the B–57s there in November, occasioned to no small degree by cramped conditions, was still fresh in everyone's mind.

Most of the aircraft recently deployed to South Vietnam had gone to Da Nang, which by March was at the bursting point. The base, a sleepy station only eight months earlier, had a permanent population of forty-two F–100s,

---

*On March 8, this became the new name for the 315th Troop Carrier Group. Three of the group's four troop carrier squadrons, the 309th, 310th and 311th, also became air commando squadrons. The fourth squadron, the 19th, already bore that designation.

Visible under the wing of a C–130 at Da Nang in 1965: a C–124, a C–123, two C–47s, and, in the far background, two F–4s.

twenty-five Vietnamese A–1Hs, twenty-four Marine helicopters, eighteen O–1s, sixteen C–123s, fourteen F–104s, four C–130 flare ships, three Vietnamese helicopters, three HU–16 Albatrosses for search and rescue, and several F–105s. Room was set aside for an average of eight transient Air Force tactical planes daily (B–57s, RF–101s, F–105s, A–1Es, or F–100s), four to six Navy fighters (F–8s and A–4s), fifteen airlift C–130s, ten transport planes, and two to four Big Eye EC–121s.

On the 13th of March, the commander of the newly arrived Marine Expeditionary Brigade, citing his inability to defend the hills west of Da Nang against either ground or air attack, asked for a third Marine battalion and two squadrons of Marine aircraft: an A–4 squadron for close air support and an F–4 squadron for air defense.[34] General Moore took a dim view of this proposal and said so to Westmoreland. He argued, in part, that:

> Da Nang air base is heavily congested and because of political restrictions all USAF jet operations into Barrel Roll, and chokepoint seeding in Laos, must be launched from Da Nang as the primary air base. And Rolling Thunder plus support aircraft, both USAF and VNAF, [fly] from Da Nang. For certain missions, augmentation aircraft make for complete saturation of all available parking areas.

Marine squadrons could be accommodated, he concluded, only by removing some nonjet aircraft from the base. Since Da Nang was one of only three

F–100s in sandbag revetments at Da Nang, March 1965.

bases in the country that could handle jets, priority should be given to these high-performance aircraft and they should remain at the northern base.[35] Although one squadron of fifteen Marine F–4s was shoehorned onto the base by moving the Marine helicopters to nearby Phu Bai, overcrowding remained a serious problem.

At a logistics planning meeting in Hawaii early in April, the conferees discussed the subject of base construction. Although the Joint Chiefs, as part of an earlier contingency plan, had arranged engineering surveys for a new jet runway at Chu Lai and a second one at Da Nang,[36] the Honolulu group decided to have surveys made for additional airfields at Cam Ranh Bay, Phan Rang, and Qui Nhon. Since this construction would be paid for by the individual services, Westmoreland spread the responsibility for the bases among his component commanders. To Moore fell the charge of planning and paying for the airfields at the three new locations, as well as improving existing air facilities at Tan Son Nhut, Bien Hoa, Nha Trang, and New Can Tho (Binh Tuy).[37]

Throughout March and April, the Viet Cong remained hidden, avoiding contact with major South Vietnamese units. The few minor incidents that did take place were initiated by Viet Cong paramilitary groups, strengthening Westmoreland's contention that the enemy was concentrating on training, reorganizing, and rearming for a full-scale offensive. Intelligence had pinpointed several enemy base camps in the country where Viet Cong preparations were under way. One such area was the notorious War Zone C in the Tay Ninh Forest, sixty miles northwest of Saigon and north of Tay Ninh City near the Cambodian border. This zone, given its name by the French, had resisted all attempts at penetration since World War II. The enemy had located his major headquarters and a signal school to train local recruits and North Vietnamese infiltrators within the enclave. Over a hundred buildings, some constructed of jungle materials and others of wood, were grouped into four complexes that included living quarters, mess halls, classrooms, arms manufacturing plants, and antiaircraft positions. Individual shelters and bunkers were everywhere, connected by shallow trenches. The entire camp sat atop an intricate network of tunnels, and since the jungle foliage had been left intact, it could not be seen from the air and was virtually inaccessible from the ground.

In mid-April, Westmoreland planned a major air operation against the complex, named after the nearby Black Virgin Mountain. In his original conception of the operation, the general envisioned an all-out air effort using Air Force planes from both South Vietnam and Thailand and, for the first time, Navy and Marine planes. In accordance with the rules of engagement, the aircraft from Thailand could not fly directly to the targets but would have to stage out of airfields in South Vietnam. The Vietnamese would participate if possible, but enough of their planes would have to remain on ground alert to take care of any emergencies in the country. Westmoreland had hoped that all other air missions in South Vietnam and Laos and Rolling Thunder in the north would stand down for this one-day operation. The entire air action was to be planned, coordinated, and directed by General Moore at 2d Air Division.[38]

Hawaii's reaction to these plans illustrates the complexity that surrounded air operations in the theater. Adm. Ulysses S. Grant Sharp, CINCPAC, questioned the idea of using planes from Thailand, because staging them through South Vietnamese fields would aggravate the congestion there. He told Westmoreland to try to get along without them and to use them only if absolutely necessary. It was all right, he said, to cancel missions over Laos that day, but the Black Virgin operation must be planned around Rolling Thunder, which was just as important as air operations in the south.[39]

To support the operation, back-up units, including Air Force search and rescue helicopters, an ordnance demolition team, and an Army medical evacuation helicopter, were moved to the Tay Ninh airport. The first bombs fell at seven in the morning, and the pounding continued without interruption for 12 hours. Air Force B–57s and A–1Es from Bien Hoa, together with

F–100s from Da Nang, flew 206 sorties; the Vietnamese contributed 54 A–1H sorties; and the newly arrived Marine F–4Bs managed 16 sorties. Bomb runs by Navy attack planes from the carriers *Midway* and *Coral Sea* brought the total to 417.

The 2d Air Division coordinated and directed the strikes through its airborne forward air controllers using their Bird Dogs to mark targets for the attackers. Hovering higher above the action, two U–10s alternated in orchestrating the operation. By midafternoon, the 3-kilometer by 6-kilometer area was engulfed in smoke from the strikes and grass fires. One explosion sent a white cloud billowing 3,000 feet into the air. As the day wore on, large sections of tree cover were ripped off, exposing hidden buildings and uncovering entrances to underground installations. By the time the attacks ended at seven in the evening, 816 tons of bombs had been dropped.

For 2 days afterward, 1,200 ARVN soldiers, flown into the area by helicopter, fanned out in search of the Viet Cong and to estimate the results of the raids. Air Force and Vietnamese A–1s and Marine F–4s provided air cover and close air support for the searchers. While the troops saw no enemy, they uncovered ample evidence of their recent departure. Sixty buildings had been destroyed from the air, and the South Vietnamese captured switchboards, radios, communication wire, 2,000 kilograms of rice, and a variety of ordnance. Captured documents indicated that at least one North Vietnamese unit had been in the area.[40]

The shift to overt American air combat in the south during February and the opening of Rolling Thunder early in March thrust the Air Force directly into the battle against both the Viet Cong and Hanoi. However, impatience and disenchantment with the results of the northern attacks were not long in coming. As early as the 13th of March Ambassador Taylor cabled from Saigon that "through repeated delays we are failing to give the mounting crescendo to Rolling Thunder which is necessary to get the desired results."[41] John A. McCone, the CIA Director, lamented the halfhearted application of the bombing, intimating that the bombing should be an attempt to compel, not persuade, the North Vietnamese. "The strikes to date have not caused a change in the North Vietnamese policy," he wrote. "If anything, [they] have hardened their attitude."[42] General Johnson noted in his report that "the tempo of punitive air strikes has been inadequate to convey a clear sense of U.S. purpose to the DRV."[43] While these leaders were opting for more bombing, General Westmoreland saw things differently. On the 27th, he reported that the air activity against the north would not have an immediate effect on the war in the south and strongly urged the commitment of American ground combat forces.[44]

A move away from principal reliance on bombing the north in favor of ground action in the south began on the 1st of April. On that day, President Johnson repeated his earlier approval of General Johnson's twenty-one measures, but stopped short of sending an American division to Vietnam. As an alternative, he agreed to double the size of American combat forces already in the country by adding two more Marine battalions and one squadron of F–4s. In response to Ambassador Taylor's recommendation for an enclave strategy, he approved a change in the Marine mission from defense to active participation in the ground war.[45]

The eleventh hour of the advisory period ended in Honolulu during the third week of April. At a one-day conference there on the 20th, Secretary McNamara and his principal military and civilian assistants, who met primarily to win Ambassador Taylor over to the new strategy, agreed that North Vietnam was more likely to respond to Viet Cong failure in the south than to the pain inflicted by bombing in the north.[46] At the urging of General Westmoreland, the short-lived, and inadequately tested, strategy of relying on bombing the north gave way at the meeting to a ground strategy in the south. The conferees backed Westmoreland, deciding to establish 4 more enclaves along the southern coast and to increase the number of troops, up to 82,000 Americans and 8,000 allies by September, to defend them. Of this number, 997 Air Force logistics people would go to South Vietnam and 3,900 others would move to other points in the western Pacific.[47] The latter would man 2 new F–100 squadrons on Taiwan and another in the Philippines; an F–105 squadron on Okinawa; F–4, RF–101, and C–130 squadrons in Japan; and another troop carrier squadron in the Philippines.[48]

At the conference, General Harris continued to lament the growing dispersion of many of his PACAF air assets, a trend which he predicted would accelerate with the new emphasis on ground warfare. In discussions with the Chairman of the Joint Chiefs, he spoke of the adjustments he felt would be necessary for the new situation. He stressed the potential that existed for aggravating the already confusing command and control arrangements in the theater. By way of example, Harris pointed to contradictory instructions that had been issued for several recent air operations, such as Flaming Dart and the early Rolling Thunder missions, which had led Westmoreland to believe that "he [Westmoreland] had operational control of all USAF forces in Southeast Asia." Harris reiterated the Air Force's long-standing discomfort with the lack of air expertise on the MACV staff and urged that PACAF be given clear control of all air operations in Southeast Asia except for the air commando and transport forces assigned to Westmoreland in the south. The need for air expertise at the highest levels, he emphasized, had become even more imperative since the recent introduction of first-line Air Force, Marine, and Navy aircraft into the conflict. Also, the escalating situation had created an intolerable load for General Moore and his staff in Saigon, who were still expected to act as both advisory staff and operators. Harris proposed remedying this by establishing a tactical air control center in Thailand to remove the large operational burden in that country from the shoulders of the 2d Air Division. He strongly recommended to the chairman that the 2d Air Division concentrate on operating the A–1Es, C–123s, O–1s, the psychological warfare program, and the tactical air control system in South Vietnam, while the Thirteenth Air Force, through an advanced echelon in Thailand, handle operations outside South Vietnam.[49]

The reconnaissance plane force, like the strike forces, was divided. Harris criticized the existing division of reconnaissance assets between MACV, who controlled the flights over Laos and South Vietnam, and PACAF, who ran similar operations over North Vietnam. This was in direct contravention, he noted, of the original CINCPAC guidance which made PACAF responsible for aerial reconnaissance throughout the Pacific.[50]

The air defense picture was somewhat brighter. The responsibility for defense of the entire Pacific was Harris's,[51] and several recent events had proved the value of having a single air defense commander. After the Gulf of Tonkin incident, for example, he had been able to move F–102s rapidly into Vietnam from other bases in the theater. In February, it had taken the 315th Air Division only two days to move the Marine Hawk missile antiaircraft battalion from Okinawa to Da Nang to protect the base against air attack from the north. Continued centralization of air defense in the PACAF defense net was critical to being able to alert the entire system rapidly and tie together both American and allied resources.

Harris opposed the establishment of a separate Southeast Asia command divorced from CINCPAC. The creation of such a command, which would encompass the entire mainland peninsula, had been included in some of the contingency plans in the event the United States took over the war. While a Southeast Asia command would have the advantage of concentrating forces on the counterinsurgency in South Vietnam, the opportunity costs, from the Air Force's perspective, would overshadow whatever advantages this might bring. Politically, to lump Thailand, Laos, Vietnam, and Cambodia together could trample on the sensitivities of these nations and create a new set of obstacles to prosecuting the war. Strategically, to separate Southeast Asia from the rest of the mainland would divide American forces in the face of the perceived Chinese threat that was common to the peninsula, Taiwan, Japan, and Korea.[52]

The change in strategy at the Honolulu conference to a ground war meant that the principal role of air power in South Vietnam in the future was support for American and allied ground forces. Within days of the Honolulu meeting, Sharp informed Westmoreland that past policy had been changed and that from now on "The first priority for all U.S. air assets in the Republic of Vietnam is support of the in-country (South Vietnam) effort." Whereas barely a week earlier, at the time of the Black Virgin operation, Rolling Thunder had enjoyed at least equal status with air missions in the south, now Rolling Thunder strikes that interfered with requirements for the south were to be cut back or canceled. Operations over Laos would continue to have the lowest claim on aircraft.[53]

This set of priorities was to continue throughout the war despite attempts to change it. For the Air Force, this meant two things. First, the Air Force was now being called on to perform a tactical mission of close air support for which two decades of doctrine, force procurement, and training had ill-prepared it. While continuing to maintain its worldwide strategic posture, which had claimed most of its attention since World War II, the Air Force was now directed to support a ground war. The story of the next three years is largely one of adaptation to this alien environment. Second, the need for close interservice cooperation would be more critical than ever before if this joint venture were to succeed. The rapid march of events in Vietnam in the spring of 1965, however, was outpacing the development of joint practices to guide them. At first, each service would continue, as it had throughout the advisory years, to plan for the future in terms of what it knew best—its own doctrine, organization, and weaponry. Many months of debate, experimentation, and, at times, acrimony lay ahead before the beginnings of joint action would emerge to match the new joint strategy.

Members of the 13th Bomb Squadron clean up the remains of a B–57 after the Viet Cong mortar attack on November 1, 1964, at Bien Hoa.

Two B–52s releasing their bombs over a target in South Vietnam.

Chapter II

Beginning of Direct Involvement
April–June 1965

Repercussions from the Honolulu conference were immediate. The first order of business for Ambassador Taylor upon his return to Saigon was to inform the South Vietnamese Prime Minister, Phan Huy Quat, of what had taken place in Hawaii. On April 22, Taylor, with his assistant, U. Alexis Johnson, discussed with Quat the deteriorating military situation in the country and his belief that the Viet Cong, reinforced by North Vietnamese regulars, would soon open an offensive. The American Joint Chiefs, noted Taylor, estimated that the thirty-one battalions of soldiers the South Vietnamese were planning to add to their forces would not be enough to stop a determined enemy. At least twenty additional battalions were needed. In his reply, the Prime Minister avoided the issue of using foreign troops, dwelling instead on the obstacles he faced in improving his own forces. His officers lacked aggressiveness. The desertion rate was high because many commanders were not paying attention to the needs of their men. There were too many officers sitting behind desks in Saigon—he wanted to send them to the field. The meeting ended without direct mention of foreign reinforcement, even though Quat was fully aware that this was what the two Americans had uppermost in their minds.[1]

The 3 men met again 2 days later, a Saturday. This time the American diplomats were more specific. "We see no way of generating the necessary forces," began Taylor, "except by an international effort." If the Prime Minister agreed, the United States could supply 32 Army and Marine battalions totaling 33,000 men. There was reason to believe that Australia, New Zealand, Korea, and the Philippines would agree to add another 4 battalions. All together, these additions should come close to what the Joint

Chiefs felt were necessary. Initially, these troops would be used, he explained, as were the Marines at Da Nang, to secure a few enclaves such as Bien Hoa, Chu Lai, and Qui Nhon, releasing South Vietnamese soldiers for combat. At the same time, they would provide a reserve strike force that could be in place in less than 2 months. Quat "received the above expose calmly and in complete relaxation," almost relieved that the subject was out in the open. While he had no difficulty, he replied, in accepting the principle of introducing an international force, he had to discuss it with Maj. Gen. Tran Van Minh and Maj. Gen. Nguyen Van Thieu of the Armed Forces Council. This he would do over the weekend and give a final answer the following week.[2]

The Council concurred with Taylor's reasoning and agreed to have American and some allied troops replace Vietnamese at several enclaves. On the 1st of May, MACV and the Joint General Staff settled on two areas to be transferred that month: the Bien Hoa–Vung Tau axis around Saigon and Chu Lai up north. The 173d Airborne Brigade would take over the former, while two more Marine battalions should suffice for the northern enclave.

The 173rd was a two-battalion airborne brigade stationed on Okinawa. Since it was the only reserve airborne force he had in the Pacific, Admiral Sharp had opposed several earlier recommendations to move it to Vietnam. He now approved the move, with the understanding that the brigade's stay would be temporary and that, should the experiment work, the paratroops would be replaced by infantry soldiers and returned to Hawaii.[3]

A seventy-man advance party from the brigade was brought into Bien Hoa by Air Force C–130s on May 3,[4] and two days later the main body started to arrive. For three days, a steady stream of these Hercules aircraft, punctuated by a handful of C–124 Globemasters carrying oversized cargo, flew troops from Okinawa to both Bien Hoa and Vung Tau. The operation went smoothly, but the congestion and unevenness of airfield facilities in the country required tight scheduling. Because of limited space, the planes could not remain overnight in the country but had to return to their home bases after discharging passengers.

The 13-hour round trip pressed against the fuel limit, and many of the carriers had to refuel for the return trip. Because this was impossible at Vung Tau, the transports landed their passengers with engines running and refueled at Taiwan on the way home. At Bien Hoa, every fourth plane refueled at the base; the others unloaded, took off, hopped the 15 miles to Tan Son Nhut and picked up fuel there.[5] By the evening of the 7th, 1,800 troops and 1,100 tons of equipment were in place at the bases and the brigade's operations center was functioning at Bien Hoa. The remaining 1,700 soldiers with their gear filtered in by sea during the succeeding weeks.

That same day, two additional battalions of Marines, accompanied by a battalion of Seabees, landed up north at Chu Lai. The naval construction battalion began immediately to build an expeditionary airfield for the three Marine squadrons of A–4s that were scheduled to follow.

Although General Westmoreland viewed the 173d and the Marine battalions as the vanguard of larger American forces, President Johnson hesitated to approve more soldiers for the war. In a series of meetings with the Joint Chiefs in April, he emphasized that he wanted to step up the war but that he also wanted new ideas on how the air forces already in the country could help the Vietnamese kill more Viet Cong.

After consulting with the Air Force field commanders and his own staff, General McConnell, through the Joint Chiefs, made several suggestions to CINCPAC for improving the effectiveness of tactical air power in South Vietnam. The most serious problem was finding the enemy. The tropical nature of the country hampered interpretation of reconnaissance photos, and spotting the Viet Cong visually was a catch-as-catch-can operation. Visual reconnaissance was usually a secondary mission for forward air controllers and helicopter pilots who concentrated on directing air strikes and airlifting soldiers into battle. Even commercial airline pilots were pressed into service to report sightings as they flew over the country. McConnell recommended that a formal visual reconnaissance program be started so that every corner of the country could be systematically monitored from the air. Besides helping to identify and attack the Viet Cong, flooding the area with small reconnaissance planes would show the Vietnamese peasants, who were out of contact with Saigon, that the United States was supporting them.

However, this in itself was not enough. The best reconnaissance information was useless unless it was relayed quickly to control centers and converted into targets. The Air Force Chief exhorted the Pacific Commander to improve procedures for channeling aerial intelligence to the targeting centers.

Another problem was the time required for fighters to respond to calls for assistance. A year earlier it had taken an average of one hour and forty minutes after a call went out from the ground commander for strike craft to arrive at the target, and sometimes they did not come at all. The problem sprang from factors both military and political. Most South Vietnamese commanders were unfamiliar with air power and were reluctant to use it. Sometimes requests went unanswered because there were not enough planes or because the requests conflicted with training or other schedules. The command line for channeling requests was long and complicated and contained built-in delays. Calls for help had to go from Vietnamese units up through battalion, regiment, division, and corps commanders and also had to have the approval of the affected province chiefs. Province chiefs, who were political as well as military leaders, sometimes saw the picture differently than the military commanders and denied the requests. After a request was approved, the response time of the planes varied, depending on whether the aircraft were diverted from other missions or were on ground or airborne alert.

In an attempt to reduce delays, General Moore had started an air request system in 1964 that allowed calls for immediate air support to go directly from the ground commander to the corps air support operations center at the same time they were going through the other command channels. If no objection was voiced by the intermediate echelons, then the target would be considered valid and the strike made.[6] However, Vietnamese Army unit commanders resented being bypassed and refused to use the system.[7] The battle at Binh Gia at the end of 1964 had been lost when a Vietnamese Army commander canceled an urgent appeal for air support from a besieged South Vietnamese Marine battalion because the request had not been made through army channels. The planes were already on their way to the scene when told to return home. The battalion, along with two South Vietnamese Ranger companies, was wiped out.[8]

McConnell made several suggestions to streamline this procedure. He recommended circumventing the politico-military coordination at the province level. He also suggested that an EC-121 be kept in the air at all times over South Vietnam to act as an airborne control center for immediate air requests. Response times could also be cut, he pointed out, by increasing the number of planes on ground and air alert.[9]

McConnell's observations were passed on to Westmoreland, whose response reflected the reality that the United States was not fully running the war and that American and Vietnamese forces were not operating under a combined command. The MACV Commander agreed that continuous aerial surveillance was needed. He was in the process of developing a plan to integrate Vietnamese, Air Force, and Army observation planes and place a unit of O-1 Bird Dogs in each of the four corps, with aircraft deployed to airfields throughout the country. However, this plan could not be put into effect until the three additional Air Force squadrons and three Army aviation companies of Bird Dogs, which were on their way to Vietnam, were in place.

Once these planes were operating, the information they gathered would flow more smoothly to the centers that developed targets—the Target Research and Analysis Center in Saigon and the corps and local sector target centers. Westmoreland rejected as "inadvisable" the suggestion to circumvent the province chief. This was a touchy political matter. Province chiefs were responsible for the safety and welfare of all the people in their provinces, and it was understandable that they would be cautious about air attacks in their areas. Also, he stated, province chiefs were needed to identify noncombatants and should not be alienated by tinkering with their authority.

The MACV Commander also took a dim view of the EC-121 proposal. It would not speed up the process of obtaining province chief approval for strikes since the chief, as both political and military leader, could not spend

Early warning EC–121s at Tan Son Nhut in 1965.

his time aloft where he would have to be to hasten approval. Furthermore, the five EC–121s that had been staging into Vietnam since April were configured for an early warning function, and their radar and radio equipment was inadequate to allow them to control fighters. Finally, no increase in either air or ground alert was possible with the present number of forces.[10] Westmoreland and Moore believed that the present tactical air control system, when fleshed out with additional O–1s and new ground radars, would do the job.

The need to improve tactical air operations in South Vietnam was reiterated by the decision at Honolulu to "increase VC pain in the South." Westmoreland, fresh from his success at that meeting, spelled out the new strategy tying air power to ground action. While missions in South Vietnam had first call on air power, he informed Moore, not all kinds of missions in the south were of equal importance. First priority must go to supporting ground troops actually engaged with the enemy. After this, air power could be used for prestrikes and air cover for units carrying out major ground operations. Escort for trains and convoys came next. Planes could be used for interdiction outside South Vietnam only after these close air support needs were met.[11] Even here distinctions were made—emphasis would be placed on hitting targets that directly affected current operations. As for other targets, perishable ones would be struck before those that could be expected to exist for a period of time.[12] Air Force planes from Thailand could not be used unless they first landed in South Vietnam and operated from there. Whenever the number of available planes proved insufficient, reinforcements would be requested from CINCPAC, who controlled the Navy carriers offshore.

The promulgation of these new air priorities fanned several smoldering issues. For one thing, it sharpened the debate between those who wanted air power concentrated against the enemy outside South Vietnam and those who believed it should be focused inside the country. Westmoreland, in effect, now had veto power over bombing, interdiction, and reconnaissance programs outside South Vietnam, many of which were PACAF programs the Air Force believed should have higher priority. The degree of future effort that would be placed on such external missions as Rolling Thunder, Steel Tiger, Barrel Roll, Yankee Team, and Blue Tree was at the mercy of the MACV Commander's judgment about how important these programs were to the progress of the ground war, rather than to their direct effect on Hanoi. There was still doubt in many Air Force circles that Westmoreland's staff, virtually devoid of air strategists, would often enough arrive at conclusions compatible with the Air Force doctrine of centralized air power. In addition, the relegation of Laotian interdiction missions to last place evoked a strong reaction from Ambassador William H. Sullivan in Vientiane. Sullivan had been pressing Moore to set aside some airplanes to support the CIA roadwatch teams that roamed the Laotian panhandle observing the infiltration. Just a month earlier, a new Steel Tiger program had been approved; and on the 3d of April, B–57s and F–100s from South Vietnam made their first strikes in the newly expanded area. Now Moore was caught in the middle, pulled by demands from several directions for his limited air assets.

Moore's attempt to carry out the McNamara air policy of "South Vietnam first" increased the tension. In his message outlining the air priorities, Admiral Sharp had once again referred to Moore as the "coordinating authority" for tactical air support and air traffic within the south.[13] An attempt by Westmoreland a month earlier to secure for Moore operational, rather than merely coordinating, authority over all aircraft (except Army) in South Vietnam had been rebuffed and now, without the power to compel compliance with the new priorities, the air division commander's task was made extremely difficult.

As it was becoming apparent in April that American participation in the war would continue to increase, the Joint Chiefs revised the operating rules (the rules of engagement) for American forces. The revision was inspired, on the one hand, by the need to give the forces more leeway and, on the other, to make sure that the military did not exceed the political and diplomatic proprieties surrounding the conflict. The rules that had been in effect since the Gulf of Tonkin incident the previous August permitted American planes to attack any aircraft or vessel that struck them in South Vietnam, Thailand, Laos, or in the territorial seas of these countries. The revised guidelines of April were more specific concerning international waters and, because of the advent of Rolling Thunder, the Chinese border. For South Vietnam the rules remained general. American planes could chase enemy aircraft across the borders of Laos, Cambodia, and North Vietnam (but not China) only if the enemy struck first and only if they were still actually engaged in combat at the time of the crossing. Even in these cases, American aircraft could not strike other enemy forces or installations they might encounter in these countries unless they were attacked first and then only to the degree necessary for self-defense. The chiefs recognized the general nature of these rules and that more specific interpretations of them would have to be made for individual missions or projects. The common denominator was that a military commander was to defend his unit with all means at his disposal against an attacking force.[14] While the operations of American forces were becoming more offensive, the rules under which they operated remained defensive.

At the time that these new air priorities were announced (April 28), slightly over 1,000 American military aircraft were in South Vietnam, half of them helicopters. Each day these Air Force, Vietnamese, Army, and Marine aircraft performed about 1,900 tasks that ranged from combat to liaison missions.* Even though the Viet Cong were still avoiding contact with the South Vietnamese and remained in their base camps rearming and retraining, the skies over the country teemed with airplanes. On the 28th, a typical day, 21 U.S. Marine helicopters in I Corps, escorted by 2 of their own Bird Dogs and 4 F–4Bs, lifted elements of the Vietnamese Special Forces in 3 waves from Da Nang to an inland camp. Farther south in II Corps, 37 Army choppers of the 52d Aviation Battalion moved a Vietnamese Marine task force from Bong Son to a suspected Viet Cong encampment nearby. The operation was covered by 16 Air Force A–1Es, 4 F–100s, and an FC–47 gunship. In II Corps, 12 Air Force A–1Es and 13 Vietnamese A–1Hs escorted several battalions of the Vietnamese 25th Division on a search and destroy mission. Following this, the planes strafed and bombed some interdiction targets. In the same corps, 23 Army helicopters lifted a Vietnamese reconnaissance company from Phu Loi, 20 miles outside Saigon, to a nearby landing zone, while 5 other armed Army helicopters flew visual reconnaissance missions. Down south in IV Corps, 16 Vietnamese A–1Hs, 12 Air Force A–1Es, 12 F–100s, and 4 B–57s escorted 68 Army and Vietnamese helicopters as they lifted Vietnamese Rangers into 2 landing zones. The target was a secret Viet Cong training base that housed 200 to 300 recruits and was guarded by 2 companies.

These combat missions were only the cutting edge of air power. Throughout the country that day, 650 resupply flights landed troops and equipment at dozens of sites. Altogether, there were 225 visual reconnaissance flights, 190 missions escorting convoys and trains, and 140 training flights. The Army flew 109 radio relay missions—flights that passed radio transmissions from ground to air, ground to ground, or air to air, as needed, between forces that did not have compatible radio equipment. Wounded

---

*Because the combat actions of helicopters and fixed fixed-wing aircraft were not counted in the same way, the traditional sortie rate was not always an appropriate measure for comparing the activities of the two types of aircraft. See Appendix 2, Sorties vs Tasks.

An Air Force F–100 escorting a convoy, South Vietnam, 1965.

soldiers were evacuated from combat areas in 42 sorties, and patients moved from one hospital to another in 13 others. In addition, 26 reconnaissance missions photographed enemy concentrations from the air. Psychological warfare, including leaflet drops and loudspeaker broadcasts, occupied 14 planes, while 7 others flew armed reconnaissance sorties against targets of opportunity. Six "flying crane" helicopters retrieved airplanes that had gone down in combat areas. Four Army Bird Dogs adjusted ground artillery fire, while the Vietnamese flew a defoliation mission to spray the sides of highways where the enemy often lurked in ambush. This plethora of air activity was supported by 339 liaison flights transporting commanders and messages between sections of the country.[15]

The task of matching available airplanes with mission requirements was complicated by two factors. In Westmoreland's view, air power in South Vietnam was the handmaiden of the ground forces; but in May, the future size and shape of American ground deployments was cloudy. Equally uncertain was the degree to which these troops would engage in combat. In fact, answers to these questions were not yet known in Washington, where they were the subject of lively debate. Far from taking the initiative in introducing ground troops, the administration was insisting that the rate of escalation of the war would be determined by the other side.[16] McNamara and Secretary of State Dean Rusk dismissed talk of a land war that would pin down American forces. With no more definite guidance than this, planners of the air war in Saigon were unable to set sortie rates more than a month or two in advance.

Efforts of the Saigon command to sort out its air requirements were further complicated by the tendency of the action in South Vietnam to absorb all available aircraft, leaving few, if any, for operations outside the country. There was no effective central air manager to put the brakes on excessive demands for aircraft from the numerous local requesting units. The air operations center in Saigon was not designed to judge the validity of the targets requested from it and had to rely on the judgment and restraint of the Army's senior corps advisors who nominated targets for attack. In an effort to "keep them honest," General Westmoreland admonished these advisors to make sure that the targets they requested were valid and arranged in priority,[17] but this failed to solve the problem. There were so many requests for air support from all over the country during the first three days of May, for example, that Westmoreland canceled all bombing and reconnaissance missions outside Vietnam and asked for ninety additional sorties each day from the Navy.[18] To honor the request, the Navy moved the carrier *Oriskany* from Yankee Station in the Gulf of Tonkin and temporarily placed it a hundred miles east of Vung Tau at a spot called Dixie Station.

Hawaii was at a loss to understand this sudden surge of requirements, especially since the enemy was dormant and the strikes were against small interdiction targets, which up until then had been neither particularly urgent nor profitable.[19] Noting that the MACV Commander had canceled the out-of-country strikes before he requested naval aircraft, the headquarters in Hawaii suggested that perhaps there were not enough aircraft in Vietnam and that the problem should be restudied. In reply, Westmoreland attributed the increase in requirements to improved targeting and to the self-generating effects of increased availability of air assets.[20]

Despite their inability to predict the future shape of the enemy challenge and the American response, the air headquarters in Saigon at the end of May estimated that, for the immediate future, they would need an average of 240 strike sorties each day. This number would rise to 345 by August when the full complement of O–1 Bird Dogs, which was being readied for delivery to the country, was in place. These figures included planes that had already been scheduled to be added to the force: a squadron of 18 F–100s destined for Tan Son Nhut in June to support the 173d Airborne Brigade, 50 new A–1Hs for the Vietnamese Air Force by August, and 3 Marine squadrons of A–4s for Chu Lai by August. These would have provided enough planes for all strike missions in South Vietnam were it not for the fact that about 14 percent of the missions were being flown outside the country. The Vietnamese were flying Rolling Thunder raids against the north and some of the B–57s were flying night armed reconnaissance missions in Laos. Westmoreland requested that three steps be taken to make up for the shortage, at least until the planned new air bases were finished. First, he wanted the Navy carrier to remain permanently at Dixie Station. The Navy obliged and ordered the *Oriskany* and its successors to launch operations regularly against targets in South Vietnam until further notice. Second, he asked that the Air Force jets already scheduled for Vietnam be rushed into place and that those already in the country be moved into more advantageous positions. Finally, the MACV commander repeated a request he had made a month earlier at Honolulu: that he be allowed to use the Guam-based B–52s against Viet Cong strongholds in South Vietnam. He estimated that 60 such sorties a month would release more than 500 tactical sorties for more profitable use elsewhere.[21]

The Viet Cong opened their anticipated "monsoon offensive" at two in the morning of May 11 when 2,500 of them, moving under the protective cover of darkness, struck the provincial capital of Song Be, 60 miles north of Bien Hoa. Their aim was to seize and hold the provincial headquarters and the compound of the Vietnamese 36th Ranger Battalion located on the edge of town. The enemy started with a heavy mortar barrage and an assault on the compound, using, besides their own weapons, guns from 2 captured armored cars. When the attack began, the Air Force liaison officer in the compound radioed to Bien Hoa for help. Within 35 minutes a C–123 appeared and dropped more than 100 flares over the advancing troops. Two A–1Es arrived shortly after three but could not strike through the low-hanging clouds. The Viet Cong penetrated the compound, killed 42 defenders, 5 of them Americans, and wounded 76, including 14 U.S. soldiers. The Americans were shot by Viet Cong who broke into the compound's medical aid station. One wounded U.S. soldier in the dispensary got up from his litter and killed an attacker with a pocket knife during fierce hand-to-hand fighting. The enemy was driven from the compound but continued the siege. Part of the insurgent force pushed on to the center of town, which it quickly occupied. By daybreak the invaders were perilously close to the airfield, preventing evacuation helicopters from landing. They had dug in at the town's market and had set up .50-caliber antiaircraft gun positions on the roof of a large church.

At first light, 4 B–57s, directed by the Air Force liaison officer on the ground and an airborne controller in a Bird Dog, struck the enemy positions ringing the compound. The planes destroyed 2 mortar positions on a ridge line, killing some 50 Viet Cong, while napalm and bombs silenced pockets of automatic weapons to the west. The jets, joined by American and Vietnamese

A–1 Skyraiders, then turned toward the town, striking 40 enemy positions including those atop the church. For 2 hours they attacked the market until it collapsed. The enemy fled the town along outlying stream beds, pursued by Vietnamese forces that had been airlifted into the area. For 2 days and nights, South Vietnamese soldiers cleared the area under an umbrella of tactical aircraft. The Viet Cong flight was so hasty that there was no time to bury most of the 279 bodies that were later found.[22] The senior U.S. Army province advisor, Lt. Col. John G. Hill, later called air power the deciding factor in the victory.

For many of the aircraft, the missions at Song Be were among their last. At a quarter after eight the following Sunday morning (May 15), a flight of four fully loaded B–57s at Bien Hoa started their engines for an armed reconnaissance mission in Laos. Three other Canberras were already at the end of the runway waiting for a takeoff delayed by the emergency landing of a Navy F–8 jet. The Navy plane had taxied to the ramp and was being inspected by maintenance people. Without warning, the lead plane of the four bombers exploded and burst into flames. Showers of red-hot fragments, flaming fuel, and incendiaries started a chain reaction among the line of planes parked wingtip to wingtip. Jet fuel from several punctured fuel bladders fed the flames. While bombs exploded, airmen towed A–1s and O–1s away from the area and firemen sprayed foam on a stock of unfuzed bombs stored near the ramp. General Moore, quickly on the scene, closed the base temporarily and sealed off a large section of the ramp containing bombs with delayed-action fuzes.[23]

Twenty-eight American crewmen and maintenance people perished and a hundred were injured. Six Vietnamese lost their lives. Ten of the eighteen B–57s were gone; but eight—the three on the runway, four out on a mission, and one at Da Nang—escaped. The Navy jet and two Air Force Skyraiders were also destroyed. The Vietnamese Skyraiders were towed from the scene, but not before twenty-five were damaged by flying fragments. Still vivid memories of the Viet Cong attack that had destroyed five B–57s six months earlier roused immediate suspicions of sabotage, but later investigation placed the blame on the malfunction of a time-delay fuze on the lead aircraft. The eight surviving bombers were moved to Tan Son Nhut where replacements from Clark joined them within a few days. The unit stayed at the Saigon base until late in June when it moved to Da Nang.

The second major attack of the spring offensive came in I Corps and, like the raid at Song Be, was directed against a provincial capital. The enemy had been gathering men in Quang Ngai Province since September and had about 4,500 there. Late in May, they began a move to isolate the capital of Quang Ngai on the coast. First they isolated the city from the rest of the country by destroying 7 bridges leading into it along the coastal highway. Then they cut the only railroad that served the city.

To its west, Quang Ngai was ringed by a string of Vietnamese Army outposts forming an outer defense perimeter near the base of the mountains. One of these positions was at Ba Gia, ten miles from the capital. On the morning of May 29, the Viet Cong caught a platoon of Ba Gia's battalion on a road-clearing operation and destroyed it. Using a tactic that was becoming more and more familiar, the enemy waited in ambush for the relief force. When the remainder of the battalion arrived, the Viet Cong surrounded it, cut it off, and poured mortar and small arms fire into the soldiers' positions. The air control center at Da Nang sent two A–1Hs, twenty-two F–100s, two B–57s, and ten Marine F–4Bs to help the trapped battalion. Fifteen tons of bombs, fourteen of napalm, and a continuous barrage of cannon and machine gun fire from the planes could not prevent the battalion's destruction.

The next morning, the government moved three more Vietnamese battalions and two Regional Force companies up from Quang Ngai to try to save Ba Gia. All day these forces were supported by Vietnamese A–1s, Air Force F–100s, and Marine F–4s. Heavy contact with the enemy was made late in the afternoon, and the planes continued their support throughout the night under the artificial light of flares. Ba Gia continued to hold.

On the 31st, both sides brought up more reinforcements. Government troops were flown into battle by C–123s and C–130s.[24] Twenty-five tons of napalm and 8 tons of bombs fell on the enemy positions that day, but the battle raged for 3 more days and nights. By the time the Viet Cong broke off contact and withdrew on June 4, 651 sorties had been flown, with 54 tons of bombs and napalm dropped and the battlefield lit with over 2,000 flares.[25] The ARVN credited air support with keeping them from being overrun.

Within the week, the enemy struck a third time, this time against a Special Forces camp at Dong Xoai, 55 miles northeast of Saigon, on the fringe of the notorious War Zone D. The battle followed what was now becoming a familiar pattern: a mortar attack, Air Force airlift of government reinforcements into the threatened area, round-the-clock bombing and strafing by tactical planes, and enemy withdrawal. The action flared around Dong Xoai for 4 days before the enemy broke off on June 13. However, the intensity of battle was increasing. On the 10th, the 2d Air Division threw the largest number of tactical aircraft to date into the fray—24 A–1Hs, 35 A–1Es, 37 F–100s, and 11 B–57s.[26] All told, 644 strike sorties were needed to keep the enemy at bay.

As the tempo of the war increased, it became obvious that more American firepower was needed. Each week the South Vietnamese were

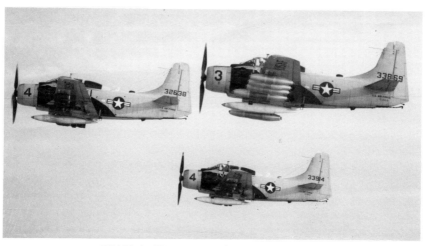

USAF A–1Es over South Vietnam in 1965.

losing the equivalent of an infantry battalion while the enemy was capturing another district capital town. The Saigon command estimated that 6 months of this would totally deplete the South Vietnamese forces.[27] These spring battles convinced MACV of the inadequacy of its small force of O–1s and forward air controllers. At the time, there were 39 airfields in Vietnam that could accommodate the Bird Dogs, ranging in quality from the 1,400-foot dirt strip at Rach Gia to the 10,000-foot concrete runway at Bien Hoa. In and out of these fields flew 50 Army, 75 Vietnamese, and 23 Air Force O–1s. The latter belonged to the 19th Tactical Air Support Squadron at Bien Hoa, which had only 44 forward air controllers both to fly the planes and to serve with the Vietnamese soldiers on the ground. On several occasions, fighter planes had to be sent home unused from a battle because there were not enough FACs to control them. The 3 additional Bird Dog squadrons that had been authorized in May were urgently needed.

On June 2, to help alleviate this problem, MACV unveiled the O–1 visual reconnaissance program it had promised in April. As with other military plans for the war, this one was designed to work within the existing decentralized military structure in South Vietnam. In this lay its strengths and weaknesses.

The basic concept was sound—since enemy movements were furtive and changes of location gradual, the best way to find the enemy was to make each pilot so familiar with a small area of South Vietnam that he would readily notice the slightest abnormality or change in the ground pattern. The country was divided into 214 areas, each small enough (about 300 square miles) so that one observation plane could cover it in several hours. The 45 areas along the coast would be monitored by 2 flights each day, and the 38 areas bordering Laos and Cambodia would each be searched by one daily flight. In the remaining 131 interior areas of the country, pilots would concentrate on those regions known to shelter the Viet Cong, making sure the areas were observed at least once each day. The reconnaissance was to be performed by Air Force, Army, and Vietnamese Bird Dogs.

The Cessna O–1 Bird Dog was the best aircraft American armed forces had in 1965 for the combined roles of forward air control and visual reconnaissance. First flown in Korea in 1950, this single-engine, 2-seat plane cruised at 100 miles an hour and could reach 18,000 feet. Excellent visibility through the wraparound and overhead windows made it relatively easy for the pilot to spot targets on the ground and fighters overhead. It was a light, reliable, and maneuverable plane that could stay aloft for about 4 hours. These characteristics, along with its ability to take off and land at unimproved sod strips, made it a natural for the role in which it was cast in Southeast Asia. However, since it was being adapted to a new environment, it had some drawbacks. Lack of armor plating exposed both pilot and vital aircraft components to ground fire. With only a single engine, its chance of being lost in the inhospitable jungle was great. While the O–1's slow cruise speed made it good for reconnaissance, it also kept the plane from reaching distant areas quickly in an emergency. The Bird Dog climbed at about 600 feet a minute, a rate that could be dangerous in mountainous terrain and under heavy ground fire. The engine was noisy, forewarning the Viet Cong of its approach. The plane carried only 4 marking rockets and did not have ideal communication and navigation equipment on board. Inadequate cockpit lighting limited its use at night. The search for an alternative began immediately.

Although each Army senior corps advisor was to develop a reconnaissance plan for his corps, planes were to operate at the subordinate province, or sector, level; and pilots would feed their information to sector operations and intelligence centers. However, operational control of the planes and pilots remained at the corps level—at the air support operation centers for the Air Force and Vietnamese planes, and at corps tactical operations centers for Army aircraft. These centers could divert flights from visual reconnaissance to other missions when there was a higher priority. The same priorities held for the Bird Dogs as for other tactical missions in South Vietnam—first call went to those missions directly supporting ground and air operations.[28] While information from these flights was fed first into the sector intelligence centers and then up to the corps level, the Air Force attempted to monitor its part of the program by setting up a common reporting system at the 2d Air Division intelligence shop.[29]

Success of the program hinged upon modifying several practices and attitudes that up till then had hindered concerted action. For one thing, Bird Dogs were being used in a variety of roles other than visual reconnaissance—

to direct air strikes, adjust artillery and naval gunfire, escort trains and convoys, vector airmobile operations, relay radio calls, transport people and messages, and even, on occasion, to evacuate casualties. The new emphasis on visual reconnaissance was going to require the Air Force, Army, and Vietnamese to modify their employment of O–1s to accommodate the increased workload. An ominous beginning was made in June when VNAF headquarters announced that visual reconnaissance for its Bird Dogs would have third priority behind forward air control and support of ground operations. At the same time, the VNAF severely curtailed the length of visual reconnaissance missions, as well as the times during the day when they could be flown. Because of the continuing shortage of fighter pilots, Vietnamese crews would be rotated each month.[30] This latter provision struck at the heart of the program by not giving Vietnamese pilots sufficient time in an area to become completely familiar with it. It became apparent from the outset that most of the visual reconnaissance would have to be done by the Air Force and Army, each of which was in the process of receiving additional observation planes for the job. If they were going to cover the entire country evenly, the three services would have to coordinate more closely than they had in the past.

Westmoreland searched for other sources of air power, in addition to the Bird Dogs, to supplement the fully committed tactical force. The thirty B–52s that had come to Guam in February were ready for missions in Southeast Asia, but no decision had been reached on how or where to use them. In March, the Joint Chiefs had proposed sending them over the north as part of the Rolling Thunder program, but they had not as yet participated. The State Department was against using them on the grounds that the B–52s could signal a higher level of escalation than American policy dictated and might cause an overreaction on the part of China or the Soviet Union. Technological and psychological factors also contributed to keeping them away from North Vietnam. Bombing techniques employed by the bombers required specific ground references, called offset aiming points, that were generally unavailable in the north; and there were problems with control in the environment of North Vietnam. Most agreed that the consequences of losing a B–52 to enemy fire would be serious.[31]

Both the Strategic Air Command and the Pacific Command, for different reasons, counseled against employing B–52s in South Vietnam. Strategists at Omaha, concerned principally with keeping the big bombers armed and ready for worldwide strategic alert, viewed their use in a tactical role as unnecessary and debilitating to the alert posture. In their estimation, there were enough tactical planes in the area to perform the role. Planners at Hawaii preferred to use the B–52s over the north.[32]

Late in March the SAC Commander, Gen. John D. Ryan, concerned about the effect the Guam planes were having on his alert posture, had wanted to return one–third of them to the United States. The Joint Chiefs, however, decided to keep them on the Pacific island, pending the outcome of developments in Southeast Asia.[33]

At the Honolulu conference in April, Westmoreland had urged using B–52s against Viet Cong base camps in the south. He had been disappointed with the results of the Black Virgin operation a few days earlier. During that attack, the area had been quickly covered by smoke, hiding targets from the later waves of fighters. As a result, the bomb pattern was spotty. The raids had used over 400 sorties and had stretched out over 12 hours, allowing time for the enemy to flee from the path of the bombs. An unacceptably high amount of ordnance had been dropped, and fighter-bombers had to be diverted from other air programs both inside and outside of South Vietnam. Westmoreland argued that the tactical fighters available to him were not efficient enough for pattern bombing. Future attacks on Viet Cong base areas, he said, should be made by B–52s, which could deliver an even pattern of bombs over a large area in a short period of time.[34]

The Joint Chiefs approved the idea, and by May details for the strikes had been worked out. While the Strategic Air Command prepared the operations plan, the 2d Air Division identified four appropriate targets for the B–52s to hit: major Viet Cong base areas in Kontum Province in II Corps, War Zone D northeast of Saigon, the Military Region 5 Headquarters in I Corps, and War Zone C northwest of Saigon along the Cambodian border in III Corps.[35] Aerial reconnaissance, using radio direction finding equipment as well as infrared and black and white photography, detected several battalions of the North Vietnamese 325th Division in Kontum Province; and the decision was made to strike them.[36]

SAC had to make one major modification to its usual bombing procedures. Normally targets on the ground were located by radar, but the radar film files were thin because of SAC's limited experience in this part of the world. Also, there were few cultural, manmade features such as cities and bridges in the country, and the jungle covered many of the geographic features that ordinarily produced useful radar returns. To make up for this lack of good radar offset aiming points, the first missions over South Vietnam used a small beacon mounted in an Army helicopter. The beacon's signal, which responded to an interrogation from the bomber, was used as a reference point to the target. It was understood that this was only a temporary expedient. The beacon crew and the helicopter carrying the beacon were vulnerable, and the beacon could be used only in safe areas. As the crews gained experience and the film file grew, they returned to normal radar synchronous bombing.[37]

In preparation for the first raid, a portable beacon was flown into Tan Son Nhut; and on the 24th, a single B–52 flew over South Vietnam to test it and take pictures of the target area. The order for the bombers to strike went out the next day, but the mission was canceled at the last minute when intelligence showed that the enemy had moved away. The big planes remained ready, and by the end of May, Westmoreland was able to include the strategic bombers in his sortie calculations.[38]

The first opportunity to use them came three weeks later. By the 15th of June, evidence pointed to a major concentration of Viet Cong forces in the area around Ben Cat, in War Zone D, forty miles north of Saigon. This base camp was the headquarters of the Viet Cong military committee directing operations against Saigon and its environs. The enemy used the base to harass the South Vietnamese and had ambushed six groups of Vietnamese soldiers in the area since the middle of May. The Ben Cat area had always been a troublesome one; and three months earlier, the Air Force had tried to clean it out by setting the forest on fire from the air. However, the foliage, damp from days of rain, refused to burn. Reconnaissance photos pinpointed fifteen one-story buildings and one two-story structure there. Air planners in Saigon concluded that the targets were too widely dispersed to be hit by fighter-bombers. Even if this were not the case, all available tactical aircraft were busy every day supporting ground forces. The planners decided that pattern bombing by B–52s was needed,[39] and Westmoreland requested the strike. On the following day, the 16th, approval came for a mission two days later.[40]

This was the first of a new type of mission, called Arc Light. The order went out before all of the details were complete. A flurry of last-minute changes passed between Hawaii, Saigon, and Guam—changes in location of the beacon and alteration of some coordinates and times. To the consternation of the military commanders, two major last minute changes were proposed from outside military channels. Twenty-six hours before the scheduled launch time, the Joint Chiefs called the Guam command asking if the mission could be moved ahead twenty-four hours—only two hours from the time of the call. The request had come from political sources in Washington. The SAC Commander said that it was too late to reschedule the ground forces that were to search the area after the attack and the mission would have to go as scheduled. Moments later he received another call, this time from Saigon, informing him that Ambassador Taylor had ordered another change. Aware of the worldwide attention that this first B–52 raid would attract and sensitive to the potential for criticism should any friendly troops or civilians be killed by falling bombs, the embassy had directed that a senior Air Force officer be aloft in the target area for "command and control." The 2d Air Division operations chief, Brig. Gen. George Simler, in a C–123, would act as interface between the beacon and the bombers. If contact between the two were not made, the general would abort the mission.[41]

The bombers were due over the target at seven on the morning of the 18th. Precisely 6 hours earlier, the first of the B–52s took off from Guam; and within 25 minutes, all 30 were airborne and heading for the refueling area off the northwestern tip of Luzon, the principal island in the Philippines. Twenty-four of the big planes carried fifty-one 750-pound bombs each—27 inside the bomb bays and 24 attached to external racks. The bomb bays of the other 6 planes were loaded with 1,000-pound armor-piercing bombs.

The armada flew toward its meeting with KC–135 tankers in ten cells of three planes each. Unexpected tailwinds from a typhoon pushed the planes ahead of schedule, causing them to arrive in the refueling area seven minutes early. To make good their rendezvous with the tankers, the three planes in the first cell made a 360-degree turn. In doing so, they flew into the path of the planes behind them. Two Stratofortresses collided in the darkness and fell in flames into the South China Sea. Four of the twelve crewmembers and a single body were recovered; the others were lost.

Twenty-seven of the remaining 28 bombers refueled and headed toward Saigon. The other plane, which had lost its hydraulic pump and radar, could not close with the tankers and aborted, landing on Okinawa. The planes crossed the Vietnamese coast at half past six; 15 minutes later, from altitudes ranging from 19,000 to 22,000 feet, began dropping their bombs on the 1-mile by 2-mile target box. The drops were controlled by the portable beacon that had been flown by helicopter the evening before to its location 11 miles from the target. Within 30 minutes, 1,300 bombs fell, slightly more than half of them in the target area.[42] The empty planes then headed south, careful to avoid the Cambodian border. Once south of Saigon, they turned eastward and, except for an aircraft that landed at Clark with electrical problems, returned to Guam. The last bomber landed there exactly 13 hours after the first had departed.

Shortly after the B–52s left the target area, thirty-two A–1Es from Bien Hoa strafed three spots north of the Ben Cat region to soften them up as landing zones. Three reconnaissance teams, each of thirty-six Vietnamese soldiers, with American advisors, were airlifted into the zones and moved southward to inspect selected portions of the target box. Overhead, Vietnamese A–1Hs and Air Force B–57s protected the scouting forces. For four hours the ground troops poked unenthusiastically through a few parts of the area but found no enemy and surprisingly little damage. There was evidence that at least one battalion of Viet Cong had been there but had left before the bombing started. The escape was later attributed to the enemy's success in infiltrating the South Vietnamese forces and learning beforehand of the mission.[43] The teams discovered several camps, training buildings, a commu-

A reconnaissance photo of the target area after the
first B–52 strike in South Vietnam, June 1965.

nication center, and defense positions and destroyed a large cache of rice.[44] This was the first time in several years that South Vietnamese troops had entered the area.

The immediately observable results of the bombing were less than spectacular. Expectations had been raised, particularly among the press corps, by the use of "strategic" aircraft. When the results fell short of those anticipated, many of the journalists became critical. A spate of newspaper articles took the Joint Chiefs and the military planners to task for using such powerful weapons against such a minuscule foe. The wisdom of "using a sledgehammer to kill gnats" became a lively editorial issue for several days.

The military leaders in Saigon and Hawaii, convinced of the effectiveness of this new weapon, remained unswayed by what they considered a misreading of the purpose of the Arc Light strikes. Placing the raids in the context of the overall military strategy of the war, they were buoyed by the results. The B–52s, pointed out Westmoreland, were one facet of a larger combined operation that included, in addition to the bombers, tactical airplanes, ground troops, and helicopters. Viewed in this light, the operation had not only been successful but justified an increased and regular use of the bombers in the future. The bombers added a dimension to the air war that had been missing. With the B–52s, Westmoreland had a weapon that could strike dug-in targets, saturate large areas, surprise the enemy, reduce his safe havens, and encourage the often timid South Vietnamese soldiers to venture into Viet Cong base areas. Further, all of this could be done without cutting into the number of tactical air missions that daily were hitting enemy troops throughout the country.[45] There were also indications that the psychological effects of the raid were as important as the physical—the number of Viet Cong defectors rose, with many bearing tales of demoralization from the unexpected bombing.

The Air Staff was less ebullient. Besides being upset by the apparently poor showing of the bomber fleet, it was disappointed by the small size of the follow-up ground force. It was also uneasy with the last-minute political attempts to alter the mission, a practice that could easily disrupt a complex military operation. His staff advised McConnell to make the other chiefs and the Defense Secretary aware of the potential danger and to encourage them to resist such changes in the future from outside the Defense Department.[46]

When Westmoreland requested a second Arc Light strike for the 27th of June, several of General McConnell's assistants suggested that MACV's enthusiasm for the big bombers was inspired by a desire to get as much air power as he could for South Vietnam, even, as plans for the Black Virgin operation had shown, at the expense of attacks against the north. McConnell quieted their fervor by saying that he did not want anyone opposing SAC going in again on the 27th or at any other time. "If SAC hasn't learned to bomb in fifteen years of extensive training," he opined, "we are not going to teach them how in a few weeks."[47]

Yet some on the Air Staff remained convinced that Westmoreland was asking for more air power than he needed. This opinion seemed to be substantiated a few days later when the MACV Commander suggested that he be allowed to use jets from Thailand for direct strikes in South Vietnam. He argued that the requirements for Rolling Thunder had stabilized while those for Barrel Roll and Steel Tiger in Laos had decreased. At the same time, the number of jets in Thailand was growing steadily. Being allowed to call them in directly without having them land first in South Vietnam would increase his flexibility and help to alleviate some of the airfield congestion in the south.[48] While nothing came of the idea at the time, it struck some Air Force leaders as a further attempt to divert air power from North Vietnam and Laos.

The proposed second Arc Light strike into War Zone D was to be followed by a ground sweep of the area. In answer to the criticism of the desultory follow-up after the first raid, this was to be a major American operation. When American Special Forces, probing the target area on the 26th, found 4 vacant Viet Cong camps and no sign of enemy activity, Westmoreland canceled the request for B–52s. Since the target area was so close to Bien Hoa Air Base, it was decided to clean it out with the ground sweep, using tactical air and artillery to soften up the area for the foot soldiers.[49] For 4 days, beginning on the 27th, the 173d Airborne Brigade, accompanied by an Australian battalion, 2 Vietnamese battalions, and a Vietnamese regiment, moved through the zone. They killed 25 of the enemy, destroyed 200 tons of supplies, and captured 50 tons of rice.[50] Unlike the halfhearted, essentially Vietnamese reconnaissance that had followed the first Arc Light raid, this was a full-blown search and destroy operation. It was the first major U.S. ground combat offensive of the war.

The 173d's first major ground mission, coupled with the planned arrival of elements of the 1st Infantry Division and the 101st Airborne Division in July and the 1st Cavalry Division in September, led to a realignment of the tactical jet and airlift airplanes that were to support them. Late in June, the 2d Air Division shifted its F–100 squadrons southward into positions better suited to the new situation. The two Super Sabre squadrons moved out of Da Nang—the 416th went to Bien Hoa and the 615th returned to the states. Their place was taken at the northern base by the B–57s, now numbering fourteen, that had been at Tan Son Nhut since the Bien Hoa accident in May. Soon after the move, their number doubled. Two new F–100 squadrons entered the country—the 481st came to Tan Son Nhut and the 307th to Bien Hoa. By the beginning of July, all the Super Sabres were south in III Corps and all the B–57s were north at Da Nang, where they were close to North Vietnam and to the Laotian trail and still in position to fly in the south.[51] A squadron of F–102 Delta Daggers and one of F–104 Starfighters were also at Da Nang. At the same time, one of the three C–123 Provider squadrons at Tan Son Nhut (the 310th) was moved north to Nha Trang where it would be in a better position to support forces in the midsection of the country. The fourth squadron, the 311th, continued to resupply I Corps from Da Nang.* American strategy had now transcended the enclave and reserve functions outlined for it two months earlier by Ambassador Taylor in his discussions with Premier Quat.

---

*See Appendix 1, Major USAF Units and Aircraft in South Vietnam, 1962–1968.

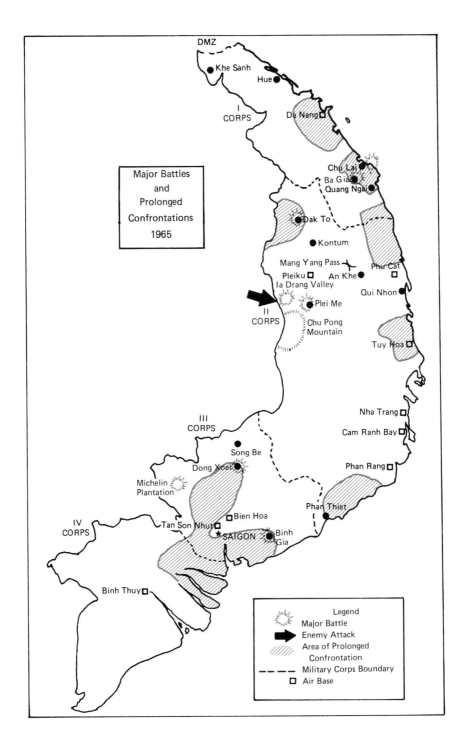

Major Battles
and
Prolonged
Confrontations
1965

DMZ

Khe Sanh

Hue

I
CORPS

Da Nang

Chu Lai
Ba Gia
Quang Ngai

Dak To

Kontum

Mang Yang Pass

Phu Cat

Pleiku

An Khe

Ia Drang Valley

Qui Nhon

II
CORPS

Plei Me

Chu Pong
Mountain

Tuy Hoa

Nha Trang

III
CORPS

Cam Ranh Bay

Song Be

Dong Xoai

Phan Rang

Michelin
Plantation

Phan Thiet

IV
CORPS

Bien Hoa

Tan Son Nhut

SAIGON

Binh
Gia

Binh Thuy

Legend

Major Battle

Enemy Attack

Area of Prolonged
Confrontation

Military Corps Boundary

☐ Air Base

Chapter III

U.S. Assumes Major Role
June–September 1965

The Viet Cong spring attacks in late May and early June 1965, which featured major assaults on Song Be, Ba Gia, and Dong Xoai, provided Westmoreland with new ammunition for his campaign to get more American reinforcements. In a dramatic communique on the 7th of June, he painted a military situation so bleak that only large doses of additional help could brighten it. Although the Viet Cong had used only 2 of their 9 regiments thus far, they were displaying new discipline and new weapons. The North Vietnamese had elements of a division in II Corps, with a second one poised just across the border in Laos. The enemy could mount regimental-size operations in any of the 4 corps and battalion-size attacks in any of the provinces. The South Vietnamese Army, on the other hand, was weakening. Four battalions had been destroyed in the northern provinces and many of the other infantry and ranger battalions were far below strength. The ARVN would now have to use its new recruits to plug holes created by the recent bloodletting and desertions, and there would be no new South Vietnamese battalions at least until November. In the interim, the decreasing force ratio between non-Communist and Communist soldiers could be reversed only by sending an American airmobile division to the central highlands. Westmoreland also asked for a Korean division of 18,500 soldiers, with an American logistic increment of 1,500; 8,000 more Marines to flesh out the Third Marine Division in I Corps; and another 8,000 Army logistic and 1,500 headquarters personnel—58,000 new troops in all, to be added to the 30,000 already in the country.

While much of this had been sought before and contingency planning for some of these troops was already under way, the new element in the request was the manner in which the general planned to use these reinforcements. "I am convinced," he wrote, "that U.S. troops with their energy, mobility, and firepower can successfully take the fight to the Viet Cong." The additional troops would be used "to give us a substantial and hard hitting offensive capability."[1]

The lack of detail that the message devoted to air resources was in sharp contrast to the discussion of ground troops. The general asked for "additional" tactical fighter squadrons to go to Cam Ranh Bay when it was completed. He concluded with the by now familiar plea for a full-time carrier for strikes in the south.[2]

Admiral Sharp backed most of these recommendations and passed them on to the Joint Chiefs, but he remained skeptical about sending an airmobile division into the interior of the country. Pleiku was in the mountains, eighty-five miles inland, deep in the heart of Viet Cong territory, and its lifeline to the coastal enclave of Qui Nhon was the vulnerable Highway 19. To send an American division there while this road was in enemy hands was an unwarranted departure from the enclave strategy.[3] The Navy-oriented command in Hawaii also balked at the carrier request. The best he could do, replied Sharp, was provide a carrier for periods of ten or twelve days at a time, at least until more of the floating airfields arrived in the Pacific.[4]

Moving with alacrity, the Joint Chiefs signed off on Westmoreland's request on the 11th of June and sent it to Secretary McNamara, who took it to the President for study.[5] The debate which the message ignited in Washington was fueled five days later when Premier Quat, who had been at loggerheads with Chief of State Phan Khac Suu over a proposed cabinet shuffle, proffered his resignation to the military National Leadership Committee. For the ninth time since the assassination of Diem in November 1963, the government had changed hands; and political stability, which had seemed within reach only a month earlier, now appeared as distant as ever.

The outlines of the new government in Saigon became clear on the 18th of June. Air Vice Marshal Ky, the Commander of the Vietnamese Air Force, emerged as Prime Minister and General Thieu as Chief of State. These men represented a younger generation of military leaders, some of whom favored a civilian government, but they had lost patience with the ineptness of those trying to create one.

In many ways, the most surprising aspect of the new government was the prominence of Ky, who until recently had not been taken seriously as a political figure. His public image had earlier been that of a flamboyant,

Vietnamese Air Force H–34 landing at a remote site marked by smoke rockets.

almost reckless, aviator unversed in politics. Born a few miles outside Hanoi in 1930, he had been commissioned a second lieutenant in the infantry in 1951. A year later he went to Morocco and then to France where he earned his wings. At the time of Diem's assassination, Ky was a lieutenant colonel commanding a Vietnamese air transport group at Tan Son Nhut. Although his role in the coup against Diem was minor, he was made Commander of the Vietnamese Air Force several weeks later.

Under Ky's direction the air force had continued to expand. When he took over, it had two fighter squadrons, one of older T–28s, the other of newer A–1s. It also had two H–34 helicopter squadrons, two of C–47 transports, and three squadrons of O–1 observation planes. At the end of his first year in command, late in 1964, three A–1 squadrons were operational, a fourth was nearing readiness, and two more were planned. The number of helicopter squadrons had doubled to four. Ky was not solely responsible for these increases—they were part of a long-range plan, being pursued under the aegis of the U.S. Air Force Advisory Group, to bring the VNAF to the level where it could fully support the Vietnamese Army against the insurgency. However, Ky was responsible for infusing a sense of pride and purpose into the air force. In a society where personal leadership still counted for much, he inspired strong loyalties to himself among his subordinates.

Ky had bolstered his reputation for flamboyance and individualism at a news conference in July 1964 when he announced that his air force was dropping sabotage teams into North Vietnam to destroy roads, bridges, and powerplants. He, himself, he announced, had led a similar series of C–47 night raids north of Hanoi three years earlier. He boasted that the Vietnamese Air Force was now in a position to wipe out whole provinces in the north and destroy Hanoi itself.[6] These were disquieting statements for the Americans who were trying to persuade the North Vietnamese and the world that the United States was trying only to defend the south and had no ambitions to invade the north. Although the American embassy curbed his enthusiasm on this occasion, Ky was clearly stiffening the backbone of the Vietnamese air arm at a time when the army was growing weaker.

Nguyen Cao Ky had first tasted true political power on the 13th of September 1964 when elements of two Vietnamese Army divisions took over downtown Saigon in a move to topple the government of Premier Nguyen Khanh. Ky stood firmly behind the premier and for several hours ran the country from his headquarters at Tan Son Nhut. By refusing to allow the air force to join the dissident army troops, he broke the back of the coup, and the rebels withdrew from the capital. General Moore, who spent most of that critical afternoon at VNAF headquarters, later drew a picture of Ky under pressure that was at variance with the popular perception of the air force commander. He described him as a man of maturity and strong character who throughout the crisis remained unshaken in his conviction that a coup at that time was not in the best interest of South Vietnam. He was not backing Khanh as an individual, Ky told the American general, but the Vietnamese people.[7]

After the September revolt, Ky had risen steadily in responsibility and respectability. By January 1965, he was a member of the Armed Forces Council that ousted yet another civilian government. At this time, he got his first purely political job as head of the Youth and Sports Ministry. Despite some objection, he retained command of the air force throughout his rise up the political ladder. On the 8th of February, he added to his prestige when he led a flight of twenty-four A–1s from Da Nang on the Flaming Dart raid over North Vietnam. Although the planes were greeted with heavy antiaircraft fire and every one was hit at least once, all but one returned to base after destroying an estimated ninety percent of the Vinh military complex. The daring and success of the raid sent a wave of pride through South Vietnam and elevated Ky to the stature of a hero.[8]

American decisionmakers, however, viewed the fall of Quat and the accession of Ky and Thieu as further evidence of South Vietnam's political instability. The military takeover, coming as it did on the heels of Westmoreland's plea for reinforcements, quickened the debate in Washington over the American military role in Vietnam. The Vietnamese, both northern and southern, were pushing Washington to a decision. At the opposite extreme from Westmoreland stood Undersecretary of State George Ball, who advised cutting losses and getting out of the country. The other actors fell between these two poles. Ambassador Taylor agreed that the situation was deteriorating, but opposed the sudden inundation of the country with American soldiers which, he said, would seriously dislocate the Vietnamese economy and morale. He recommended instead that American troops be introduced gradually. The Joint Chiefs, who up till then had been leading the move toward massive American involvement, now yielded that role to Westmoreland.[9] While they had supported the MACV Commander's request of June 7 and agreed with his estimate that increased American action was necessary, the chiefs were no closer to consensus on what form that action should take than they had been in March.[10] General McConnell still felt strongly that it would be a mistake to send large numbers of American fighting troops to Vietnam without first knocking out the North Vietnamese with air power. He warned against rushing an untrained and untested airmobile division to the highlands until it was clear how it would be supported.[11]

The Air Force Chief was reflecting a long-standing difference of opinion with the Army over the role and control of tactical support aircraft. Unlike other Army divisions, the airmobile division had over 430 of its own aircraft, both helicopters to move troops and strike the enemy and some fixed-wing planes for reconnaissance and supply. Over the years, the Air Force had watched the steady growth of Army aviation, attempting to check it when it appeared to infringe on the Air Force's own close air support function. Despite several agreements between the services since 1951, a gray area still remained between the respective roles of Army and Air Force aircraft in supporting ground forces.[12] Some still felt the Air Force should control all aerial support for the Army, including helicopters, but this was patently unrealistic in light of earlier agreements. As much as it rankled, Army helicopters to move troops from home base to the combat zone appeared there to stay. To Air Force eyes, the Army's armed helicopters to clear landing zones for the troops, OV–1 Mohawks for reconnaissance, and CV–2 Caribous for airlift appeared as violators of the earlier agreements and duplication of the functions of Air Force tactical fighters, reconnaissance planes, and C–123 airlift planes.

McConnell's reservations about deploying the division resided on several levels. The division was not ready—in fact it had not yet been activated. An experimental airmobile division had been pieced together from other units for a stateside field test the preceding fall, but since then, most of the elements had returned to their original units. It would take time to reassemble, replace, and retrain them. Further, since the stateside test had been carried out unilaterally by the Army, rather than jointly with the Air Force, McConnell and his staff could only guess at what tactical air support the division might need from the Air Force.[13] Above all, the Air Staff viewed air power as an

U.S. Army OV–1 Mohawk observation plane.

indivisible entity, with a life and rules of its own, which was most effective and economical when planned and controlled rationally from one central place. To place globules of single-purpose aircraft in Vietnam appeared wasteful and inefficient. The implications of the division going to Vietnam reached far beyond the war in that country; the success or failure of the experiment could have an important bearing on the future force structure of both services.

It was still not clear in mid-June whether the division would be sent or, if it were, where it would go and what it would do after it arrived. The Joint Chiefs had altered their earlier position and now wanted to send the division first to Qui Nhon, rather than inland to Pleiku, "to ensure base and lines of communication prior to deploying to the highlands."[14] The Chairman, Gen. Earle G. Wheeler, USA, assured the Army Chief, however, that once the division was in the country, Westmoreland could use it as he saw fit. Still the President made no decision as to whether it would go at all.

The chiefs continued to debate the issue. At a meeting late in June, McConnell told the other chiefs that if they recommended sending the division to Pleiku without providing for a secure link with the coast, either by road or by air, they would be "criminally responsible." His remark was greeted with silence around the table.[15] A week later, during an Air Staff discussion as to how the Air Force would supply the American division at Pleiku should it be sent, McConnell said he did not think it would go there, but if it did, it would not have to be supplied for long, since the Viet Cong would destroy it.[16]

The Air Force Chief's planning staff warned him that the recent JCS approval of Westmoreland's request, made on a crash basis, was but the latest in a series of ad hoc steps toward an irreversible American commitment to protracted, large-scale warfare on the Asian mainland. It lamented the absence of any systematic analysis of where the United States was heading and exactly what the new troops were supposed to accomplish. Pointing to a four-year history of poor intelligence, underestimation of the enemy and overestimation of American capability, and faulty strategies and programs for Vietnam, the planners warned against going along with MACV and CINCPAC "simply because they were on the scene." They argued that the Joint Staff and the service staffs, some of which had not been consulted on the original JCS endorsement, should look closely at where the proposed war of attrition would lead. Before going further, some searching questions should be addressed. Will the troops requested by Saigon be enough? How many more will be needed later? Is it truly possible to convince the North Vietnamese that they can't win? Will the reserves have to be called up? If so, will the country go along with this? Is the administration likely to come through on such a tough political decision? The theater commanders were not in a position to answer such questions, the staff noted, and the stakes were too high to allow the decision to be made by the Pacific actors.[17]

During a visit to Saigon on the 17th of July, Secretary McNamara was briefed by Westmoreland on a program for taking the initiative in Vietnam. The first part of the program would stop the enemy's momentum by year's end and would require 154,000 ground troops and 23 American squadrons of strike planes. For the second phase, which would put the allies on the offensive during the first half of the next year, the general would need 95,000 more men, including 7 more Air Force strike squadrons.[18] McNamara asked Westmoreland to let him know in detail what forces and equipment he would need. No sooner had the Secretary arrived back in Washington than the answer came, on July 20, in the form of a shopping list of 133 items. In his cover letter to the Secretary, Westmoreland noted that, since he had been pressed for the list, he had not had time to coordinate it with CINCPAC. He would do so as soon as the items were justified.[19]

His list contained details of military units, personnel, transportation, equipment, munitions, funds, and communications systems. To support the forty-four maneuver battalions* that would be in the country by the end of

---

*Thirty-four of these would be American. The remainder would be mainly Korean, with a sprinkling of Australian and New Zealand soldiers. The term "maneuver battalion" as used in these plans included infantry battalions (whether airmobile or airborne), tank battalions, mechanized battalions, and armored cavalry squadrons. Other types of forces that would be in the country but not included in the term 'maneuver battalion" were air cavalry squadrons and division reconnaissance units.

the year, he would need nine Air Force and six Marine jet fighter squadrons and four C–130 airlift squadrons (table 2). The Air Force's fighter squadrons would be positioned along the coast—three at Cam Ranh Bay, three at Phan Rang, and three at Qui Nhon—and would all be in place by October when these bases were scheduled to open. For the second phase during the next year, the United States and its allies would add twenty-eight more maneuver battalions, calling for eleven more Air Force fighter and two troop carrier squadrons. The fighter squadrons would go to Cam Ranh Bay, Bien Hoa, and Phan Rang. A new C–130 squadron would be stationed at Tan Son Nhut in March and another at Nha Trang in April.[20]

Table 2
Fighter Squadrons Needed for the 1965–1966 Ground Buildup*

		Battalions in country	Jet Sorties Needed	Squadrons Scheduled			Total Squadrons Needed
				USAF	USMC	USN	
1965	Sep	21	9,820	5	6	4	15
	Oct	35	12,130	5	6	8	19
	Nov	44	14,350	9	6	7	22
	Dec	44	14,840	9	6	8	23
1966	Jan	48	15,670	13	7	5	25
	Feb	49	15,850	15	7	3	25
	Mar	50	15,920	17	7	1	25
	Apr	51	16,100	17	7	1	25
	May	56	17,000	17	10		27
	Jun	57	17,180	17	10		27
	Jul	57	17,180	17	10		27
	Aug	66	18,880	19	10		29
	Sep	66	18,880	19	10		29
	Oct	66	18,880	19	10		29
	Nov	72	19,880	20	10	1	31
	Dec	72	19,880	20	10	1	31

*Based on the number of non-South Vietnamese maneuver battalions predicted to be in South Vietnam, the chart was drawn up at the Secretary of Defense's conference in Honolulu, September 27–30, 1965, and contains only minor changes to Westmoreland's July 1965 predictions.

Westmoreland arrived at these squadron figures by using a number of arbitrary planning factors. The overall strategy of the war was a factor only in the most remote sense, since there still was no specific scheme for fighting the enemy. More important to the calculations were several numerical assumptions.* The first was that each non-Vietnamese maneuver battalion would be allotted six tactical sorties a day, a far from scientific number. Since the enemy held the initiative and was expected to do so until the end of the year, it was impossible to foresee in detail how many of what kinds of strikes would be needed. According to the priorities, tactical planes would first be used to support ground troops who were actually in contact with the enemy and after that used for prestrike, air cover, escort, and interdiction missions. With such an open-ended list of tasks from which to choose, it seemed that however many planes were sent to Vietnam, they would all be fully employed.

A second assumption was that each strike plane would fly, on the average, 1.2 sorties a day, or 36 each month. As the number of non-Vietnamese maneuver battalions in the country grew from the existing 12 to 44 by the end of the year, the number of monthly sorties would rise correspondingly from 7,500 to almost 15,000. This would require 23 squadrons of jets. Since the Marines had 6 and 2 Navy carriers provided the equivalent of 8, the Air Force would supply the other 9 squadrons.

Projecting ahead into 1966, the Air Force would need 17 jet squadrons in Vietnam by midyear, part of them to replace the Navy planes (whose use Secretary McNamara was seriously questioning), and 20 squadrons by the end of the year. By that time, the Marines would have 10 squadrons in the country. Therefore, according to the long-term projections, by the end of 1966, there would be the equivalent of 30 jet squadrons of 18 planes each in the country, flying close to 20,000 sorties a month to support 72 non-Vietnamese battalions. These calculations did not include the Air Force and Vietnamese A–1s that were flying 2,900 sorties a month for the Vietnamese Army.

As methodical and logical as these plans appeared, they were grounded in assumptions concerning the nature of the enemy's response, the ability of the Army to get all its battalions into operation, the rapid construction of airfields, and the degree of naval jet participation in the south. These assumptions were not to be realized in the succeeding months, and the figures would be altered accordingly. The number of troop carrier squadrons that would be needed was based on an expected requirement to move 2,000 tons of supplies by air each day by the end of the year.[21]

More reconnaissance planes and equipment were also needed, according to Westmoreland. Although the additional O–1 Bird Dogs were beginning to arrive in the country, more jets were needed for countrywide coverage. The shopping list called for twelve RF–101s and nine RF–4Cs at two sites in Vietnam.[22] The two C–130s flying air cover reconnaissance missions over the

---

*A 1966 PACAF study examining the responsiveness of tactical air in South Vietnam from December 1965 through April 1966 also considered the effect of these factors. See Appendix 3, Planning Factors for the Tactical Air Buildup.

gulf should be increased to five.[23] Also needed were more sophisticated aerial sensors that could provide inflight infrared readouts.[24] The Air Force's 13th Reconnaissance Technical Squadron at Tan Son Nhut, which was processing the film brought in by the jets, was in wretched shape.[25]

Getting the necessary Air Force units into the country quickly, however, would require changes in personnel practices. One of the more intractable problems was the existing limit on the number of Air Force people who could be stationed permanently in Vietnam. Another was the length of time—4 to 6 months—it took to get the Defense Department's approval and to move an airman into the country. To skirt these restrictions and keep operations going, the Air Force had been sending men on temporary duty while the approvals for permanent replacements were being processed. As a result, one-third of the airmen in the country were on temporary tours of from 60 to 120 days.[26] Not only were the personnel of the jet squadrons temporary, rotating back and forth every few months from the United States or from other Pacific bases to Vietnam, but so were other support people in the country. This meant that 12 percent of all the American forces in South Vietnam were there for only a few months. Besides the disruption to planning and continuity, this use of temporary people was costly. Per diem and travel expenses for a man on a 4-month temporary assignment exceeded the cost of stationing him there for a year. While this system had succeeded in keeping down the number of Air Force people in the advisory force, it was inadequate for the new combat environment. Westmoreland, in his memo, asked McNamara to streamline the approval procedures and, at the same time, give the Air Force a block of spaces it could use to assign people rapidly. If this were done, a man could be on the job within 45 to 60 days after he was requested and remain there for a year.[27]

The timetable for introducing Air Force units also depended upon how quickly the new airstrips were built and the older ones improved. Construction of new 10,000-foot airstrips at Cam Ranh Bay, Phan Rang, and Qui Nhon and of second parallel runways at these bases and at Tan Son Nhut, which had been approved in March, was running into obstacles. Some of the methods being used could not adapt to the rapid change. For one thing, the system for funding construction delayed the process. Westmoreland could approve only construction that cost less than $25,000. Airfield construction costing between $25,000 and $200,000 had to be approved by Air Force headquarters even before the design stage could begin. Higher amounts needed Secretary McNamara's sanction. Since it was estimated that the building and upgrading of these fields would cost over $3 million, the approval system needed streamlining. Westmoreland asked for authority to control larger amounts of construction money. The MACV Commander, he said, had to have the freedom to approve the necessary money on the spot.[28]

Construction at Cam Ranh Bay in 1965.

Airfield building was also being slowed by the paucity of construction people. There was only one construction firm (RMK/BRJ*) in the country under the Navy Construction Agency. Although the firm was large and had just completed the airfield for the Marines at Chu Lai, it would have to expand considerably to handle the task ahead. Westmoreland suggested that additional architectural engineering firms come to Vietnam[29] and that Army and Navy construction battalions might be needed to help.[30]

The urgency to get the three airfields finished added a further complication. Each airfield was being built in two stages: first, an "expeditionary" or temporary runway of aluminum matting was laid in about four months and put to immediate use. Then a permanent parallel concrete runway was built, and the traffic was shifted to the second runway. In some cases, the aluminum on the first strip was taken up and replaced with permanent concrete. It was originally planned to reuse the aluminum matting at other fields after it was taken up. However, to have the fields ready in time, the runways were built concurrently, ruling out reuse of the matting. Also, the geographic locations of the fields and the lack of good roads and railroads in the country made it impractical to transport the matting from one location to another. The MACV Commander informed the Secretary that a much

*Raymond International, Morrison-Knudsen, Brown and Root, and J. A. Jones.

Installation of aluminum matting at Cam Ranh Bay.

larger amount of matting was going to be needed than had been planned: three million square feet at Cam Ranh Bay by mid-August and three million at Phan Rang and Qui Nhon each by mid-September. At least as much again would be needed in the succeeding months.[31]

During his trip to Vietnam, Secretary McNamara had discussed giving some jet aircraft to the Vietnamese. In his shopping list, Westmoreland passed on a strong plea from Ky for at least a token jet force to boost the prestige and morale of both the Vietnamese Air Force and the civilian population. Pointing to the presence of jets in the air forces of Thailand, Cambodia, the Philippines, and North Vietnam, he recommended that four B-57s from the Da Nang squadron be marked with Vietnamese insignia and flown by Vietnamese pilots. Six Vietnamese pilots had already been checked out in the Canberras, and there were fifteen more with jet training, along with about forty mechanics. These pilots could join in strikes against the Viet Cong; and later they, along with the mechanics, could form the nucleus of a Vietnamese F-5 squadron that was then being considered.[32]

Westmoreland also noted in his memo that the change from advisory activities to combat was putting a strain on ammunition supplies. The quick buildup of forces and the rapid acceleration in the number of sorties was depleting his stocks of many types of ordnance. Some items had become so critical that supplies of them were being flown from one base to another as a stopgap measure to keep the planes in the air. The stock of 250-pound bombs would be gone by September and that of 500-pound bombs by November. Rocket launchers would be depleted by October. Leaflet bombs and flares were also being used up. While some of the shortages were being offset by dipping into worldwide assets and by borrowing between the services, the ultimate solution, as proposed by the MACV Commander, lay in releasing more from existing stocks and increasing production.[33]

Westmoreland's memo, a masterpiece of staff work, represents one of several turning points in the conflict. While complete in its tactical details, it made no mention of a strategy for using the requested reinforcements. Although the Saigon commander's briefing to McNamara on the 17th had included a three-phased program for "winning the war," this was more a hopeful plan than a strategy. Now his shopping list had the effect of diverting the minds of military planners away from the larger strategic questions to the more familiar and more easily managed subjects of force structures and deployments. The types of questions raised earlier by the Air Staff planners were overwhelmed by this subsequent request for men and equipment. At work seemed to be the unspoken assumption that strategy would flow from, rather than be a determinant of, the types and locations of American forces in Vietnam.

The strategic discussions going on in Washington at the same time were of a higher level. The whole question of where the United States should go in Vietnam was once again explored in a marathon series of White House meetings beginning on the 21st of July. The service chiefs' turn with the President came on the following afternoon. Before crossing the Potomac to the White House, they gathered in the Pentagon to discuss their position.[34] While they agreed on the need for more strenuous military action, service differences persisted, and these surfaced that afternoon during discussions with the President. The Army's Chief, General Johnson, argued strongly for granting Westmoreland all that he asked. General McConnell and the Chief of Naval Operations, Adm. David MacDonald, while supporting some additional ground forces to defend the enclaves, insisted that the MACV plan would be fruitless unless it was accompanied by concentrated bombing of the north to prevent the enemy from matching American increases. President Johnson was clearly concerned with the political effect at home of increasing the bombing, as well as the military effect in South Vietnam and the diplomatic effect in China and the Soviet Union. This was not a new concern for him. Earlier, in April, he had told McConnell that, while he believed that going north was the right thing, he was catching so much hell over the bombing from both the American public and foreign countries that it was politically tough to maintain that strategy.[35] Despite McConnell's plea on the afternoon of the 22d that the bombing had been ineffective because the raids were flown against the wrong (politically chosen) targets, it became obvious as the afternoon wore on that political rather than military considerations were powering the drive toward a decision.[36]

Falling back on political criteria, the President eliminated the alternatives to Westmoreland's proposal one by one. He said that the American people would not accept bombing the north into submission. He ruled out disengagement on the grounds that it would weaken American credibility and cast doubt on the country's promises elsewhere in the world—he would not be the President to back down on commitments made by his two predecessors and by himself. He could not continue the present strategy—it was not working and prolonging it would lose more territory and people. Since none of his civilian and military advisors had been able to convince him of a better course, he had no choice but to follow the route laid out by General Westmoreland. Although he was far from persuaded by the military arguments, the other choices seemed worse.[37] At a press conference on the 28th, the President announced that he had ordered to Vietnam the airmobile division and other forces that would raise the American fighting strength there from 75,000 to 125,000 at once, with the possibility of later increases.[38]

While these decisions were being made in Washington, the Viet Cong, bolstered increasingly by North Vietnamese soldiers, continued their attacks on district capitals. Having suffered severe casualties from air strikes in their unsuccessful drives against Song Be, Ba Gia, and Dong Xoai in May and June, they now tried several new techniques to neutralize the air power that had frustrated them. Waiting until the flying weather was poor, they captured two district capitals in Kontum Province: Toumorong on the June 25 and Dak To on July 6. During this period, they carried out a series of night hit-and-run raids on the airfields at Da Nang, Nha Trang, Cheo Reo, Soc Trang, Bac Lieu, and Can Tho, with the most serious attack at Da Nang on July 1. A Viet Cong special mission team slipped onto the base at half past one in the morning and trained its newly acquired Chinese 81-mm mortars and 57-mm recoilless rifles on the alert area, destroying two flare-laden C–130s and two F–102s armed with Falcon missiles and rockets. Four F–102s were towed to safety out of the path of the exploding ordnance. After an hour and a half, the assailants withdrew into the darkness. One airman had been killed, and the flare ships continued to burn out of control until midmorning.[39] The enemy also developed new antiaircraft techniques, including increasing their density of fire and training it at attacking aircraft rather than at opposing ground troops.[40]

Spurred in part by the renewed enemy offensive and partly by dissatisfaction with the lack of centralized control of air power in Southeast Asia, the Air Staff intensified its search for ways to make air power more effective. The steady rise in air activity had bloated the 2d Air Division to the point where it was becoming as large as a numbered air force. General Moore, who had been given yet another job as deputy to Westmoreland for air operations and had pinned on his third star, was still reporting to the major general commanding the Thirteenth Air Force at Clark. Several proposals were discussed for alleviating the command situation, including one to divorce the operations in Thailand from the 2d Air Division and place them under an advanced echelon of the Thirteenth Air Force in Thailand.[41] This solution would have satisfied the Thais, who were uneasy about having the planes in their country controlled from Saigon. McConnell, seeking to centralize rather than fragment control, preferred to elevate the 2d Air Division in status, if not yet in name, to the level of the Thirteenth Air Force by taking it out from under the Thirteenth Air Force and placing it directly under PACAF.[42] This change was made on the 8th of July. The units in Thailand were reassigned to the Thirteenth Air Force, but the 2d Air Division would continue to control their operations through a deputy commander at Udorn.

At the same time, the Air Force structure in South Vietnam was tightened up. Fighter wings replaced the existing groups at Bien Hoa and Da Nang, while the groups at Tan Son Nhut and Nha Trang were upgraded. The many heterogeneous tactical and support units that had proliferated at these bases were clustered under the new organizations.[43] This introduced an embryonic wing structure that could be expanded quickly as more forces entered the country. Several weeks later, the Defense Department approved the future movement of five tactical fighter wings and two C–130 wings to Southeast Asia.[44]

Throughout July and August, the recently refurbished Air Force and Army O–1s and their newly trained pilots arrived in South Vietnam. At Hurlburt Field in Florida, the Air Force pilots had been practicing the seemingly endless variety of tasks they would have to perform—directing air

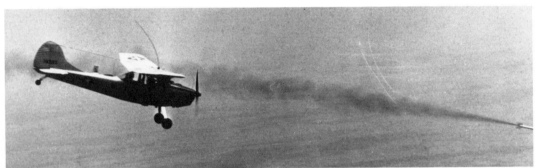

FORWARD AIR CONTROLLERS
Clockwise from top left—a forward air controller lining up for a landing at a small dirt strip; an O–1 on a visual reconnaissance mission; an artist's rendering of an O–1 directing a strike by an F–4; an O–1 over smoke from a marking rocket; an O–1 on convoy escort; a forward air controller about to drop a smoke grenade; a typical forward base; a forward air controller directing strikes from the ground; a forward air controller assessing damage after a strike; an O–1 firing a marking rocket.

strikes, flying visual reconnaissance, escorting convoys, adjusting artillery, and calling in Army helicopter fire teams. To prepare for this alien environment, these jet pilots had to adjust their highly technical skills to the more rudimentary procedures of the Bird Dog. Each forward air controller learned how to navigate by reading maps, how to view the ground in such a way as to be able to pass on critical information to jet fighter pilots (who during a strike had only seconds to comprehend the battle situation), how to mark targets with rockets and grenades, and how to orchestrate one and sometimes several flights of fighters onto the target. To do this well, he had to be familiar with several radio systems, the capabilities of forty-seven types of bombs, three sets of rockets, four kinds of missiles, five varieties of guns, and half a dozen kinds of flares. The sense of bemusement among these aerospace fliers can be imagined as they learned, for example, that the easiest way to make a sight for shooting marking rockets was to place a grease pencil mark on the windshield.

For visual reconnaissance, the pilot was shown practical techniques for getting to know his own area of Vietnam intimately. He was encouraged to become aware of the eating, sleeping, working, traveling, and social routine of the people in his region. He should know how crops in his area were harvested, processed, distributed, and stored. As he flew over villages and fields, he should check for the normal percentage of men as compared to women and children—the sudden disappearance of men could indicate an enemy military muster. Since the Viet Cong traveled and operated primarily at night, the forward air controller should check roads and trails at sunset and again at sunrise for signs of use. There were many ways to discover the enemy's presence without seeing him—reading shadows to determine the presence and height of structures, checking shorelines for footprints when the tide was out, investigating road cuts and signs of digging that could indicate mining, and keeping alert for telltale marks of human presence, such as camp fires or disturbed flocks of birds.

When escorting marching troops or convoys of trucks, the air controller's job was to scout the road one or two miles ahead of the vehicles for signs of ambush, blown bridges, or other suspicious activities and to keep an accurate count of the vehicles. He was to see that the trucks did not use roads that he had not reconnoitered. The Bird Dog's main purpose was to serve as a deterrent. Were the convoy attacked, the controller, with no guns of his own, was to call in air or artillery relief. Since a large part of the controller's work would be in support of ground tactical units, he had to appreciate the benefits and hazards of the ground artillery, which was being fired constantly over much of the battle area. To avoid being hit by artillery and to be able to adjust the artillery from his high vantage point, the pilot needed to learn the artilleryman's vocabulary and capability and to work closely with the fire support people on the ground. There would be times when he would have to direct Army helicopter gunships. He had to know when it was better to use them rather than fixed-wing planes and what kinds of results he could expect from them.[45]

By early September, the new Air Force Bird Dogs and pilots had spread out into the field, creating 3 new tactical air support squadrons: at Da Nang (the 20th), Pleiku (the 21st), and Binh Tuy (the 22d), each with about 30 planes. With the 19th TASS still flying its 30 O–1s out of Bien Hoa, there was now a unit in each corps. Using these points as home bases, the Bird Dogs and tactical control parties were operating in and out of 65 locations. The Army had added 100 of the observation planes to its original 50, and these were spread throughout the country, with the largest concentrations at Hue–Phu Bai, Pleiku, Tan Son Nhut, and Can Tho. Recent additions to the Vietnamese Air Force had increased their Bird Dog strength to 85, divided between Da Nang, Nha Trang, and Bien Hoa. All told, there were 360 of the craft in the country.

At month's end, all of South Vietnam was under O–1 surveillance,[46] and the number of visual reconnaissance sorties being flown by Air Force Bird Dog pilots had surpassed the number of strike control sorties they flew. At the beginning of July, before the buildup, Air Force O–1s had been averaging 41 reconnaissance and 71 strike control flights each day; but 3 months later, they were flying 150 visual reconnaissance sorties a day, while the number of strike control sorties remained unchanged.[47]

With changes taking place on so many fronts, McConnell brought his staff to Hawaii in mid-August to discuss with the field commanders the Air Force's role in the new environment. In these meetings, he was acting not as a member of the Joint Chiefs, who were responsible for the overall strategy of the war, but as Chief of the Air Force, whose job in the conflict was to support PACOM and MACV, the two unified commands fighting the war. However, these two roles could not always be easily divorced.

Following a discussion of Rolling Thunder and agreement that future attacks should concentrate on the targets and go after the surface-to-air missile sites only incidentally, the conferees focused on the war in the south. McConnell informed the group that the Joint Chiefs had agreed on a three-pronged air strategy: supporting the ground forces now pouring into South Vietnam, bombing in the north to discourage the North Vietnamese from continuing to support the Viet Cong, and deterring the Chinese from entering the conflict. The first objective, in the planners' view, worked against the third one. The presence of large numbers of American ground forces in South

Vietnam would probably signal to the Chinese that the United States was concentrating efforts there, rather than on air attacks against the north. Although this would be a misreading of how far the United States was prepared to go to counter Chinese intervention, as long as the United States showed questionable resolve, deterrence would be difficult. Concerning the second objective, while no one at the meeting was rash enough to guarantee that bombing the north would bring an immediate halt to Viet Cong activities in the south, they did agree that the Viet Cong would never stop as long as the north supported them. Nevertheless, the nation's policy now was to fight a war of attrition in the south, and while the Air Force had never favored this strategy, it would support it.[48]

General McConnell predicted that American ground forces alone could not defeat the enemy. The United States could never put enough troops into the country to do the job, and American soldiers were unfamiliar with this type of war. McConnell believed that the guerrillas could be defeated only from the air. It would be expensive, but it would have to be done, even if it required placing four fighter-bombers on every Viet Cong squad. The chief noted that President Johnson wanted the Air Force to kill Viet Cong and that is what would be done. He felt that things would "rock along" for two or three months; and if they continued to deteriorate, there would be a change. In the meantime, he and his staff would provide whatever support they could for Westmoreland's first phase in hopes that the second phase, scheduled to start at the turn of the year, could be averted by forceful action against the north.[49]

As for command relations for fighting the war, McConnell said that some of his staff had been recommending that the 2d Air Division become a numbered air force with two divisions, one in Vietnam and one in Thailand. He had not yet decided what to do. General Moore, reflecting the on-the-scene perspective, favored such a plan. The Army had set up a major headquarters in Thailand, and the Navy had upgraded its command there. Since all American activity in the country worked through Ambassador Graham Martin in Bangkok, it was important that the Air Force be strongly represented. McConnell said he was against pyramiding headquarters and wanted to keep the organization from becoming any more complicated than was necessary. The outfit that did the best job would get the credit, he said, not the one with the biggest headquarters. He saw no need for divisions in Southeast Asia but wanted the existing wing structure strengthened.

Although Moore had been appointed Westmoreland's air deputy in May,[50] it was still not clear how much actual control he would have over air power. The MACV plans division, the only one of the staff agencies headed by an Air Force general, had proposed giving Moore operational control of all the planes in Vietnam, but Westmoreland had rejected this idea. The terms of reference (the job description) for his new position enjoined Moore

An F–4 Phantom II armed with missiles and bombs over Vietnam in 1965.

to take a broad view of air operations and recommend the best ways to use air power. He was also empowered to coordinate operations of all "air forces" under MACV with the Vietnamese Air Force. However, centralized control, considered vital by the Air Force, still eluded him.[51] When he visited air units in the country, Westmoreland had informed Moore, he was to wear his MACV hat. McConnell told Moore at the meeting that he should spend most of his time as air deputy and turn over the 2d Air Division business to his deputy, Maj. Gen. Gilbert L. Meyers. In this way, he could use whatever leverage he had to work toward centralization. One of the main obstacles would be the Marines, who continued to insist that their aircraft were there to support Marine units and would contribute to 2d Air Division's effort only after their own requirements were met.[52] *

On the buildup of people, McConnell was told that the Air Force would need 40,000 military and 7,700 civilian personnel in the country to handle all the operations. The biggest hurdle would be getting 1,900 more pilots. Within the next few months, all the rotational units from the Tactical Air Command would be replaced by troops permanently assigned to PACAF.

The general was given a status report on aircraft production and the new technology that was being developed. Unlike the situation immediately before the Korean conflict, when the United States had been producing 35 different types of planes, there were now only 7 coming off the assembly lines. None of these were bombers, and only the F–4 and the F–5 were fighters. The former

---

*Since there were no Army troops in I Corps, Westmoreland in July had agreed to allow the Marine air-ground system in I Corps to remain outside MACV's control.

was the only one being built for the Air Force, as the F–5 was for foreign sales. The aircraft production base was weak. Lead times were at times a limiting factor. It took 12 months to speed up a production line and 18 to 24 months to reopen a line once it was shut down. Only 25 F–5s were being built each month, and it would require 18 months to double this output. Thirty months would be needed to reach 175 fighters of both types a month. The research and development section of the air staff was in close contact with General Moore in Saigon to keep him abreast of progress and to find out what he needed. The research people had 64 new munitions projects under way, and almost half of these were in the testing stage. Many new items "to dig out the Viet Cong" would be arriving in the theater. Researchers were also developing improved aids for reconnaissance—flares with 5 million candlepower, lamp pods for the C–123s, and improved forward-looking infrared equipment. In addition, they were working on a smaller, more compact version of the long-range navigation system (LORAN) that could be adapted from large aircraft and installed in tactical fighter planes. They were also experimenting with jet engines for the C–123.[53]

The commanders asked McConnell's help on a flood of matters. Construction of the new airfields was still going too slowly for the Air Force to give full support to the first phase of Westmoreland's strategy. One problem was security. The Army had agreed to send enough engineer battalions to do the job,[54] but MACV had delayed asking for them because some of the areas chosen for fields were not yet secure. Since May, the Air Staff had been looking into the possibility of the Air Force building some of its own fields. McConnell had in the past consistently maintained that this was the Army's job and they should do it "even if it requires them to have half a million more people."[55] The situation had now reached the point where McConnell told the field commanders to let his program director know what help the Air Force could provide. He told them that he would support an Air Force organization, including manpower and a one-star position, to get the job done.[56]

Supplies of some munitions were still dwindling, and the shortage would get worse before it improved. Because of the escalating sortie rate, many munitions were being used up faster than they were being produced; and the missions were starting to cut into reserve stocks. Although production would increase from 7,500 tons a month to 60,000 by the end of 1966, this would not solve the immediate problem. Until production caught up with demand the following May, the planes would be dropping 250-pound bombs as a substitute for 500-pound and 750-pound bombs, which the B–52s were using up. General Moore also pointed out that many ships were bringing munitions to Vietnam with incomplete rounds—napalm tanks had fins missing and bombs were lacking fuzes. McConnell told his logistics chief to check with the depot at Ogden, Utah, to see if munition loads were being shipped improperly or if the depot was counting on assets already in Vietnam to make up complete rounds.[57]

Although the O–1 Bird Dogs were doing an adequate job, they were not designed for the combined role they were performing and were hampered by lack of armament. What was needed was a plane that could fly both reconnaissance and strike missions. North American was now building the first 7 of a new light armed reconnaissance aircraft, the OV–10, that could cruise at 240 miles per hour and land at 60 miles per hour. The planes were expensive; each cost half as much as an A–1. McConnell ordered the first 2, which were scheduled to be off the production line in 6 months, sent to Vietnam for testing.

By the end of the meeting, a host of tactical and logistic matters had been reviewed. General Harris was told to work directly with the TAC Commander on how that command could support the war, to let headquarters know how many more revetments were needed in South Vietnam to protect the planes, and to recommend what the duty and combat tours should be for the airmen in the combat zone. General Moore was enjoined to come up with predictions of future requirements for B–52 sorties and to present a detailed picture of the bomb shortage so it could be reported to Secretary McNamara. Gen. Gabriel P. Disosway of the Tactical Air Command was directed to send one of his command's C–130s to Vietnam to act as an airborne command post and to get two more ready to go. Many items needed further study. It had yet to be decided if the 2d Air Division should become a numbered air force, whether the fighter planes in the Pacific would continue to be included in the worldwide quick reaction alert or be dedicated solely to the war in Vietnam, and whether new C–130 airlift squadrons should be located in Vietnam or in the Philippines.

By the end of August, MACV had produced a formal concept for the new program.[58] The Saigon command noted that the plan was necessitated by President Johnson's announcement on the 28th of July that the United States would commit massive military forces. The appearance of this concept a month after the commitment of forces substantiated the Air Staff's earlier observation that large numbers of American troops were going to Vietnam before a master plan for their employment had been developed.

The program included three phases. During the remaining months of 1965, the United States and some Third World allies would send enough forces to Vietnam to stop the losing trend. In the first half of the 1966 (Phase II), the allies would go over to the offensive and begin rebuilding the rural

The air strip at An Khe in late 1965. A U.S. Army CV–2 Caribou and an OV–1 Mohawk are visible on the pad at center right.

economy. If the enemy still refused to quit, an additional year and half should be enough (Phase III) to destroy his remaining forces. It was assumed that the Chinese would not intervene militarily, that the United States would keep control of the air over North Vietnam, and that the Viet Cong would give up the struggle when they realized it was fruitless.

The plan outlined specific programs for each of the four corps areas. In the northernmost I Corps, the Marines were responsible for strengthening their three enclaves at Hue, Da Nang, and Chu Lai and for joining with the South Vietnamese in destroying Viet Cong forces and resources in the coastal plain. After the first of the year, as they moved into the second phase, the Marines would secure the entire coastal region by first connecting the three existing enclaves and then spreading out north and south until the entire coast was clear. Once the enemy was gone from the plain, the Marines would move into the piedmont and the western mountains beyond, spreading South Vietnamese authority and pacification as they went. While the American and Third World forces were destroying the enemy, the South Vietnamese Army would bend its efforts toward pacification. If the enemy had not lain down his arms by the end of the second phase, an intensified campaign against him would continue until he did so. The effort in the enemy-infested II Corps would also begin along the coast with the U. S. Army establishing major bases at Qui Nhon and Cam Ranh Bay and a smaller base forty miles inland at An Khe. From these bridgeheads, the American and South Vietnamese would attack the enemy's inland bases around Pleiku, Kontum, Cheo Reo and Ban Me Thuot but not occupy any of the territory. During the second phase, as in I Corps, the allied forces would move westward extending South

Vietnamese control to the Laotian and Cambodian borders. The key to this strategy was to keep Route 19, the main artery to Pleiku, open. Korean soldiers would protect the bases. In III Corps the strategy differed slightly. Here the American forces would strengthen bases at three points (Bien Hoa, Ben Cat, and Phuoc Vinh) north of Saigon to relieve pressure on the capital and its environs. This would continue through the second phase with stepped-up attacks on the Viet Cong base areas in War Zones C and D. American troops in this corps would also act as a reserve reaction force that could move anywhere in the country when needed. The 173d Airborne Brigade at Bien Hoa had already been doing this, and it was decided to keep it in the country to continue doing so. No American troops would go into the Mekong delta, which made up IV Corps. There the South Vietnamese were on their own to establish bases at Can Tho, Vinh Long, and Soc Trang as springboards against enemy supply bases.

Some of the forces were already in the country when the plan was announced. In mid-July, a brigade of the 1st Infantry Division had gone to Bien Hoa; and later that month, a brigade of the 101st Airborne Division had landed near Qui Nhon. The rest followed quickly. By September, there were 38,000 Marines in I Corps—23,000 at Da Nang, 13,000 at Chu Lai, and 2,000 at Hue. The Army's airmobile 1st Cavalry Division, which had inspired the earlier debate, arrived at Qui Nhon in the middle of the month. With the deployment of the remainder of the 1st Infantry Division to Vung Tau and a Korean division to Cam Ranh Bay and Qui Nhon early in October, the major ground units planned for 1965 were in the country.[59]

The enemy's offensive slackened off during the late summer months. Throughout August and September, the small-unit actions seesawed back and forth as allied forces, increasingly taking on an American complexion, searched out the enemy while the Viet Cong assaulted outposts and villages. During these months, the enemy assaults were frustrated primarily by air power. Some of the most significant actions occurred around Route 19 in the mountainous midsection of the country. While clearing the road west of Pleiku early in August, South Vietnamese soldiers ran into large concentrations of Viet Cong and North Vietnamese. The enemy did not stand and fight but melted into the jungle on either side of the road and took up defensive and ambush positions. It took 2 weeks for the South Vietnamese soldiers, supported from above by 244 strike sorties, to eliminate the pockets of resistance and reach the border.[60] In September, while preparing the way for the airmobile 1st Cavalry Division's move to its inland base at An Khe, part of the 101st Airborne Division moved westward from Qui Nhon to sweep Route 19 of Viet Cong. Near An Khe, it ran into trouble. Letting the first 2 waves of helicopters land American troops, the Viet Cong opened a vicious barrage against the third wave, driving the choppers off and isolating the 2 American companies. Bird Dogs from Pleiku flew to the scene and directed fighters against the besieging enemy battalion. Persistent pressure from the air and from ground artillery allowed a relief column to reach the beleaguered soldiers who then, still under tactical air cover, cleared the region. The airmobile division took over responsibility for the area on the 1st of October.[61]

Elsewhere in the country, principally in the northern provinces of Quang Nam and Quang Tri, American planes drove attackers away from government posts and bombed suspected caches of enemy supplies. They flew over 11,000 tactical attack sorties in each of these months, about one-third of them Air Force flights. Being larger, and thus able to carry more ordnance than the other American and Vietnamese planes, Air Force aircraft dropped almost half of the total weight of bombs.[62] The B–52s were quickly adapting to the new environment as their number of missions kept pace with the increase in tactical air sorties. After their initial Arc Light strike in June, the bombers returned to South Vietnam 5 times in July and twice that often in August. By early August, the crews had become more familiar with the terrain and pinpointed their targets for the first time with radar rather than with the beacon on August 2.[63] With a few exceptions, the big bombers continued to use this method for the remainder of the year.

The first half-dozen Arc Light missions had been individual,thirty-bomber flights planned and flown one at a time against targets selected in Saigon. There was some criticism of these missions, particularly by the Air Staff in Washington. Besides harboring the suspicion that Westmoreland was using them in part to divert attention from the north, there was a growing feeling that there were not enough good targets to justify using the Stratofortresses. Also, there was dissatisfaction with Westmoreland's hesitancy to provide ground followup, the best way to evaluate missions and improve future ones. General McConnell agreed that there were no truly good targets in South Vietnam but that, since the Air Force had pushed for the use of air power to prevent Westmoreland from trying to fight the war solely with ground troops and helicopters, the Air Force would continue to use the bombers.[64]

Some important changes were made in August. By the middle of the month, it was agreed that the flights would be more effective if they were flown more frequently but with a smaller number of planes on each mission. The crews could also react more quickly, while the targets were still active, if most of the planning was done ahead of time. Five "free bomb zones" were created, and target folders were prepared on each so that the bombers could

A B–52 releases its load of bombs over South Vietnam, October 1965.

be called in on short notice. Two of the target boxes were in the stubborn War Zones C and D north of Saigon. Two others were at the southern tip of the country in An Xuyen Province. The fifth zone was in the north, southeast of Da Nang, the suspected location of the enemy's regional headquarters.[65] Most important, from the Joint Chiefs' view, was that they now received authority to approve these strikes in South Vietnam. Up until then, the power to authorize Arc Light strikes had rested in the hands of the President. Also, Westmoreland said that only American troops could be counted on to do a thorough job of ground followups, and that the chances of a mission being compromised were greater when combined American-Vietnamese operations were planned. Therefore, he would schedule followups only when American troops could be spared.[66]

The first of these smaller B–52 missions took place on the 26th of August in an area north of Bien Hoa; and from then on the missions ranged in size from five planes upwards, with occasional full-scale, thirty-bomber raids. Several times in October, two and even three missions were carried out simultaneously.[67]

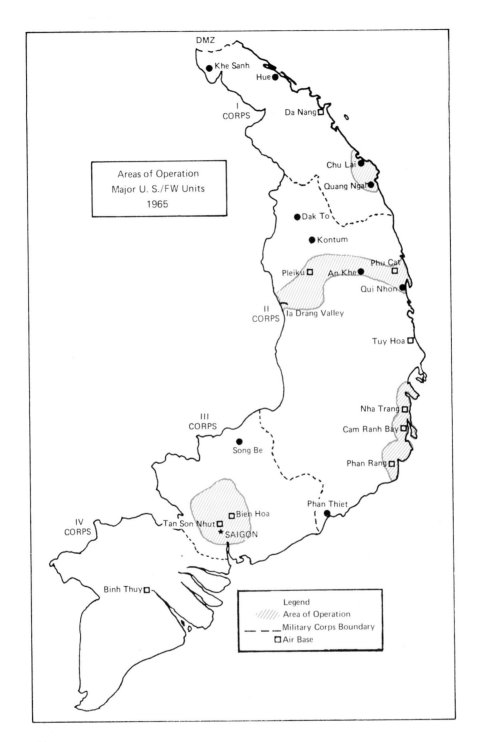

Areas of Operation
Major U. S./FW Units
1965

DMZ

Khe Sanh

Hue

I
CORPS

Da Nang

Chu Lai

Quang Ngai

Dak To

Kontum

Phu Cat

Pleiku   An Khe

Qui Nhon

II
CORPS   Ia Drang Valley

Tuy Hoa

Nha Trang

III
CORPS

Cam Ranh Bay

Song Be

Phan Rang

Phan Thiet

IV
CORPS

Bien Hoa

Tan Son Nhut
★ SAIGON

Binh Thuy

Legend
Area of Operation
Military Corps Boundary
Air Base

84

Chapter IV

Air Force Deployments and Air Operations
September–December 1965

While planning and carrying out the deployment of forces to Southeast Asia in late 1965, the Joint Chiefs remained acutely aware of American military commitments to other parts of the world. These requirements flowed from the "two-and-a-half war" strategy that called for the United States to have enough forces to respond simultaneously to a major nonnuclear attack in Europe by the Soviet Union against NATO, to a full-scale conventional outburst by the Chinese in the Pacific (most likely against Taiwan or Korea), and to a third conflict anywhere in the world that, while minor in nature, would require an immediate answer by the United States. The westward flow of forces across the Pacific led to recurring evaluations by the chiefs of the total American force structure.

Their analysis of the situation in September 1965 was far from encouraging. Air Force planners pointed out that, if all the airplanes that were supposed to go to Southeast Asia by December did so, the Air Force would have two-thirds (53 of 83) of its tactical fighter squadrons committed overseas, nearly one-fourth (20) of them in Southeast Asia. The percentage of deployed reconnaissance squadrons would be even higher—of the 16 squadrons in the inventory, 14 (88%) would be outside the United States, 3 of them in Southeast Asia. Sixteen of the Air Force's 25 C–130 troop carrier squadrons and 10 of its 14 air commando squadrons would also be deployed overseas, 4 and 6 in Southeast Asia, respectively. The increase in forces being sent to the Pacific was cutting severely into the force structure that was coming perilously close to being unable to handle all its responsibilities. The Air Force needed more aircraft and personnel, not only to send overseas, but also for the training and rotational base at home supporting the overseas force. The planners estimated, for example, that more than 800 fighter aircrews would rotate annually through Vietnam. This placed an added burden on training and rotational facilities that also had to support the other 33 fighter squadrons stationed abroad, both in Europe (22) and in the Pacific outside Southeast Asia (11).

To support the Southeast Asia war, to have forces positioned against potential Chinese intervention, to be ready to defend Europe for thirty days against a Soviet attack, and to have enough planes and people for rotation and training, the Air Force would need by the end of the year eleven new fighter squadrons, seven additional reconnaissance squadrons, five more troop carrier squadrons, and four air commando squadrons. The other services were equally hard pressed to support the global strategy. To restore their strategic reserve while fighting in Vietnam, the Army estimated that it needed seven more aviation companies, the Navy needed another carrier, and the Marines needed an additional expeditionary force. None of this could be done, in the chiefs' view, short of calling up reserve units, extending involuntarily the term of military service, expanding the industrial base, and increasing the ceilings that limited the size of the armed forces.[1] Each of these prescriptions was fraught with political and economic implication; and the administration, as yet feeling no sense of urgency, was willing to postpone action on them.

These JCS estimates assumed full implementation of the Phase I deployments. By January 1966, however, only nine of the thirteen Air Force tactical fighter squadrons scheduled to be in South Vietnam were there. A main factor slowing down Air Force reinforcements was the difficulty in building and improving air bases.

The temporary runway at Cam Ranh Bay had been finished in mid-October 1965. Earlier, between June and September, U.S. Army engineers had prepared the Cam Ranh area by building 30 miles of roads, setting up quarries, lengthening a pier that they had built there 2 years before, and building equipment platforms, fuel storage areas, and motor pools. In September, they had turned the project over to the civilian construction combine of RMK/BRJ, which up till then had done most of the construction in South Vietnam. The initial work force of 76 Vietnamese quickly mushroomed to 1,500, mostly women, and within 50 days the runway was ready for use. A week later, aprons and taxiways were complete and living quarters and supply buildings were ready for occupants.

While 3 squadrons of F–4 Phantoms at MacDill Air Force Base, Florida, were being readied for deployment, a temporarily assigned squadron (the 43d) arrived at Cam Ranh Bay on the first of November and began flying missions in South Vietnam the next day. A week later, members of the 12th Tactical Fighter Wing headquarters arrived; and by the middle of the month, the planes and personnel of 2 more Phantom squadrons (the 557th and 558th) were in place. The 43d, being there first, flew most of the sorties in November (295); but by December, the other 2 squadrons, now in full operation, flew over 840 sorties in both Vietnam and Laos. The 43d returned to MacDill on the first day of the new year[2] and was soon replaced by a third permanent Phantom squadron, the 559th. At the end of January, these 3 squadrons were joined by a fourth, the 391st, which was diverted from the still uncompleted base at Phan Rang.

Cam Ranh Bay, however, was the only one of the new or improved jet bases proposed back in April that was ready by the end of the year. The Army engineers had encountered a host of problems at Phan Rang. A shortage of aluminum matting, compounded by heavy rains and an unanticipated increase in the amount of earth that had to be moved, pushed back the estimated completion date from December to April of the next year.[3]

The situation at the third of the new bases, Qui Nhon, was even worse. The original survey of the site had been made from the air since the ground had not yet been secured. When the architectural and engineering people finally inspected Qui Nhon from the ground, they found that they would have to move three million cubic feet of earth and spend many months preparing the soil for the aluminum matting and many additional months preparing for the permanent runway. These changes would add three to four million dollars to the original cost.

In September the project was halted and a search began for a replacement. Two other coastal sites—Tuy Hoa, forty-five miles south of Qui Nhon, and Phan Thiet, east of Saigon—were suggested. A feasibility study and coastal survey in September and October inclined CINCPAC toward the former. In November, however, MACV objected to building a new base at Tuy Hoa, pleading that it could not afford to pay the price. Security in the area was poor and stationing enough troops there to protect the workmen and the completed base would weaken the military offensive just getting under way. Since the number of construction people and the amount of construction equipment in Vietnam were finite, to build a base at Tuy Hoa would delay other projects with equal or higher priority. Logistic support for the base would have to come through Vung Ro Bay, twenty miles distant, and the problems created by this made the site impractical. Finally, transportation personnel would have to be taken away from Vietnamese ports already backed up with ships waiting to unload. The tactical sorties that would be flown from Tuy Hoa could be launched from a Navy carrier instead.[4]

MACV agreed reluctantly with CINCPAC early in December to begin construction at Tuy Hoa the following month, but the decision was postponed in January in favor of examining another site fifteen miles north of Qui Nhon at Phu Cat. Still another airfield would be needed; and discussions during the first two months of the new year centered on the Air Force's contention that fields were needed quickly and on MACV's stand that

The first F–5s in Vietnam attract attention at Bien Hoa, October 1965.

resources were limited, that other projects came first, and that the Air Force would have to wait its turn. By February, the issue had escalated to the level of the Air Force Secretary.

Other Phase I programs pushed ahead despite the delay with the new fields. Late in October, a dozen F–5 Freedom Fighters landed in two waves at Bien Hoa after a transoceanic flight from Arizona. The planes made up a provisional tactical fighter squadron, the 4503d, that was to spend four months in Vietnam testing the lightweight fighters in combat and comparing them with other jets already flying against the enemy. Earlier, in July, when Westmoreland had asked for twenty-five of these planes for the Vietnamese Air Force, Secretary McNamara was unenthusiastic and postponed a decision until the planes could be tested in combat.[5] To satisfy the Vietnamese request for jets, they were "given" four of the B–57s at Da Nang in August,[6] although the planes remained a detachment of the USAF squadron there;[7] and twenty Vietnamese had been sent to Clark to train as pilots, navigators, maintenance officers, and mechanics.[8]

The Freedom Fighter was a light, twin-engine supersonic jet that the United States was distributing to its foreign customers both through its military assistance program and through direct sales. It was designed to support troops in action, intercept enemy aircraft, attack supply lines and communications, and fly armed reconnaissance missions at high and low altitudes. Forty-seven feet long, with a wingspan of 26 feet and a weight of only 13,000 pounds, it could carry close to 3 tons of missiles, bombs, rockets, and napalm as well as machineguns, reconnaissance gear, and extra fuel.[9]

Since the Air Force, having emphasized over the years larger aircraft for general war situations, lacked combat experience in any lightweight, low-cost tactical jet fighter, it decided in July to test the F–5 in Vietnam. General McConnell resisted a suggestion by the other chiefs that he make a formal recommendation to give the planes to the Vietnamese when the tests were finished. He did not yet want to tie the tests to the issue of jets for the Vietnamese lest it cause Secretary McNamara, who was still not sold on the idea, to cancel the tests.[10]

The twelve planes were camouflaged and fitted with aerial refueling equipment, armor plate, jettisonable pylons, and a new gyro system. When they arrived in Vietnam in October, they were quickly dubbed Skoshi (little) Tigers. A team of evaluators accompanied them to monitor the accuracy of their weapons, the ease of maintaining them, and how well they could maneuver and survive in a hostile environment.

For the first two months, the F–5s flew against targets inside Vietnam, seldom venturing farther than forty miles from Bien Hoa. Their performance was compared with that of the F–100s from the same base, the F–4s from Ubon in Thailand, and the F–104s from Da Nang. The F–104s were dropped from the test when they left the country in November. Early in December, as they moved into full operation, the new F–4 squadrons at Cam Ranh Bay replaced the Ubon Phantoms in the evaluation.[11]

In the interest of realism, the F–5s were folded into the operations in Vietnam and treated just like the other jets. The 2d Air Division planned the missions, which, like the other strike sorties in the country, were often diverted after takeoff to high-priority, last-minute targets ranging from Viet Cong troops to sampans, trucks, and buildings. By the end of December, the Skoshi Tiger squadron had flown 1,500 sorties and dropped over 3 million pounds of ordnance. One plane was lost to ground fire on the 16th of December.

The reviews of this first phase of the text were mixed. Pilots and ground crews were enthusiastic about the plane. The twelve F–5s flew twenty-four sorties a day and could readily have flown twice that number. They were easy to maintain. Some, however, still preferred the nonjet A–1s, which carried a larger load and loitered longer. Some minor equipment problems surfaced. The 20-mm machineguns were not holding up. Aircraft engines, damaged by debris sucked in from expended ammunition and rockets, had to be replaced, on the average, after every twenty-six hours of flying. The same debris scratched and smoked the plane's canopy, making it difficult for the pilot to see, especially when it rained. Most of the logistic and planning totals worked out in the states for the experiment had to be multiplied by a factor of four or five for operations in Vietnam.[12] On the first of January, the squadron moved to Da Nang for a one-month test to see how well the planes would do over North Vietnam and the trails of Laos.

While this experiment was in its early stages, another was being completed and transformed into a permanent operation. On the 14th of November, twenty venerable C–47s landed at Tan Son Nhut to form the 4th Air Commando Squadron.[13] For almost a year, one—at times several—of these thirty-year-old cargo planes had been flying test missions as gunships in Vietnam. The idea of mounting a side-firing gun at the door of a transport, wired so that the pilot could fire it from his seat up front, had been pushed by several fighter pilots in the Air Force Systems Command. Two of these officers, Capt. John C. Simons and Capt. Ronald W. Terry, had fought a wall of opposition before the idea was taken seriously. There was concern about the vulnerability of the lumbering Gooney Bird in a hostile environment. There was also sensitivity about the Army's growing role in close air support. The Air Force had been opposing, on doctrinal grounds, the Army's use of armed helicopter transports as gunships. Were the Air Force to use the C–47 in this fire support role, it could be construed as tacit approval of the Army's practice and could lead to an increase of armed Army transports. The strongest opposition to gunships had come from Gen. Walter C. Sweeney, Jr., the TAC Commander, who earlier had felt that the development of this (and other) weapons specifically for Vietnam could distract the Air Force from its main focus, Europe and NATO. He had feared that acceptance of such a vulnerable plane as a permanent part of the force could spell trouble in a future war on that continent.[14]

However, stateside tests of the gunships were promising enough to overrule these objections. Early in December 1964, two of the Gooney Birds at Bien Hoa were fitted with guns, gunsights, and flare dispensers; and by the middle of the month, they were repelling attacks on Vietnamese outposts. Just before Christmas, one of them flew the first night gunship mission. The results were sufficiently gratifying to raise hopes that one of the Air Force's more intractable problems, supporting troops at night, was on the road to solution. Tests continued for several months; and in May, the Air Force decided to go ahead with the C–47 as a first-generation gunship. The plane's endurance; the space to carry flares, spare guns, and ammunition; and the crew's ability to reload, repair, and replace guns during a mission made it the best vehicle for the job. The plane showed that it could deliver heavy and quite accurate fire from 3,000 feet, an altitude that put it safely above ground fire and allayed fears about its vulnerability. An added bonus was its quick reaction time from airborne alert to the target. At the same time, it was evident that the C–47, as with other aircraft (such as the O–1 and the F–5) that were being adapted off the shelf for use in the conflict, had shortcomings that would have to be corrected in later models. The C–47's successor would require more cargo compartment space for a greater payload, it would have

An early AC–47 with ten .30–caliber machineguns mounted for side firing.

to be better protected with armor, and it would need an improved system for cooling the guns.[15] Even as the Air Force was sending these gunships to Vietnam, it was searching for a more satisfactory replacement.

The gunships (now labeled AC–47s) went to work immediately and, by the first week in December 1965, had expanded their operations to include strikes and flare missions against enemy soldiers moving down the trails of Laos.[16]

On the same day that the gunships arrived at Tan Son Nhut, three C–123s were added to one of the airlift squadrons there (the 309th ACS). These planes, modified with equipment for spraying herbicides and designated as UC–123s, joined four other spray planes that, since early 1962, had been defoliating the jungle that hid the enemy from the air. During their first year in Vietnam, these four original planes, making up a detachment called Ranch Hand, flew a small number of missions clearing roadsides, power lines, railroads and areas around depots, and airfields. MACV's initial skepticism about the operation had turned to support at the end of the first year as enemy attacks decreased markedly in the sprayed areas.[17]

While the UC–123s continued to fly periodic defoliation missions during the early years, Washington resisted suggestions from Saigon, often Vietnamese-inspired, that the planes spray enemy crops. The strongest objections within the American government came from the State Department, where it was felt that the advantages of such an operation would be more than offset by the propaganda barrage that was certain to follow. Although President

A Ranch Hand UC–123 with spraying arms under the wings at Tan Son Nhut.

Kennedy gave his approval late in 1962 for Vietnamese helicopters to spray enemy crops, these flights did not begin until May of 1964. Within 6 months, the Vietnamese had destroyed 6,400 acres of crops in Viet Cong areas. When the Vietnamese refused to fly these missions in War Zone D, Ambassador Taylor turned to the American planes. The 4 aircraft flew their first crop destruction missions early in October 1964 and added 34 more missions by the end of the year. Restrictions on the crop-spraying flights eased gradually early in 1965; and by midyear, Ranch Hand was flying as many crop destruction as defoliation missions. The success of the operation led to the decision to add 3 additional spray planes to the detachment. Like the gunships, the UC–123s soon expanded their operations and flew their first defoliation mission in Laos early in December 1965. Unlike the gunships, however, missions on the trails were never to become an important part of Ranch Hand operations.[18]

The American buildup late in 1965 was accompanied by attempts to centralize and improve several psychological warfare programs already under way. On the 20th of November, the cargo ship USS *Breton* docked in Saigon, its hold filled with the crated parts of seventeen U–10 Super Courier light observation planes. The aircraft were assembled and flown to Nha Trang to join four C–47s in a recently organized Air Force squadron.[19] The new squadron, the 5th Air Commando, was the Air Force's contribution to a joint public affairs program recommended in March by the United States Information Agency and organized two months later in Saigon.

For nearly a year, a handful of Vietnamese light planes had been beaming broadcasts and dropping leaflets in both North and South Vietnam. Their equipment, however, was unequal to the task, and the mounting

An Air Force U–10 drops leaflets on a psychological warfare mission.

volume of enemy ground fire was forcing them to higher altitudes from which their messages could not be heard. Loudspeakers mounted under the wings of the U.S. planes were 4 times as powerful as those of the Vietnamese, allowing the ships to fly safely at 3,000 feet and the messages to be heard from that altitude. The program sought to gain support for the government among the listeners on the ground. The planes were viewed as a way of spreading information that otherwise could not reach the populace. Leaflets and broadcasts warned of impending airstrikes and herbicide missions, provided information on current events, and explained government programs.* Over regions controlled by the enemy, the propaganda aimed at discrediting the insurgents and inducing defections.

By early December, the planes were dispersed from Nha Trang to forward operating bases throughout the country. Like the fighters, their missions were planned in advance either locally or in Saigon, while some planes remained on alert for immediate reactions. In December, these psyop aircraft flew 287 missions, a tenfold increase over the previous month; and by early January 1966, they were starting to speak to the North Vietnamese troops in eastern Laos.[20]

By the end of 1965, the Air Force had 20,000 people and slightly over 500 planes stationed in South Vietnam that flew 144,000 sorties during the

---

*See Appendix 4, Psychological Warfare Leaflets.

93

year.* An additional 9,000 people and 205 planes were stationed in Thailand. The aircraft in Southeast Asia ranged from the largest to the smallest planes in the inventory. This seemingly incongruous situation, which, paradoxically, was criticized by some as too sophisticated and by others as not sophisticated enough, resulted from factors whose importance the critics on both extremes underestimated. Most influential of these were the existing American global strategy and the rapidity with which U.S. strategy changed in Southeast Asia during the summer of 1965.

American global military strategy since the Second World War had focused on strategic, particularly nuclear, deterrence of the Soviet Union and on maintaining the ability to fight a nuclear war should deterrence fail. Equipment had been designed and airmen trained primarily to give the Soviet Union pause in executing any plans it might have to attack the United States or one of its allies. After the Korean conflict, this strategy was expanded to include deterrence of nuclear and conventional war in both Europe and the Pacific. While the new, more flexible strategy extended the American umbrella to nonnuclear warfare, it fell short of preparing the country for conflicts on the smaller insurgency level.

The sudden shift to a military ground strategy in Vietnam in 1965 deprived the Air Force of the lead times it needed for research, development, and production to retool for that kind of war. American policymakers in mid-1965 saw the situation in South Vietnam as extremely critical and decided on immediate action. Once the decision was made to stop American withdrawal and to intervene in force, there was no alternative but to rely, initially at least, on the men, equipment, and planes that were on hand. The result was the deployment of aircraft designed for a different age and a different kind of conflict.

Aside from being further squeezed on its own bases, the Vietnamese Air Force was surprisingly little affected by the American military rush that swirled about it. This was due fundamentally to the American policy, adopted early in the 1960s, and reaffirmed as late as July 1965, not to merge the Vietnamese and American armed forces. Despite frequent importuning from Washington and numerous suggestions over the years that closer integration of the two armies might be beneficial, Ambassador Taylor and General Westmoreland remained firmly convinced that more harm than good would result from amalgamation. The decision was partly political, partly

---

*See Appendix 5, USAF Tactical Sorties in South Vietnam, 1965–1967.

military. Those on the scene in Saigon were acutely aware, as Westmoreland put it, that "subordination might give credence to the enemy's absurd claim that the United States was no more than a colonial power."[21] A combined command, moreover, would contradict the publicly stated American objective of creating a viable government and military force that could stand alone after the Americans withdrew.[22] "Subordinating the Vietnamese forces to U.S. control," in the eyes of the general, "would stifle the growth of leadership and acceptance of responsibility essential to the development of Vietnamese armed forces capable eventually of defending their country."[23] Besides, the MACV Commander believed he informally could reap the same benefits that a combined command would bring without suffering the drawbacks. His relations with the Vietnamese Joint General Staff (JGS) were close and compatible, and the almost total logistic and financial reliance of the Vietnamese on the United States gave him all the influence he needed.[24] A formal sharing of command with the Vietnamese, on the other hand, would inhibit the more aggressive Americans. As a result, there remained two sovereign military structures tenuously linked by informal personal relationships and a more formal advisory group. The Chief of the Air Force's Advisory Group, Brig. Gen. Albert W. Schinz, described the relationship between the two as one in which Americans could not "command, direct or order our counterparts, but must use tact, diplomacy and persuasion."[25] However, what were intended to be suggestions by the Americans were often interpreted by the Vietnamese as commands, with the result that the Vietnamese came to rely on the Americans to a greater degree than the Americans maintained they wanted.

The structure of the Vietnamese Air Force also was little changed by the events of 1965 because its buildup, begun 3 years earlier, was virtually complete when the American inundation began. By May of 1965, the VNAF organizational structure was almost totally Americanized; and by the end of the year, there were 13,000 men and 359 planes in the force—numbers that would not change substantially until the 1970s. Of the 5 tactical wings, 2 were in III Corps (Bien Hoa and Tan Son Nhut) and a single wing was in each of the other corps (at Da Nang, Pleiku, and Binh Thuy). A fifth fighter squadron of A–1s (the 522d) had been activated at Tan Son Nhut in May, and the sixth and final squadron (the 524th) came into being at Nha Trang in August, bringing to 146 the number of Vietnamese Skyraiders. The 4 H–34 helicopter squadrons and 4 O–1 liaison squadrons were up to strength and 2 of the 3 planned transport squadrons of C–47s were operational. This was as large a force as the country could afford, and it was deemed sufficient to defend postwar South Vietnam. Until that day arrived, the United States could handle any additional requirements. Besides these tactical wings, the VNAF had a logistics wing at Bien Hoa, a base support group at Pleiku, and its French-founded Air Training Center at Nha Trang.

By late 1965, the American advisors were turning from expanding to modernizing the Vietnamese air arm.[26] Plans were taking shape in December for modernization over the next three years. Two of the six fighter squadrons would gradually convert to F–5s (if McNamara could be persuaded), the H–34 helicopters would give way to newer UH–1s, and at least one of the C–47 squadrons would receive C–119 transports.[27] Major improvements were envisioned for the forward air controller program, the air defense net, and in the realm of communications, which was particularly weak.

While the Americans did not have direct formal control over the VNAF, there were many subtle, indirect ways in which the bulging Air Force presence touched the Vietnamese flyers. Except at Cam Ranh Bay, the arriving American air units were crowded onto existing VNAF bases. The Vietnamese base commanders lacked the experience and resources to cope with the influx. Conditioned to thinking of the war in terms of decades, these senior officers were frequently suspicious of the American's piecemeal approach to such matters as real estate, ramp space, and base facilities. The American tendency to get the job done as quickly as possible and the system of short individual tours for American airmen occasionally led to misunderstandings and strained relationships. Americans also found the environment unfamiliar. Accustomed to controlling their own bases, the Air Force had to make many adjustments.

The imposition of the Air Force's type of command structure on the higher levels of the Vietnamese Air Force did not always result in changes down the line. In some cases adjustments were made. The massive injection of Americans into both the central tactical air control center (formerly the air operations center) at Tan Son Nhut and each of the local direct air support centers (formerly the air support operations centers) set an example of combat management their allies attempted to emulate.[28] The Air Force people at these centers set about gaining control of air operations by increasing the number of forward control missions, by creating a current intelligence structure to deal with immediate requests, and, for the first time, by demanding targets from South Vietnamese Army units. The control system began to change from a post facto recorder of air operations to the positive planner and controller of air strikes it was originally meant to be. The Vietnamese gradually came to see the benefits of this centralized control. In December 1965, they copied the Air Force system by taking their own local air control centers, which were located alongside the USAF ones, out from under their tactical wings in each corps and tying them directly to their own central control center, which existed side by side with the Air Force's in Saigon.[29]

Although the Air Force advisory group was limited to training and modernizing the VNAF, its work was augmented informally by the vast American resources that were pouring into the country. The very presence of massive amounts of American equipment and skilled people alongside the Vietnamese led to increased cooperation in air operations. Gradually the Vietnamese came to use, in some cases by joint agreement, the American aircraft and control warning system, weather stations, the vast skein of navigational aids strung out across the country by the United States, the communication network, fire and crash rescue vehicles, and the aerial port system.

In other areas, however, adaptation came slowly, if at all. The Vietnamese air headquarters in Saigon found it difficult to control and manage what still remained at core a decentralized force. This was due in part to the fact that the Vietnamese Air Force had to compete with the Vietnamese Army, usually with little success, for attention and resources. The army, for example, was responsible for maintaining the air bases, but its support of the air force in providing materials and skilled labor was marginal.[30]

The Vietnamese Air Force, moreover, suffered an even greater management drain than it had earlier. Its commander, Prime Minister Ky, pulled his best people with him into the government, leaving to the American advisors the task of training replacements. The difficulties of that were noted by General Moore who observed that, although several young field grade officers were showing promise as good leaders, "daily siestas and weekend slackening of effort is still a way of life."[31] A midyear evaluation of the Vietnamese helicopter and liaison operations in the delta illustrated the effects of poor management:

> The helicopters and liaison aircraft in Can Tho are commanded by very junior officers who exercise little, if any, control over the detachment. The aircrews cannot be located at times. They take two-and-a-half to three-hour lunch periods, during which time they are away from the base and no one is available for flight.[32]

The aircraft at the base were not being used properly. Pilots, lacking training and confidence, refused to fly at night and would not use their helicopters for medical evacuation missions in the face of enemy action. Liaison pilots were assigned for only two weeks and then moved away to another province, undercutting MACV's ambitious visual reconnaissance program. Once sent into the field, Vietnamese forward air controllers were on their own. As a result, American FACs directed virtually all the Vietnamese fighter strikes.[33]

As part of trying to create a self-sufficient Vietnamese air arm, the United States Air Force in late 1965 began to deemphasize stateside training and stress preparation of their counterparts in South Vietnam. While the ideal was to have the Vietnamese train themselves at home, this had to be supplemented by on-the-job training, with American units and mobile

Vietnamese Air Force A–1H Skyraiders over South Vietnam.

training teams that traveled the country teaching a wide range of technical and professional subjects. Only when training could not be done at home would Vietnamese airmen be sent abroad.

Substantial as they were in peacetime, the problems of training were magnified in war. In the midst of combat, Vietnamese air commanders were reluctant to release men for training. With the war all around them, pilot trainees were thrown into action as soon as they became minimally qualified, leaving little time to learn instrument and night flying. As a group, the commanders operated from day to day rather than programming and training their way out of their skill shortages. Often the men resisted being sent for training since this meant leaving their home stations. The program was weakened by the low pay that forced the men to moonlight, by the family separation, and by the relatively poor facilities at Vietnamese training bases.[34]

The two cultures clashed in other small, but important, ways. Flying safety, for example, was hampered by the absence in Vietnamese law of immunity against self-incrimination. It was not unusual for a pilot, after giving testimony helpful in determining the cause of his accident, to find himself behind bars. In one instance, one such unlucky pilot was transferred to the army with the rank of private. Although some officers were trained in flying safety in the United States, they did not ever work in the area when they returned to Vietnam. Highly promising in the first place, they were quickly promoted out of the field.[35] To a people being introduced to the complexities of western technology, the concept of preventive maintenance was alien; and the tradition of postponing maintenance until equipment broke down or failed to function continued.[36] Medical facilities and procedures for flightline and aviation medicine were primitive. Although many of the Vietnamese doctors had been trained well in France, Hanoi, or Saigon, they did not have adequate resources. Medical buildings were substandard, lacked running water, and were often equipped with makeshift partitions and a few inadequate lights. "One dispensary," as described by an Air Force advisor, "had only a black aluminum pan, a dirty hot plate, and a pair of forceps to pick up the questionably sterilized syringe."[37] There was no concept of military public health, occupational medicine, or food inspection. Aircraft accidents were never investigated medically. The challenge to the Americans was to move the Vietnamese Air Force toward self-sufficiency while the weight of their own effort was shifting from giving advice to performing combat.

The number and ferocity of enemy attacks began to escalate again in October, as did the quality of the American response. The Viet Cong and their tutors, the North Vietnamese, were employing a strategy perfected in the early days of the struggle against the French—using a "neutral" neighbor's land as a supply conduit, a sanctuary, and a training ground. Just as the Viet Minh in 1950 had gathered and trained their soldiers in camps across the border in China for attacks into Vietnam, their successors were now using Laos and Cambodia in similar fashion.

Alarmed at the influx of American troops into the country, the North Vietnamese launched an offensive in the central highlands to cut the country in two before American troops became too strong and too numerous. The first step in this plan was to seize the South Vietnamese outposts just inside the border. Although the enemy had overrun one of these border posts at Dak To in June, they were driven from it within 2 days. Another attack in August on the camp at Duc Co was beaten back, largely by 280 tactical strike sorties.

The final major enemy assault of the spring offensive came in mid-October in the II Corps area, which just several weeks before had become the responsibility of the airmobile division. The Communists' objective was the small triangular fort at the Montagnard village of Plei Me, 20 miles inside Vietnam from Cambodia and 25 miles south of Pleiku. The post was manned by 350 local irregular troops and a 12-man American advisory team.

For six days preceding the assault, a North Vietnamese general rehearsed the operation with his two northern regiments and the Viet Cong. One regiment and the Viet Cong were to take up positions west of the camp, while the other regiment was to be seven miles to the north astride the road

Air delivery of supplies from a USAF C–123 Provider.

that ran to the camp from Pleiku. The first regiment would surround the camp and attack it. As reinforcements came down the road from the north, the second regiment would ambush them. The two forces would then join to capture the isolated camp. Special measures were taken against airplanes. The soldiers were instructed to concentrate their 50-mm and .30-caliber machine-guns on the attack planes and helicopters. They were also ordered to stay close to the camp's wire perimeter in hopes that the planes, fearful of hitting their own troops, would not attack.

Just after sunset on Monday evening, the 19th of October, the enemy overran a small outpost in a clearing below the camp. The American Army captain in charge of the advisors did not take this too seriously until four hours later, when the insurgents launched a full-scale assault on the camp itself. In response to his call for assistance, a C–123 flare ship arrived from Da Nang, followed five minutes later by a pair of A–1Es. The fighters threw back the human wave attack against the camp, but the enemy continued to rain heavy fire on the defenders. As the seriousness of the situation became evident, more air and ground resources were funneled toward the camp. The next day C–123s from Nha Trang began flying in food and ammunition. Since the small runway was unusable, they dropped the supplies from the air. Four cargo planes were hit the first day, but none was shot down. As the battle raged, an Army advisor in the outpost radioed to the forward air controller overhead and asked, "Do you have any influence? We're low on ammunition and need supplies badly." The pilot replied, "Why, yes...as a matter of fact, three 'birds' are circling the area now, preparing to make a drop." "Boy," came the pleased reply, "you really do have influence."[38]

Canberras from Da Nang and Super Sabres from Bien Hoa continued to hold back the enemy on Tuesday with strafing and napalm strikes. Throughout that night and all day Wednesday, the Plei Me camp continued to receive mortar fire and ground probes. At half past two on Thursday morning, the enemy tried another all-out assault, only to be driven back by the planes that hit them within ten feet of the camp's fence.

Two relief elements were on their way by Thursday. Helicopters landed two Vietnamese Ranger companies three miles north of the camp, and the force began to work its way toward the fort. At the same time, a South Vietnamese Army regiment prepared to set out down the road from Pleiku. The convoy had about fifty vehicles, tanks, armored personnel carriers, and artillery. Another hundred sorties kept the enemy at bay as the first relief column of rangers entered the camp.

The enemy realized that the camp could not be stormed until the two regiments were joined. They poured their heaviest fire yet into the fort on Friday morning. American planes responded with 114 sorties throughout the day, dropping bombs, napalm, and rockets and strafing the North Vietnamese troops and gun positions.

The armored task force from Pleiku was within 7 miles of the camp on Saturday evening when the enemy sprang the ambush. The first attack left several vehicles burning. Between sunset and dawn, 74 air strikes pummeled the ambushers. An AC–47 gunship lit up the area with flares and sprayed the enemy with its miniguns. At daybreak, the North Vietnamese broke contact. Elements of the 1st Cavalry Division that had moved from An Khe to Pleiku took up positions on either side of the road that evening, and the convoy proceeded on to the camp. The failure of the ambush broke the back of the enemy's battle plan. They halted their attacks on the camp, and their firing dropped to sporadic harassment and occasional mortar rounds. The strike planes turned to firing on the fleeing troops and bombing escape routes, and the number of sorties dropped gradually from 109 on Sunday to 9 on Thursday the 29th, the last day of the operation.

This was the largest air-supported combat operation of the war so far, using almost 600 strikes. Two-thirds of these were flown by the Air Force, with the Navy, Marines, and the Vietnamese providing the rest. Airlift planes flew 643 tons and 3,300 troops, in 163 sorties, to the scene of the battle. General Moore was encouraged by the quick response of his planes and by how well they worked together with American and South Vietnamese ground troops to save the camp. For the first 3 days of the battle, only air power stood between the garrison and the enemy.[39]

At the height of the action, General Westmoreland flew into An Khe. When it became apparent that the camp would be saved, he decided to send the American troops to pursue the fleeing North Vietnamese. This was a major departure from previous actions. Although the enemy had been repulsed in similar, albeit smaller, attacks in the past, he was always allowed to retreat, regroup, and retrain because the South Vietnamese Army lacked the reserves and initiative for pursuit. With the 1st Cavalry Division now in place in the area, the general ordered a search and destroy mission that was to provide the first major showdown between Americans and North Vietnamese—the month-long battle in the Ia Drang Valley between Plei Me and the Cambodian border.

On the first of November, three days after the siege of Plei Me ended, one third of the 1st Air Cavalry Division (its 1st Brigade) began fanning out westward from the camp to pursue the attackers. In keeping with Westmoreland's program for the first phase of operations in II Corps, the brigade was to harass and attack the enemy wherever found but was not to seize territory.

The region between Plei Me and the Cambodian border 20 miles away was marked by 2 prominent geographic features—the Ia Drang River that snaked through the area from Cambodia, carving out a sheer valley, and the Chu Pong Range that formed the valley's southern wall. The highest elevation was the Chu Pong Mountain, a 2,800-foot rise 15 miles west of Plei Me that sloped down into Cambodia.

Like War Zones C and D to the south, the Chu Pong was thought to shelter a major enemy redoubt, the hub of operations for the central highlands. Strategically situated at the foot of the Ho Chi Minh Trail, it provided easy access to Cambodia and gave the enemy a secure area to store supplies, train soldiers, make and repair arms and equipment, and use as an operating base for combat units. The besiegers of Plei Me were believed to have emerged from this base. In all the years of warfare, the Vietnamese Army had never ventured into the area; and until early in November 1965, it remained inviolate.

The American search and destroy mission into the Ia Drang Valley, called Silver Bayonet, was the first full-scale combat test of the Army's new airmobile tactic that relied heavily on organic Army aircraft for both close air support and logistic airlift. Helicopters flew the soldiers into combat and provided support for them in their contact with the enemy, while other helicopters and twin-engine Army Caribou transports delivered supplies to rear and forward bases. At the beginning of the operation, the Army corps-level commander, adhering to airmobile doctrine, ordered the division to use its own aircraft for all airlift within 150 miles of the battlefield.[40] Helicopters and Caribous were directed to fly supplies from the division's main base at An Khe to the fighting units. It was expected that Highway 19 from An Khe to Pleiku would remain in friendly hands and that most supplies could move by road at least to Pleiku.[41] Were the road closed, 150 tons of supplies would have to be flown in daily.

More was riding on the outcome of this operation than the immediate improvement of the tactical ground situation in Vietnam. General McConnell remained skeptical of the airmobile idea and believed that the best force for fighting a ground war was a regular Army division with Air Force tactical support. He had consistently opposed moving the airmobile division into the highlands, at least until its lines of communication with the coast were firmly established, either by securing Route 19 or by planning to rely on the Air Force to keep An Khe and the forward bases supplied by air. All eyes were now riveted on the Army's attempt to prove that it could sustain itself.

Both the Army and the Air Force were looking closely at the division's conduct as a key to future requirements. Secretary McNamara was leaning toward converting another of the Army's 16 divisions into an airmobile force and increasing the number of Army aviation companies during the next few years from 78 to 109. He felt that the expensive airmobile division would be worth the cost if it modified the concept of battle and lowered casualties by increasing the tempo of operations and reducing the time troops were exposed to enemy fire. Doubting that this would be the case, the Air Force Chief told his commanders in Hawaii and Saigon to keep detailed statistics on every phase of the operation, including the amount of nonorganic (other than Army) air support requested by the division, both for strikes and airlift; the order of battle of both friendly and enemy forces; and the enemy losses of soldiers and equipment, particularly to tactical aircraft and B–52s. He also asked them to keep a sharp eye out for the Army's success or failure in keeping the ground lifelines open.[42]

The operation began on the first of November, and for a week, elements of the 1st Brigade swept the area between Plei Me and the base of the Chu Pong Range. Several minor skirmishes took place. On the first day, the Americans made contact with enemy troops 5 miles west of Plei Me and, by nightfall, had killed 78 North Vietnamese and uncovered a major enemy hospital with tons of supplies. Emboldened by this initial success and convinced that the besiegers of Plei Me were fleeing westward toward Cambodia, they planned an ambush. On the next day, an air cavalry squadron leap-frogged over the heads of the retreating enemy to a landing zone near the border. For 3 days, the American soldiers fought with the enemy, killing 150 of them. During this first week of the operation, the Air Force supported the division with 68 sorties.

On the 9th of November, the 3d Brigade replaced the 1st and began sweeping the southern portion of the Ia Drang Valley along the base of the Chu Pong Range. Contacts were sporadic for the first few days, but when a battalion of Air Cavalry soldiers on deep reconnaissance flew into a landing zone at the base of the Chu Pong on the morning of the 14th, the enemy was stung into action. Three North Vietnamese battalions were poised on the slope above the landing zone to defend the ground leading westward into the mountain and the border. The first three American companies landed unopposed and began securing a perimeter around the landing site. Helicop-

An Air Force A–1 attacking a Viet Cong position in South Vietnam.

ters were delivering the fourth company around noon when the enemy struck. Air delivery of troops was halted as the Americans fought off the attackers. Tactical aircraft, armed helicopters, and artillery pounded the North Vietnamese troops for seven hours before they broke contact. Air Force A–1Es, F–100s, B–57s, and F–4s and Marine A–4s helped to hold the enemy at bay; but staggering losses did not prevent the North Vietnamese from attacking again at nightfall. As Air Force planes lit up the area with flares, tactical fighters strafed the attackers and AC–47 gunships raked the mountain slopes to the west.[43] By then the perimeter had been firmly established, and the enemy death toll mounted as attempts to pierce it failed.[44]

The North Vietnamese opened the action at a quarter to four the next morning with a three-company attack on the American positions. While savage hand-to-hand fighting took place around the perimeter, A–1Es from Pleiku hit the attackers with general purpose and white phosphorous bombs. By six, the highly accurate air strikes had stopped the assault.[45] The enemy struck again an hour later; and by eight, F–100s were on the scene with napalm as A–1Es, B–57s, and F–4s drove off the assailants. Reinforced by several additional infantry companies, the Americans attacked the two-mile-long Communist defense line that consisted of bunkers covered with logs and dirt and was defended by machineguns. The fighting lasted until five in the evening, when the enemy retreated from that area.[46]

A request made the night before by the division bore fruit at four in the afternoon, when 18 B–52s, diverted from a bombing campaign farther south, dropped over 900 bombs into the enemy's area close to the fighting.[47] For the first time in the war, the huge bombers were used in direct support of the fighting on the ground. Although specific results of the raid were not immediately available, General Westmoreland was sufficiently gratified to request daily strikes by the B–52s. At the same time, to reduce the reaction time of the big bombers, he sought permission to deal directly with the bombers' headquarters, the 3d Air Division on Guam.[48]

There was no letup in the battle on the 16th until late in the afternoon. Fighting broke out before sunrise that morning when first 2, then 4, enemy companies attacked the cavalry units. From six until noon, Air Force and Marine planes hit the North Vietnamese with napalm and strafing,[49] while American artillery pounded away at them. That afternoon, an Air Force U–10 flying over the enemy dropped 30,000 leaflets and 50,000 safe conduct passes while its loudspeaker blared appeals to surrender.[50] Westmoreland's request for daily B–52 strikes was approved, and the Joint Chiefs agreed to let him deal directly with the 3d Air Division. The chiefs, however, modified this approval by making it "subject to monitoring and possible veto by higher authority."[51] The proximity of the fighting to the border of Cambodia made Washington reluctant to relinquish full control to the MACV Commander.

Westmoreland used the B–52s in daily strikes against the ridge lines of the Chu Pong and used the tactical planes against the attacking North Vietnamese closer to the American positions. Two-kilometer by three-kilometer grids were drawn over the map of the battle area, and the B–52s hit 3 of these on the 17th and 2 more each 24 hours thereafter. By the time of their last mission over the valley on the 22d, the bombers had flown 96 sorties and dropped close to 5,000 bombs on enemy positions and supply routes.[52]

On the morning of the 17th, elements of two American battalions probing the ground north of the landing zone were ambushed and split into two perimeters by the North Vietnamese. Enemy snipers kept the soldiers pinned down as other enemy forces drove a wedge between the two groups. Fighters were called in and slowly drove the enemy back with 20-mm strafing until they had sufficient room to drop napalm and bombs. The fighting was at such close quarters that some Americans were singed, but the enemy was beaten off.[53] For three days after the ambush, cavalry troops moved west and south through the valley, establishing a crescent of landing zones along the river around the northern rim of the Chu Pong. On the 18th, they were joined by a South Vietnamese airborne battalion, which set up a blocking force along the Cambodian border. Two days later, the 3d Brigade relinquished command to the 2d Brigade, which spent the following week mopping up the valley.

Midway through the campaign, the Joint Chiefs informed McNamara there was strong evidence that the enemy was using Cambodia as a sanctuary and a staging area for attacks into South Vietnam.[54] When it appeared likely that the Americans would drive the enemy across the Cambodian border, Admiral Sharp asked the Joint Chiefs to relax the rules of engagement and allow the Americans to pursue the enemy across the border. In his view, Cambodia had forfeited its neutral status by harboring the enemy and the United States had to protect itself by chasing and destroying the enemy there.[55] On the 21st of November, the chiefs authorized air strikes, ground artillery firing, and troop maneuvering into Cambodia when it was necessary to defend against enemy attacks from that country. However, attacks on enemy base areas were prohibited unless these could be justified as self-defense in terms of continuing engagement or threats to allied forces.[56]

The action wound down as the North Vietnamese, realizing it was suicidal to stand and fight in the open valley, retreated to the hills. At the same time, the Americans decided that a single brigade could not storm the Chu Pong without unacceptable losses. The operations ended on the 28th of November.[57]

In terms of casualties, the campaign was highly successful. Almost 2,000 of the enemy were killed, while 215 Americans died and 358 were wounded. According to captured prisoners, the fighting ability of the Americans impressed the enemy, who had been told before the battle that U.S. soldiers were poor fighters who would turn tail and run. A recurring theme among the captives was the physical and emotional havoc wrought among them by the constant bombing.[58]

In a postmortem on the action, Air Force commanders were more convinced than ever that nonorganic planes, both strike and airlift, were essential to airmobile operations. During the month-long action, strike planes flew 753 sorties, 330 of them during the critical 7-day period in mid-November.* These sorties supported only 2 battalions in the field and averaged, during the most important week, 23 sorties a day for each battalion. This was far in excess of the 5 tactical strike sorties per day for each battalion that was being used as a planning factor in deciding how many squadrons were needed for the war. The operation was successful largely because of its hit-and-run nature aimed at keeping the enemy off balance. However, should the division ever have to commit its full resources, it could need as many as 276 sorties a day. The need for tactical air support would be even greater were the division committed in two or more widely dispersed areas. After the Ia Drang battle, several battalion commanders commented on the decisive role of the tactical air strikes, and General Westmoreland questioned whether the division as then constituted had the necessary firepower and endurance to meet requirements in South Vietnam.[59]

Air Force airlift had proved to be even more important than had the fighters. Although Korean troops kept the ground supply routes open from Qui Nhon to An Khe, the Army could not spare from combat the battalion it would have needed to keep the road open from An Khe west to Pleiku.[60] At

---

*See Appendix 6, USAF Support of Major Ground Operations, 1965–1967.

A Royal Australian Air Force Caribou landing at Tan Son Nhut, 1965.

first the Army tried to resupply itself with helicopters and Caribous. In attempting to do so, however, it diverted sorely needed air resources from its maneuver battalions, causing its aircraft availability rate to plummet. After five days, when the fuel supply for his nearly 300 helicopters had sunk to 7,000 gallons (70,000 gallons a day were needed), Maj. Gen. Harry W. O. Kinnard, the division commander, requested Air Force assistance.[61] A steady stream of fuel and ammunition in C–130s and C–123s began to be delivered from Tan Son Nhut to Pleiku and then to Catecka, 10 miles to its south. The division later reported that without the deliveries, "we would have had to grind to a halt for lack of fuel."[62] In the campaign, an average of 300 tons of supplies a day were flown to the division, double the prebattle estimate. The Army provided 40 percent of this through its organic air capability and by land means. The remaining 60 percent was flown in by the Southeast Asia Airlift System, essentially Air Force C–130s and C–123s and some Australian Caribous. Overall, 15 percent of the total airlift within all of South Vietnam went to the division, a figure that rose to 25 percent during the mid-November surge.[63] Air Force airlift was clearly indispensable for the airmobile division.

General Kinnard did not disagree with this conclusion. In a letter of thanks to General Moore in Saigon, he noted that the airmobile division had an even greater need of Air Force close air support, reconnaissance, and cargo aircraft than did other Army divisions.[64] In summing up the operation, the Army commander stated that the division lacked the ability to airlift supplies to the battlefield from 150 miles away. Any time major quantities of fuel and supplies had to be airlifted over ranges beyond 25 miles, he said, the airlift requirement would start cutting into his division's operational capability.[65] As a result, he concluded, airmobile doctrine should call for Air Force, not organic Army, planes to fly supplies from the depot to brigade bases.[66] This was the only way he could be certain of having enough planes for tactical operations.[67]

The matter was put most succinctly by the division's logistics chief who, in briefing the Defense Secretary after the battle, noted that the division had attempted to provide all support with organic airlift. However, because it had to "look both backwards to the Qui Nhon port and forward to fighting forces, it was unable to handle the requirement so the Air Force was called in."[68] The Ia Drang action brought the Air Force and Army a step closer toward resolution of their doctrinal differences over the respective roles of the two services' aircraft.

The same could not yet be said for coordination between Air Force and Marine air operations. General Westmoreland had so far enjoyed scant success in trying to incorporate Marine planes into his air deputy's central control system. The best he had achieved had been a pledge from the Marines to let MACV use any sorties left over from their commitments to their own ground troops in I Corps. The 2d Air Division was largely excluded from supporting ground operations in the northern corps. Even though Air Force liaison officers and forward air controllers were stationed with the ARVN and Marine divisions there, these officers were often ignored or circumvented. During the first week in December, for example, the Marines planned a combined operation, Harvest Moon, with the 2d Vietnamese Division to destroy a sizable Viet Cong force that had interposed itself between the two Marine enclaves at Da Nang and Chu Lai. Although heavy ground fighting and a substantial need for close air support were anticipated, neither the Air Force liaison officer with the Vietnamese division nor the one with the Marine regiment was included in the precampaign briefings. Yet these officers had been flying daily over the region as part of MACV's visual reconnaissance program and knew the terrain better than anyone in the area.[69]

The plan called for two Vietnamese battalions, one a ranger unit, to move westward by road from the coast to deliberately provoke an ambush. It was expected that they would contact the Viet Cong on the second day. At that time, two U.S. Marine battalions would be lifted by helicopter to the enemy's rear, catching him between the Americans and the South Vietnamese. The Vietnamese battalions set out as scheduled on the morning of the 8th, but with no Air Force or Vietnamese observation planes overhead to scout the way. The rangers were to the right of the road; the other battalion to the left. Early that afternoon the Viet Cong launched an unexpectedly heavy attack against the rangers. The four-man Marine ground control party, which accompanied the rangers and was responsible for calling in air support, lost contact in the ensuing retreat. The Vietnamese commander called for Air Force assistance and two forward air controllers from Da Nang flew to the area and took over control of the air operations. Since they had not been involved in the planning, the controllers were at first unfamiliar with the code signs, radio frequencies, and the location of the troops on the ground.[70] Orienting themselves quickly, they called in forty-seven Air Force and Marine sorties to protect the fleeing rangers. The enemy broke off the fight late in the day, and the rangers regrouped and established a perimeter.

An Air Force flare ship with a controller aboard supported them through the night. At first light the next morning, the Viet Cong struck the second Vietnamese battalion, which began a disorganized withdrawal eastward toward the operation's command post. Two Air Force Bird Dogs from Quang Ngai, flying a routine visual reconnaissance mission over the area, saw what was happening and, in the absence of any overall air coordination, began to direct the retreat from above. Spotting 150 Viet Cong on the road between the retreating unit and its destination, one of the forward air controllers called in 2 Marine F–4s from Da Nang and they scattered the ambushers. An AC–47 arrived, and the other controller directed it against another 100 enemy soldiers moving along the road behind the Vietnamese troops. After the gunships swept the road, the enemy was nowhere to be seen. During the action, the forward air controllers lost sight of the Vietnamese forces. When they located them 15 minutes later, they were 3,000 meters from where they should have been and moving directly toward 200 Viet Cong waiting in ambush. The controllers put a series of strikes on the enemy and directed the gunships to sweep a crescent east and north ahead of the South Vietnamese. There was no shortage of strike planes. Jets from Da Nang remained overhead throughout the day. The tactical air control center in Saigon advised the local control center that all its resources were at its disposal.

Without centralized control of air power countrywide, however, coordination of air support during this battle was poor.[71] Marine fighters arrived over the battle area with no one to direct them until the Air Force controllers took over. Several times on the 9th, the controllers had to interrupt their strikes as other Marine fighters, controlled by unknown agencies, flew into the area.[72]

By noon, the remnants of the Vietnamese battalion reached their destination and set up a defensive perimeter surrounded by the enemy. The air controllers continued to direct continuous strikes around the perimeter to hold back the Viet Cong. While the air controllers were directing strikes in a ring around the besieged South Vietnamese, a Marine helicopter came in suddenly, unannounced, and began directing Marine fighters preparing a landing zone for the Marine battalions. In one perilously narrow area, Marines in helicopters were directing F–4s on prestrikes, while Air Force controllers were placing close support aircraft around the Vietnamese units.[73]

The two Marine regiments were landed by afternoon, and by dusk some of them had linked up with the South Vietnamese. By noon the next day, the Marines had relieved the Vietnamese soldiers, who were evacuated from the area. The Vietnamese corps commander, Maj. Gen. Nguyen Chanh Thi, bitter over the poor air support he had received, withdrew his units from the combined operation. From then until the 19th of December, when the operation ended, the Marines operated in one area with their own air support while the Vietnamese searched another, supported by their own O–1s and A–1s.[74]

Confusion in the air over the Harvest Moon battlefield highlighted what Air Force leaders considered a major weakness—the divorce of the Marines from MACV's control. A week after the campaign closed, General Westmoreland called Lt. Gen. Lewis W. Walt, the Marine commander, and General Moore together to discuss the problem. As the first item of business, the MACV Commander agreed to ask for ten more Marine fighter-bomber squadrons for Vietnam, but only with the understanding that a number of sorties equivalent to two of those squadrons would be made available for general support throughout the country "and not be reserved for use by the Marines."[75] Westmoreland was extremely upset by the existence of three air forces in I Corps, which he called inefficient. With the fervor and exactitude of theologians, the Marine and Air Force representatives defended their respective doctrines as the best way to use air power in Vietnam.

The most important person in the Marine system was the ground commander, whose requests for air support were not to be questioned. In the Marine view, the battlefield and the air above it were inseparable, and it was the ground commander's responsibility to weave artillery, helicopters, reconnaissance aircraft, and close air support planes into his pattern of maneuver. To the Marines, tactical air strikes were another form of artillery to be subordinated to the overall fire support that the ground commander had at his disposal. To take away his control over this important facet of his artillery would weaken his ability to orchestrate the elements of battle. During a crisis, for example, when the commander needed air strikes that had not been planned and scheduled beforehand, it was more efficient for him to scramble aircraft that were on ground alert than to divert planes from scheduled missions. To do the latter would leave someone else without air support. The ground commander should get everything he wanted when he wanted it, even if this resulted in great surges of air strikes at one time and inactivity at another. In a Marine phrase, tactical air power had to be "consumer-oriented."[76] Further, to vest control of tactical air power in some distant controller, who was unfamiliar with the flow of the ground battle and to whom a request for close air support had to be weighed against other demands being made upon him, increased the time it took for aircraft to respond to emergencies and could result in "a radical disruption to the Marine's organization for combat."[77]

The Air Force disagreed on virtually every one of these points. In its view, air space was a continuum, each part to be looked at in relation primarily to other air space rather than to the ground below. Since air resources were limited, they had to be meted out judiciously by a central agent who understood the areawide needs and could shift his planes as the tactical situation changed. It was much more efficient to operate the total air resources at a sustained, relatively constant, sortie rate than to surge to meet fluctuating requirements and then have planes sit idly by. Fighters could respond more quickly to urgent calls for help if they were already airborne and diverted from lower priority missions than if they were sitting on alert. The Marine system was probably the more efficient for traditional types of Marine operations—support of relatively small ground forces during an amphibious assault to secure a beachhead. However, for the combined operations of Vietnam, in which air power was needed for bombing, interdiction, airlift, reconnaissance, and air-to-air combat, as well as for close air support, such single-mission dedication of aircraft was wasteful.[78]

Confronted with these diametrically opposed positions, Westmoreland sought a compromise. He asked General Meyers, the 2d Air Division Deputy Commander, to develop a doctrine comparable to that of the Air Force, but with enough safeguards to appease the Marines. A decision on the matter would wait until the study was complete.[79] Westmoreland believed that he needed a single air commander, but felt that service politics were such that he had to move slowly. Too precipitate a move to bring air power together in his hands, in his view, would create a swirl of controversy that could interfere with his ability to get the job done. His commission to Meyers was but a small step in this doctrinal dispute. Although temporary resolution of the dispute in the Air Force's favor would be reached two years later, the search for accommodation was to resume after the war.

Tents of the 555th Civil Engineering Squadron, Cam Ranh Bay, February 1966.

Chapter V

Settling in and Sorting Out
January–April 1966

The first months of 1966 were a time of settling in and sorting out for the Air Force in Southeast Asia. The first wave of deployments was completed during this time, while plans for additional reinforcements were being refined. The Air Force tightened up its organizational structure to bring it into line with the demands of the ground war in South Vietnam. At the same time, units arriving in Vietnam were assimilated; and in many cases, their plans and practices were modified so they could work more effectively, not only with each other, but also with the other services, both American and Vietnamese.

The United States met its goal of 44 non-Vietnamese maneuver battalions in the country by the first of the year (the South Vietnamese had 149).[1] However, of the 13 USAF tactical fighter squadrons earmarked for their support by January, only 9 were in place; the rest were without airfields to house them. The 2d Air Division did some shuffling of units that allowed the remaining squadrons to enter the country by the middle of March, although not at their scheduled bases. In January, the Farm Gate A–1 squadrons were moved out of Bien Hoa, one to Pleiku (the 1st ACS) and the other to Nha Trang (the 602d ACS), to make room for a new F–100 squadron (the 90th TFS) from the states. Since the air base at Phan Rang was still not finished, 2 of the F–4C squadrons scheduled to go there were sent elsewhere for the time being—the 391st to Cam Ranh Bay and the 480th to Da Nang. The arrival in mid-March of the 389th Phantom squadron at newly opened Phan Rang marked the end of the first phase of Air Force deployments.*

---

*See Appendix 1, Major USAF Units and Aircraft in South Vietnam, 1962–1968.

The enemy had answered the buildup with an escalation that kept pace with the allied forces. By the beginning of 1966, the North Vietnamese were sending 4,500 men into the south each month, and the combined strength of the Viet Cong and the men from Hanoi was believed to be about 230,000.[2] Although the arrival of U.S. forces late in 1965 had prevented a collapse of the Saigon government, continued infiltration was making it difficult for the United States to turn the corner and take the offensive. Planners in Washington set about reexamining their plans in light of this enemy reaction. The earlier estimate that 28 more battalions would have to be added to the 44 already in place was proving to be far too low.[3] During a visit to Saigon at the end of December 1965, McNamara was persuaded that, taken together, the Phase I forces and those planned for Phase II could accomplish only the Phase I goal of stopping the enemy. Increases above those already planned would be needed for the shift to the offensive. That same month, Admiral Sharp brought the issue to a head with a request for 486,500 U.S. and allied forces in South Vietnam by the end of 1966 and 169,000 more in Thailand and the rest of the Pacific. Ten more tactical fighter squadrons would be needed for South Vietnam and 6 for Thailand.[4]

The decisionmakers were three months into 1966, however, before reaching agreement on this heightened request. The process was slowed by divergent opinions on several issues: the overall strategy of the war, the effectiveness of the earlier deployments, and the repercussions that future deployments would have on service resources and on commitments in other parts of the globe.

General McConnell had not abandoned his strategic views of the previous summer. While he had concurred in the Joint Chiefs' approval of ground forces at that time (a step he took to avoid presenting the President with divided counsel), the Air Force Chief was still uncomfortable with the ground strategy. In his view, the United States was playing to the enemy's strength instead of exploiting its own aerial and naval advantages. There were not enough people in the United States, he said, to fight the North Vietnamese and Chinese in their own countries on their own terms. He still believed that air power in the north should receive at least as much emphasis as foot power in the south. He insisted, as he had on numerous earlier occasions, that this is what the Joint Chiefs had agreed on in August.[5] If things continued as they were going, it was just a matter of time until the United States would have either to leave the country or get serious and direct the full force of its air power against the north.[6] The Air Force had gone along with things, he told his staff in January, but the time had come for a stronger approach. There were enough brains on the Air Staff to figure out a way to sell the Air Force's position.

The general's dilemma was a classic one: his ideas, no matter how reasonable and well thought out, were not selling themselves automatically and, in this case, the cards were stacked against the Air Force vendors. The President was still being advised by those whose earlier counsel had initiated the ground strategy and who, accordingly, were unlikely to accept sweeping changes. To be acceptable, any successful proposal for an air strategy would have to allay these advisors' fears that the conflict would escalate beyond Vietnam, that the Soviet Union and China might be provoked into further aiding Hanoi or taking even more drastic action, and that the United States might be tarred with the brush of indiscriminate bombing. McConnell's staff came up with new editions of earlier proposals that stressed air power for all of Southeast Asia and sounded moderate enough to defuse these concerns.[7] With the decision already made, however, these proposals went nowhere. The chief continued to take the position that more U.S. troops could not be justified without intensified air attacks against the north.[8]

On less strategic grounds, also, the Air Staff was reluctant to go along with Sharp's request. No serious evaluation had been made of the effect the 195,000 U.S. and non-Vietnamese troops already in Vietnam were having on the war and, until such a judgment was made, it seemed fruitless to keep adding people. McConnell and General Greene, the Marine commandant, asked the Joint Chiefs to make such an evaluation on which they could judge the size of future deployments.[9] Although the Joint Chiefs provided an evaluation on February 2, the Air Force and Marine Corps disagreed with its methodology and asked that it be studied further. An acceptable analysis was not finished until June, long after decisions had been made on the Sharp proposal.[10]

McConnell's most serious reservations, however, centered around the effect further deployments would have on the United States' ability to respond to the more important potential challenges from the Soviet Union and China.[11] To satisfy Sharp's needs, the Air Force would have to withdraw most of its reconnaissance aircraft from Europe, add fighter squadrons to the Tactical Air Command, and shift many people from overseas bases. The size of the Air Force would have to be increased and some National Guard units activated.[12]

At a Honolulu meeting in late January and early February, Sharp refined his requirements. He now asked for 459,000 U.S. troops for Vietnam by the end of the year, accompanied by 10 more Air Force fighter squadrons for Vietnam, 6 for Thailand, and 61 more reconnaissance planes for the theater. The Hawaii planners also asked for a jump in the number of monthly B–52 sorties to 400 in February, to 450 in April, and to 600 in July. These figures could be met by calling up some reserves, by reassigning people from other overseas areas, and by extending the term of service for those on active duty.[13] General Harris noted that these estimates for South Vietnam had been prepared by Westmoreland and his staff, while those for the air campaigns in North Vietnam and Laos were the work of Sharp's advisors. The component services of the Pacific Command, PACAF and PACFLT, had not been asked seriously to contribute. Before sending the recommendations to the Joint Chiefs, Sharp gave Harris one and a half days to comment—hardly sufficient time for such weighty matters.[14]

McNamara asked the Joint Chiefs and the individual services for their opinions on Sharp's request. He ruled out a callup of reserves and extension of the term of service. By the end of February, McConnell concluded that his hopes for a strategy change were in vain. The secretary had been sold on a ground war, and it was obvious that a decision to that effect had already been made. The general felt that the least he could do was to point out to the other chiefs that the ground strategy was not the one they had earlier agreed on and that they should again state this view in their response.[15] The JCS reply to McNamara approved Sharp's request for forces, but recommended that, since all the forces would not be available by year's end, the deployment should be spread out over the next sixteen months, until the middle of 1967. Reflecting McConnell's view, the chiefs also recommended that Sharp's strategy be replaced with their own earlier one that placed bombing of the north and of the Laotian trails on an even level of importance with pressure in the south.[16]

The Air Force's response to the secretary pointed out that it could send all sixteen fighter squadrons in 1966 if it made adjustments elsewhere. To do so, the Skoshi Tiger F–5 test squadron then in South Vietnam would have to be converted into a permanent squadron and kept there. Another F–100 squadron could be squeezed out of Europe by replacing three squadrons that were temporarily assigned to Turkey with two permanent ones in Spain. Two more F–102 squadrons could be assigned to Southeast Asia and a third one, already temporarily on Okinawa, could be stationed there permanently. Some reserve personnel would be needed to beef up the training program in the states. To control these planes and strengthen the visual reconnaissance program, eighty-one more Bird Dogs should go to South Vietnam.[17]

Near the end of March, McNamara reached his decision. The goal for the end of the year was 79 U.S., 23 allied, and 162 South Vietnamese maneuver battalions in the country. Once again, the secretary's analysts used fixed sortie figures to decide how many additional fighter squadrons would accompany these troops and also would be needed for the war outside South Vietnam. They set a figure of 18,500 sorties for the month of June, building up to 23,300 by December. These figures broke down to a monthly sortie rate of 150 supporting each U.S., Korean, and Australian Army maneuver battalion and 200 for each U.S. and Korean Marine battalion. The South Vietnamese Army would get 7,800 sorties a month, Laos 3,000, and North Vietnam 7,100 to 7,500. Based on this, the secretary concluded that 11, rather than 16, new Air Force squadrons would be needed.[18] Four fighter squadrons would go to Phan Rang between April and November, 2 more would be added at Bien Hoa during July and August, while 4 would make their home at Qui Nhon between July and November. In addition, a reconnaissance squadron would go to Tan Son Nhut in August.[19]

The Defense Secretary approved the transfer of fourteen B–66s from Europe to Southeast Asia, six for reconnaissance and eight for strikes, and the formation of an F–5 USAF squadron, using the Skoshi Tigers as a nucleus. Four RF–101s would come from France, which had just withdrawn from military participation in the North Atlantic Treaty Organization.[20]

Washington's reliance on fixed sortie figures and rates carried inherent dangers for the Air Force. While useful in deciding how many forces were needed, such "scientific" calculations bore the seeds, soon to be germinated, of becoming measurements of effectiveness. A field commander, supplied with a certain number of planes and a monthly sortie rate, could easily find himself judged (or at least suspect he would be) by how close he came to that figure and could be tempted to fly his planes to meet that number, even at times when there were no lucrative enemy targets. Missing from this analytical procedure were allowances for such unpredictables of the battle-field as the fluidity of the enemy, the changing requirements of the monsoon seasons, and the unexpected surges of activity that form part of any war. This use of fixed sortie rates presented a strong challenge to the air commander's flexibility and to Air Force doctrine.

These deployment plans, as it turned out, had to be modified by two realities of Vietnam: the shortage of air munitions and the snail's pace at which airfields were being built. The munitions shortage, which had developed during the buildup the prior year, was reaching serious proportions and by April was beginning to affect operations. Many Air Force sorties were canceled that month—233 on the 7th, 134 on the 8th, and 515 between the 11th and 14th.[21] Air Force planes were running out of iron bombs, 20-mm ammunition, and some rockets.

The shortage resulted from a conjunction of events, including a slowness in gearing up production, late ship arrivals in Vietnam, and the delivery of many incomplete rounds. Several temporary measures were in force to cope with the situation. During the first 3 months of 1966, nearly 1,000 airlift sorties were flown within Southeast Asia shuttling munitions from one base to another. The Air Force was borrowing bombs weighing 100, 250, 500, and 1,000 pounds from the Navy.[22] As an emergency measure, the Air Force contracted for 19 "Special Express" surface vessels, at about $5,000 a day, to carry munitions nonstop from the United States to Vietnam. To conserve what he had, General Moore extended his order of the previous December

A Skoshi Tiger F–5 releases bombs at a Viet Cong target, March 1966.

that pilots stop dumping unexpended bombs and bring them back to their bases. Munitions were curtailed for aircrews training in the United States for assignment to Vietnam, and a cutback was also ordered in the use of ordnance for firepower demonstrations and exercises at home.[23]

Pressure from the Defense Secretary to maintain high sortie rates, lest the ammunition shortage become generally known, resulted for a while in planes flying with token ordnance loads often unsuitable for the targets. "We often used white phosphorous bombs and things of this nature," recalled General Meyers later, "which had no relationship to the target at all just to put something on the airplane because we were forbidden to cut down the sortie rate."[24]

In April, McNamara sent a team to Hawaii to look into the problem. Not surprisingly, different service representatives at the conclave saw the issue differently. General Harris noted that his command had received only 88 percent of the 150,000 bombs it was supposed to get since the first of the year. More seriously, only one-third of the 750-pound and less than one-half of the 500-pound bombs were complete. Fins were missing on the 500-pound bombs and fuses on the larger munitions. General Moore complained of ships being late getting to Vietnam. Admiral Sharp accused Harris of not reporting the shortages properly. In general, it was felt that management of resources had not been good and that commanders were not keeping each other informed.

The conferees then turned to the question of how to support the CINCPAC bombing plan until munitions became plentiful. As a temporary measure, the Hawaiian command agreed to release the bombs it had set aside for use in Korea. Since it would be nine months before the situation would ease, the conferees had to choose, for the longer range, between reducing the number of sorties for the rest of the year or flying the planned number of sorties with lighter loads. Admiral Sharp, wedded to sortie rates as a measure of effectiveness, told the conference that he was going to fly as many sorties as were planned regardless of the size of their loads.[25] Reporting effectiveness based on sortie rate favored Navy planes, which carried lighter loads from carriers, more than it did Air Force aircraft. The Air Force was against sending its planes on missions with less than complete loads, for to do so required more sorties and more pilots exposed to danger to drop the same amount of ordnance.[26]

Following the team's return to Washington, several steps were taken to ease the burden. General McConnell persuaded the Joint Chiefs to reduce the number of sorties rather than have the aircraft fly with lighter loads.[27] This meant that fewer planes would be needed than were originally planned. President Johnson assigned the highest national priority to production of 250-, 500-, and 750-pound bombs; 20-mm cartridges; and 2.75-inch rockets.[28] At the same time, the Defense Secretary set up a new office in the Pentagon to improve the flow of munitions.[29]

Full deployment of the squadrons planned for 1966 depended also on the completion of enough airfields to receive them. Although four F–4 squadrons were operating out of Cam Ranh Bay at the beginning of the year, the temporary aluminum taxiways and runway had problems. A twenty-three-inch rainfall in December raised the water table to the level of the aluminum, and emergency draining had been required. Rain made the runway slick, and landings had to be made with drag chutes. At the first sign of rain, barrier crews rushed to their stations, crash recovery people took up positions near the runway, strobe lights were turned on, and quick decisions were made whether to let the planes land or divert them elsewhere. With the advent of the dry season, the challenge had turned to one of coping with a shifting runway. The dry sand under the aluminum moved with the wind, while the runway shifted in the direction of landing aircraft. During the first months of 1966, a constant north wind pushed the taxiway three feet south, while the runway edged north under the weight of planes landing from the south. Landing the traffic to the south for three weeks moved the runway back, and taking daily stress measurements and periodically changing the direction of the traffic kept the shifting under control. The moving sand created bumps and dips, and construction crews were continually at work replacing sections of the aluminum runway and smoothing out the sand below.[30]

Phan Rang was still not open at the beginning of the year because the heavy December rains delayed work on that field; but by mid-March, a temporary runway, taxiway, and apron were in place. A squadron of F–4s, the last of the jet fighter squadrons due under Phase I, arrived on March 14. Along with it came the headquarters of a new fighter wing, the 366th, to prepare for the arrival of additional squadrons. No sooner had the squadron bedded down, however, than unseasonable rains damaged the field, causing further postponement of the transfer of the other two F–4 squadrons from Cam Ranh Bay and Da Nang.

Money had been set aside for two new jet airfields in 1966; but, as with the munitions, airfield construction became mired in service differences. Despite USAF pressure on the Hawaiian headquarters and on MACV, the building program lagged dangerously behind operational commitments. CINCPAC's indecisiveness and General Harris' differences with Admiral Sharp over the issue were frustrating to General McConnell. The problem, in his view, was threefold: there was not enough construction capability in the field to do all that had to be done; the commanders in Southeast Asia favored a ground war and were busy building to support it; and, finally, Admiral Sharp, as a naval officer, favored sea-based over land-based aircraft. The Navy, according to McConnell, would welcome the opportunity to move another carrier into the South China Sea rather than see another airfield built.[31]

While CINCPAC dragged its feet over the question of new fields, MACV tried to decide the best site for the third air base. The earlier plan to begin work at Tuy Hoa had been halted in mid-January and a study was undertaken to compare that site with another one at Phu Cat fifteen miles north of Qui Nhon. The survey concluded that it would take until the summer of 1967 to build the base at Tuy Hoa, while the one at Phu Cat could be finished by the coming November. MACV decided on the Phu Cat site late in February.

McConnell, appalled at the delays in choosing the third site and convinced that air bases were not receiving their share in the military construction program, overcame his earlier reluctance and urged the Air Force Secretary, Harold Brown, to get permission for the Air Force to build a fourth base itself. Early in February, Brown sought McNamara's blessing for the Air Force to hire its own contractor to work independently of other construction efforts in South Vietnam.[32]

Brown's proposal met strong opposition from Hawaii, MACV, and the Navy. At first, Westmoreland opposed the suggestion, principally on organizational grounds. Such a plan, he noted, would change priorities and deprive MACV of control over design and construction standards. The erection of ports, depots, and airfields had to be "balanced," and it was unlikely that any one service could successfully isolate itself in this way. It was hard to imagine a new contractor coming into the country and building a field without using local labor and material. MACV's construction chief, the Navy officer in charge of construction, had forty-eight million dollars worth of equipment in the field and could do the job by the end of 1966. Finally, the construction people in South Vietnam were experts on local conditions, logistic problems, the soil, and the terrain; it would take a new agency at least several months to match this experience.[33]

Brown countered these objections by noting that several American construction companies had assured him that they could complete an expeditionary field in six months and a permanent one in a year, while staying within the budget already agreed on. Further, the Air Force contractor would not compete with the construction combine already in Vietnam but, rather, would complement it and relieve MACV of part of its burden. Overall control of the contractor would remain with MACV's construction chief. Brown disagreed with MACV's suggestion that the new firm be merged with RMK/BRJ, which he pictured as "already top heavy in management."[34]

Discussion continued through March, April, and May, concerning not only who would build the base, but also where it should be. Hue–Phu Bai, in I Corps, became a leading candidate for a while, until serious civilian unrest there convinced the planners that a base there would not be secure enough. By the end of May, there was general agreement to locate the next airfield at Tuy Hoa.

In the meantime, however, General McConnell was having second thoughts about using an Air Force contractor. When he was first won over to the idea three months earlier, two contractors assured him that they could do the job. Now, in late May, there was only one and McConnell believed the chances were only about even that the work could be done in time. The contractor's estimate was a third higher than the $52 million originally set aside for the project. McConnell was concerned that, by letting the contractor work under the MACV construction chief, the Air Force would lose control of the project. Since opposition to the idea was so extensive, he felt the Air Force could get a bigger black eye by going ahead and failing, even though it did not control it, than by not having an airfield. On the other hand, the Air Force might end up with no airfield and the Navy with another carrier on the line. The chief began to think of alternatives. By adding ramp space to the fields in Thailand, the Air Force could move 130 planes there, which would be the equivalent of building a new base in Vietnam.[35] The general suggested that Brown try to get McNamara to change priorities so that the fourth base could be built by the MACV combine on a priority basis. The Air Force Secretary foresaw too many obstacles to these ideas and decided that the Air Force had no alternative but to get its own contractor if it wanted another field in time. McConnell swallowed his doubts and agreed.

Gen. John P. McConnell, Chief of Staff, U.S. Air Force, left,
and Gen. Harold K. Johnson, Chief of Staff, U.S. Army.

On the 27th of May, the Air Force signed a contract with Walter Kidde
Constructors, Inc. to build its base at Tuy Hoa.[36]

To get around the problems of the saturation of MACV's construction
capability, the inflationary impact on the Vietnamese economy, the shortage
of native skilled labor, overextended supply lines, and the difficulty of finding
heavy construction equipment, the Air Force contract with Kidde was based
on a new single-package philosophy, called the Turnkey concept. The
contractor was responsible for the complete project, except for supplying the
real estate and keeping the area secure. Kidde had to provide the design and
engineering work and the materials and equipment, as well as all the
transportation, shipping, offloading, logistic support, and labor and management. The contractor was prohibited from competing with other construction
in Vietnam for labor, materials, and shipping facilities. Kidde agreed to
complete interim facilities in seven months and a permanent base in one year.
The contract included incentives for early delivery, for control of inflation,
and for control of the conduct of the employees. To circumvent clogged port
facilities, which would lead to delays, supplies were to be brought in over the
beach where the new site was located. The contract called for permanent port
facilities to be in place within fifteen months.[37]

Not all the interservice competition occasioned by the new posture in
Vietnam remained unresolved. On a Saturday morning late in March,
General McConnell and the Army Chief, General Johnson, in the quiet of the
latter's Pentagon office, sketched out the draft of an agreement that would

dampen, for the moment at least, a long-standing squabble between the two services. In the draft, Johnson agreed that the Army would give up its claims to all fixed-wing airlift aircraft and would transfer those it had to the Air Force. McConnell, for his part, agreed to abandon the ancient Air Force claim that it should operate all helicopters, including those in a combat theater that moved troops, provided fire support, and supplied Army forces. In a bow to existing realities, the two chiefs allowed some exceptions to this stark statement. The Air Force could still use helicopters for special air warfare operations and for search and rescue. The Army could continue to fly small fixed-wing liaison planes for administrative purposes. Where the situation demanded, Air Force fixed-wing airlift planes could be attached to ground commands if a joint or unified commander wanted them used that way.[38]

Although this doctrinal controversy dated back to the 1950s when Army planes first began to expand in size and mission, it was brought to a head by Army airmobile operations in Vietnam. The Army had six CV–2 Caribou companies in the country, each with sixteen aircraft. These planes were, in Air Force eyes, usurping the mission of the C–123s and were not doing it well. The Caribous were controlled by ground commanders and remained outside the common, USAF-run Southeast Asia Airlift System. They were used principally by the 1st Air Cavalry Division, the Special Forces, and by higher U.S. Army headquarters for battlefield supply and to carry passengers, mail, and medium cargo. With its sixteen planes, each company was averaging ten missions a day, a low rate in Air Force eyes.[39] The recent airmobile operations around Pleiku and the Ia Drang valley had given further weight to the Air Force's contention that Army fixed-wing planes could not supply an airmobile division adequately.

McConnell had inherited this doctrinal controversy from his predecessor, General LeMay, whose firmness on the subject had ruled out compromise with the Army. From the beginning of his tenure, McConnell had been thinking of ways to settle the matter, along the lines of a fixed-wing/helicopter division of labor. Both chiefs had worked on the problem quietly, conferring privately for six months before arriving at a meeting of the minds. The need for secrecy between the two men stemmed from the strength of the opposition to compromise within their respective services, which would have made agreement in a larger forum impossible. Hovering over the negotiators was the prospect that, if they could not settle the matter themselves, it would likely be done for them by the Defense Secretary. To elevate the matter to the level of the Joint Chiefs would give the Navy and Marines the chance to exercise influence in a issue that was of no great doctrinal import to them.[40]

The two service staffs also had to be considered. Over the years, the controversy had taken on deep doctrinal overtones and become embedded in

U.S. Army CV–2 Caribou transport over South Vietnam.

both staffs as bedrocks on which the services' future rested. McConnell and Johnson, convinced that lack of agreement would hurt operations in Vietnam, wanted to work toward a decision on pragmatic, rather than theoretical, grounds. To retain flexibility to negotiate, they had to distance themselves as much as possible from the more doctrinaire counsel of their staffs. On the air side, for example, it was a long-held conviction among many that it was wrong for the Air Force to deny itself the right to use any aerial vehicle necessary for military tasks. It was also seen as quite reasonable to impose limits on the Army, several of whose aircraft had exceeded the weight limits placed on them by earlier agreement.[41] There were those on the Army side who, with some relish, saw the growth of the Army's fixed-wing fleet as "the nose of the camel within the tent of tactical air support" and encouraged it.[42]

McConnell sought opinions from wide-ranging sources. At one point, he discussed the Army's use of Caribous with a former Air Liaison Officer attached to the 1st Cavalry Division. The officer knew of only one occasion when an airstrip had been built that could handle a Caribou but not a C–123. In his estimation, the C–123 could do everything the Caribou did, plus more. One of the Army's objections was that the C–123 carried too big a load and a smaller plane was needed. It was the liaison officer's opinion, based on his personal observations, that it was better for the bigger plane occasionally to carry a smaller load than not to be able to lift enough when more was needed. He also informed the chief that the Air Force could do a better job for the Army if it had all airlift under its control.[43]

As negotiations proceeded, McConnell and Johnson briefed only a handful of people on their respective staffs but discouraged proposals or changes from them. When the final agreement was sketched out, it was sent to staff members with the caveat that anyone who tried to change the meaning of the agreement would be fired.[44] The final text, as signed on the 6th of April, was identical to the draft. Soon after the agreement, work began to convert the 104 Caribous in Vietnam from the Army to the Air Force. The first day of 1967 was set for completion of the changeover.

During the intervening eight months, two major changes would have to take place. The Army companies would become Air Force squadrons, which would mean a gradual replacement not only of pilots but of maintenance, equipment, and procedures. The Air Force would have to learn to operate an entirely new aircraft system and become steeped in ground force problems, both under combat conditions. However, although the agreement stipulated that the Caribous (and the C–123s) could be placed under the control of ground commanders if Westmoreland decided it was necessary, this flew in the face of the Air Force's attempts to centralize air resources in Vietnam. Before the end of the year, it would have to be decided whether the new airlift planes would be placed under the Air Force's Southeast Asia Airlift System or remain outside and be set aside for the exclusive use of ground commanders. The Air Force was provided a further challenge by the Army Chief's contention that the Air Force would be unable to match the Army's performance record with the Caribous in Vietnam.[45]

One of the first tangible effects for the Air Force of McNamara's March decision on deployments was the conversion of the F–5 Skoshi Tiger planes into a permanent squadron. The planes had moved from Bien Hoa to Da Nang on the first of the year for a thirty-day evaluation over North Vietnam. Due to the moratorium on bombing the north, however, which lasted through the month of January, the planes could fly only interdiction missions against the trails in Laos. They returned to Bien Hoa early in February for the third phase of the experiment, a maximum support effort in III Corps. For three weeks, squadron pilots flew six planes five times each day supporting Vietnamese and American troops. Maintenance proficiency increased to the point where ground crews were changing engines in less than two hours.

The test was originally scheduled to end on the 20th of February, but instead, on that day, the planes returned to Da Nang to try again over the north. Bad weather drove them to Laos the first week, but finally, on the last day of the month, they flew for the first time above the Demilitarized Zone. For a week they bombed targets and flew high altitude escort and MiG combat patrol missions. The tests ended on the 8th of March, and the planes returned to Bien Hoa, judged capable of service in Vietnam. Since the planners in Washington were nearing a decision on the fate of the squadron, it was kept in the country and authorized six additional planes.[46] A month later, it became the 10th Fighter Squadron, the first operational F–5 unit in

125

the Air Force. Earlier plans to give the planes to the Vietnamese were postponed in the face of the need to add USAF squadrons in Southeast Asia without depleting Europe.

To get a better control of past and future units coming to Vietnam, the Air Force tightened its organizational structure. The reconnaissance units at Tan Son Nhut were facets of the operation that had escaped centralization. The variegated requirements for reconnaissance in the diverse areas of Southeast Asia had produced a three-way split of the reconnaissance effort at the Saigon base: geographical, command and control, and support. Anticipating that the coming influx of reconnaissance planes from Europe would increase the problem of divided control, the 2d Air Division in mid-February consolidated its seventy-four planes into a reconnaissance wing, the 460th, with four flying squadrons and one technical support squadron. It now had a central point of responsibility for all reconnaissance activities, from scheduling and flying missions through developing and distributing the film.[47]

Most of the reconnaissance jets—RF–4s, RF–101s, and RB–66s—were ferreting out targets in Laos and North Vietnam, while a small detachment of RB–57s, called Patricia Lynn, was flying infrared reconnaissance missions looking for concentrations of enemy soldiers and supplies in South Vietnam.

There was no separate Air Force intelligence net between the 2d Air Division and its subordinate units or its higher headquarters.[48] The data from the Patricia Lynn flights went to MACV, where it was combined with other reports to develop targets. Intelligence reports had to compete for priority over the MACV command net, and perishable ones often died.

The prohibition against the Air Force developing its own targets for its own planes in South Vietnam was frustrating. Some Air Force leaders believed the Air Force could do a better job if the data were read by professionally trained Air Force eyes and the targets were picked by people who appreciated the strengths and weaknesses of air power. Instead, ground commanders chose the air targets. Circumscribed as they were by terrain, they were understandably unable to select interdiction targets that were outside their view. Yet interdiction targets were those the Air Force was best trained to hit. As a result, the vast interdiction capability of the Air Force was throttled back in South Vietnam, to become only one of several forms of fire support for troops fighting on the ground.[49] Targets for B–52 strikes, which began the summer before, were chosen by ground officers in MACV unfamiliar with the potentialities of the big bombers. Jet reconnaissance products did not get to the air liaison officers in the field who could best use them. The Air Force was denied the function of choosing targets from reconnaissance photos. The Air Force's effectiveness depended largely on having this information, yet the Air Force was kept from it. As in other facets of the air support mission, air leaders were sensitive to the fact that they might be criticized for doing a poor job, even though the constraints placed upon them made it difficult for them to do better.

Not all the reconnaissance difficulties stemmed from this doctrinal and command issue. The tropical nature of the terrain, as well as the unconventional techniques of the enemy, posed formidable challenges to sophisticated aerial systems designed to discover less concealed and less transient adversaries. High hopes had been entertained the year before for infrared photography, which depended not on light, but on heat emanating from enemy encampments. However, the capabilities of infrared equipment lagged behind the demands being put upon it by the Southeast Asian environment. The Canberras had enjoyed some success early in 1965 in the flat southern regions of the delta, but when the action moved north to the mountains of I and II Corps later in the year, the need to fly at higher altitudes lowered the quality of the photographs.[50] Pilots had to fly at an altitude high enough to give them broad coverage, yet low enough to take suitable pictures. The best compromise was 2,000 feet, but at this altitude they could not get sufficient clarity to identify individual gun emplacements, troops, trucks, and small boats. The planes did not have full infrared systems, but only scanners rather hastily installed and poorly maintained. Westmoreland characterized the program as a "shoe-string operation."[51] During the first part of 1966, the number of monthly infrared missions was cut in half, to 38, while day photo flights doubled, to 75.[52]

The rapid buildup overwhelmed the photo processing cell (the 13th Reconnaissance Technical Squadron) at Tan Son Nhut, which was sorely in need of better equipment, more space, and more people. Part of the photo lab was crowded into a ramshackle building, and the rest was scattered in trailers and shacks. The supply of electricity to the laboratory was always tenuous. Air conditioners worked at half capacity most of the year and not at all during the hottest months. The automatic processing equipment was subjected to temperatures of 130° and high humidity, causing frequent breakdowns. Emulsion melted from the film, and the efficiency of the photo personnel declined. Technicians had to suspend plastic-wrapped ice in the chemical solutions to achieve correct temperatures for developing film. While demands on the photo lab increased, no additional workspace was provided.[53] By January 1966, the lab was processing three million feet of film a month, a sevenfold increase over a year earlier. Yet the number of people to interpret this deluge of photos had only doubled. At one point, the squadron borrowed twenty-two people from MACV to help with the work. All hands were employed processing the film, with little time left to interpret or monitor the quality of the photographs.[54]

MACV's monopoly of the air intelligence role within South Vietnam sprang from several factors. Among these was the nature of the war. With both friendly and enemy forces spread throughout the country, it seemed logical to many, even some in the Air Force, that ground commanders should propose targets and that MACV should choose them. Yet the inadequacy of USAF intelligence to meet MACV's air intelligence needs was a contributing, if not critical, factor. At one point MACV offered the target function to the Air Force, but the 2d Air Division could not man it. Some in the Air Force believed that its own lack of readiness and capability in this area gave MACV the opportunity to take over a traditionally Air Force function.[55]

The search for a complement to photo and infrared reconnaissance within South Vietnam turned early in 1966 to electronics. The enemy's widespread use of radios in the field was tailormade for eavesdropping. Five years earlier, the Air Force had tried to use a C–54 based at Tan Son Nhut to home in on the enemy's radio transmissions. The test failed, but a second one, begun in October 1965 with a single C–47, was showing more promise. In mid-December, the C–47 detected a Viet Cong battalion within a few hundred meters of its location near the Michelin Plantation, and the plane was kept on past its original testing period. During the first 4 months of 1966 it flew 300 missions.

At this time, the Army had fifteen small planes using airborne radio direction finding (ARDF). A major limitation of the Army equipment was that the plane had to turn directly toward the source for accurate detection, which alerted the Viet Cong that they had been discovered. Equipment in the Gooney Bird (designated an RC–47) allowed it to fix enemy transmitters without changing direction, reducing the chance of compromise and allowing the crew to detect radios transmitting in short bursts.

General Moore asked for thirty-five of the RC–47s for his command, and the Joint Chiefs agreed in March. Discussions the following month between McConnell and Johnson, paralleling those that surrounded the Caribou issue, led to a division of the ARDF mission between the Army and the Air Force. The former had fifty-six U–6 planes, the latter forty-seven RC–47s. South Vietnam and its immediate environs was divided into thirty–nine ARDF areas, including four over the trails in Laos and one off the coast of North Vietnam. These five, and three others in the mountainous region of South Vietnam, were assigned to the Air Force because the RC–47s were more rugged than the Army planes. The remaining thirty-one areas were split between the two services. The Air Force grouped its planes, under the reconnaissance wing, into squadrons at Tan Son Nhut, Nha Trang, and Pleiku. The first of these, the 360th Tactical Reconnaissance Squadron, was set up at the Saigon base during the first week of April and within a month had its full complement of planes.[56] The second squadron, the 361st, was activated at about the same time at Nha Trang; but it would be later in the year before it received all its planes. By the time the third squadron, the 362d, was operating from Pleiku early in the following year, all three had been redesignated as tactical electronic warfare squadrons and the planes as EC–47s.

Partly as a reflection of the northward spread of the war and partly to make room for the consolidation of reconnaissance operations at Tan Son Nhut and jet fighters at Bien Hoa, most of the propeller-driven aircraft were moved off those bases by March and assigned to a new air commando wing, the 14th, at Nha Trang. The two A–1 Farm Gate squadrons (the 1st and 602d Air Commando Squadrons) were placed under the new wing. By year's end, the former was flying from a forward location at Pleiku and the latter had been transferred to Thailand. The AC–47 gunship squadron from Tan Son Nhut (the 4th ACS) went to the new wing, along with the 20th Helicopter Squadron. A fifth squadron, made up of psychological warfare C–47s and U–10s (the 5th ACS), which was already at Nha Trang, rounded out the new composite wing.* Although most of these planes continued to operate out of smaller inland fields, their headquarters were consolidated at the coastal base.

As a result of the rapid accumulation of American forces, the 2d Air Division was elevated to a numbered air force, the Seventh, on April 1.[57] During World War II, the Seventh Air Force had supported U.S. island-hopping operations by bombing and strafing Japanese installations throughout the central and western Pacific. Bombers and fighters from its two commands had participated in the capture of the Ryukyus; and in the final months of the war, Seventh Air Force fighters from Iwo Jima and Okinawa escorted B–29s and B–24s from Okinawa that struck the home islands of Japan. Now the Seventh Air Force was reactivated for the conflict in Vietnam.

The change from an air division was largely cosmetic, since the 2d Air Division had for sometime been both large enough and important enough to be a numbered air force. By the time of the change, the Seventh Air Force controlled over 1,000 aircraft, with close to 30,000 people on its rolls. The change was titular also in that it brought no alteration in its mission or its command and control arrangements.[58] The new air force simply stepped into the air division's shoes, remaining a component of MACV, but responsible for only one-third of the aircraft in South Vietnam. Army helicopters, B–52s,

---

*See Appendix 1, Major USAF Units and Aircraft in South Vietnam, 1962–1968.

and most of the Marine aircraft continued to be directed from elsewhere. At the same time, the Seventh Air Force remained PACAF's control point for Air Force missions in Laos, North Vietnam, and Thailand. General Westmoreland stuck to his position that as long as he did not control these operations outside Vietnam, Air Force representation and responsibility on the MACV staff would not be realized.[59]

While most leaders subscribed to the tenet that centralized air power was a good thing, none could agree on the level at which this centralization should reside. The Marines, whose aircraft wing expanded during the year to eleven helicopter and ten fixed-wing squadrons, fought tenaciously to keep control of these airplanes out of the hands of MACV and at their own wing level. The Commander of the Seventh Air Force deplored the time he had to spend coordinating aircraft from five separate air organizations in South Vietnam and another in Thailand, while the majority of the aircraft, Army helicopters, remained outside his ken. General Westmoreland was miffed and hampered by being arbitrarily confined to controlling air power only in South Vietnam, and most Seventh Air Force leaders agreed with him.[60] Admiral Sharp in Hawaii, seconded by his Air Force commander, felt strongly that his responsibility for the entire Pacific area dictated that he retain the authority he had over the strategic bombers and retain his control of the airlift and tactical air forces operating outside South Vietnam in the event he needed them in other parts of his theater. One man's centralization was another's dispersion.

This situation placed the Seventh Air Force Commander, more than the others, on the horns of a dilemma. As Westmoreland's air deputy, he agreed that control should be centered in MACV. By doing so, however, he placed himself in opposition to the Air Force's traditional resistance to parceling out air power below the theater commander level, which in this case meant below the level of the Pacific commander in Hawaii. The air commander in Saigon had to walk a narrow line.

The Air Force early in 1966 was molding its planes and people in South Vietnam into an effective supporter of ground troops, both U.S. and Vietnamese. At the same time, it was learning much about how to adjust to the demands of the counterinsurgency environment. Largely unconcerned with the doctrinal controversies that swirled above their heads at higher levels, junior Air Force officers were learning to work well with their Army and ARVN counterparts at the many points where their duties intersected. Since the previous July, when U.S. Army troops began arriving in South Vietnam in great profusion, two Air Force controllers had been assigned to each U.S. maneuver battalion, as well as to higher echelons. One remained on the ground and moved with the battalion commander to forward areas, advising him as to the best way to use strike aircraft. The second air controller covered the unit from above in his O–1 Bird Dog. Always in contact with his ground counterpart, the airborne FAC performed visual reconnaissance of the battlefield and relayed intelligence to the ground. When fighters were called in he controlled their strikes. The nearly disastrous loss of the Marine ground control party in the Harvest Moon operation, coupled with an increasing shortage of qualified Air Force pilots, led to the disappearance after March of ground controllers with the U.S. Army below the brigade level. For the remainder of the war, the main job of the FACs with battalions was to carry out reconnaissance and control strikes from their Bird Dogs. This represented no change as far as the ARVN was concerned, since Air Force controllers had seldom accompanied Vietnamese battalions on the ground. Ground FACs continued to advise U.S. ground commanders at brigade, division, and higher levels.

The Air Force controller's job was complicated, not only by his need to learn ground tactics and procedures, but also by the complexity of the institutional arrangements that had grown up within the Air Force structure in Vietnam. The controller and his Bird Dog received administrative, maintenance, personnel, and supply support from the tactical air support squadron (TASS) in his corps. Yet his mission orders came from the direct air support center (DASC) through the air liaison officer (ALO), who was located elsewhere in the corps. This arrangement was likened by one TASS commander to a "three-headed monster with no common nerve center." The people running the show, the DASC and the Corps ALO, were making command decisions that virtually prevented the TASS from operating as a tactical unit.[61] This dichotomy of control often left the FAC ignorant of who his boss was.[62] The DASCs themselves fell between two stools. In I Corps, for example, the DASC director pictured his operation as an "unwanted stepchild." Theoretically it was supported by the 20th TASS, but since the DASC was located with the Army, the Air Force did little to help it with its problems. Similarly, because the DASC was an Air Force organization, neither the Army nor the ARVN felt responsible for it. The operation was housed in a rundown shack that needed repainting, rewiring, new windows, and air conditioning.[63]

The 4 tactical air support squadrons were under a tactical control group in Saigon, while their planes flew out of 65 small airstrips around the country. Supply was a recurring problem, with frequent shortages of airplanes, marking rockets, spare parts, and personal items. The Air Force still had only 120 Bird Dogs, which were hard pressed to keep up with the demands for their services. In Kontum Province, for example, 4 O–1s were supposed to support 10 Special Forces camps, each of which carried out at least a long-range patrol every day. Only 2 planes were assigned, and frequently one or the other was grounded for lack of parts. The FACs at times borrowed O–1s from the Army,[64] but the Army planes were just as overcommitted and not always available.[65] The problem arose in part from the Air Force's success in

USAF O–1 Bird Dogs at a remote field in South Vietnam.

selling air support. The U.S. Army and the ARVN were relying more and more on air strikes for their ground operations.[66]

Besides directing strikes, the FACs were in constant demand to fly visual reconnaissance missions, both the routine daily ones that were part of the MACV program and special ones that were requested either by the provinces or by MACV to assess the results of B–52 raids. From January through April 1966, the O–1s flew 26,000 strike control and visual reconnaissance missions, compared with 39,000 the entire preceding year. Of these, 60 percent were reconnaissance flights.[67]

A shortage of forward air controllers contributed to the problem. This was due in part to the Air Force's insistence that all FACs be qualified fighter pilots, and there were not enough to go around. More of the FACs were assigned to the Special Forces CIDG* camps than to the ARVN. In II Corps, for example, six ARVN regiments (the equivalent of six U.S. Army brigades) were without air liaison officers. Some Vietnamese resented the preponderance of tactical air resources that were going to the U.S. and other allied ground forces and looked on the DASC that supplied air power as a private air force.[68] Since the aggressiveness of the Vietnamese troops ebbed and flowed in direct proportion to the amount of air support they received, the pilot shortage was having a direct effect on the Vietnamese operations.[69] Attempts to wean the ARVN from dependence on U.S. controllers were getting nowhere. Vietnamese Army commanders seldom trusted the VNAF

---

*The CIDG (Civilian Irregular Defense Group) program was initiated in 1962 with the support of the U.S. Mission in Saigon (MACV assumed support in 1963). The program was created to strengthen the counterinsurgency effort of the South Vietnamese government by developing paramilitary forces from the minority groups, primarily the Montagnard, in South Vietnam.

and wanted USAF FACs who could command jet fighters rather than their own controllers who could not. In many ways they were justified, as the VNAF controllers were slow in mastering the techniques of strike control and visual reconnaissance.[70]

As American pilots gained experience in this makeshift environment, most of them came to feel that their planes should be armed. Although the FACs carried sidearms, and occasionally M–16 rifles, many believed they could do a better job if the planes were armed. On reconnaissance missions, small arms fire from the ground kept the planes too high for the pilots to see all that was going on. When diving to mark a target for the fighters, the Bird Dog was vulnerable to ground fire, often causing the pilot to miss his mark. Were the O–1 equipped with attack rockets that could scatter the ground assailants, it would have a better chance of surviving and of placing its marking rockets accurately. Further, maintained many of the controllers, an armed Bird Dog could break off some attacks and ambushes. This would cut down on the number of friendly casualties that were being suffered before the heavy airstrikes arrived 30 or 40 minutes later and would, in some cases, eliminate the need for the costly and, at times, inefficient fighters.[71] Typical of the comments from the controllers were those of a pilot who flew Bird Dogs for a year in the delta. Many times during that year he spotted 2 or 3 Viet Cong moving across the ground. He did not call in strikes on them because they would be gone before the fighters arrived and they did not warrant expenditure of the heavy ordnance carried by most fighters. He estimated that he sighted between 100 and 150 of the enemy in groups of 2 or 3 who, in his words, "live to fight another day."[72] The Seventh Air Force resisted suggestions to arm the Bird Dogs, fearing that to do so would tempt the FACs into rash attacks and larger losses.

Day-to-day experience in the field highlighted some serious deficiencies of the Bird Dog. While the O–1 was the best off-the-shelf plane available the summer before, many inadequacies that seemed minor at the time were proving major early in 1966 as the plane was called on to fly more, as well as different kinds of missions. The most frequent complaint was its lack of armor. Pilots were being wounded, sometimes fatally, by small arms fire that penetrated the cockpit from below. Some FACs fashioned protection by wiring pieces of plastic around the aircraft's seat.[73] Performance was also limited by the plane's radios that did not allow the pilot to talk to all the people he should—ground controllers, fighter pilots, the DASC, and the emergency channel. The Bird Dog was overweight and underpowered for the mission. Its slow rate of climb exposed it to enemy fire, and its relatively short range cut down its effectiveness. Four marking rockets were not enough to do the job in a heavy action where as many as a dozen could be used. The planes were restricted at night by poor lighting in the cockpit and inadequate navigation equipment.

A temporary replacement, the O–2 (Cessna Super Skymaster), was being readied and a more permanent controller plane, the OV–10 Bronco, was being tested. For all the Bird Dog's technical drawbacks, however, some forward air controllers were concerned that, with the advent of these replacements, they would lose much of their versatility. The O–1 was cheap and easily maintained and allowed them to fly many types of missions in addition to strike control and reconnaissance—short notice flights into out-of-the-way forward bases, deliveries of documents and equipment, and orientation flights for ground personnel. The controllers had been able to perform these services for the Army because they were not under rigid central control. The flights were helping to create excellent relations with the Army. The FACs valued highly their freedom of action and the wide latitude they had to make decisions. Some feared that the introduction of higher performance and better equipped planes would also bring stronger central control and less freedom for them to work informally with the Army. In their eyes, more expensive planes that were more tightly controlled could destroy this carefully nurtured relationship that was important for day-to-day operations.[74] Too much sophistication in the new aircraft could hurt this relationship.[75]

Night tactics was another area where constant attempts at adaptation were made. Moving and attacking under the cover of darkness and during foul weather was the enemy's most successful tactic. Air Force countermeasures had increased in sophistication since 1962 when VNAF Gooney Birds dropped flares over attacking enemy troops to illuminate them for its strike planes. A year later, C–123s joined the C–47s in dropping flares. When jets were first used in 1965, they too helped with the night problem and soon were dropping bombs under the light of their own flares. By early 1966, the AC–47 gunships were doing most of the flare illumination in night actions and were proving extremely versatile. Not only could they respond to calls for help in thirty minutes or less, they also sometimes resolved the issue with their own guns. When the enemy was too strong for this, the gunships became control planes and directed fighters. Every night a few of the eighteen gunships stayed on airborne alert, while the others were ready on the ground to replace them when their flares or ammunition were spent.

Even under these conditions, however, this tactic had limitations. Flares that did not ignite, as well as those that drifted from the battle scene, made it difficult to keep the battle area continuously illuminated. Since most of the experiments with night tactics were being devised on the spot, without the benefit of joint training, perfect coordination between flare ships, fighters, FACs, and the people on the ground was seldom achieved.[76]

Although these tactics worked fairly well on clear nights, jets found it almost impossible to locate and hit the enemy when weather moved in and low clouds sheltered the battlefield. This had been brought home again early in March when the Viet Cong seized a Special Forces camp in the A Shau Valley near the Laotian border. Waiting for an umbrella of low clouds to protect them, they attacked at two in the morning and enjoyed immunity from overhead punishment for two days. The few planes that pierced the clouds could not find them. With their speed, the jets needed more room to maneuver than the 300-foot ceiling provided.[77]

The Air Force had been experimenting with a new bombing technique for over a year; and on the first of April, installed a ground radar at Bien Hoa, which, under the right conditions, could direct pilots to unseen targets. A second radar was set up at Pleiku the following month; and the system, called Skyspot, gradually expanded by early 1967 to cover the entire country from five sites. Skyspot was an adaptation of a radar scoring system that the Strategic Air Command used to evaluate the accuracy of its bombing practice. When flares could not be used, the fighter pilot got his headings, airspeeds, and altitudes by radio from a ground controller who was tracking his plane by radar and computer. As the pilot neared the target, the controller told him when to release his bombs. The pilot was freed from the need to see the enemy, to coordinate with friendly ground troops, and to fly into the range of enemy fire. Most planes dropped their bombs from between 10,000 and 20,000 feet. Skyspot caught on quickly, and soon one quarter of the tactical strikes were radar-controlled.[78] The B-52s started to use the system in July, and by the end of the year, it was their principal bombing method.

Yet Skyspot was not the hoped-for single solution to the problems of night and bad weather bombing and, from the point of view of sortie rates, was not the most effective system. Its radars could reach out only 50 miles. Although special beacons on fighter planes could amplify the signal and extend the range to 200 miles, there was a shortage of such beacons in 1966 and only the F-100s at Bien Hoa carried them. Since a Super Sabre carried only one-fourth the weight of bombs carried by a B-57, three or four F-100 sorties were needed to do what one Canberra flight could do.[79] Like all radar, furthermore, the Skyspot beam could not pass through obstructions and needed an unimpeded path to the airplanes, limiting how low the fighter planes could fly. The radar could control only one flight at a time against one target, much less effective than using a forward air controller, who often found himself simultaneously orchestrating several flights over a target.

A series of technical factors further reduced Skyspot's accuracy. Were the plane only one degree off its proper heading when it released its bombs, for example, the bombs would miss the target by as much as 350 feet. Errors occurred if the plane's wings were not level at the time of release; and to fly straight and level while releasing their bombs, the fighters needed smooth air, a rare occurrence in Vietnam. Since the radios from the ground were usable for only 150 miles, Skyspot missions were seldom flown farther than that from the stations.

The understandable reluctance to drop bombs on enemy soldiers who were close to one's own troops led to a ban on Skyspot strikes within 1,000 yards of friendly forces, unless the ground commander specifically approved. Some pilots, trained to dive against a visible enemy, were uncomfortable with the system and believed they were more accurate when bombing what they could see. There continued to be general frustration among pilots with the lack of follow-up evaluation of their strikes–evaluations they needed to improve their tactics and the composition of their bomb loads.[80]

Despite its imperfections, however, Skyspot gave the Air Force a much better, if still limited, ability to hit the enemy at night and in bad weather. It was incorporated gradually into the system. The rules that had restricted air strikes to those under the control of a forward air controller were relaxed to allow strikes under Skyspot control. For the tactical planes, however, the new system remained a backup method that was used only when FACs and flares could not be used.

Reflecting the influx of additional planes, the increase of targets, and the organizational superstructure that was being created, Air Force planes during the first third of 1966 doubled their rate of flying in South Vietnam over that of the previous year. By the end of April, they had logged 97,000 sorties, compared to 144,000 during all of 1965. The largest surge was in airlift and forward air controller flights. The airlift figures were swelled by the burgeoning number of C–130 missions, which in these 4 months alone was 3 times that for all of 1965. Jet reconnaissance and fighter missions increased 85 and 62 percent, respectively. The AC–47 gunships that had begun operations in earnest the previous November had, by the first of May, flown over 2,000 sorties, 4 times the number flown the year before. Several of the older types of planes were flying less because their missions were being taken over by newer craft. Among the fighter-bombers, A–1 and B–57 flights were down 10 and 20 percent as the F–4s, F–5s, and F–100s assumed larger strike roles. The reconnaissance B–66s, still waiting for reinforcements from Europe, flew at one-third their former rate. C–130s and C–123s were rapidly replacing the older airlift C–47s, whose sortie rate dropped 40 percent. The Vietnamese flying rate was also up by 25 percent, the largest increase coming in strike missions by A–1s.[81]

Indicative as these figures are of the increase in air activity, they say little of the specific results of the missions. Unfortunately, for the planners at the time and for subsequent researchers, reliable quantitative indications of results were unobtainable. For one thing, the Air Force had no clear-cut objective of its own to measure results in South Vietnam. Its role, along with the air elements of the other services, was to support ground operations. Air power was viewed, outside the Air Force, as but one of several types of supportive firepower at the call of the ground commanders. While the Army and Air Force Chiefs had agreed on this ancillary position for air power in the spring of 1965,[82] MACV further codified it in mid-1966 by directing that all air strikes in South Vietnam be reported as close air support missions.[83] Although this decision faithfully reflected the MACV position that all of South Vietnam was part of the battlefield, it made it difficult for the Air Force to measure the results of what it considered its own contribution to the war.

The problem was compounded by the lack of precision in terminology. The time-honored distinction between those air strikes that join with artillery against an enemy in contact with friendly forces (close air support) and those unilateral air strikes against the enemy's supplies and lines of communication at a distance from the battlefield (interdiction) tended to break down in the unconventional environment of South Vietnam. Westmoreland's ground-oriented injunction that all of these be called close air support missions simplified the reporting system but made Air Force evaluation difficult.

Adding to the confusion, the reports of strike results were neither complete nor accurate. The absence of ground surveillance after air strikes was endemic. Reports filed by the pilots after each strike were inexact estimates limited by the reporting system and by geographic and climatic conditions, enemy tactics, and less than perfect equipment. Attempts at separating the damage inflicted by Air Force planes from that achieved by other air and ground fire was tantamount to deciding whose blade caused which wound in Caesar's body. Probably most important, there existed no way to measure the long-range, as opposed to the immediate, effects of air strikes on villages, road security, morale, and infiltration.[84]

In the absence of credible quantifiable data, the Air Force relied on the best information it could get to measure how it was doing. The number of sorties, the weight of bombs dropped, and the amount of ammunition expended, as well as testimonials from ground customers and impressions gleaned from captured or defecting enemy soldiers, often provided the best available information. Conclusions drawn from such relatively "soft" material were necessarily couched in qualified and conditional terms. The lack of specific, quantifiable assessments, in turn, made it difficult for air leaders to plan improvements for the future with certainty.

Yet even with all these impediments, the Seventh Air Force, PACAF, and the Air Staff produced some incisive analyses of the air war. Analysis shops at each of these levels monitored and interpreted developments in every phase of the war—fighter tactics, airlift, loss ratios, weapon effectiveness, enemy responses, and personnel and organization suitability—that frequently led to tactical and technical improvements.[85]

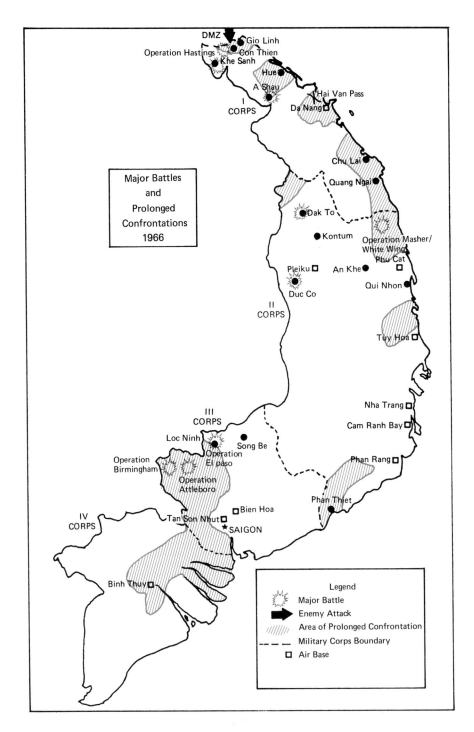

Major Battles
and
Prolonged
Confrontations
1966

DMZ
Gio Linh
Operation Hastings • Con Thien
Khe Sanh
Hue •
A Shau
Hai Van Pass
I
CORPS
Da Nang □

Chu Lai •
Quang Ngai •

Dak To
Kontum •
Operation Masher/
White Wing
Phu Cat
Pleiku □
An Khe •
Duc Co
Qui Nhon •

II
CORPS

Tuy Hoa □

Nha Trang □

Cam Ranh Bay □

III
CORPS

Loc Ninh
Song Be •
Operation
El paso
Operation
Birmingham
Operation
Attleboro

Phan Rang □

IV
CORPS

□ Bien Hoa
Tan Son Nhut □
★ SAIGON

Phan Thiet •

Binh Thuy □

Legend

Major Battle
Enemy Attack
//////// Area of Prolonged Confrontation
— — — Military Corps Boundary
□ Air Base

138

Chapter VI

Setbacks for Centralized Air Power
May–December 1966

As it began its fourth month in operation on July 1, 1966, the Seventh Air Force received a new commander, Lt. Gen. William W. Momyer. General Moore moved to Hawaii as second in command of the Pacific Air Forces. Momyer was the logical choice to take over the air war in Vietnam. For over two decades, while the Air Force devoted most of its resources to its strategic mission, the new Seventh Air Force Commander had remained a strong and tough advocate of tactical air power. He participated in the birth of tactical air doctrine and close air support techniques in the Army Air Forces when he commanded a fighter group in North Africa during World War II. After the war, as Assistant Chief of Staff of the newly created Tactical Air Command, he increased his experience with tactical fighter planes supporting ground forces in battle. During the early fifties, Momyer was on the faculty of the Air War College, which gave him the opportunity to apply his practical fighter experience to the improvement of fighter doctrine. A tour as a tactical wing and air division commander in Korea plunged him once again into the day-to-day challenges of fighter operations. Between 1958 and 1964, Momyer brought his operational and doctrinal background to bear as chief planner for the Tactical Air Command and as part of the Air Staff in Washington. Responding to President Kennedy's initiative, these were watershed years for the Air Force; and counterinsurgency, with its concomitant revival of tactical air power, was added to the traditional emphasis on nuclear weapons and strategic operations. In the Pentagon, Momyer was closely involved with building the force structure and molding a doctrine for tactical fighters in Vietnam.

Having dealt over the years with questions of tactical air power's relation to joint operations with the other services and to the Air Force's own strategic resources, the general now entered on an assignment where both of these relationships were being put to the test. He would succeed in translating some of his ideas into action in Vietnam, but others would be modified by the realities of the war.

His belief that air power was most efficient when it was centrally controlled was foremost among his convictions. One of the strongest challenges to this idea was coming from the airlift operation in South Vietnam, which, in his estimation, needed tighter organization and direction. Even though the April agreement between the Army and Air Force Chiefs had ended any lingering hopes that the Army's vast number of helicopters would be drawn into a centralized airlift system, the Air Force could still, in Momyer's view, centralize the airlift planes it controlled—the C–123 Providers, the C–130 Hercules, and, shortly, the CV–2 Caribous (that the Air Force redesignated as C–7s).

The ordinary pattern of deployment and resupply, with the bulk of people and materiel moved by surface transportation into and around a war theater while the priority cargo went by air, was modified in South Vietnam during the early stages of the war. Congestion at the few Vietnamese water ports often forced ocean-going vessels bearing cargo for Vietnam to deposit their loads at outlying ports in Okinawa or the Philippines. The loads were then flown into Vietnam. Once inside the country, the cargo once again had to be moved by air, since the inadequacy and insecurity of roads and railroads ruled out the more normal and less expensive surface distribution.[1] The result was an unprecedented reliance on the Air Force's tactical airlift fleet, both the C–123s stationed within Vietnam and the C–130s borrowed from PACAF and flown into the country from outside to complement the Providers. By mid-1966, these planes were already hauling 50,000 tons a month, a figure that was expected to double before the year ended.

The planes of the four C–123 squadrons still belonged to the 315th Air Division in Japan, although they were stationed in Vietnam and their crews came from the Seventh Air Force. The C–130s, which had already surpassed the C–123s in deliveries, also belonged to the command in Japan and were flown into Vietnam on two-week rotations. Major maintenance and support were performed for the C–130s outside South Vietnam. Even though the Provider and Hercules people had arrived at informal working relationships to ameliorate some of the harsher inconsistencies of this divided command, two separate airlift systems remained, with different, and at times, conflicting, priorities and schedules.[2] This divided management had not yet hurt deliveries, but Momyer felt that the projected increase in airlift sorties would strain the system beyond the point of efficiency. He believed that all airlift planes should be brought under his command.

Radiating out from Tan Son Nhut, Nha Trang, and Da Nang, the four Provider squadrons kept a stream of materiel and passengers flowing steadily

Livestock Transport—cattle are crated for air drop (top), dropped with parachute from C–123 (right), arriving unhurt at a remote Special Forces camp (bottom).

into the small, isolated outposts in the Delta, midlands, and the northern reaches of the country. Each squadron kept some of its planes on alert to drop flares, evacuate the wounded, and aid in the search for downed airmen. In addition, several of the planes of the 309th squadron at Tan Son Nhut were flying herbicide and defoliation missions.

The bulk of the cargo flights were flown into areas with small unimproved air strips. When the planes could not land, they dropped their supplies from the air. Most routine supply missions were short, less than an hour long, but the sixty planes were each flying about five sorties a day. The types of cargo the planes carried mirrored the nature of the Vietnamese war and society. Besides such military items as ammunition, loaded fuel bladders, aircraft parts, and vehicles, the aircraft moved Vietnamese war refugees, coal, live pigs, cows, chickens, ducks and peacocks, rice, wine, mail, and whatever else was needed and could fit into the holds.[3]

The 311th Air Commando Squadron (ACS) at Da Nang mainly flew scheduled flights—a daily roundtrip passenger flight down the coast to Saigon with stops along the way and shorter daily cargo flights to coastal and mountain Special Forces camps in I Corps.[4] All squadrons helped out in emergencies. During the Masher/White Wing operation early in 1966, for example, the Da Nang C–123s moved air cavalry soldiers and over 700 tons of supplies from Pleiku and An Khe forward to Bong Son, while the Nha Trang squadron, the 310th ACS, flew critical flare and evacuation missions.[5] The Providers were in on virtually every major ground operation in 1966.

Small arms fire from the ground posed an ever-present threat to these operations, particularly during airdrop missions and when bad weather forced the planes to hug the ground. About fifteen aircraft were hit each month, although few were downed. In January, a C–123 from Da Nang, carrying seventy Vietnamese soldiers to nearby An Hoa, was forced by bad weather to fly low and visually follow the course of a river. Automatic weapon fire struck the plane from both sides of the river; but the pilot got the plane and its passengers safely back to Da Nang without an elevator cable, throttle cable, or altitude indicator.[6]

The following month, a C–123 from the 19th ACS at Tan Son Nhut, while dropping rice to the small outpost of Duc Phung north of Saigon, was hit repeatedly and broke off the mission. Several days later the plane returned, and through a combination of new approach headings and expert maneuvering, the pilot dropped the remaining five tons of rice on the target.[7]

In March, another of the squadron's planes was struck by ground fire while lifting off from Bien Hoa with six tons of artillery shells destined for Song Be. A fuel line rupture caused the left engine to burst into flames that quickly became uncontrollable. The cargo was jettisoned in ninety seconds as the plane turned back for Bien Hoa. While on the final approach, the fire spread through the heater ducts and into the right wing. The pilot landed the plane with most of the left wing burned away and the right wing already starting to burn.[8]

That same month, the 311th assisted in the unsuccessful defense of the A Shau Special Forces camp. On the 9th, one of its planes headed for the camp to drop 15,000 pounds of ammunition and medical supplies. The weather was bad, and the pilot followed an A–1E down through a hole in the overcast. Although he dropped his bundles successfully from 50 feet, ground fire ripped through the plane's electrical cables cutting off most flight and engine instruments. The return to Da Nang was made by dead reckoning, with sound being the only method for the pilots to adjust the propellers.[9]

Not even the scheduled passenger flights were immune. In March, a Da Nang plane was fired at while landing at Quang Ngai. One hit entered the fuselage at the forward entrance door, penetrated the air duct at floor level, and came to rest inches from a passenger.[10]

In another instance, while taking off from Dau Tieng, a small strip forty-five miles north of Saigon, a C–123 from the 19th squadron was riddled by ground fire, which caused liquid fire to drip from ruptured hydraulic lines in the ceiling. The thirty-five Vietnamese military passengers grabbed parachutes and tried to force open the emergency door. Five of them burst into the cockpit and attempted to climb out the side window. Turning back to the airfield, the pilot realized that if he crashlanded (the landing gear would not go down) with the passengers out of control, they would be tossed about the plane on impact. Near the end of his approach he intentionally nosed the aircraft down hard and dragged it through some treetops, throwing everyone to the floor. The plane crashlanded without a fatality.[11]

Second only to ground fire as a headache for the airlift crews was the poor condition of many of the landing strips whose surfaces deteriorated under heavy use. Landings on substandard runways blew tires, ruptured hydraulic lines, and wore down brakes and bearings. Runways were frequently closed by planes unable to taxi or to park because of blown tires. Many of the 135 strips used by the C–123s were less than 2,000 feet long and located in places where approaches at night and during bad weather were precarious.[12] A large number of the outposts had dirt strips that became soft and unusable when it rained.[13] In May, a Provider got mired in runway mud when it landed at sunset at Tuyen Nhon, an 1,800-foot strip in the delta. Rather than abandon the aircraft to the enemy attacking in the area, the crew and some Special Forces troops worked through the night to free the plane. Helicopters flew in air bags and, while several crew members stood guard with M–16 rifles, pierced steel planks were placed under the wheels and parts of the runway ahead of the plane were built up with mud and dirt. At three in the morning, the plane took off and returned to Tan Son Nhut.[14]

By mid-1966, the number of C–130 squadrons in the Philippines, Okinawa, Taiwan, and Japan had increased to 12, with 140 planes shuttling

A C–123 making an assault takeoff from a short field in October 1966.

supplies into and around South Vietnam. At any given time, 40 of these cargo planes were in the country at either Tan Son Nhut, Nha Trang, or at the new Cam Ranh Bay air base, from which they flew into many of the forward airstrips. The Hercules' presence in Vietnam had grown dramatically in the year since the first 4 had been sent there temporarily to ease a cargo backlog, and they were carrying two-thirds of the tonnage distributed throughout the country.

What integration there was of the C–130s into the airlift system during the intervening year had not been accomplished without difficulty. Generals Westmoreland and Momyer wanted the large planes stationed permanently in the country and assigned directly to them. In arguing their case, they cited the inefficiency of shuttling the planes back and forth between the islands and the mainland, usually empty on the return trip. They also argued that flying the mission in Vietnam required pilots with an intimate knowledge of the challenging terrain and often treacherous airstrips—knowledge that could not be acquired on two-week tours in the country. Hawaii and the Air Force, on the other hand, argued that the C–130s had to serve the entire Pacific and must be ready for missions outside Southeast Asia if they were needed. PACAF also pointed out that Vietnam was crammed with airplanes and support units and keeping the C–130s there permanently would require maintenance and support elements that would further tax an already saturated situation.

Until February 1966, the 315th Air Division in Japan kept tight control of the C–130s by scheduling the planes, determining the fields into which they could fly (very few), setting cargo loads, and handling virtually all the details that surround airlift operations. As a result, many of the organizations and practices of the C–123s were unnecessarily duplicated. The situation was modified somewhat in February when the 315th group in Saigon was upgraded to a wing and given control of the C–130s during the time they were temporarily in the country.[15] However, there was no change to PACAF's position that the planes should continue to be based outside Vietnam.

General Momyer was not satisfied with the arrangement when he arrived. Although it had operational control of the C–130s while they were in Vietnam, the Saigon wing still could not program the aircraft, reorganize their units, or integrate them with the other airlift forces. Having to depend for its planes on another command located 2,400 miles away, the wing could not easily adjust the C–130 missions to unforeseen emergencies, shift airplanes and crews about to fit unique situations, plan the maintenance workload that ebbed and flowed with the tide of war, nor "get the last hour out of the planes and men."[16] The cargo handling terminals, called aerial port squadrons, still reported back to Japan. The division there tried to install its own control centers in Vietnam alongside those of MACV.[17] In short, the general saw himself without command of the forces he needed to carry out his responsibilities.[18]

At the same time, the question remained of how the Air Force would use the Army Caribous it was to inherit at the end of the year. Consistent with the April agreement giving the planes to the Air Force, Army commanders in Vietnam were asking Westmoreland to allow the aircraft to be used exclusively for specific units rather than have them put into the larger airlift system. The MACV Commander and Momyer agreed that the Caribous would be assigned directly to the Seventh Air Force, but, at least for the first month, they would continue to support the same Army units they had been supporting. After that they would reexamine the arrangement and decide if the planes should be incorporated into the common airlift system.[19]

When Momyer arrived at the Seventh Air Force, PACAF was already considering placing an air division in South Vietnam to consolidate the C–123s, the Caribous, the aerial port squadrons, and the airlift control centers. General Harris remained firm, however, in insisting that the C–130s would remain outside of this new organization. There was a general feeling at the Seventh that Harris did not want to give control of the planes to them because that would mean giving control of the planes to MACV. However, since Westmoreland was getting whatever he wanted and had de facto control of the planes anyway, the air leaders in Saigon felt they were being handicapped unnecessarily.[20] General McConnell in Washington agreed with Harris. An Air Staff study convinced him that fewer planes were needed under the shuttle system, which was more flexible and better suited to

Southeast Asia. This was so because the number of C–130s moving in and out of South Vietnam could be increased or decreased rapidly (even daily) as peaks and valleys occurred.[21]

Momyer favored the idea of an air division but pleaded that the C–130s be part of it. Only in this way, he noted, would he have clear-cut command and control of the Hercules, which were rapidly becoming the mainstay of the airlift system.[22] Although General Moore, while commander in Vietnam, had also urged basing the C–130s in the country, in his new position at PACAF and with a new perspective, he now opposed the idea.[23] So did virtually everyone else outside Vietnam. The PACAF plan was approved, and in October, the new airlift division (the 834th) began operating at Tan Son Nhut as part of the Seventh Air Force. The 315th wing, with its C–123s, was placed in the new division, giving the Seventh Air Force, for the first time, full command of the Providers. A second wing for the division (the 483d) was created at Cam Ranh Bay, also in October, to get ready for the Caribous. An airlift control center was established to serve as a focal point under MACV for airlift operations throughout the country.

The keystone of Momyer's plan, inclusion of the C–130 wing, remained unfulfilled. The general continued to press for the Hercules after the air division was created, arguing for efficiency and for sustained exposure of the airlift pilots to the country.[24] General McConnell was persuaded, however, by another study from his analysis shop showing that basing the transports in Vietnam would require more planes, would cost more for facilities, and would destroy the shuttle system's flexibility to provide increasing or decreasing numbers of planes as the fluid situation changed.[25] The argument for keeping the planes at the PACAF level won the day; and for the rest of the war, the C–130s were to retain their home bases outside Vietnam. The delegation of full operational control of C–130 operations and maintenance to the Seventh Air Force the following August did not solve the problem. Questions of skill, motivation, and effectiveness remained. "That airlift remained a problem," Momyer later wrote, "was primarily correlated, in my mind, with the failure to assign a C–130 wing to the Air Component Commander" (i.e., to himself).[26] His deputy commander was less restrained. He recalled, "We violate our own principles. We complain about the Marines not coming in wholeheartedly with us. We complain about the Navy not doing it. We don't even do it in the Air Force."[27]

Between July and December 1966, the Air Force converted the six Army Caribou companies into troop carrier squadrons. For the first time since the creation of the Air Force in 1947, a major Army unit was transferred to the Air Force. The Army had been flying the ninety-six CV–2s from five locations in South Vietnam. According to the plan for their conversion, the squadrons at An Khe and Qui Nhon were to move to the new field at Phu Cat, two more were to go from Can Tho and Dong Ba Thin to Cam Ranh

Bay, while a third pair were to remain at Vung Tau. During these months, Air Force personnel replaced their Army counterparts on a one-for-one basis as Army tours expired. In this way, the transfer was made without interrupting operations, and the Air Force people gained experience gradually in a combat environment.[28]

In July, the first three Air Force officers joined the 17th Aviation Company at Camp Holloway, near Pleiku, where it was supporting the 1st Cavalry Division. By September, thirty more airmen had joined the company, which had moved to An Khe, and went through an unusual orientation program. Besides ironing out differences with the Army over maintenance, supply, and administrative methods, the Air Force men had to learn to defend themselves against ground attacks. They were formed into an infantry company and taught by members of the 1st Cavalry Division how to use weapons and ground tactics. Throughout the transfer, Army procedures gradually yielded to Air Force methods.

Increasingly, Air Force pilots flew resupply missions into short and rough fields during major operations—Thayer II, Irving, and Paul Revere IV. The move to the new location at Phu Cat began on December 23 as tons of cargo and vehicles were moved by air and by road to the still half-completed airfield.[29] The new troop carrier squadron, the 537th, was in place by the first of January. It was joined at Phu Cat that day by the 459th from Qui Nhon. The field was not yet finished, and the newcomers were greeted by a 3,000-foot dirt strip and a parking ramp that had been hastily constructed of aluminum matting. The flyers had to share many of the facilities with the civilian construction company building the field.[30]

The story was similar in the other squadrons. In August, the first 2 Air Force officers arrived at the 135th Aviation Company at Dong Ba Thin, several miles north of Cam Ranh Bay. They lived in rain-soaked tents and shaved out of their helmets. By the time it moved to Cam Ranh Bay on the first of the year as the 458th Troop Carrier Squadron, the unit had 44 officers and 137 enlisted men. Normal combat operations went on without interruption throughout the transition period. On the day of the move, 5 of the Caribous took off from Dong Ba Thin, flew their combat missions and, with the sorties completed, landed at their new home. Another 5 flew directly to Cam Ranh Bay, while the remaining 5 flew to Nha Trang to set up an operating location there.[31] The airplanes of the other squadron coming to Cam Ranh Bay, the 457th from Can Tho, also arrived on the first; but their equipment, shipped by LST, was diverted and off-loaded at Saigon. It did not arrive until two weeks later.[32]

The conversion of the two squadrons at Vung Tau, the 535th and 536th, was smooth. Among all six squadrons, the change from the more relaxed Army methods to more formal Air Force practices took place with little friction and much cooperation. By January the changeover was complete, with all the squadrons plugged into the Air Force operating and reporting system.

The frustration that General Momyer experienced over the C–130s was matched by his inability to gain more control over the B–52s. Momyer considered Air Force doctrine obsolete and not sufficiently flexible to serve the needs of Southeast Asia.[33] This doctrine, which held that strategic air power was indivisible and would lose its punch were it parceled out to theater commanders, had led in 1946 to the creation of the Strategic Air Command directly under the Joint Chiefs of Staff. Sensitive to its worldwide responsibilities, the command, over the years, had resisted proposals by theater commanders to share its control of the strategic force. While the Strategic Air Command retained control of the bombers in Southeast Asia, one important element of that control, the power to nominate targets, had been given to General Westmoreland.

The Seventh Air Force, however, shared none of this control and had little to say in choosing targets or in controlling the strikes. When the first B–52 missions were flown in 1965, targets were sent up to MACV from the Army field commanders. Appropriate ones were then forwarded to the Joint Chiefs, the Defense Secretary, the State Department, and the White House. In April 1966, the political leaders, more confident in bomber operations, delegated to CINCPAC the power to approve MACV's targets. This basic arrangement for controlling the B–52s had matured when Seventh's predecessor, the 2d Air Division, was still small and lacked the power and resources for a full-fledged targeting operation. The same system was still in effect when Momyer arrived, even though the Seventh Air Force had by then grown to the point where it could have done the targeting. Although the Seventh did suggest some targets to MACV, so did all the ground commanders and the Seventh enjoyed no special priority. During the B–52 missions, the Seventh's role was limited to coordinating the bombers with the other tactical missions being flown in the country and to providing aerial protection for the Stratofortresses.

Momyer considered this highly inefficient. To him, Arc Light missions should be no different from the other flights he controlled in South Vietnam. To get the most out of the bombers, the B–52s should obey the same rules as the other planes. The Seventh Air Force, the organization closest to the battlefield, should decide which type of planes, B–52s or tactical ones, was best suited for particular targets and what kinds of ordnance, fuzes, and tactics would produce the greatest results. This could best be done by incorporating the Arc Light program into the Seventh's tactical control system.[34]

Soon after he arrived, Momyer began to press for more control over the B–52s and for fewer missions by the big bombers. He was motivated not only by doctrinal questions of command and control but equally by a practical concern of how to use the bombers most effectively. To him, Westmoreland's employment of the B–52s as long-range artillery to suppress "what may or may not be suspected concentrations or supply areas" was questionable and relatively ineffective.[35] In the absence of massive enemy formations or logistic concentrations, it was wasteful to increase the number of Arc Light sorties. Instead, the bombers should be used selectively against specific targets, and 2 squadrons of them flying no more than 150 sorties a month should be enough.[36] In cases where the enemy was believed to be gathering his forces for an attack, there were enough fighter-bombers on hand to contain any attack until the big bombers could be brought in.[37]

This difference of opinion over how to use the bombers was encouraged by the uncertainty that existed about how productive the raids were. Unable to obtain specific, quantifiable assessments, each general adopted a position that fit his preconception of the role of air power. Westmoreland was using the bombers to harass the enemy and to break up enemy concentrations before they jelled, while Momyer believed they should be used only to interdict definable targets of massed men or supplies. Momyer argued that he, as Seventh Air Force Commander, was in the best position to nominate targets to Westmoreland and to control the Stratoforts as they flew over South Vietnam.[38]

Since the B–52 operation had grown so large and was taxing MACV's resources, Westmoreland at first appeared receptive to this idea.[39] In Washington, McConnell was placed in a dilemma. On the one hand, SAC could not relinquish a portion of its worldwide strategic responsibility by turning over part of its forces to a local commander. On the other, McConnell was sympathetic to the Seventh Air Force's position and hoped to get the planes more under the aegis of the senior airman in Vietnam. By way of compromise, he proposed that Momyer be given control as Westmoreland's air deputy, rather than as Seventh Air Force Commander. Momyer pointed out that this would change nothing since his job as air deputy was merely advisory and carried with it neither authority nor responsibility. Because the planes were being used in tactical roles, he repeated, they should be folded into his operations like the other tactical planes. Momyer continued to emphasize that MACV was using the bombers differently than the Seventh was using its tactical planes and that, as long as Westmoreland picked the targets, the aircraft would continue to be used for close air support rather than for interdiction.[40]

McConnell then suggested that a SAC contingent be placed in the Seventh Air Force headquarters to do the operational planning, at the same time stressing that SAC's role would not be diminished.[41] All sides—USAF, SAC, MACV, and the Seventh Air Force—held firm to their positions.

Finally, in December, the Joint Chiefs modified the organization with an arrangement that, in practical terms, changed little. Acting on McConnell's suggestion, the chiefs suggested moving the small existing SAC liaison office from MACV to the Seventh, increasing its size from five to seventeen planners, and attaching it to Momyer as the MACV Air Deputy. This new SAC advanced echelon (ADVON), as it would be called, would plan and coordinate Arc Light requests, monitor the missions as they flew over South Vietnam, determine the requirements for ground radar (Skyspot), and schedule the refueling tankers.[42] Westmoreland agreed to all the points in the proposal except its heart. "It is not the intention of COMUSMACV," he replied, "to assign the function to plan and coordinate strike requests to the SAC ADVON. This function will be retained in . . . MACV headquarters."[43]

Although the ADVON was installed in the Seventh Air Force's headquarters early in January 1967, its day-to-day work continued to be with SAC's 3d Air Division on Guam. The Seventh Air Force remained outside the Arc Light decisionmaking process. What it had gained, in effect, was a slightly more efficient instrument for orchestrating its own planes with the B–52s. However, its input to missions came only after the substantive planning had been done elsewhere.

This controversy had been occasioned in part by the steady increase in Arc Light sorties that had taken place since the first mission in June 1965. By the end of July 1966, the bombers had flown 4,309 sorties in 471 missions, all but a few in South Vietnam, to harass the enemy and keep him off guard.[44] The bombers struck in Laos for the first time in December 1965; and in April 1966, dropped their first bombs on North Vietnam. Westmoreland believed the enemy was reacting to the increased American ground pressure by massing more frequently, by stepping up his infiltration of troops from the north, and by building new supply areas.[45] To counter this, the MACV Commander used more B–52s and attributed the enemy's failure to launch a planned monsoon offensive in the summer of 1966 to MACV's spoiling actions, in which the Stratoforts played a major role.[46] As the Arc Light program grew, so did the need to improve it. Modifications developed by April 1966 had more than doubled the number of bombs each B–52 could carry, from 51 to 108. At the same time, other steps were taken to reduce the time it took the bombers to reach their targets.

With Skyspot equipment aboard, the B–52s could be diverted, either before they left the runway or while they were in flight, to secondary targets if the primary ones had vanished. Since this entailed giving Westmoreland authority to approve the secondary targets and since well over 80 percent of

A modified B–52 releases an internal load of 84 bombs in a test over Eglin AFB, Florida, in March 1966 (above). The bomb bay of a B–52 with a load of 84 bombs (right). The bombers can carry 24 more bombs on wing racks.

the B–52 raids were flown over South Vietnam, CINCPAC in November gave the MACV Commander the authority to approve all Arc Light targets in South Vietnam. His refusal to delegate this power down to the Seventh Air Force was a further indication that the bombers were viewed as a form of artillery whose main contribution to the joint effort was as a backdrop to the ground commanders.

Starting in July, to respond more quickly to requests from Saigon, six bombers on Guam were kept on continuous alert as a quick reaction force and were supported by six tankers on Okinawa. The quick reaction force and the diversion system, however, did not get to the heart of the reaction time problem. Under the best of conditions, the bombers, once summoned, still took six hours to arrive over Vietnam.

Table 3

Possible Sites for New B–52 Bases

Air Base	Distance to Nha Trang (miles)	Runway Length (ft)	Runway Width (ft)	Runway Weight Bearing Capacity (lbs)
Ban U Tapao, Thailand	650	11,500	200	400,000
Clark AB, Philippines	770	10,500	150	300,000
Mactan AB, Philippines	910	8,500	150	350,000
Ching–Chuan Kang AB, Taiwan	950	12,000	200	470,000
Tainan AB, Taiwan	950	10,000	148	207,000
Kadena AB, Okinawa	1,370	12,100	300	364,000
Andersen AB, Guam	2,100	11,200	200	400,000
Minimum Needed for B–52s		11,000	200	400,000

Throughout 1966, all headquarters worked to find an additional home for the planes closer to Vietnam. At first, it was planned to improve the facilities on Guam so that seventy planes could fly from there. When Westmoreland in July called for still more B–52 sorties,[47] the Joint Chiefs began to investigate Taiwan, the Philippines, Okinawa, and Thailand as possible sites (table 3). They quickly rejected Taiwan and the Philippines for political reasons and because construction costs would be too high. General McConnell favored the Thai base at U Tapao, which in June had become the home of some KC–135 tankers. In September he asked that the matter be explored by the ambassador in Bangkok. During a visit to Guam in November, McNamara ordered the chiefs to draw up plans for increasing the facilities on Guam and for placing fifteen of the big planes at Tuy Hoa in South Vietnam. The idea of B–52s at Tuy Hoa roused strong opposition from Admiral Sharp, Air Force Secretary Brown, and the Joint Chiefs on the grounds that it would be too expensive and insecure. Meanwhile, Brown continued to push for Thailand; and early in January, the ambassador in Bangkok was asked by McNamara to discuss the matter with the Thai government.[48]

Westmoreland had persuaded the chiefs early in 1966 to increase the number of monthly B–52 sorties to 450 through March, to 600 through June, and to 800 during the second half of the year. The 450 mark was reached by August, but the bomb shortage kept the rate at about that level until November. The easing of the shortage, accompanied by the MACV commander's insistence on 800 sorties a month as quickly as possible, pushed the rate to 600 in December, with 800 reached in March 1967.[49]

McNamara was uncomfortable with the cost of the Arc Light program. The ordnance alone for 800 monthly sorties in 1967 would reach half a billion dollars. With other expenses, the bill for the year could surpass $780 million.[50] Gnawing at the Defense Secretary, whose penchant for quantifiable results was well known, was the paucity of hard data on what the B–52s were accomplishing. The primary sources for measuring results, visual and photo reconnaissance, were often hampered by dense foliage, poor weather, and the enemy's cleverness in covering his tracks. Ground reconnaissance teams entered the bombed areas after about only 10 percent of the Arc Light strikes. The location of targets deep in enemy territory, as well as the frequent unavailability of airlift, usable roads, and soldiers, kept this low rate constant throughout the war. Forced to quantify, the closest the chiefs could come were detailed (and very impressive) statistics on the number of missions and sorties, the weight of ordnance dropped, the accuracy of the bombs, and what percentage (99.7) of the bombs planned were actually dropped.

If qualitative measurements were meager, however, subjective valuations abounded as Westmoreland continued to press for increases. He portrayed the Arc Light raids as extremely effective in lowering the enemy's morale, increasing desertions, forcing changes in tactics, and causing disruptions to the enemy's economy.[51] The MACV chief derived these conclusions primarily from prisoner-of-war reports and the testimony of his field commanders. Captured enemy soldiers were fairly consistent in what they said. They had frequently been forced to evacuate their camps and seek refuge across the border. Many wanted to desert after each raid, but conditions often prevented them from doing so. The element of surprise, however, decreased somewhat with the passage of time as the enemy came more and more to receive advanced warning of the raids and was able to take some protective measures.[52] The most consistent picture that emerged from the prisoners was one of terror, panic, demoralization, and confusion.[53] American ground commanders, who selected the targets as a means to disrupt the enemy, considered B–52s the most effective weapon system used in South Vietnam.[54] Thus, the anomaly persisted with the Army enthusiastic about the big bombers, which it viewed as "flying artillery," while elements within the Air Force objected to them in this role because they were not being used effectively.

By late 1966, some of the problems engendered by the 1965 buildup were on the road to resolution. By November, the air munitions shortage, which had been critical during the summer, was improving rapidly. Most critical had been the 2.75-inch rockets that forward air controllers used to mark targets and to create fires on the ground. In April, the Air Force had been forced to borrow 15,000 of these rockets from the Army, barely enough to avert the immediate crisis. Forward air controllers tried to substitute smoke grenades for marking rockets, but that did not work. The low point in supply came in July, when PACAF received only 65,000 of the 186,000 rockets it needed.[55]

The inventory of bombs reached its nadir at the same time. When the shortage first became noticeable in April it affected only the smaller (250 and 500 pounds) general purpose bombs. As heavier ordnance was substituted for these, however, its availability too began to dwindle. By July, 8 types of bombs, ranging in weight from 250 to 3,000 pounds, were on the critical list. In March, the Army began to run out of flares they fired from their mortars and artillery pieces and turned to the Air Force and VNAF to light up the battlefields. Soon the Air Force was running low on flares.[56]

Steps taken during the spring and summer were paying off near the end of the year. The creation of an Air Munitions Office in the Pentagon, the release to CINCPAC of reserve munitions from Korea and the United States, increased production, adjustment of the sortie rates, and improved surface deliveries combined to raise the stock level in the Seventh Air Force from fifteen days in June to almost the normal forty-five days by November. The supply of 20-mm ammunition used by the jets, however, was still lagging behind. The two million rounds provided for December fell far short of the three million that were needed. Tighter controls on this cannon ammunition carried over into the new year.[57]

The airfield picture also brightened in the latter part of the year. The new 10,000-foot runway was opened at Phan Rang in the middle of October, ending a string of construction travails that had required herculean efforts to surmount. The 18 F–4s of the 389th squadron, which had arrived in March, had operated for 4 months off the temporary aluminum plank runway, whose usable length varied with the weather from 6,000 to 10,000 feet. When the rains hit in May, 6-inch gaps opened up between the aluminum and the ground and quickly filled with water. At times, the ordnance hanging from the wings of the Phantoms dragged along the ground as the planes raced down the runway for takeoff. Since the aluminum became too hot during the daytime to touch, Air Force engineering teams replaced the runway piece by piece at night when takeoffs and landings were restricted.[58] The civilian contractors, meanwhile, worked around the clock and finished the permanent concrete runway in October. By then, 4 squadrons of F–100s had arrived along with the 20 B–57s from Da Nang. At the same time, an interchange of wings took place. The 366th Tactical Fighter Wing with its squadron of F–4s moved up to Da Nang, while the 35th wing came down to Phan Rang from the northern airfield. By the end of the year, Phan Rang was fully operational.

General McConnell's earlier reservations concerning the ability of the Air Force contractor (Walter Kidde Constructors, Inc.) to complete the base at Tuy Hoa on time proved unfounded. An advance construction party arrived in June; and within six months, with the completion of interim airfield facilities, the base was in operation. The Turnkey project was so successful because the Air Force exercised extraordinary control over the contractor and because the incentives in the contract encouraged the company to meet its schedules and demobilize its force as early as possible.[59] The first squadron of F–100s (the 308th) touched down on November 15, forty-five days ahead of schedule. Within a month, it was joined by two others (the 306th and 309th); and by the end of December, another operational fighter wing (the 31st) had been added to the Air Force's roster.[60]

Construction did not move as smoothly at the Phu Cat site north of Qui Nhon, even though, unlike the other bases, no interim runway was planned. The site for the base, which had been agreed on in February, was a former Viet Cong training center only five miles from An Nhon, the birthplace of the Communist insurgency in South Vietnam. The Phu Cat Mountains, an enemy redoubt the South Vietnamese had yet to penetrate, were only eight miles away. In April, soldiers of the Korean Tiger division moved into the area to clear the way for the MACV and Korean construction workers. The work force arrived in May; and for two months, the Korean soldiers, who lived in the camp, had to accompany the workers whenever they left the site.

Twenty-five days had been allowed for local villagers to remove and relocate some 300 graves of relatives from the planned runway sites. When the villagers entered the area, however, they collected fire wood, stole runway stakes, set booby traps, and on one occasion, committed a murder. Not a

PRIME BEEF PROJECTS
Clockwise from top left—pouring cement
at Da Nang; Quonset huts at Da Nang;
water tower at Da Nang; cutting wood for
new buildings at Da Nang; aluminum
matting at Tan Son Nhut; spreading
cement at Tan Son Nhut; barracks at Tan
Son Nhut; a bomb dump shelter at Pleiku.

single grave had been removed by the end of the period, and the job fell to the Americans.

Earth moving began in June and went well despite Viet Cong harassment. Leaflets left by the Viet Cong were frequently found in the work and living areas. The operator of the water treatment plant was discovered to be a Viet Cong. Mines and booby traps were a constant source of concern—one Korean soldier was killed and three injured by a mine. The American excavation superintendent emerged unscathed from his truck after a mine blew it fifty feet into the air. Two Korean officers were killed by snipers near the construction site; and in August, the Koreans repulsed a Viet Cong attack on the workers.

Nevertheless, work progressed at a record rate until the rains began in September.[61] Due to delays and escalating construction costs there and at other bases, the Seventh Air Force, which was responsible for paying for all airfield work, had to cut back on its Phu Cat contract. The civilian contractor's responsibility was reduced to only the runway, roads, utilities, the ammunition area, and the control tower. Air Force engineering teams took over construction of all else.[62] The first concrete for the runway was poured on December 20, and eleven days later the two Caribou squadrons arrived.

Meanwhile, Air Force Prime Beef* emergency construction teams had been sent to Vietnam and were transforming the faces of the bases at Tan Son Nhut, Bien Hoa, Da Nang, Nha Trang, Pleiku, and Binh Thuy with aircraft revetments, barracks, Quonset huts, parking aprons, guard towers, and new plumbing and electrical systems. They finished a second 10,000-foot runway at Da Nang in July and the first permanent runway at Cam Ranh Bay in November. (The Military Airlift Command began flying its C–141 transports into the base that month, relieving some of the pressure on overburdened Tan Son Nhut.[63]) In some instances, including the runway at Cam Ranh Bay, the Air Force teams completed projects begun by the civilian agency when the money ran out.

By the end of the year, the Air Force had 834 planes in South Vietnam (table 4), now the home for a numbered Air Force, an airlift division, and 9 wings—5 jet fighter, 2 airlift, a reconnaissance, and an air commando. The 5

---

*Prime Beef—combination of a nickname (Prime) and an acronym (BEEF—Base Engineering Emergency Force).

Table 4
USAF Aircraft in Southeast Asia
1965–1967

Aircraft	Dec 1965 SVN	Dec 1965 Thai	Dec 1966 SVN	Dec 1966 Thai	Jan 1968 SVN	Jan 1968 Thai
Fighter/Bombers						
A–1	53	6	20	18		35
A–26				7		12
A–37					25	
B–52						15
B–57	22		20		23	
B–66		5				
F–4	68	32	135	38	116	97
F–5	11		15			
F–100	76	3	203		193	
F–102	9	4	12	10	12	10
F–104				18		
F–105		90		135		106
T–28				11		8
Transports						
C–7					80	2
C–47	7		6		16	3
C–123	49		60		53	
C–130					73	17
Reconnaissance						
RB–57	3		3		4	
RB–66	3	7				
RF–4	9		40	22	34	40
RF–101	13	13	14	15	17	
Observation						
O–1	118		197	23	181	
O–2					103	34
Helicopters						
CH–3	10	1	4	9		14
HH3		2	3	7		7
HH–43	11	21	15	9	20	9
HH–53						4
UH–1				15	12	
Electronic						
EC–47			25		40	
EC–121	4		4			30
EB–66				22		24
Other						
AC–47	20		19		27	
HC–54		5				
HC–130			3	4	12	
HU–16	5		6			
U–2			2		2	
U–6				15		
U–10	18		16		15	12
UC–123			12	6	18	4
KC–135		16		31		40
	509	205	834	415	1,085	523

Source: PACAF Status of Forces Reports

fighter wings had 338 jet fighter-bombers* distributed among 18 squadrons. Eleven squadrons of F–100s were flying from Tuy Hoa, Phan Rang, and Bien Hoa, while 7 F–4 squadrons were based at Da Nang and Cam Ranh Bay. Twenty B–57s, 15 F–5s, and 12 F–102s brought the total of jet attack planes to 385. The old airlift wing (the 315th), still at Tan Son Nhut, controlled the C–123s, while the new wing at Cam Ranh Bay prepared to receive the Caribous. All reconnaissance units were operating from the wing at Tan Son Nhut, and a new air commando wing (the 14th) had been pulled together at Nha Trang from other bases in the country. This wing included the gunships (4th ACS), psychological warfare planes (5th ACS), the helicopters (20th HS), and the A–1s of the 602d ACS, one of the two remaining Farm Gate units. The other A–1 squadron, the 1st ACS, was at Pleiku.

The 768 nonairlift planes, along with 134 Vietnamese A–1s, were guided in their tactical missions by the Air Force's tactical control system, which had its trunk—the tactical air control center—at Tan Son Nhut. The branches of the system—the local direct air support centers, the radar control posts, the forward air controllers, and the Skyspot stations—extended throughout the country. Calls for air support increased during the year; and refinements to the system, originally designed for a smaller war, adapted it to the new situation.

In April, MACV had turned down a Seventh Air Force suggestion to place all the Army and Air Force O–1 Bird Dogs under the Seventh's control.[65] Adhering to his preference for "coordination" rather than "control," Westmoreland drew the Army's air-to-ground system closer to the Air Force's system the next month by placing the two networks under a new MACV joint air-ground operations system. This was an attempt to improve the Air Force's responsiveness to Army calls for air support. By placing Army and Air Force officers side by side at each combat level from the battalion up to MACV, the joint system made it easier for the ground commander to orchestrate Air Force planes with his artillery and helicopters when all of these converged on the battlefield.[66]

The Air Force, however, still had no voice in the use of the helicopters that belonged to Army combat units and senior corps advisors or, in the case of general aviation, to MACV. The only interface between these helicopters and the Air Force's control system was through a vague MACV injunction that the Army's commanding general in Vietnam "prepare joint operating instructions to ensure integrated and coordinated air operation."[67]

The opening of the SAC ADVON within the control center shortly after the beginning of 1967 served the same kind of purpose with regard to the

---

*These 338 jets, when added to the 20 A–1s in Vietnam and the 226 fighters in Thailand, represented 80 percent of PACAF's fighter aircraft and 18 percent of USAF's worldwide fighter resources. In January 1965, these figures had been 30 percent and 3 percent, respectively.[64]

Joint Air–Ground Operations System

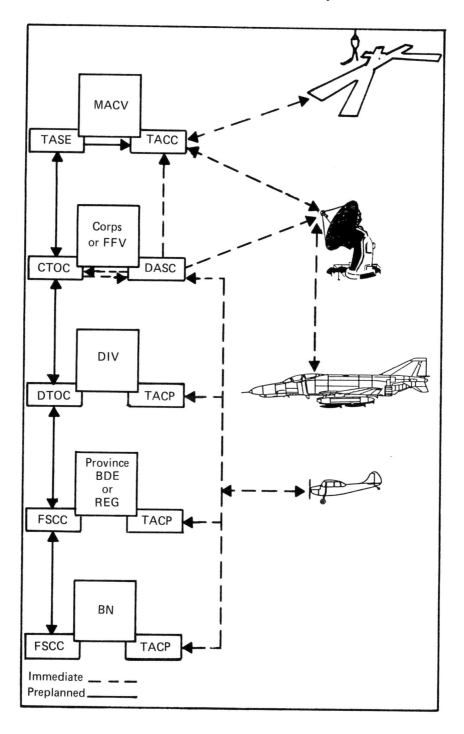

B–52s. While it improved coordination somewhat, it added not a whit to the Seventh Air Force's control over the big bombers.

Meanwhile, the Marine fighters in I Corps, which had grown to 10 squadrons and 165 planes, were controlled by the Marines' self-contained, air-ground system, despite Westmoreland's instructions the year before that they coordinate their flights through the Air Force.[68] The MACV Commander had tried again in June to draw Marine aircraft into the countrywide war. In a directive that month, he stipulated that Marine and Navy planes were to be brought under the tactical air control system during operational emergencies.[69] It would be a year and a half before such an emergency arose. In the interim, three separate American fighter air forces continued to operate in South Vietnam: the Marines, supporting their own ground troops; the Seventh Air Force, controlled by MACV; and the carrier–based naval tactical aircraft, which were outside of MACV's jurisdiction.

One of the more critical branches of the Air Force's control system, the forward air controllers, was also the one posing most of the problems. The most pressing of these was a shortage of pilots. A year earlier, the Air Force had agreed to supply two controllers to each U.S. Army battalion and at least one to each of the higher Army levels—the brigade, the division and, if necessary, the corps or field army. At the same time, however, the Seventh Air Force was providing controllers to the Vietnamese Air Force, the Vietnamese Army, the other allies in South Vietnam, and for such varied operations as herbicide flights, covert activities, rocket-watch patrol, and armed reconnaissance missions. The subsequent rapid buildup of battalions and the many new programs under way in 1966 stretched the Air Force's inventory of controllers. Two factors compounded the problem. The Air Force insisted that the controllers first be fighter pilots. Since it took nearly three years to train a pilot and convert him into a controller, the supply was sluggish. At the same time, the increasing tempo of combat in Vietnam put an even higher premium on fighter pilots. The Tactical Air Command, which was supplying the pilots and controllers, had to spread its limited resources thinly.

After reviewing a study late in 1965 that concluded the Army was satisfied with a single forward air controller in each battalion, General McConnell sought relief from the agreement; but the Joint Chiefs demurred. At the end of 1966, when the number of non-Vietnamese maneuver battalions in the country had passed the century mark, the Air Force was 100 short of the 570 controllers it was authorized to have in South Vietnam. Caught in a squeeze between declining supply and increasing demand, the Seventh Air Force began pooling its controllers at the brigade level and assigning them temporarily to battalions.[70] Although born of necessity, this pooling arrangement was viewed by many controllers as a positive step in giving them additional flexibility. Their arguments in favor of pooling were analogous, in some ways, to those advanced by the advocates of centralized air power.

At the root of the controller shortage was the overall pilot shortage. Higher than expected combat losses and a policy permitting pilots to go home after one hundred missions over North Vietnam combined to keep the demand ahead of the supply. The Air Force had been seeking ways to ameliorate this drain of pilots since its squadrons in Southeast Asia had become permanent in November of 1965. It first shortened some pilot training programs, which cut several months from the time it took to create flyers.[71] At the same time, the Tactical Air Command set aside four of its wings as a pool of trained pilots ready to replace those in combat. The first of these replacements became available in May 1966.[72] By assigning pilots returning from Southeast Asia to fighter units in the Tactical Air Command and in Europe, qualified pilots were released from these two commands to go to Southeast Asia. Gradually European tours were cut by as much as two years to squeeze more pilots out of the system.[73] The Fifth Air Force in Japan lent some of its pilots to the Seventh during particularly critical periods.[74] Late in the year, the Air Force considered putting navigators in the rear seats of the Phantom jets to release yet more pilots. The theater Air Forces (Seventh and Thirteenth) opposed the idea on the grounds that the back seater might be called upon to fly the plane and, during an emergency, land it.[75] The idea was dropped in November mainly to avoid disrupting the pilot replacement programs that were well under way by then.[76]

Late in 1966, Momyer made a serious attempt to clarify the indistinct arrangements that existed between the forward air controllers, the tactical air support squadrons, and the direct air support centers. Since each of these branches of the control system was at times serving different masters, it was not possible to combine them in one, clear-cut organization. The direct air support centers, as well as their parent tactical air control center in Saigon, had originated as (and still maintained the outward appearance of being) instruments for controlling Vietnamese planes. As the war had escalated and USAF planes came increasingly to be used by U.S. ground forces, control lines became tangled. Forward air controllers belonged to one unit, their planes came from another, and their operations were directed by yet a third. In December 1966, the four tactical air support squadrons in Vietnam (and a fifth in Thailand), along with their planes, pilots, and two maintenance squadrons, were brought together into a new group (the 504th) at Bien Hoa. The Air Force now had a more compact, two-headed system for managing its

ALO/FAC Units and Related Organizations in Southeast Asia

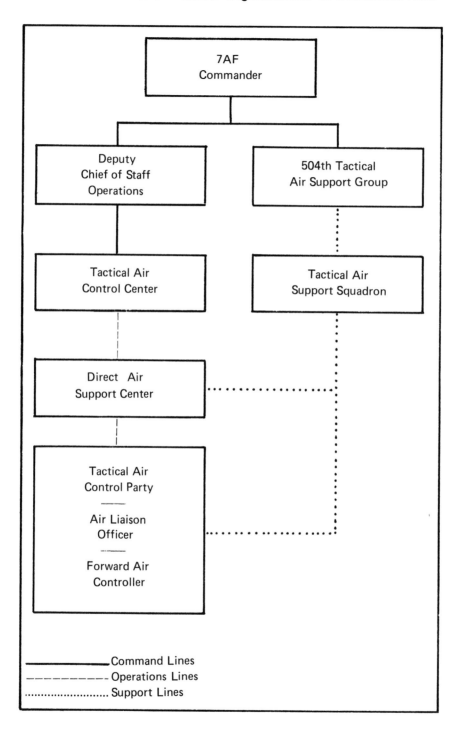

fighter planes inside South Vietnam: the tactical air control center at Tan Son Nhut, which controlled the planes' operations through local control centers and radars, and the tactical air support group at Bien Hoa, which, through its tactical air support and maintenance squadrons, supplied the planes, men, communications equipment, and maintenance for these operations.[77]

The airlift planes, however, remained outside the fighter-bomber system and continued to be controlled separately by the 834th division. While this divorce between airlift and strike forces contravened Air Force thinking on centralized control, its effectiveness in Vietnam was to lead to a revamping of the doctrine to permit such split control in cases where one control center could not manage the force efficiently.[78]

Modifications of the Air Force's structure and practices during 1966 were made in the fluid milieu of combat, with a view toward improving air support for U.S. and allied ground forces. That some of the changes clashed with Air Force doctrine was to be expected. The Air Force's approach to these adaptations was less than monolithic. Commands closer to the action, burdened with improving day-to-day efficiency, were often less wedded to larger doctrinal and interservice issues than were the more distant headquarters, which were responsible for the larger implications of the war. The decisions that flowed from these divergent views came to rest most often on the middle ground. While this left room for further disagreement and, at times, disillusionment, these decisions moved the military machine gradually towards a state of higher efficiency.

A chaplain and two assistants help build the Chaplain's Office at Pleiku.

Chapter VII

The "Frontier" Spirit
1966

The ability of its members to adapt to the physical and social conditions they encountered was as important to the Air Force's operations in Southeast Asia as tactics, technology, and doctrine. The alien environment of South Vietnam required considerable adaptation, even though it was, in some ways, less oppressive to airmen than to those fighting on the ground. The bulk of institutional adjustments took place during the period of the vast influx in 1965 and 1966. During this time, airmen assisted in raising their working and living conditions to an acceptable, if not ideal, plateau and learned to perform under climatic conditions and within a social and economic milieu they had little power to alter. While the degree of accommodation varied with individuals, the overall reaction to the situation was the emergence of a "frontier" spirit, with both individuals and units relying to a large degree on their own devices to cope with the uncertainties of the war. The phrase that echoed with the greatest regularity from the reports of the period was "self-help."

During the deployment, the urgency of getting the tactical cutting edge of the force into place as quickly as possible was a principal reason why operational personnel were often called on to create and improve their own facilities in the midst of fighting the war. As a result, support units lagged behind by months, forcing tactical organizations to initially provide much of their own support. This situation continued well into 1966, and it was not until late in the year that, as one fighter squadron commander noted, "the attitude has become one of the base supporting the fighter units and not the fighter units supporting the base, which was prevalent at first."[1]

Throughout the year, the Air Force moved gradually closer toward its goal of decentralizing aircraft maintenance and other support functions by locating as many logistic organizations as it could at the lowest possible field level. While this decentralization had been a goal for many years, planning in the 1950s for massive nuclear retaliation or limited brushfire wars did not anticipate the problems that arose in Vietnam, where combat continued not for months but for years. When the squadrons there were converted from temporary to permanent in late 1965, they at first performed their own light maintenance, while depending on bases outside the country—at Clark in the Philippines, at Naha and Kadena on Okinawa, and those on Taiwan—for heavy repairs, overhauls, and inspections. As the rapid buildup in 1966 saturated these facilities, field maintenance was gradually moved onto bases within Vietnam. The decision to continue to press on toward the goal of "maximum base self-sufficiency" was not made lightly. Enemy mortar and artillery attacks posed threats to units in the country. Nevertheless, the risk was deemed preferable to the amount of time lost shuttling planes thousands of miles across the South China Sea and to the frequent loss of parts in transit from offshore depots. In one instance, when the Air Force contracted with Air America to overhaul its U–10s on Taiwan, the program was seriously delayed because wings were misplaced when the aircraft were dismantled for shipment.[2]

The movement toward decentralization also affected the engineers. When the escalation began in mid-1965, the Air Force's civil engineering contingent in Saigon numbered six people. By the time an adequate logistic and maintenance structure began taking shape near the end of 1965, combat units were already in place and in great need of operational and maintenance facilities. The engineers spent most of 1966 catching up, resorting to several ad hoc measures to bridge the gap until permanent organizations were functioning. Prime Beef teams, which were rushed into Vietnam for 120 days at a time, proved a useful expedient, but were far from a long-range solution. The Red Horse* engineering squadrons, 5 of which were in the theater by 1966, provided more permanent help but were often hobbled by lack of supplies.[3] The inventiveness of operational personnel and their willingness to undertake much of the smaller construction went a long way toward easing the situation.

Creation of a permanent civil engineering structure throughout the country was slowed by the shocks the supply system experienced from many unanticipated elements in the Vietnamese environment. In the United States, supply organizations were manned for a system in which many items were bought on the open market and did not have to be handled or stocked. This was not the case in Vietnam where virtually all supplies were brought in from the outside. Supplies for the engineers and combat materiel competed for shipping priorities, both from the states to Vietnam and from the docks of

---

*Red Horse—Rapid Engineering and Heavy Operational Repair Squadron, Engineering.

Vietnam to the field. Frequently three to four months intervened between the time goods landed at the dock and arrived at the base where they were needed. In the states, moreover, stocks of supplies were automated for efficient inventory. The absence of adequate computer equipment in Vietnam during these early days often resulted in items being in the country and even on the base where they were needed, but hard to locate. At Phan Rang, for instance, when ground crews needed parts for the F–100s, they went to the supply warehouse to locate those they could readily identify from experience. Larger items were found about half of the time after several hours of searching. Delivery times, after the items were located, varied from thirty minutes to six hours.[4] Finally, competition for the limited number of communication lines inside Vietnam slowed the supply system. The most time-consuming activity in the country was often that of higher headquarters trying to contact the field. At times, it took several days to get in touch with subordinate units.[5]

Although construction in Vietnam came under the supervision of the Navy's Officer in Charge of Construction and the heavy work was contracted out to the combine of RMK/BRJ, these two organizations worked closely with the Air Force's engineering and materiel directorates in Saigon whenever air bases were involved. New bases were constructed according to priorities. "Horizontal" construction (runways, ramps, taxiways, and other elements essential to support the incoming weapon systems) came first. Second priority was accorded to "vertical" construction of facilities needed to maintain the airplanes. Facilities for personnel and administrative needs were built last. In the interim, these personnel and administrative needs were met by Gray Eagle kits, the initial supply packages that contained minimum support equipment such as tents, electric generators, field kitchens, portable runway lights, and vehicles. As horizontal and vertical maintenance facilities were completed, barracks replaced tents and permanent generating plants supplanted the portable ones.[6]

The transfer of logistic services into Vietnam continued throughout 1966 and into the following year, accompanied by much experimentation and some disruption of personnel and plans. As a result, working space throughout the country was at a premium and conditions were less than ideal as more and more units entered the country. The number of people at the air bases escalated more rapidly than did working areas to accommodate it.

At Tan Son Nhut, the Air Force population skyrocketed from 7,780 at the beginning of the year to over 15,000 at its end;[7] and the U.S. airmen added their own structures to those built earlier by the Vietnamese, the

French, and the Japanese. Units vied with one another for existing space—facilities for the new reconnaissance wing, for example, were at first wholly inadequate. Until November, the headquarters staff, whose numbers rose from 55 when the wing was created in March to 839 by the end of the year, operated from an open-air, poorly lighted, and crowded area alongside a busy helicopter pad. Dust and dirt were everywhere. Although the unit moved into remodeled offices in November, ancient French plumbing was unequal to the task. Frequent water outages gave rise to unsanitary conditions. A severe shortage of telephones hampered efficiency; and during a large part of the year, several offices shared the same numbers. It was difficult to contact many agencies because of busy lines.[8]

Demands for computerized information grew steadily throughout the year. Initially installed and equipped to keep track of base supply items, the data automation unit at Tan Son Nhut exploded with requests for information on personnel, maintenance, the payroll system, airlift, and a host of smaller recurring and one-time projects. Yet this sensitive equipment, which was being used around the clock, was housed in a Quonset hut on the base's perimeter, where it was subjected to dust from passing vehicles and to temperatures and humidity changes that led to frequent breakdowns. The absence of dehumidifiers, plus exasperatingly long waits for replacement parts, led to lengthy periods when the equipment was not operating. Although technicians were flown in regularly from other bases to repair the equipment, this provided only temporary relief.[9]

Efforts at self-improvement were at times frustrated by the overtaxed situation. Members of the C–123 squadrons at Tan Son Nhut spent much of their spare time renovating their crowded offices by insulating the walls, tiling the floors, rewiring the building, and installing air conditioners. When the work was complete, however, the power generator failed and the base could not provide a replacement. For 2 months, the airlifters used the modernized building without lights or ventilation.[10] Finally, after much cajoling, engineers tied the facility into the base power lines.[11] In another part of the base, the gunship detachment managed to acquire a 3-room air-conditioned trailer as sleeping quarters for its crews, but the nearest latrine was 500 yards away.[12]

Da Nang experienced a similar increase of Air Force people, from 3,300 to 6,200.[13] Virtually all the office buildings on the base were clustered around the two parallel runways and the taxiways. Work, meetings, and conversation were continually interrupted by the noise from aircraft taxiing and taking off 24 hours a day.[14] The operations building of the airlift squadron consisted of one large room with two small offices. It served as a weapons storage area, a radio facility for air-to-ground communications, a scheduling and operations office, a storage area for crew and aircraft equipment, a records section, and a sleeping area for the night duty officer, with another area set aside for the

Da Nang Air Base, 1966.

paperwork, weather briefings, and for posting the performance data needed by the crews on their daily missions. Squeezed in among all this was a crew lounge and refreshment center, flanked by a bulletin board on one side and a large intelligence map on the other. "It is a most compact structure," understated one officer, "serving as a continual reminder that we are indeed at war here."[15] The squadron's administrative building, badly in need of repair, contained four small offices used by the commander, the administration officer, and the navigation officer.[16]

Adverse weather conditions gave rise to unexpected difficulties with motor vehicles. Sandy soil, kicked up by water during the rainy season, wore down brake shoes and drums within 500 miles. Vehicle lubricants lasted less than a week on the bumpy, flooded roads. Twice as many vehicle maintenance people were needed as had been planned.[17]

Two of the biggest headaches at Bien Hoa were caused by inadequate electricity and water. Available commercial electrical power, set for 50 cycles, wreaked havoc with U.S. equipment, which ran most efficiently at 60 cycles. Until a new power plant was completed in November, portable generators were used, which proved costly in manhours and equipment. The water came from an antiquated Vietnamese Air Force system that was in such poor shape, it operated only 4 hours each day. The Air Force purchased a well from the Vietnamese that provided enough water for everything but drinking. The base engineers processed drinking water at a central point and distributed 30,000 gallons of it to 75 points each day. Large rubber water storage tanks holding 3,000 gallons were set up outside mess halls and clubs to reduce the number of trips by the tankers.[18]

By December, Cam Ranh Bay, now a year old, was still working its way out of its growing pains. Some of the earlier operational problems had been solved, but others remained. Although the new concrete runway had opened in November, the taxiways were still of aluminum planking and many flights still used the old aluminum runway, which, in the words of one squadron commander, "continues to be a sporty proposition."[19] Soft shoulders and the lack of an overrun and aircraft barriers caused planes frequently to sink into the soft sand when they veered off the runway. Air traffic control remained a problem. The volume of aircraft traffic had built up to over 27,000 movements a month, and constant taxiway repairs caused frequent changes of taxi routes and increased ground time. The F–4 squadrons were assigned offices so small that aircrew members had to carry on their business in their own quarters when they were not flying. Severe shortages of spare parts, a common plaint throughout the country, slowed down operations. The item in most critical demand was aircraft tires, which wore out at a phenomenal rate due to the nonstabilized shoulders of the taxiways, rocks blown onto the taxiway by aircraft, and the additional taxiing that was required to avoid construction.[20]

The base at Pleiku blossomed during 1966 from an outpost of 150 men with no tactical mission to a base of over 2,100 Air Force personnel supporting and flying propeller-driven fighters, psychological warfare planes, gunships, forward air control observation planes, and rescue helicopters. The controller contingent with its 12 Bird Dogs was moved around the base to 3 different locations during the year, ending up in an area devoid of toilets at the opposite end of the base from the living quarters. Difficulty in getting transportation increased reaction time for alert launches; and if the base had come under attack, the ramp area would have been almost unreachable. In addition, there were no revetments to protect the planes in this extremely vulnerable area.[21]

Working conditions were equally disruptive at the newer bases as fresh units arrived and older ones were reorganized or moved about. The Air Force population at Phan Rang leapt from 118 in March, when the base opened, to over 4,500 in September, when the fourth F–100 squadron joined the original F–4 unit. The initial units had taken over a base with virtually all facilities still in the planning stage. For example, the maintenance shops were located in tents; and the maintenance people lacked a hangar, a power check pad, a test cell pad, a fuel cell repair area, wash rack facilities, a loading crew training area, and a radar calibration area.[22] Although there was a parachute loft, it contained no dehumidifying equipment for drying the chutes. As material filtered in during the late summer, tents were set up to house it. Summer rains transformed the dirt around the shops into 6 inches of mud, creating problems with the equipment. Many maintenance personnel, lacking equipment, were assigned to such other jobs as filling sandbags, building hootches, driving buses, and laying fences.[23]

The first F–100 squadron, the 612th, arrived at Phan Rang on the first of July, followed two weeks later by the 615th, even though the base was still being built. Squadron members set up tents to house an operation center, an administration office, and flight planning and briefing areas. Clouds of dust, stirred up by heavy construction equipment, settled everywhere, complicating the operation of everything from typewriters to sophisticated electrical machinery. Until engine repair and test equipment began to arrive in October, the squadrons curtailed their flying, since as high as eighty percent of the new engines were rejected. The aircraft parking area was particularly troublesome. Rainwater gathered under the aluminum matting, displacing the sandy soil and causing dips and ridges to develop. Red Horse teams were constantly at work replacing sections of the ramp. There was barely enough room to park the planes, and aircraft had to be towed or taxied with extreme care. Runups were performed at minimum power settings lest panels, covers, and other loose equipment blow across the ramp. Whenever a plane had its engines running, the exhaust blast forced a halt to maintenance on nearby aircraft. Here, too, there were no concrete revetments to shield the planes from mortar attacks. Until the new concrete runway was finished in October, there was insufficient room to separate the planes to make them less vulnerable. When the new runway became operational, the old aluminum one was used for dispersal.[24]

Although an airstrip had been at Nha Trang for many years, it became a major base in 1966 when most of the Air Force's nonjet aircraft were moved there and placed in the 14th Air Commando Wing. A large part of the increase during the year was caused by the arrival of C–47s which, under the codename Phyllis Ann, began flying radio direction finding missions. The expansion presented problems similar to those experienced at other installations. The Red Horse team from Cam Ranh Bay built maintenance shops, storage sheds, billets, parking ramps, roads, ditches, and wells to catch up with the population explosion. Between July and December, the team completed twenty-two major construction projects. The familiar trio of dust, noise, and heat rendered otherwise simple activities difficult and slow.

The new base at Phu Cat took shape during the second part of the year. Work progressed as rapidly as materials could be delivered over the narrow, dangerous Highway I from Qui Nhon. In August the base could accommodate 150 Air Force personnel. By January, when the Caribous arrived, the base contained 15 two-story wood frame hootches; a 1,200-man mess hall; a dispensary; an administration building; a laundry; a recreation building; and a complete water, sewer, and electrical utility system.

Along with the working conditions, the living conditions of Air Force officers and enlisted men in Vietnam were important for morale and efficiency. These, too, improved in the course of the year to where they were at least acceptable. Even more than with working conditions, the improvements in living conditions were the result of voluntary self-help. The single most important item was housing. Quarters ranged from tents surrounded by mud to hotels and villas in nearby towns and cities. Soon after he arrived in April, General Momyer launched a drive called "Operation Spruce Up" to improve living conditions throughout his command. In addition to setting in motion plans for better housing on the bases, the operation sought to improve morale by tightening up on discipline and improving the appearance and cleanliness of the bases. Rules for wearing the uniform and for military courtesy were more stringently enforced. Living and working quarters were scoured and flowers appeared along the main streets and around offices and barracks at many stations.[25]

At Tan Son Nhut, a paucity of quarters on base forced most enlisted men and officers to live in Saigon in quarters that were below standard and outrageously overpriced,[26] and the Vietnamese government was unable to guarantee the security of those living off the base. Frequent terrorist attacks against private dwellings, culminating with the bombing of the offbase Victoria Bachelor Officers' Quarters on the first of April, caused a flood of people to move back onto the already overcrowded base.[27]

Quarters at Bien Hoa at the beginning of the year consisted of open, screened, slate-roofed huts measuring sixteen by thirty-two feet. These hootches housed seven officers or twenty enlisted men.[28] Rats and mice scurried everywhere. There was no hot water for the showers and the one hot water heater for shaving accommodated forty men—if they hurried. This situation inspired the saying heard around the area: "Many flowers but no hot showers."[29] By summer, the increase of people forced the supply group to erect tents to handle the overflow. After several months of negotiations, the Vietnamese base commander agreed to give the Air Force a small plot of land on the base. This new area, dubbed the New Cantonment Area, had three dilapidated masonry buildings, which were rehabilitated, and contained land enough to build seven new dormitories. In return, the Air Force agreed to repair twenty-four wooden dormitories and latrines the VNAF were using on another part of the base.[30]

To relieve overcrowding in the mess halls, enlisted men at Bien Hoa were given an allowance to eat their meals at the club or elsewhere. The group commander organized a committee of First Sergeants, Sergeants Major, and the Housing Officer that set about cleaning up the cantonment area and eliminating many of the unsanitary conditions. In November, the first two-story barracks was ready in the new housing area, and two were completed each month until the housing situation eased.[31] Even in these barracks, enlisted men slept in bunk beds, were crowded together into open bays, and shared wall lockers. Since some squadrons were flying around the clock, there was constant traffic through the barracks, making it hard for those who worked at night to get adequate rest.[32] Even such simple activities as changing clothes or writing letters were difficult.[33]

Officers at Cam Ranh Bay fixed up the interiors of their Quonset hut barracks. The shortage of such common items as water and electricity required judicious rationing. Each housemaid was allotted two pans of water for each clothes-washing cycle, and water to the shower rooms was cut off for four hours each day. Lighting was restricted to eight 100-watt bulbs in each hootch. Roofing slate, which insulated the huts, was in short supply, causing many aircrews to sleep in hot and humid areas that were not airconditioned.[34]

Until summer, most officers at Da Nang lived in rented houses and villas in the city. Following civil disturbances downtown in April and May, the city was placed off limits and personnel began moving onto the base. By September, officers, like the enlisted men, were housed in open-bay barracks and screened-in buildings where daytime sleeping was hot and uncomfortable.[35] There were frequent complaints about rats and mice—in the lockers, running along the rafters, climbing onto beds while the occupants slept, and darting about in broad daylight in populated areas. Dust and aircraft noise were constant companions.[36]

The troops at Nha Trang faced special problems as large numbers of people poured into the existing space. At the beginning of the year, officers and NCOs had to live off base, while the enlisted men were housed in barracks on the base.[37] Untold hours were wasted commuting back and forth to messing facilities and quarters in town.[38] Rising inflation caused those living off base to pay exorbitant rents, and Vietnamese landlords required 3 to 6 months' rent in advance. MACV tried to curb these excesses—a directive issued in January set a maximum price that servicemen could pay for rent and required that all leases be approved by the Judge Advocate's office.[39] However, these rent ceilings were unenforceable.[40] As more airmen arrived at the base during the summer, the amount of available living space dwindled. The American billeting area was adjacent to the ARVN ammunition depot that, while built for 1,500 tons of ammunition, was crammed with 5 times that amount.[41] After lengthy negotiations, the ARVN agreed to let the Americans have the depot area for construction of 2-story barracks if the Americans would build a new depot north of the city at Chut Mountain. As an interim measure, the Air Force sought more land from the U.S. Army. At first the Army told the base commander to restrict the arrival of additional personnel. However, the Army later grudgingly offered 11 acres of land at a location that proved too distant to sustain operations.[42] By October, when the base was over 1,100 billets short, a self-help program to erect tents began on every available piece of ground on the base.[43]

The housing situation was still poor at Phan Rang as late as September, when the fourth (the 614th) and last of the F–100 squadrons arrived. Only twenty of the twenty-seven tents needed by the enlisted men were available. Of these twenty, only eleven had floors and electricity. Six hootches were available for officers, but one had been stripped of all electrical sockets and outlets before it could be occupied. On the night the squadron arrived, seventeen beds disappeared from the enlisted area.[44] The town was off limits, but there was no compensating recreational facility on the base. The local "Sin Strip" just outside the base gave rise to a high rate of venereal disease.[45]

The housing eased somewhat at Phan Rang in October when the 389th moved its F–4s to Da Nang. However, the personnel moving to the already crowded northern base were packed into three and a half barracks in one area and two tents in another, with hardly enough space to move around.[46]

On a single day in January 1966, 500 officers and enlisted men moved into tents at Pleiku as construction began on open-bay barracks. By September, 13 of these, housing over 900 men, were finished; and 10 more were ready for occupancy by NCOs and enlisted men in October. More Army and Air Force personnel arrived, and the buildings became crowded as soon as they were inhabited.[47] Crew members of the gunship squadron, who flew 4 out of every 5 nights from eight in the evening until six the next morning, were averaging 4 hours of sleep during the day. High temperatures, aircraft noise, building maintenance activities, and sounds from passing vehicles constantly interrupted their rest. Since the average age of these officers was in the 40s, the lack of proper rest aggravated the fatigue factor.[48]

During the buildup, Air Force engineers at many bases relied on Vietnamese from surrounding areas to build facilities, and the U.S. airman's perception of his job and his motivation were affected by his relationships with the Vietnamese people. Given the shortness of tours and the gap between the two cultures, Americans came in contact mostly with Vietnamese who were either workers or domestics on the air bases, fellow fighters against the Viet Cong, or neighbors in the towns and cities where they lived.

Through an aggressive recruiting and training program, the Air Force group commander at Phan Rang, Col. Lewis R. Riley, increased the number of Vietnamese working on the base from 623 in May to over 1,000 by the end of the year. He did this by searching the countryside and visiting villages that had not been previously entered by Americans. As part of his campaign to attract workers, he studied the history, customs, beliefs, and social pressures that were operating in Ninh Thuan Province, where the base was located, and passed this knowledge on to his officers and NCOs at briefings and staff discussions. Through a string of formal and informal practices, he developed good relations with the Vietnamese. He got to know all the white collar

Vietnamese civilians put up fencing at Phan Rang, January 1966.

employees and many of the laborers, stopped to chat with them during his daily tour of the base, and picked up employees walking from one work site to another. Vietnamese were invited into the clubs for "friendship evenings," and local children attended the base movie theater and used the beaches. The commander frequently dined at the homes of employees and often invited Vietnamese military and civic leaders to the base for lunch or dinner.

At Phan Rang, as at most other bases, Vietnamese worked as carpenters, laborers, maintenance men, painters, masons, electricians, auto mechanics, drivers, warehousemen, equipment operators, cooks, busboys, and kitchen helpers. Thirty of them occupied professional and technical positions. The Vietnamese proved to be quick learners and very receptive to training. The turnover rate for the labor force at Phan Rang was about ten percent each year, only half for lack of ability or inclination to improve. A daily record of absenteeism was kept, as much to gauge sudden increases in Viet Cong pressure as to keep track of the workers.[49]

Over 300 Vietnamese civilians were extremely helpful at Bien Hoa in providing manpower for the building program there. The civil engineering chief praised their ability as tradesmen and artisans.[50]

The number of contacts between Americans and Vietnamese increased in the second half of 1966 as new life was injected into the pacification and civic action programs. While individual Air Force members had been helping village and hamlet dwellers before this, they had done so on a piecemeal basis and without formal command support. With the establishment of civic action organizations at ten bases in the summer, voluntary participation in assistance programs increased. Air Force and other U.S. and Vietnamese service personnel supervised the construction and repair of schools, churches, clinics, sanitation facilities, roads, culverts, and drainage systems. At Tan Son Nhut, efforts to improve the conditions of the people living around the perimeter of the base at first led to estrangement between the U.S. and Vietnamese airmen who worked together on the projects. VNAF members were embarrassed by their inability to match the progress of the Air Force volunteers and were dispirited as the living conditions of the civilians around the base began to surpass their own.

Even though relations slowly improved throughout the country, many Americans were never able to adapt fully to some aspects of Vietnamese society. One of these was the unsanitary conditions, by western standards, of the country. In an effort to show the citizens of Nha Trang the benefits of cleanliness, a detail from the base helped clean up the streets, parks, and beaches of the city in May. No sooner had the job been completed, however, than people resumed throwing trash, garbage, and human waste in the streets.[51] Unsanitary conditions in the clubs and messing facilities at Da Nang and elsewhere were attributed to the Vietnamese who worked there. Squadron members complained of workers who washed their hands in the water used to rinse glasses or cleaned their noses with their fingers before handling utensils and glasses. When the base late in the year stopped the practice of hiring Vietnamese housegirls and houseboys to clean the living quarters, there was a noticeable rise in cleanliness.[52]

A further irritant was the perceived dishonesty of many of the Vietnamese, particularly in the larger cities. In Saigon, where the 750,000 people of the late 1950s had swollen to 3 million, mostly refugees from the fighting in the countryside, the more affluent Americans were viewed as likely economic targets. In the view of an NCO at Tan Son Nhut, the Vietnamese he dealt with found the war personally profitable and were not at all averse to its continuation. In his extensive commercial dealings, he found the Vietnamese had two prices for everything—one for a Vietnamese customer and another, vastly higher, for Americans. He found this a curious way for the Vietnamese people to express their gratitude for the defense of their country. It was impossible for an American to proceed far down a Saigon street before being accosted by young and able-bodied procurers, money changers, or black marketeers. Many Americans found it difficult to reconcile the presence of this untapped supply of manpower with the concept of a country struggling for survival in a supposedly popular war.[53] Quickened by the inflation that accompanied the U.S. deployments, the black market thrived as American goods appeared for sale all over Saigon. Airmen at Bien Hoa complained that the black market was draining numerous items from the exchanges and supply warehouses.[54] As Pleiku built up, neither the hut maids, nor the prices they charged, came under supervision. A girl fired for

Enlisted men's quarters at Bien Hoa, October 1966.

theft or incompetence was often quickly rehired by occupants of another hut. Gradually these maids came under the purview of the billeting office. There was a set price for their work and those fired could not be rehired.[55]

Living conditions, as uncomfortable as they were at times, did not appreciably hurt morale. A series of personnel practices, both formal and informal, more than offset the harsher elements of the situation. In many cases, the challenge of constructing their own housing and recreational facilities motivated airmen by giving them a goal. In addition, the knowledge that many U.S. soldiers and marines were living under tougher conditions helped to place the situation in context.

Despite its drawbacks for operations, the one-year tour was frequently cited as an excellent policy.[56] The rest and recuperation program was very popular, with airmen flown at government expense to spend five days with their wives and families at Pacific areas outside Vietnam, such as Hawaii, Tokyo, Singapore, Bangkok, Hong Kong, Australia, Taipei, Manila, Kuala Lumpur, or Penang. Family separation and the inevitable drudgery of war were also partially alleviated by the generally efficient flow of news, the privilege of free mail, and the slow but steady growth of recreational facilities.

Financial incentives also helped ease the strain. Foreign service pay and family separation allowances were added to regular salaries, as was a monthly combat pay of $65. Those living off a base received a cost of living allowance. In addition, airmen on bases that did not have mess halls received a daily subsistence allowance of $2.57, which dropped to $1.30 a day when

179

Newly completed all–faith chapel at Pleiku, September 1966.

government messing facilities were available. The enlisted man's total pay was exempt from income tax, and the first $500 of an officer's pay was similarly excused. By enrolling in an overseas deposit program, all military personnel received 10 percent interest on savings at a time when normal bank interest rates hovered around 4 percent.[57] The proliferation of excellent medical facilities and adequate libraries, churches, base exchanges, and clubs throughout the year helped to dissipate much of the boredom.

Working conditions came in for more criticism than did living conditions. Factors that adversely affected the airman's ability to do his job, which threatened his own career goals, or factors that interfered with the effectiveness of air power were of greater concern to Air Force personnel than the absence of personal comfort.

The 4th Air Commando Squadron at Nha Trang experienced such a career problem. Many of the younger pilots in the gunship squadron resented the large number of older officers flying as crew members. When the squadron had been formed in the states for duty in Vietnam, flyers were chosen for their experience in the C–47. Half of the original contingent of thirty-nine were senior field grade officers with an average age of forty-four, many with experience in World War II and Korea. Their presence in such large numbers forced senior captains and junior majors to fly as buck pilots, in many cases a step backward from earlier, more responsible positions they had held as flight commanders. Deprived of the chance to command and to develop their managerial abilities, they felt they were being hurt in their evaluations where such talents figured prominently. Already at the midpoint of their careers, they felt the loss of experience that would equip them to supervise combat operations in the future. They argued that the Air Force was putting itself in a position where it was unable to determine which of its younger officers in this type of operation possessed command ability. Some became discouraged and seriously entertained the idea of resigning.[58]

The continual shifting of personnel around the theater disquieted many of the fighter pilots.[59] For the most part, pilots remained in squadrons for only a few months and then, when they became proficient in the mission, were transferred elsewhere and replaced by new men. Of the forty-six pilots that passed through the 416th Tactical Fighter Squadron at Bien Hoa between July 1966 and March 1967, for example, only sixteen completed a one-year tour with the squadron. Six came from other F–100 squadrons and spent less than a month with the 416th before returning to the states. Three others joined the unit for a few months to complete tours they had begun as forward air controllers. The remaining twenty-one pilots served with the squadron for an average of less than four months before being reassigned elsewhere in Vietnam. Only five of these pilots stayed longer than six months; one pilot was with the squadron for only one month, five others for only two.

Such excessive turbulence decreased combat effectiveness by causing havoc with flying schedules, additional duty assignments, and evaluation reports.[60] A similar situation existed in most other fighter squadrons. Although the turnover rate of enlisted men was less severe, averaging ten percent each month, even this created a need for additional training and supervision. The rapid and continuous reassignment of forward air controllers from one part of the country to another, often with only a few hours notice, created great individual inconvenience, a loss of already critical manpower, and disintegration of unit continuity.[61] The loss of unit integrity caused by people moving in and out, with its concomitant negative effect on morale, led to suggestions to reinstate the earlier rotational system in which units stayed together and moved as a whole.

The need for combat crews to perform many administrative jobs in the squadrons as additional duties detracted from their concentration on combat and discouraged some. Typical was one of the F–100 squadrons at Phan Rang where the pilots, after finishing one or two sorties a day, took on responsibilities for mail, mobility, small arms control, the central base fund, security, paying the troops, education, controlling ration cards, physical training, voting, squadron transportation, disaster control, information, on-the-job training, unit casualty reporting, awards and decorations, classified document control, and a host of other assignments.[62]

Eager to do the best job they could, the fighter pilots' enthusiasm was often diminished by the paucity of information they received on the nature of their targets before they took off and on the results of their mission after they landed.[63] Pilots also chafed at the minimum altitude restrictions under which they had to operate. Since most of the planes that were lost were downed by ground fire, the pilots were ordered to stay above 1,000 feet when using napalm or strafing and above 400 feet when releasing high drag weapons. After each pass, they had to return to at least 2,000 feet. Many of them saw a direct conflict between this emphasis on safety and their ability to carry out the mission. As minimum altitude increased, effectiveness decreased. In their view, the potential of both napalm and strafing was almost totally negated by the restrictions. Dropped from such high altitudes, the effect of finned napalm canisters covered an area only 10 feet in diameter, the size of a good campfire, rather than the 200-by 25-foot area that could be covered at lower altitudes. Strafing at the higher altitude hindered the pilot's ability to see the target and often caused the rounds from the cannon, designed for a smaller slant range, to fall short. The requirement to return to 2,000 feet after each pass prevented pilots from seeing the result of their strikes. Many felt that unnecessary sorties and expense were being used to destroy targets. More confidence by higher headquarters in their ability and judgment, according to them, would have increased their initiative and morale.[64]

Some forward air controllers were unhappy with the existing situation in which their commanders were not their bosses. The tactical air support squadron provided the FACs with planes, maintenance, and logistical support, but the pilots were under the operational control of the Seventh Air Force through the direct air support center. This situation often led to confusion and much duplication of effort.[65] In addition, the controllers resented the requirement to call in a psychological warfare plane to warn villagers before directing strikes on them. By relinquishing the element of surprise, this made it virtually impossible to call in immediate air strikes on villages filled with enemy troops discovered on routine visual reconnaissance missions.[66]

Another frequent complaint of the controllers was the lack of spare parts for their Bird Dogs, which resulted in canceled missions. The absence of an automated supply system produced chronic shortages of carburetors, piston and cylinder assemblies, propellers, windshields, starters, brakes, tires, and wheel assemblies.[67]

In many units, the manning documents, which spelled out how many and what kinds of people were needed, were unrealistic and slow in adapting to the wartime environment of Vietnam. Ideally, each squadron was to have one and a half crews for each of its airplanes. However, some units exceeded that rate, for example, the sixty officers of an eighteen-plane F–4 squadron at Cam Ranh Bay. These officers, at the most, flew only every other day, but more normally flew every fifth day, with a dampening effect on morale.[68] Other squadrons were undermanned—the gunship squadron, most of the time, had one crew for each plane, with each crew flying almost daily. Included in these crews were the commander and the operations officer, pilots whose daily ground duties removed them from regular flying. In addition, whenever the squadron was deployed to separate locations throughout Vietnam, as many as five pilots, who served as detachment commanders, were lost to the regular flying schedule. The brunt of the flying fell on the remaining officers, who quickly experienced fatigue and declining spirits.[69]

Maintenance unit manning was also slow in adjusting to wartime conditions and the radical organizational changes of 1966. With the establishment of permanent wings in Vietnam early in the year and the gradual movement of maintenance facilities into the country, it took experimentation throughout the year to align the right numbers and kinds of people with the requirements of the new situation.

There were inequities at first, and some units had too many people. The wing's maintenance squadron at Nha Trang, according to its supervisor, had enough chief master sergeants to man the organization for five years— authorized twenty-six, there were forty-two on duty. Twenty master sergeants were assigned, while there were but six slots. Other units, on occasion, had the wrong type of people. Flight mechanics at Nha Trang, whose principal job should have been to troubleshoot aircraft maintenance problems when away from home, were assigned to flight crews where they did little more than refuel the planes. This put an added burden on ground crews. "There are many disgusted and disillusioned personnel," noted one maintenance supervisor, "as to the urgency of their need in Vietnam and the waste of manpower when they could be used at many bases in the states."[70] The wing's First Sergeant echoed these sentiments. Alluding to the inflated number of senior maintenance NCOs, he pointed to a morale problem caused by transferring so many from stateside bases, where they were needed, to jobs where they felt they were not useful.[71]

At Phan Rang, twelve senior officers, half of them with previous experience as chiefs of maintenance at stateside bases or numbered air forces, were assigned to eight slots in the field maintenance squadron. Morale suffered.[72] Unneeded enlisted maintenance people, about one hundred strong, were detailed to assist the Red Horse outfit and the base engineers with self-help construction projects. At first this was beneficial. However, the precedent had been set, and as the number of assigned people came to match the authorizations by year's end, it became difficult to keep these other projects going.[73] Overmanning at Bien Hoa placed a severe strain on housing and working facilities and lowered morale among NCOs in the 3d Fighter Wing.[74]

At the same time, other units were short of men. The civil engineers at Phan Rang were constantly undermanned.[75] A shortage of people in the support group at Nha Trang placed an extra workload on already overloaded messing, billeting, administration, and personnel functions.[76] The number of skilled automotive mechanics authorized for the transportation squadron at Da Nang would have been adequate for a base that size in the states, but was woefully small to keep vehicles operating in the unfriendly terrain and extreme climate.[77] At Bien Hoa, many sections of the 3d Fighter Wing had the same number of people to run a 7-day, round-the-clock operation as in the states for a 40-hour week.[78] At the same base, the 3 Air Force men and 3 Vietnamese civilians who had been responsible for mail distribution to 3,400 people early in the year were not increased in number as the population of the base climbed to 5,400 by December. The message center, a hub of wing operational activities that operated all day, every day, was run by these 6 people, who worked 8 hours a day, 7 days a week.[79] The Air Police squadron at Bien Hoa, responsible for the protection of Air Force personnel and planes, had only three-quarters of the people it needed,[80] while the Air Police squadron at Pleiku was short of sentry dog handlers throughout the year.[81] Only a single technician was assigned to maintain the 50 pieces of data processing equipment at Tan Son Nhut. To handle frequent breakdowns, Air Force technicians were often flown in from other bases and civilian technical representatives were employed.[82]

As nettlesome as many of these factors were, they represented little more than adaptation pains of the Air Force settling down to a war different from the one for which it had been preparing. Sporadic discontent among some airmen had little detrimental impact on operations. In spite of crowded conditions, imbalances in manning, periodic bottlenecks in the supply system, and less than ideal living conditions, the Second Air Division/Seventh Air Force kept seventy-five percent of its attack planes flying in Southeast Asia throughout 1966, well above the seventy-one percent the Air Force used as a standard.[83]

A wide variation in operational readiness resides within this average figure, from almost ninety percent for B–57s and O–1s to a low of fifty-one percent for the F–4s during September and October.[84] Three-fourths of the unflyable planes (eighteen percent of the attack aircraft) were grounded for maintenance, while lack of parts accounted for the others (table 5).

Not only did the maintenance units keep an above average number of planes ready for combat, but the pilots also flew about ninety-six percent of the scheduled sorties.[85] While the original criteria used to decide deployments called for 1.25 sorties a day for each aircraft, this was not necessarily an operational figure. Among combat aircraft during the year, each F–5 flew, on the average, 1.31 sorties a day, with 1.07 for the B–57s, 1.02 for the A–1s, 1.00 for the F–100s, and 0.84 for the F–4s (table 6).[86]

Table 5

Aircraft In-Commission Rates*
January 1966–June 1967
(percent)

	1966												1967					
	Jan	Feb	Mar	Apr	May†	Jun	Jul	Aug	Sep	Oct	Nov	Dec	Jan	Feb	Mar	Apr	May	Jun
Operationally Ready																		
A–1	85	85	84	87	83	87	86	87	87	81	88	86	89	81	84	82	83	85
F–4	59	60	67	69	72	67	65	66	51	51	55	58	56	58	60	62	63	69
F–100	75	75	67	74	67	63	71	74	75	68	65	70	73	76	73	73	75	74
F–105	67	62	63	69	77	75	68	67	59	64	64	65	61	57	59	60	64	72
B–57	84	89	87	76	88	84	83	86	84	82	91	91	88	91	86	88	93	90
RF–4	74	79	76	73	63	66	71	69	69	64	59	65	67	65	65	71	75	77
RF–101	74	70	85	79	83	80	75	72	62	65	68	69	72	67	65	71	72	72
C–7A													64	70	75	76	75	71
C–123	58	58	70	74	76	73	74	72	74	72	71	74	74	72	77	76	77	77
UC–123	85	72	90	68	86	90	90	86	78	88	81	75	83	88	83	80	77	79
O–1	89	91	90	90	89	84	90	89	90	91	92	94	92	92	92	91	92	92
Total	75	75	76	77	78	75	75	75	72	72	72	74	74	74	75	75	76	78
Hours	512	527	621	577	628	640	696	761	807	868	844	913	1007	901	993	968	978	948
Not Operationally Ready, Maintenance (NORM)																		
F–4	12	28	24	24	22	26	25	21	31	30	32	32	34	32	34	33	30	25
RF–4	17	15	14	20	26	21	19	18	17	22	30	25	22	24	27	24	19	19
C–7A													28	22	19	21	22	25
C–123	34	31	24	19	19	17	18	18	19	19	19	20	20	21	21	21	20	19
Not Operationally Ready, Supplies (NORS)																		
F–4	20	9	8	8	7	7	10	14	18	19	13	11	11	9	6	5	8	6
RF–4	10	6	10	7	9	13	10	13	14	15	11	10	11	12	8	5	6	4
C–7A													8	8	6	3	3	5
C–123	8	10	7	7	4	10	9	10	7	9	9	6	7	7	3	2	3	3

*Selected SEA Aircraft under Seventh Air Force Operational Control
†Estimated

Source: 7AF Hist, 1 Jan 66–30 Jun 67, App IV

Table 6

Sortie Generation Rates of USAF Aircraft in Southeast Asia
June 1965–December 1967

		A-1E			A-26			F-100			F-4C			B-57			F-5A	
		Sorties	No*	Rate*	Sorties	No*	Rate*	Sorties	No*	Rate*	Sorties	No*	Rate*	Sorties	No*	Rate*	Sorties	No*	Rate*
1965	Jun	873	47	.63				1,207	51	.79	203	18	.38	424	26	.56			
	Jul	691	49	.47				1,769	55	1.08	391	18	.73	630	26	.81			
	Aug	908	50	.61				1,747	57	1.03	433	18	.80	591	22	.89			
	Sep	1,064	54	.65				1,860	61	1.01	1,260	53	.79	533	21	.84			
	Oct	1,360	53	.85				2,050	60	1.14	1,158	55	.71	515	20	.84	155	12	1.62
	Nov	1,290	53	.81				2,191	77	.95	1,537	76	.68	537	20	.89	719	12	2.00
	Dec	1,568	59	.86				2,134	79	.87	1,768	99	.58	542	20	.87	643	12	1.80
Total/Ave		7,754	52	.69				12,958	63	.96	6,750	48	.68	3,772	22	.80	1,517	12	1.37
1966	Jan	1,522	57	.86				2,132	78	.88	2,662	99	.86	471	20	.76	421	10	1.25
	Feb	1,371	48	1.07				2,371	88	.96	3,261	134	.87	500	20	.89	595	11	1.93
	Mar	1,481	36	1.33				3,118	94	1.06	4,788	165	.93	763	20	1.21	413	11	1.20
	Apr	1,165	41	.94				1,859	94	.69	4,834	186	.86	643	20	1.07	267	11	.80
	May	1,165	34	1.08				2,689	90	.96	4,313	184	.75	588	20	.95	353	11	1.03
	Jun	1,148	33	1.13	65	8	1.14	3,139	91	1.14	5,465	182	1.00	684	20	1.13	367	11	1.10
	Jul	1,081	32	1.40	137	6	.65	4,066	119	1.10	5,864	185	1.02	774	20	1.24	457	10	1.40
	Aug	972	30	1.02	170	7	.73	4,773	131	1.17	5,155	189	.87	698	18	1.20	390	8	1.42
	Sep	762	26	.98	247	8	1.03	5,158	156	1.10	4,365	172	.85	697	20	1.16	451	11	1.36

	A-1E			A-26			F-100			F-4C			B-57			F-5A		
	Sorties	No*	Rate*	Sorties	No*	Rate*	Sorties	No*	Rate*	Sorties	No*	Rate*	Sorties	No*	Rate*	Sorties	No*	Rate*
Oct	1,020	36	.91	296	8	1.19	4,505	159	.91	3,810	180	.68	661	20	1.07	614	18	1.10
Nov	1,154	35	1.10	232	8	.96	5,275	159	1.11	3,674	177	.69	691	21	1.40	805	18	1.49
Dec	1,056	38	.80	205	8	.83	5,288	190	.90	3,659	173	.68	660	20	1.02	708	16	1.43
Total/Ave	13,897	37	1.02	1,352	8	.78	44,373	121	1.00	51,850	169	.84	7,830	20	1.07	5,841	12	1.31
1967 Jan	931	36	.83	216	11	.63	6,642	202	1.06	4,158	176	.76	685	20	1.10	727	17	1.38
Feb	1,002	36	1.00	208	10	.74	5,979	195	1.10	4,344	178	.87	614	20	1.10	595	17	1.24
Mar	951	36	.85	184	9	.66	7,418	199	1.20	5,246	178	.95	754	20	1.22	769	16	1.55
Apr	1,055	35	1.00	193	9	.71	7,162	200	1.19	5,369	178	1.01	731	21	1.16	(transferred		
May	1,083	35	1.00	201	9	.72	7,468	195	1.23	5,168	179	.93	813	20	1.30	to VNAF)		
Jun	881	30	.98	170	8	.73	6,800	194	1.17	5,272	182	.97	721	21	1.14			
Jul	942	33	.92	154	9	.55	7,561	195	1.25	5,381	176	.99	738	20	1.19			
Aug	958	33	.94	202	8	.81	7,089	196	1.17	5,695	193	.95	744	20	1.20			
Sep	948	33	.96	140	8	.58	6,809	194	1.17	5,413	197	.92	694	21	1.10			
Oct	1,048	31	1.09	203	11	.59	7,225	194	1.26	5,746	203	.91	735	20	1.18			
Nov	1,104	31	1.18	251	11	.76	7,295	193	1.26	6,084	228	.89	680	20	1.13			
Dec	1,140	35	1.05	266	12	.71	7,214	195	1.19	6,273	222	.91	712	20	1.15			
Total/Ave	12,043	34	.97	2,388	10	.68	84,662	196	1.18	64,149	191	.92	8,621	20	1.18	2,091	117	1.42

*Daily average

Source: PACAF Summary of Air Operations in SEA, volumes XIV, XXIX, XXXIII, XXXVIII, and XLI

Measured by the original criteria of five daily sorties for each maneuver battalion and 1.25 sorties for each plane, the Air Force, Navy, Marines, and VNAF together flew about eighty percent of the sorties demanded by these calculations. This in no way prevented the services from supporting ground troops in contact with the enemy, since each day there were six times as many sorties available as were needed for close air support missions. Planes scheduled for other types of missions, particularly direct air support, interdiction, and escort, were readily diverted when needed to support ground troops without hurting the overall air campaign in the south.[87]

The ability of airmen to adapt quickly to the situation and to produce a good flying record in 1966 can be seen by examining naval air operations. The Navy's carrier, which had been at Dixie Station since June 1965, was moved north to Yankee Station in August to join in the air war against the north. The fourteen-month presence of the carrier provided a rare opportunity to compare the results of land-based and sea-based aircraft performing the same combat mission. The Air Force and the Navy faced some common limitations. Both operations were restricted by the rules of engagement that banned attacks on civilian communities regardless of their composition. The ordnance shortage in midyear affected the carrier and airfield planes equally. Continuing political instability within South Vietnam also had an effect on both ground-based and sea-based programs.

Carrier operations had some inherent advantages over the land-based aircraft. The carriers deployed quickly and, unimpeded by the need to construct facilities, immediately went into full-scale operations after arriving at their station. They possessed a large degree of flexibility in that they could move up and down the coast as needed. Further, carriers were not threatened by mortar and artillery attacks. Finally, the carriers had their own logistic system divorced from that inside Vietnam, and consequently, they were not in competition with MACV priorities.

These advantages, however, were largely offset by living and working conditions aboard the carriers. Due to the compactness of the carriers, which carried up to 5,000 personnel, living and working conditions required the most precise planning and the highest degree of personal discipline. Close personal contact, combined with continuous noise and fatigue, dictated that the carriers be rotated back to port regularly. Enlisted men averaged 16 hours a day of hard, dirty work.[88] At night, the men worked on the aircraft under low-intensity red light. Rest came hard during the flying cycles when the carrier operations were at full tilt, and pilots often flew with less than the

A U.S. Navy F–8 Crusader lands aboard the USS
Ticonderoga after a mission over North Vietnam.

desired rest.[89] The most serious limitations, however, flowed from the limited
amount of space on the carriers, which imposed weight and size constraints
on the aircraft and on their scheduling.

Three significant factors, not bothersome to the Air Force ashore, with
which naval aviation had to contend were rough seas, steam catapults to
launch the planes, and the need to launch and recover all mission aircraft
within narrow periods of time. Each of these tended to downgrade the overall
efficiency of air operations and cancel many of the advantages of mobility and
flexibility.

During high seas between December 23, 1965, and January 2, 1966, the
USS *Ticonderoga* at Dixie Station canceled 295 sorties because of pitching
decks. (The F–8 was the aircraft most affected by pitching decks.) Besides
interfering with the safety of the airplanes, high seas occasionally forced
postponement of resupply efforts, which, in turn, also affected sorties.[90]

Catapults were limited in the amount of weight they could bear, and this
placed a restraint on the size of loads of the planes.[91] The smaller carriers had
two catapults, the larger four. A malfunction of one catapult, which was
frequent, could double the launch time and delay recovery of incoming
flights, which then had to be refueled from aerial tankers.[92]

The most constricting factor on ordnance and fuel loads (and, consequently, on sortie length) was the need to recover all the planes from each
mission within a period of 20 to 30 minutes after the subsequent mission had
been launched.[93] The smaller carriers had seventy planes and the larger ones

upward of one hundred aboard; eighty percent of these aircraft were attack planes. Cycles were scheduled to accommodate the predominant type of aircraft in each group, usually the A–4. The number of sorties a carrier could launch was tied directly to these launch and recovery cycles. The need to get the planes of different types back at the same time forced compromises between the desired sortie length, the types of missions, and the divergent capabilities of the different aircraft. Higher performance aircraft had to "throttle back" to fit the cycle.[94]

While land-based planes, too, had to take into account takeoff and landing weights, these were far less critical than they were for carrier planes. It was not unusual, for example, for an Air Force F–4 to land with four missiles and four 750-pound bombs and up to 6,000 pounds of fuel on a 7,000-foot runway. Navy F–4Bs, on the other hand, could not safely land with similar ordnance on a 1,600-foot carrier deck with more than one-third that amount of fuel.[95] As a result, many planes took off with less than maximum fuel and ordnance, of necessity reducing both the length and punch of their missions.

Table 7

Ordnance Tonnage per Sortie
January–July 1966

	USAF			USN			USMC			VNAF		
	Sorties	Tons	Ave*	Sorties	Tons	Ave*	Sorties	Tons	Ave*	Sorties	Tons	Ave*
Jan	4,257	6,509	1.53	3,521	2,972	.84	2,671	1,748	.65	2,520	1,931	.76
Feb	4,675	5,948	1.27	3,160	2,597	.82	2,778	2,426	.87	2,836	2,848	1.00
Mar	6,090	8,149	1.34	3,474	3,156	.91	3,530	2,958	.84	2,920	3,074	1.05
Apr	3,446	5,741	1.67	3,184	3,497	1.10	3,093	1,970	.63	2,500	2,286	.91
May	4,309	3,968	.92	2,810	2,793	.99	2,817	1,937	.68	2,573	2,048	.80
Jun	5,288	4,997	.95	2,597	2,570	.98	3,011	1,964	.65	2,789	2,867	1.03
Jul	6,302	5,094	.81	2,607	2,730	1.05	4,237	3,537	.83	2,991	2,317	.77
	34,327	40,406	1.18	21,353	20,315	.95	22,137	16,540	.75	19,129	17,371	.91

*Tons/sortie

Source: Intelligence inputs to CY 66–67 Requirements, DIC, Seventh Air Force.

As with their counterparts on land, naval aircraft mechanics, loading crews, and pilots performed well under trying conditions. Light maintenance was done on board and the operationally ready rate of carrier aircraft was comparable to that of the Air Force in Vietnam—between 70 and 75 percent.[96] The Navy stressed sortie rates more than did the Air Force; and as a result, its average daily rate for aircraft (1.21) was higher than that of the Air Force (0.93). In the more important area of ordnance expenditure, however, weight and size limitations held carrier planes on runs over South Vietnam down to an average expenditure of 0.94 tons of ordnance per sortie. Larger aircraft, longer runways, and the ability to schedule with more flexibility permitted the average Air Force plane to drop 1.21 tons per sortie.[97] With the Air Force flying over 47,000 attack missions and the Navy 20,000 between January and August, the amount of ordnance each plane carried made an important difference (table 7). Contrary to the opinion of some at the time that the Air Force was severely hindered by overcrowded airfields and logistic facilities, evidence indicates that airmen made the necessary adjustments to conditions and produced a maintenance, logistic, and flying record at least equal to that of the other services.[98]

Navy F–4s launch from the catapults of the USS *Franklin D. Roosevelt* against targets in North Vietnam, November 1966.

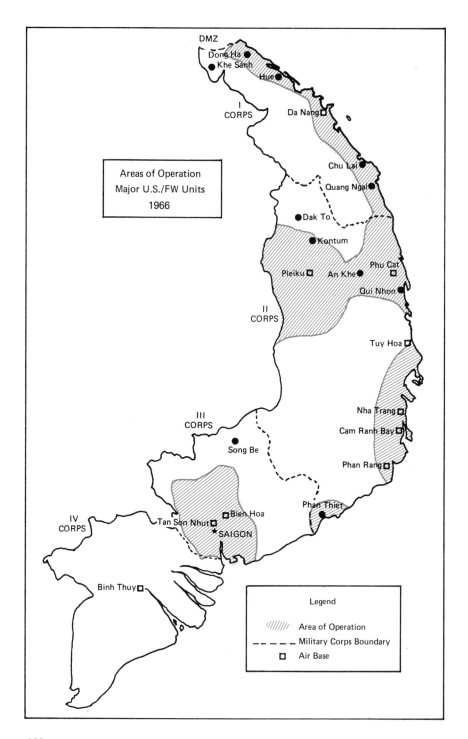

Areas of Operation
Major U.S./FW Units
1966

DMZ

Dong Ha
Khe Sanh
Hue

I
CORPS

Da Nang

Chu Lai
Quang Ngai

Dak To

Kontum

Phu Cat
Pleiku   An Khe

Qui Nhon

II
CORPS

Tuy Hoa

III
CORPS

Nha Trang
Cam Ranh Bay

Song Be

Phan Rang

Phan Thiet

IV
CORPS

Bien Hoa
Tan Son Nhut
SAIGON

Binh Thuy

Legend

//////// Area of Operation

— — — Military Corps Boundary

☐ Air Base

Chapter VIII

Air Operations
1966

With U.S. and worldwide attention focused at the beginning of 1966 on events surrounding the bombing campaign against North Vietnam, which was then temporarily suspended, the war in the south was receiving relatively less detailed direction from the policymakers in Washington. The United States' national policy for South Vietnam remained unchanged from what it had been the previous year. In its broadest exposition, as restated by President Johnson early in the year, the aim was still to maintain a military barrier behind which the South Vietnamese could construct a viable political and economic state.[1]

While this policy implied that military defense was the means, and nation building the end, of American activities in South Vietnam, Washington's reliance on its ground commander, General Westmoreland, assured that these priorities would be reversed. As the policy filtered down and was interpreted, in turn, by the Joint Chiefs, CINCPAC, and MACV, it took on an increasingly military coloration.

CINCPAC translated the objective into a plan for all of Southeast Asia. Adhering to the goal of a stable and secure non-Communist government in the south, the Hawaiian headquarters called for selective attacks on North Vietnam's warmaking capability, the protection of the southern people, the wrenching of certain areas from the Viet Cong, and the destruction of enemy soldiers and supply bases in the south.[2]

The MACV program for moving toward this objective, while acknowledging its political, economic, and social aims, stressed even more strongly the military measures to be taken within South Vietnam. Given the training, resources, and tradition of the military, it could hardly have been otherwise. As proclaimed by Westmoreland almost a year earlier, 1966 was to be the year when the anti-Communist forces in South Vietnam went on the offensive. The campaign plan stressed two major goals for the year: enlarging and purifying those areas already under government control and whittling down the enemy's influence outside these areas.[3]

These goals included bringing, during the course of the year, an additional 235,000 Vietnamese under the protection of the Saigon government by gradually increasing the size of the four relatively secure National Priority Areas: the region around Saigon, a large section of the Mekong Delta centered on Can Tho, and two smaller enclaves along the coastal plain in the northern provinces of Binh Dinh and Phu Yen. Once the enemy had been driven from these areas by "clearing and securing" operations, the United States would help the Vietnamese develop the areas politically and economically through pacification. In the delta region of IV Corps, where there were few U.S. ground troops, the task would fall to the Vietnamese Army. Prospects looked bright; the infusion of U.S. forces into other parts of the country had relieved regular Vietnamese troops from defensive duties, freeing them to participate in clearing operations. In the other corps, however, the brunt of these operations would be performed by U.S. troops.

Outside these National Priority Areas, principally in I and II Corps, the goal was to defend the major political centers and food-producing areas by a war of attrition against both enemy soldiers and their supply bases. Unlike the clearing efforts, these search and destroy missions sought not to seize and hold territory, but to kill soldiers and deprive them of support. MACV's expectation for the year was to kill the enemy at a rate at least equal to that of reinforcements coming in, while eliminating half of the enemy's base areas.[4] In addition to these two types of missions, the command found it increasingly necessary to mount quick spoiling attacks against enemy forces building up around the borders of South Vietnam.

Intelligence estimates at the outset of 1966 placed the enemy's strength in South Vietnam at 37,000 North Vietnamese and 200,000 Viet Cong.[5] During the first 4 months of the year, the enemy, still stinging from the defeats of late 1965, avoided contact in most parts of the country, attempting instead to build up forces in the border areas opposite the highlands in II Corps and in the northernmost province of Quang Tri. Air attacks against these preparations constituted the bulk of the U.S. response until the U.S. ground strength could reach the levels necessary to take the offensive.[6]

Incidents on the ground trailed off steadily in I Corps between January and April. The Viet Cong struck only when certain of victory. In III Corps the number of attacks declined even more sharply as the Viet Cong concentrated on isolating the capital. Action in the delta also remained at a constant low level. Here the Viet Cong strove to detach this southernmost corps from Saigon by keeping pressure on the umbilical cord, Route 4, that connected them.

Only in II Corps did ground action pick up during the early months of the year, due largely to the heavy North Vietnamese and Viet Cong pressure on both the central highlands and the central lowlands. In the highlands, the U.S. 25th Infantry Division carried out a string of search and destroy operations aimed at keeping the enemy pinned against the Cambodian and Laotian borders and away from their comrades in the coastal plain. In the lowlands, the largest concentration of coastal rice paddies outside the delta stretched along the coast in the hundred miles that separated Qui Nhon from Quang Ngai. The enemy held virtual control in this area through a field force that had at its command a Viet Cong main force regiment (the 2d) and a North Vietnamese regular regiment (the 18th). Two other back-up regiments were believed to be nearby. It had been over a year since the South Vietnamese Army had patrolled the region.

Beginning near the end of January, elements of the 1st Air Cavalry Division, an ARVN division, and a Korean battalion engaged in the first division-size search and destroy operation of the war. For six weeks, the U.S. forces chased the enemy, moving counterclockwise in four stages around the village of Bong Son, located seven miles inland on Route 1, midway between Qui Nhon and Quang Ngai. The ARVN area of operations was to the north and east of the 1st Cavalry, between the coast and Route 1, while the Korean units were responsible for keeping the roads secure. The first phase of the operation, called Masher,* began northeast of the village when U.S. soldiers landed to surround the enemy.[7]

Air Force planes backed up each part of the operation. On opening day, January 24, C–123s helped move air cavalry soldiers from their base at An Khe into Bong Son. Forward air controllers directed A–1Es from Nha Trang in softening up landing zones during the next few days. On the 26th, the commando planes struck one hundred khaki-clad Viet Cong moving toward one of the landing zones. Each night C–123s, AC–47 gunships, and C–47 flare ships kept the area lit and warded off enemy attacks while U.S. units established their positions. The main attack began on the 28th in poor weather. The following day, as the Air Cavalry linked up with the South Vietnamese and moved north, their way was blocked by an enemy dug into trenches, bunkers, holes, and tunnels. More A–1Es were called in, and the Skyraiders cleared out the obstacles with bombs, napalm, and white phosphorous rockets. As the soldiers moved forward, the planes struck villages on their flanks from which sniper fire was peppering them. From overhead, a U–10 from the 5th ACS dropped leaflets and beamed messages through its loudspeakers. After each period of heavy fighting, the psyops plane broadcast funeral dirges and wailing sounds to play on the enemy's superstitions.[8]

---

*See Appendix 6, USAF Support of Major Ground Operations, 1965–1967.

With rotary bomb-bay door open, an Air Force B–57 prepares to bomb a target during Operation Masher/White Wing in February 1966. The photo was taken from an O–1 directly underneath the bomber.

While trying to cross a river, the cavalrymen were pinned down and had to dig in for the night. Flare ships kept the area bright all night, but the enemy continued the sniper and mortar harassment, with the intensity of the firing increasing noticeably each time a flare failed to ignite. At first light the next morning, the barrage intensified until returning A–1s forced the Viet Cong and North Vietnamese to pull back.

On the first day of the new month, B–57s from Da Nang entered the fray, striking dug-in enemy positions that blocked the advance. The following day, B–52s helped clear the way for the cavalry troops. The enemy retreated westward over the Da Dan mountain range and into the An Lao Valley beyond, northwest of Bong Son where the second phase of the operation was to take place. During this first phase of the campaign, the Air Force had flown 213 sorties, one-fifth of them diverted from other missions.

Sensitive to the wide publicity the operation was receiving and to the potentially negative reaction to the cruel and inhuman implications of the name Masher, MACV changed the name of the operation to White Wing for the second phase.[9] For 5 days the A–1s helped carve out landing zones in the northern part of the An Lao Valley and assisted the soldiers sweeping southward, pushing the enemy before them. At night, Air Force C–123s kept the valley lighted. The U.S. forces made little contact with the enemy until they reached the southern end of the valley on the 11th of February. A–1s were again called on to break up concentrations of Viet Cong blocking the way. The strike planes flew 126 sorties in clearing the valley.

Action then shifted to the southwest of Bong Son. For two weeks the 1st Cavalry scoured the region, often calling on air strikes to dislodge the enemy from stubborn pockets. The A–1s were joined by F–4s from Da Nang. Two B–52 raids on February 21 hit a particularly tenacious Viet Cong stronghold. Ground troops met with no resistance when they entered the area after the bombing, but found many bodies and weapons.

The final phase of the campaign took place during the first week of March in the mountains southeast of Bong Son. Landing zones were unusually difficult to clear because of the extremely dense foliage. Air strikes first removed enough of the cover so that soldiers could be lowered into the area by ladder to finish the job with chain saws.[10] The troops found few enemy soldiers, and the forty-day operation closed down on the 4th as the allied forces evacuated the area.

Over 2,000 of the enemy died, a command post was destroyed, and the survivors dispersed westward. The Air Force had flown 600 sorties, 400 of them planned 24 hours in advance, the remainder diverted from other missions or scrambled from alert pads to the battle areas. For those missions planned in advance, the long lead time between scheduling and striking (they were scheduled at ten in the morning the day before they were needed) decreased somewhat the ground commander's ability to make last minute changes. Since the ground commander chose the targets and the ordnance for these missions and the enemy often changed his position or complexion by the time the planes arrived, many missions were wasted.

When calling for planes to be diverted from other missions or scrambled from alert pads (one-third of those in the Masher/White Wing operation), the ground commander was concerned with two things—how quickly they arrived and how successfully they bombed the target. Planes diverted from other targets normally arrived in less than twenty minutes. Those called from alert took twice as long, due to the time needed to get airborne.[11] Since the diverted flights were armed for other missions, their ordnance was not always suited to the changed missions they were flying.

Many Air Force pilots expressed discomfiture with the operation. Often the A–1 fliers found too many planes over the battle area when they arrived, and they either returned home or had to hold for long periods of time. Some landed back at Nha Trang with live ordnance still suspended from their wings. To the strike pilots, a "cry wolf" situation was developing which, if not changed, could some day deprive ground troops of the immediate air support they might need.[12] The pilots' observations agreed with those of the forward air controllers. Ground commanders, in their estimation, were still not sufficiently discriminating in their requests for air support.

The persistence of several other minor problems became evident during the Masher/White Wing operation. Communications between ground stations and between the ground and the air were still not totally satisfactory. The cluster bomb units the fighters dropped were not particularly effective. Many of them did not explode because of the dense foliage; and in several cases, the troops picked them up, not knowing what they were.[13] On the whole, however, the operation went more smoothly than Silver Bayonet and Harvest Moon, its predecessors in November and December.

The day after the campaign came to a close, two North Vietnamese deserters walked into the Special Forces camp at A Shau, in I Corps near the Laotian border, and announced that their comrades were preparing to attack the camp. A Shau was one in a growing string of Vietnamese border outposts that had been providing bases since 1961 for allied attacks on enemy guerrillas and for keeping watch on enemy infiltrators. By early 1966, the number of these camps had increased to almost fifty. At each camp, a small detachment of U.S. Army soldiers advised a handful of paramilitary Vietnamese CIDG companies normally recruited from the local area. Isolated as they were from the more populous coastal plain, the outposts relied upon aircraft to bring them supplies and to defend them against major assaults.[14]

Since the opening of a new American aerial campaign against the trails in Laos the previous December, many of these outposts had come under increased pressure. Air Force, Navy, and Marine planes concentrated attacks against the trails in a 125-mile section of the southeastern corner of Laos, an area called Tiger Hound. Two task force headquarters, one at Tan Son Nhut and one at Da Nang, directed Air Force Bird Dogs at Khe Sanh, Kham Duc, Dong Ha, and Kontum that controlled Air Force F–100s, F–4s, A–1Es, AC–47s, B–57s, and defoliation UC–123s, as well as Army OV–1s and Navy and Marine jets. The Tiger Hound area was becoming an integral part of the war in South Vietnam; and by the end of January, soldiers, trucks, sampans, bicycles, and whatever else was seen moving toward South Vietnam, attracted over 100 sorties a day. As a result of this disruption to supply lines, the enemy began to look for more base areas across the border in the northern part of South Vietnam, with the first resistance encountered in the south coming from these Special Forces camps. The latest attack on one of these camps had taken place in January when an enemy force tried unsuccessfully to overrun the outpost at Khe Sanh, far to the north.

The camp at A Shau sat two miles inside Vietnam from the Laotian border at the base of a mile-wide valley dominated on two sides by high mountains. A barbed wire defense perimeter surrounded the walls of the triangular fort, and a 2,300-foot airstrip lay just outside this perimeter. From the camp, 210 Vietnamese irregulars and their 10 American advisors blocked the enemy's movement into the valley. Through preparations reminiscent of those preceding the attack on Dien Bien Phu a dozen years earlier, the Viet Cong and North Vietnamese in late February began moving troops toward the fort along covered back trails to avoid detection. At the same time, they secretly set up antiaircraft traps by positioning camouflaged guns and mortars on the hills above the camp. On the ridge lines just northeast of the valley, they placed four antiaircraft positions, each with seven 12.7-mm machine guns for use against aircraft and hidden mortar pits to saturate the zones where helicopters were likely to land. By early March, 2,000 soldiers surrounded the camp. They dug a labyrinth of covered trenches and siege works extending inward from the maximum range of small arms fire to within 100 yards of the camp's southern wall.[15]

After learning of these preparations from the defectors on the 5th, the camp's inhabitants called in air strikes on the enemy. Two days later, 7 more Americans and 149 ethnic Chinese tribesmen, the Nung, were flown in to reinforce the garrison.[16]

The enemy's tactics against the camp resembled those employed against the Plei Me outpost 5 months earlier. Attacking at two in the morning of March 9 under a cloud cover at 500 feet, the Communists destroyed the camp's supply area before breaking off the assault at daybreak. During a second enemy attack later that morning, an AC–47 gunship was able to penetrate the ceiling and made a pass at the camp at tree-top level. On its second pass, the plane's right engine was torn from its mount by ground fire, and it crashlanded on a nearby mountain slope. The grounded crew drove off the first enemy attack, but 2 crewmembers were killed in a second assault. As a USAF helicopter dropped down to pick up survivors, the Viet Cong rushed at the crew a third time. While 3 men were being lifted to safety, the plane's copilot, Lt. Delbert R. Peterson, charged the enemy's machineguns with his M–16 rifle, allowing the rescue to take place. The chopper took off under heavy ground fire leaving Peterson, who was never found, and the 2 dead men behind.

Two Farm Gate Skyraiders from Pleiku, aloft on another mission, were diverted to the scene. Finding a hole in the clouds, the flight leader, Maj. Bernard F. Fisher, led the two planes through it and down the valley to the camp. Learning by radio that the enemy was planning a third attack, Fisher told his wingman to take care of the gunship while he directed other incoming planes through the hole to the camp. First he brought in a second flight of Skyraiders to strafe the enemy within a half mile of the walls. Then he directed a CH–3C helicopter into the fort to evacuate the wounded. Returning above the overcast, he led two C–123s in to drop medical supplies and ammunition. Next Fisher guided a pair of B–57s through the hole to

Maj. Bernard Fisher and Maj. Dafford Myers shortly after landing at Pleiku following Major Fisher's rescue of Major Myers from the runway at A Shau.

bomb enemy positions and destroy the gunship. Two VNAF A–1Hs also made it through the clouds to bomb the enemy. The enemy's attack was forestalled. Poor weather throughout the day had limited the aerial response to only twenty-nine sorties. After sunset, the defenders repaired their positions and dug in for the night. A pair of C–123s and a gunship remained overhead until morning dropping flares.

At half past three the next morning, one of the C–123s received the message that the camp was under full-scale attack. Protected from the air by a 200-foot cloud layer, the enemy broke through the barbed wire and breached the south wall. The ceiling lifted somewhat to 800 feet, allowing a few more sorties than the day before. Between five and six, Marine jets, using radar, dropped bombs through the clouds. At nine, a forward air controller directed a napalm attack against the south wall, but at eleven, the defenders radioed that they could hold out for no longer than an hour. Four Skyraiders, again led by Major Fisher, got in under the clouds and began strafing the enemy. On its third pass, the plane piloted by Maj. Dafford W. Myers was hit and crashlanded on the debris-strewn airstrip. Fisher, learning that it would take 15 or 20 minutes for a helicopter to arrive, decided to rescue Myers himself. After one unsuccessful attempt to land on the runway from the smoke-engulfed northern approach, he wheeled his plane around and landed from the other direction, dodging bullets, oil drums, cans, and pieces of Myers' plane littering the runway. Myers darted from cover alongside the runway and was pulled into the plane by Fisher, who then took off and headed away to safety at tree-top level through a stream of ground fire.

The 210 sorties flown on the 10th were unable to save the camp, which was evacuated that evening by air. Arc Light strikes, planned for that day, were canceled due to the rapid exodus from the valley. The fall of A Shau was a substantial victory for the enemy and a setback for the MACV campaign against Viet Cong supply areas.[17] The enemy set about at once converting the valley into a major logistic base and building roads linking it to the Ho Chi Minh Trail. The Saigon command, with a relatively limited number of forces in I Corps, decided reluctantly against trying to retake the camp. Instead, it shifted its energy northward to counter a major enemy force that was gathering in the Demilitarized Zone. It would be 2 years before U.S. forces would return to the valley.[18]

The loss of A Shau, coupled with pessimistic intelligence reports, convinced the military leaders in Saigon that the North Vietnamese were working hard to take advantage of the two remaining months of good weather in the south to consolidate their forces for a major summer offensive. Recounting the gradual increase in the size of the forces the enemy was slipping into the country, from small companies in 1960 to the appearance of the first division in 1965, Westmoreland in mid-March described the enemy as having the framework of six divisions in South Vietnam. The North Vietnamese goal, he said, was to spend the remaining period of good weather bringing those divisions to full strength.[19]

To prevent this, the number of air attacks on the Laotian trails was stepped up dramatically between April and June, particularly against the passes where these trails emerged from North Vietnam. B–52s flew almost 400 sorties against the trails and, on April 12, in their first strike within North Vietnam, flew against the eastern side of one of the passes. As the rains began to turn the southern trails to mud in June, the enemy shifted the infiltration effort to the north, where the roads were hardening in the returning good weather.[20]

The North Vietnamese were now adopting a new strategy. Upset by the failure of the guerrillas to take over the populated regions of South Vietnam, Gen. Vo Nguyen Giap, the North Vietnamese commander, turned to a border strategy of concentrating large numbers of his troops in the northern provinces of South Vietnam in hopes of drawing U.S. troops into these remote areas. His local forces could then press toward victory further south.

North Vietnamese soldiers were entering the northern provinces of South Vietnam through both the Demilitarized Zone and the Laotian panhandle, using the zone despite their agreement in 1954 to refrain from

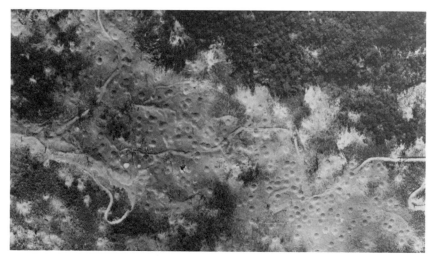

Bombing by B–52s in April 1966 produced heavy cratering on Route 15, a major artery leading to the Mu Gia Pass between North Vietnam and Laos.

military activity in the ten-kilometer strip that separated North from South Vietnam.[21] Quang Tri and Thua Thien, the two northernmost provinces, are separated geographically from the rest of South Vietnam by a mountain spur that runs across the country and meets the sea just north of Da Nang. Only one narrow winding pass (Hai Van) connects the region with the rest of the country. Hue, the major city in the area, was the old Imperial Capital and was politically and culturally important to all Vietnamese. Westmoreland was convinced that the two North Vietnamese divisions (324B and 341) poised in and around the Demilitarized Zone were preparing to seize the two provinces and establish a "liberation" government at Hue, drawing the Americans and South Vietnamese away from Saigon, their ultimate target.[22]

After a visit to I Corps in July, Westmoreland decided on a two-pronged assault on the 324B Division of the North Vietnamese, which had descended by then into the northern province. Unable to send ground troops openly outside South Vietnam, he would use his soldiers along the inside edges of the country to block the enemy's advance and rely on air power to hit the enemy from behind. He moved the 3d Marine Division up into Quang Tri Province where, with the ARVN and supported by the Air Force, it was to meet the enemy head on. Air Force and Marine planes were to simultaneously attack supplies and reinforcement routes in the lower part of North Vietnam and the western side of the Demilitarized Zone in Laos.

These latter areas, being outside South Vietnam, were not totally Westmoreland's to do with as he pleased with air power, but their importance to the battle inside the country gave the general an increasingly stronger voice in operations on these fringe areas. The tangled command and control relationships in effect for North and South Vietnam and Laos prevented him from unilaterally ordering air campaigns in this triborder region. Instead, he had to acquire air resources through persuading CINCPAC and also, in the case of Laos, the American ambassador in Vientiane. The Joint Chiefs, through CINCPAC, were responsible for the Rolling Thunder bombing of North Vietnam, and the embassy in Vientiane had to seek the Laotian government's approval, tacit or otherwise, before striking the trails.

For the Rolling Thunder campaign, North Vietnam was divided into six areas, called route packages. It was Westmoreland's view, as he expressed it to CINCPAC, that the two southernmost packages, those directly above the Demilitarized Zone, should "properly fall into the tactical category since they are closely linked with and in part contiguous to the battlefield of South Vietnam."[23] In short, they should be considered an extension of South Vietnam and belong to him. He pictured the other route packages, and their westward extensions into Laos, as the enemy's strategic rear or base establishment. Using this distinction, he requested a cutback of strikes in the strategic areas to be able to concentrate air attacks on the tactical areas abutting South Vietnam.[24]

General Momyer did not fully agree with this interpretation. If Westmoreland's argument were carried to its logical conclusion, he noted, all of North Vietnam should be placed under MACV's control, since the entire air campaign against the north was designed to affect the battle in South Vietnam.[25]

Westmoreland's request placed the Seventh Air Force Commander once again in an ambivalent position. Route Package I, directly above the zone, became Westmoreland's responsibility, and Momyer, as his deputy, had to support it with aircraft. However, Momyer also controlled the Air Force's resources for Rolling Thunder, and he felt he could not eviscerate the northern campaign in favor of the extended battlefield.

The ground campaign opened on July 15 as 3,000 South Vietnamese soldiers swept through 2 areas just below the Demilitarized Zone and 8,000 American Marines maneuvered through a third area. The allies attempted to fix the enemy, estimated at between 8,000 and 10,000, and call in air strikes to attack and scatter these men.[26] Friendly ground troops were prohibited from entering the Demilitarized Zone except when they were in contact with the enemy. Even then, they had to withdraw as soon as contact was broken. In no case could friendly troops cross the mid-zone demarcation line into the northern half of the zone.

Air Force controllers were assigned to the South Vietnamese division, while the Marines planned to use their own aircraft from Chu Lai for their part of the operation, called Hastings.* The countrywide shortage of FACs

---

*See Appendix 6, USAF Support of Major Ground Operations, 1965–1967.

Rolling Thunder Route Packages

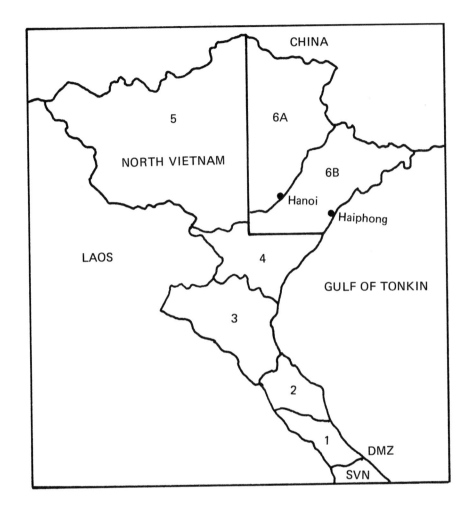

forced the Air Force to borrow nine O–1s and fourteen pilots from II and III Corps and send them to the northern province.[27] Although the FACs were assigned to the ARVN division, Momyer ordered them to give the Marines whatever assistance they could.

For ten days, South Vietnamese contact with the enemy was light. The Marines, on the other hand, ran straight into the North Vietnamese. When it became evident that they did not have enough of their own controllers to direct all their planes, they requested help from the Air Force. After that, a

USAF controller remained overhead each day from sunrise to sunset. Unfortunately, one of the Bird Dogs collided with a Marine helicopter over the battlefield on the 23d, killing the Air Force pilot.[28]

During a 4-hour battle on the 18th, as 2 Marine platoons were under attack from 1,000 khaki-clad North Vietnamese using bugles, whistles, and arm-and-hand signals to direct their assault,[29] the FAC called in napalm strikes on the attackers. On the 23d, a FAC flying along the southern rim of the zone was fired on from within the zone. Invoking the "inherent right of self-defense," the Marine commander ordered air strikes against the gun position. The FAC led strikes that destroyed what proved to be a 37-mm cannon. The following day, the rules of engagement were relaxed to allow air strikes against any confirmed military targets within the zone.

Between the 15th and the 27th, Air Force controllers directed 250 Marine air strikes, while 51 B–52 sorties hit 7 targets. Hastings ended on August 3 with almost 900 of the enemy dead and the division driven back into the Demilitarized Zone.[30] Since the enemy was expected to return, the Marines left a battalion in the area (Operation Prairie) to keep track of him.

Although billed as a combined Marine/ARVN operation, Hastings was in reality two different operations, with separate support channels for the Marines and for the ARVN. Aside from the collision between the Bird Dog and the USMC helicopter, there were few problems between the Air Force and the Marines over airspace, artillery interference with aircraft, requests for FAC support, or diversion of air strikes from one sector to another. The use of two different air control systems worked fairly well, however, only because the enemy did not move from one area to another. The Air Force liaison officer who was in charge of the forward air controllers noted, with prescience, that, had the enemy appeared in force on the boundaries between the ARVN and Marine jurisdictions or crossed from one into the other, USAF and USMC planes would have intermingled and their effectiveness would have suffered.[31] This problem, still only a potential problem in 1966, would become actual a year later, when the U.S. Army moved in force into I Corps to carry out combined operations with the Marines.

The campaign again illustrated the vulnerability of having too few forward air controllers and O–1s in the country. By having to divert a large number of planes and pilots from other corps, the Air Force weakened the tactical control system in the other areas.

During a brief appearance, the Vietnamese Air Force performed miserably. On the 18th, two of their Skyraiders, out of radio contact with the ground, struck uncomfortably close to some ARVN troops. The Vietnamese ground commander banned the VNAF from his area, declaring that he would work only with American planes directed by American controllers. That same night, a VNAF flareship on ground alert at Da Nang failed to answer a request from the other Vietnamese ground force because the pilot was ill.[32]

The Vietnamese Army still lacked confidence in the VNAF, a problem that was to plague the U.S. Air Force throughout the war.

The ground and air actions during Hastings were but one part of the attempt to forestall the enemy's offensive. Since American and Vietnamese planes were at first banned from bombing in the zone, they had to slow the enemy down by striking his bases and infiltration routes north and west of the zone. The Seventh Air Force began a concentrated effort to do this on July 20, while Hastings was in progress farther south. The new interdiction area, called Tally Ho, encompassed the thirty miles directly above the Demilitarized Zone in Route Package I. Several major arteries, including Route 1A in the plain near the coast and Route 102 through the western mountains, ran through the region into the zone. The enemy was hauling supplies from the termination of these roads in the zone into South Vietnam on their backs or on pack animals.

During the planning for this air campaign, the Marine commander requested that he be allowed to use his aircraft independently in the Tally Ho area. Momyer again voiced to Westmoreland the importance of keeping air operations centrally controlled, and the request was denied.[33]

Westmoreland, ever a firm advocate of B–52s, wanted to use the big bombers in the Tally Ho region, in the Demilitarized Zone, and in Laos around Tchepone.[34] His conviction that the military and psychological effects of the Stratofortresses would stop the enemy drive was not shared by Ambassador Sullivan in Vientiane, the Joint Chiefs, the State Department, nor by General Momyer. Sullivan opposed any B–52 bombing in Laos that could not plausibly be reported as having taken place within South Vietnam, and Tchepone was too far (twenty miles) from the border for that. The chiefs at first applied the same rationale in disapproving strikes in Tally Ho. The State Department was equally set against B–52 bombing in the zone, fearing it would signal an escalation and jeopardize a current diplomatic initiative aimed at embarrassing the North Vietnamese for violating the zone. Momyer, who, in general, favored only limited use of the B–52s anywhere in the theater, was bolstered in his position by a Seventh Air Force study that cast doubt on the effectiveness of the bombers in inflicting either physical or psychological harm on the enemy.[35] He continued to maintain that they should be used only against clearly defined targets and doubted that they would be useful in spoiling an intended attack.[36] The question of using B–52s in these areas was still hanging fire when the Tally Ho campaign got under way on the 20th.

Tally Ho Area and Route Package 1

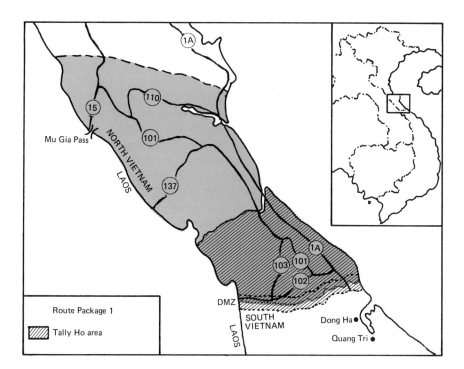

The MACV Commander's desire to divert tactical planes based in Thailand from Rolling Thunder to Tally Ho also went unrealized. One reason was the Thai government's opposition to using planes stationed in its country to strike in South Vietnam. Since the air campaign was taking place in conjunction with Hastings, some strikes in I Corps were likely. Further, Momyer convinced Westmoreland that there were already enough strike planes available without weakening Rolling Thunder. As a result, all the planes first scheduled for Tally Ho were tactical aircraft from South Vietnam—Air Force B–57s and F–4s from Da Nang and F–4s from Cam Ranh Bay along with Marine A–4s and F–8s from Da Nang and F–4s from Chu Lai—directed by the Tiger Hound forward air controllers. Later, planes were allowed to be diverted, if needed, from canceled missions in the northern route packages, but they had to remain north of the Demilitarized Zone.[37] A small sector was set aside in the southwest corner of Tally Ho for the Vietnamese Air Force. Daily flights were to be orchestrated from above by the flying command post C–47 located at the western end of the zone, which relayed requests for immediate strikes from the forward air controllers to the control center.

Tally Ho was the first experience with the O–1 Bird Dogs in a heavily defended area. The enemy's reaction was intense, particularly in the eastern coastal plain that contained most of the passable roads. The North Vietnamese had developed countermeasures against the FAC and strike planes. To avoid giving away their positions, the enemy withheld their fire while the Bird Dogs reconnoitered an area. As soon as the FAC would roll in to mark a target, however, the enemy would let loose a barrage of ground fire—at times 30 or 40 people firing semiautomatic weapons, at other times heavier 37-mm or 57-mm guns. This forced the O–1s to remain above 2,500 feet, an altitude too high to be very effective. Concerned primarily with the safety of the O–1s, General Momyer in August ordered that they be confined to the mountainous western portion of Tally Ho, where enemy reaction was lighter, and ordered A–1Es into the plain. Most of the strikes in the plain were carried out by "armed reconnaissance" missions against targets of opportunity that required no forward air controllers.

Despite lucrative strikes outside the Demilitarized Zone, the prohibition against hitting the enemy in the zone continued to provide sanctuary until the restriction was lifted on the 24th. Before the restriction was lifted, the United States had honored the 1954 prohibition against military activity in the zone. Since the North Vietnamese had long since abandoned any pretense of respecting the zone's neutrality and were firing at friendly planes from it, the State Department dropped its long-standing objection to retaliation. The newly approved strikes were to be made only against clearly defined military targets, they were to be controlled by FACs, and every effort was to be made to minimize civilian casualties.[38] The Bird Dogs immediately began to uncover widespread networks of roads and trails and large caches of enemy supplies in the zone. Pilots confirmed that Route 102 in the west was being used as a major infiltration corridor.

On July 25, a FAC spotted a major ammunition depot just north of the Demilitarized Zone. Fifty strike planes from Da Nang, Chu Lai, Cam Ranh Bay, and Pleiku pounded the target throughout the day, setting off over 200 major explosions. It was believed that this was a major supply depot for the 324B Division and that its destruction weakened the division's ability to hold out against the Americans and the ARVN to the south.[39]

Despite gratifying success of daytime raids against depots and truck parks, reconnaissance pilots saw little movement on the ground. Aware that the enemy was moving under the protection of darkness, the Bird Dogs began flying night reconnaissance missions. Using binoculars and starlight scopes, which intensified what little light there was, the FACs spotted heavy traffic moving through the zone. Due to heavy air congestion, however, they were still prohibited from directing strikes against these targets. When they spotted lucrative targets, the FACs turned them over to Skyspot, which controlled the fighter strikes.

For almost two months, as tactical aircraft kept the 324B Division off balance in and above the zone, Westmoreland continued importuning to get the B–52s into the fray. Picturing the big bombers as "a major innovation of the war," he repeatedly requested them as essential to blunting the offensive, which he still expected.[40] By early September, he had wrung reluctant permission from Washington and Vientiane. Between the 15th and 26th, the Strategic Air Command flew eight missions in the Demilitarized Zone and struck targets around Tchepone. For ten days in October, the Stratoforts returned to the zone. Late in the month, when SA–2 surface-to-air missile sites were discovered north of the zone and along the North Vietnamese border with Laos, the B–52 bombing was suspended, but the tactical planes continued to fly.

The monsoon winds changed in November, and the weight of the air interdiction effort shifted back to southern Laos. A reduced number of tactical sorties, however, continued in the Tally Ho area into the next year. Airmen had amassed an impressive record. They had destroyed over 70 trucks, 1,200 structures, 80 watercraft, and 90 antiaircraft positions. Untold amounts of ammunition had been blown up. Most telling of all, the North Vietnamese offensive did not materialize.

The Tally Ho operation highlighted practices where improvement was needed. Some of the problems encountered by the controllers and fighters in both Hastings and Tally Ho were identical to those they had experienced in Tiger Hound, while others were spawned by the divided command structure that characterized these two northern operations. Many controllers in both Tally Ho and Tiger Hound complained of the lack of current intelligence and of the absence of a centralized Air Force intelligence system to provide them with more lucrative targets. Although the Bird Dog pilots spotted numerous targets and reported them, no followup took place.[41] As in South Vietnam, Air Force missions were flown based on MACV, rather than Seventh Air Force, intelligence. The critical job of selecting targets and the ordnance to hit them, rested with the Army, and as a result, many targets the Air Force deemed important went unattended. Further, given the Army's unfamiliarity with air ordnance, planes often arrived with bombs and other ordnance ill-suited to the target.[42]

Another continuing complaint, engendered by the divided command situation, was that ground artillery at times interfered with the controller's visual reconnaissance and strike direction. On one occasion, for example, while a controller was leading a C–123 on a defoliation mission west of Hue, the refusal of the Marines to stop shelling the area forced the pilot to call off the mission. At another time, while flying near Quang Tri, the same

A C–130 sets down near Tay Ninh during Operation Birmingham.

controller was bracketed with artillery shells above and below his plane and hastily departed the area.[43]

Paradoxically, at least one of the difficulties stemmed from too much centralization. A recurring criticism made by the controllers was the penchant of Air Force fighter pilots to make only one pass at a target before heading home. One fighter wing, in fact, had made this a rule for its pilots. To the FACs, who were controlling Army, Navy, Marine, and Vietnamese fighters as well as Air Force planes, this wasted ordnance and made the Air Force appear less committed than the others.[44] While aware that this procedure was at times dictated by fuel considerations, the controllers believed the decision as to the number of passes to be made should be decentralized and left up to the flight leaders who were most conversant with the particular situations.

There was still discomfort with the Air Force's internal command structure that had one organization (the tactical air support squadron) responsible for the FAC planes and men but gave another (the air control center) control of their activities.[45] The controllers were also uncomfortable with the blanket rule requiring a warning to the inhabitants before a village was bombed. This rule of engagement often delayed strikes beyond the fuel endurance of the Bird Dogs and resulted in numerous missed opportunities.[46]

The operations in and above the Demilitarized Zone provided further evidence that the days of the Bird Dogs were numbered. The enemy's severe reaction to the FAC planes, particularly in these border areas, was restricting the O–1s to the point where a more survivable replacement was imperative. Although the O–2 was about to be introduced into South Vietnam, it was not expected to be any more effective than its predecessor in the heavily defended border regions. This would lead the following year to experiments with jet planes in those areas for visual reconnaissance and control of strikes.

The MACV command was under no illusion that the enemy had been stopped for long. The 324B Division had crept back into I Corps, where the Marines' Operation Prairie continued to harass it. The North Vietnamese offensive to seize Quang Tri Province failed, however, having fallen victim to the combined air and ground campaigns that cut off its supplies and slowed its advance. The campaign also illustrated what air leaders had been saying all along, namely that, while air power alone could not completely halt the infiltration of a determined enemy, it could cause him to divert enough of his energy toward replenishing destroyed supplies and routes to weaken his military thrust. This was to remain the Air Force's conception of interdiction throughout the war, even later, when more sophisticated attempts were made to slow down the North Vietnamese infiltrators.

To the south, the most immediate and substantial military thorn in the Saigon government's side remained those enemy forces encamped in an arc forty miles north of the capital in War Zones C and D and in the intervening Iron Triangle. Despite the pounding of Zone C by tactical aircraft in the Black Virgin operation a year and a half earlier and the attacks by B–52s against Zone D in their maiden mission in June 1965, Communist soldiers continued to use these heavily forested sanctuaries as supply and staging areas. Roaming through the area was the Viet Cong's 9th Division, which had defeated the government's forces at Binh Gia late in 1964 and had attacked the South Vietnamese at Song Be, Dong Xoai, and at the Michelin rubber plantation in 1965. In this last action late in November, the three regiments of the 9th Division had ambushed and almost annihilated the ARVN 7th Regiment. These sanctuaries also sheltered the strategic hub of the Viet Cong military effort, the Central Office of South Vietnam (COSVN).

Clearing the enemy from these war zones was one of MACV's goals for 1966. Although the Viet Cong had retreated into War Zone D early in the year and tried to avoid contact, U.S. and South Vietnamese units continued to harass them. During Operation Silver City in March, the 173d Airborne Brigade killed over 500 of the enemy in the zone and seized large quantities of supplies and equipment, driving the survivors westward into War Zone C, close to Cambodia. From these havens, the enemy prepared for an offensive during the coming rainy season.

To disrupt these preparations, the U.S. 1st Infantry Division, with strong aerial support, again struck elements of the division in April (Operation Birmingham). Two months later, the American division, aided by the ARVN, went on the offensive again (Operation El Paso II), this time seriously mauling the Viet Cong in 5 battles. Close air support was decisive in 3 of these battles.[47] Almost 350 well-timed strike sorties by F–100s from nearby Bien Hoa and F–4s from Da Nang swung the balance. In one of these battles, on July 2, the Air Force used its newly installed Skyspot radar bombing system for the first time to support fighting ground troops. Two flights of Super Sabres and one of Phantoms dropped their bombs from 10,000 feet through an 800-foot overcast. The ordnance landed within 500 feet of the friendly forces, driving back the enemy.[48] Unfortunately, it also fell close to two FACs who had slipped in under the overcast and were flying at 250 feet. The controllers got the Skyspot turned off until they finished directing their strikes.

The next and largest operation during 1966, aimed at chasing the 9th Division from its sanctuary, began in September under the codename Attleboro.* Late in the month, the enemy division, back up to strength, began to consolidate its regiments in War Zone C northwest of Dau Tieng and gird for a winter offensive against Tay Ninh Province. The tactical philosophy was to contact and fix the enemy with ground units, using close air and artillery as the prime "killer," and then mop up with infantry.[49] For over a month, both sides jockeyed for position as contact remained light. Throughout October, the Air Force flew only a single immediate and 140 preplanned flights in support of roving Army patrols. Then on the last day of the month, U.S. ground units penetrated the area, capturing nearly 1,000 tons of rice and bringing an immediate reaction. Both sides rushed in reinforcements for a showdown. A North Vietnamese regiment moved in from nearby Cambodia, while elements of the U.S. 1st Infantry Division were brought in to back up the U.S. 25th Infantry Division. The stage was set for a major confrontation that, over the next 2 weeks, saw some of the heaviest fighting of the war up to that point.

The fiercest battles of Operation Attleboro took place during the first week of November, as the deeply entrenched enemy stubbornly defended extensive supply areas against the approaching U.S. forces. The fighting started in earnest as the enemy began to be routed from bunkers between Tay Ninh City and Dau Tieng. A steady stream of C–123s and C–130s flew troops from all over South Vietnam into Tay Ninh and forward airstrips. For five days and nights, fire fights continued throughout the zone as F–100s from Bien Hoa, B–57s from their new home at Phan Rang, and F–4s from several South Vietnamese bases successfully beat back waves of attacking Viet Cong and North Vietnamese. The entire arsenal of Vietnam-based Air Force planes took part—flareships, gunships, defoliation flights, psychological warfare missions, airlift, and medical evacuation.

---

*See Appendix 6, USAF Support of Major Ground Operations, 1965–1967.

By the 8th, the fighting died down as the enemy retreated toward the Cambodian border. That same day, the first B–52s hit the area. For 17 days, the big bombers continued to pound the jungles of War Zone C, destroying much of the enemy's headquarters and killing several COSVN leaders. Advancing U.S. soldiers captured enormous caches of supplies, including arms, weapons, mines, rice, peanuts, documents, engines, bicycles, medicine, cloth, bugles, tools, uniforms, trailers, tractors, animals, refrigerators, and tires. Over 300 buildings, 500 bunkers, 90 tunnels, 9 base camps, and a claymore mine factory were destroyed.[50]

By the time the operation ended on the 25th, the Air Force had flown over 1,700 strike sorties in November, 485 of them immediate. In addition, 225 Arc Light sorties had dropped over 4,000 tons of bombs. In 3,300 sorties, Air Force transports moved over 11,000 troops and 9,000 tons of cargo into the battle.[51]

During Attleboro, Air Force representatives at each of the infantry division headquarters (the 1st and the 25th) were organized along the lines of a fighter squadron. The ranking Air Force officer, the division's air liaison officer, was in on all the planning and advised the commanding general on daily requirements for air support and the appropriate type of ordnance for various missions. For a staff, he had an assistant and an operations officer and his assistant. Below the division air liaison officer, each brigade had an Air Force control party consisting of a brigade air liaison officer, his assistant, and three forward air controllers. This arrangement provided both flexibility and centralization. The division air liaison officer and his people, in addition to advising the ground commander, supervised the overall aerial portion of the operation and flew visual reconnaissance missions to bring back firsthand information to the Army commander. The brigade liaison officers kept track of operations within the brigades' battalions and often acted as forward air controllers or advisors to the battalion commanders. To do their jobs properly, the liaison officers and controllers had to know every detail of the ground plan—the participating units, call signs, frequencies, planned artillery, probable ground force advance routes, and the types of ground actions likely to occur along these routes. Only through intimacy with all of these ground details could the Air Force officer advise the ground commanders on the types of strikes, and particularly the kinds of ordnance, they should request. The ordnance needed in preparing landing zones was different from that used in softening up areas through which ground troops would be moving and from that needed to best uncover dug–in emplacements or supplies. The liaison officer also advised the ground commanders on coordination of air with artillery strikes.[52]

In Attleboro, the liaison officers frequently had more to do than they could manage, particularly when two or three battalions of a brigade were engaged. In these cases, the system's flexibility permitted the division air liaison officer and his people to fill in at the brigade level, either in the air or on the ground.[53]

One reason why the Air Force control parties at the brigades often became overcommitted was the practice of having one of their members aboard the Army commander's control helicopter as it maneuvered over the battlefield. The Air Force officer's job on board was to advise the commander and act as liaison with the ground forces. In reality, he was a captive passenger who served no function that was not already being performed by the forward air controller on the scene in his Bird Dog.[54] The liaison officers successfully recommended that their presence in the control helicopters be discontinued to make better use of the scarce pilots.[55]

As dramatic as the larger campaigns (such as Masher, Hastings, and Attleboro) were, they represented only the cutting edge of the Air Force effort in South Vietnam. In 1966, the Air Force flew over 355,000 "tactical" sorties* and close to 4,300 Arc Light sorties. Nearly half of the tactical sorties were by fixed–wing airlift planes that delivered men and supplies, while 17 percent of the sorties sought out the enemy through visual, photographic, and electronic reconnaissance. Forward air controllers directing air strikes consumed another 8 percent of the total. Four percent of the sorties were used to drop flares, spray defoliants, and work on the enemy psychologically, while the small number of Air Force helicopters flew another 4 percent carrying troops and supplies, searching for downed airmen, and evacuating the wounded. Only one-fifth (74,000) of all the tactical flights flown that year in South Vietnam were strike sorties that dropped bombs and other ordnance.[56]

The nature of the reporting system in South Vietnam made it difficult to fit these 74,000 strike sorties neatly into the time-honored categories of close air support and interdiction. The distinction between these two types of missions, to which proponents of air power had become accustomed, had grown up during an era of conventional wars with clearly defined battlelines. Flights in these earlier wars had traditionally been defined as close air support sorties if they hit hostile targets close enough to friendly forces to require coordination with other supporting fires and coordination with the movement of these forces.[57] However, flights that struck supplies and lines of communication beyond the front without the need to coordinate were interdiction sorties. Air leaders looked on the latter as one of the distinct, and therefore more important, functions of air power.

---

*See Appendix 5, USAF Tactical Sorties in South Vietnam, 1965–1967.

A C–130, part of the airlift in Operation Attleboro, rolls to a stop on the narrow air strip at Dau Tieng in early November 1966.

The absence of front lines in South Vietnam blurred this distinction. In the Army's view, the entire country was a front line and all air strikes, including those made by the B–52s, were lumped together as close air support efforts. The term "interdiction" seldom appeared in the reporting system. Stressing its own terrestrial priorities, MACV understandably evaluated air power primarily on the basis of how well it helped its ground troops carry out their missions. While its judgment on this score was almost universally laudatory, the Army displayed little interest in evaluating air power's economy or in distinguishing between its various forms of expression. Air strikes were combined in the MACV reporting system with mortar, artillery, and helicopter gunships and entered under the general rubric of close support.[58]

The Air Force, on the other hand, vitally interested in measuring the efficiency and effectiveness of its missions over and above the immediate assistance they rendered to ground troops fighting with the enemy, needed a clearer delineation of the types making up these 74,000 sorties. Even here, the many ways in which airplanes were being used inundated the reporting system. Constant attempts were made to adapt the traditional notions and doctrine to a radically and continually altering situation. Many of these 74,000 strike sorties fell into a gray area between those missions that were clearly close air support in the traditional sense and those that would formerly have been called interdiction. These hybrid missions, to which the Seventh Air Force and PACAF gave the name "direct air support,"[59] struck enemy supplies and communications away from battles (the interdiction element) while remaining, technically at least, under political control and in some proximity to the ubiquitous friendly troops (the close air support element). During the first 10 months of 1966, a large majority (77 percent) of strike sorties were of this halfway variety. Only 15 percent were reported as close air support.* The subjective and largely unreliable nature of these reports was echoed by an F–100 squadron commander at Phan Rang who, at the end of his tour there, admitted:

> Records of close air support and direct air support missions show an overwhelming majority of direct air support missions. However, since there is no clear dividing line which separates direct air support from close air support missions, it is left to individuals to decide and an untrue picture is presented.[60]

Until the end of October 1966, a mere 3 percent of all Air Force sorties in South Vietnam, according to the reports, struck enemy soldiers actually engaged in combat with allied forces.

On November 1, the Seventh Air Force, possibly in an attempt to bring the reporting system closer to the realities of the command and control arrangements, expanded its definition of close air support by including several types of strikes that until then had been considered direct air support sorties, notably strikes that prepared landing zones.[61] As a consequence, the figures for November and December showed a dramatic switch between close and direct air support sorties, with two-thirds of them suddenly falling into the former category and only one-third into the latter.† Yet the Air Force had not altered its pattern of flying during these two months from what it had been previously. This change of definition raised the annual percentage of close air support sorties only slightly from three to five percent of the total. However, this modification in definition did not legalize the reporting of interdiction missions as such, a change that would have shown a truer picture of what Air Force aircraft were doing.

Even though the Air Force received plaudits from the Army for the effectiveness of its strike planes when they were called upon to help, the Army requested strikes for only one out of every ten ground clashes. Ninety percent of the ground battles in South Vietnam were fought without the benefit of tactical air support. One reason for this was that half of all ground contacts lasted less than twenty minutes, too short a time to bring air power to bear.[62] Further, many of the clashes, in the eyes of the Army commanders,

---

*The remaining eight percent were either air defense, combat patrol, or escort sorties (see Appendix 5, USAF Tactical Sorties in South Vietnam, 1965–1967).

†See November–December 1966 in Appendix 5, USAF Tactical Sorties in South Vietnam, 1965–1967.

were too small to warrant assistance from outside their units. However, since Army commanders used artillery or helicopter gunships in many of these battles, some Air Force analysts were convinced that airplanes could have been, and should be, used twice as often as they were for close support work.[63]

This relative unemployment of planes for close air support was emphasized by an Air Staff study late in the year. While one of the original deployment criteria a year earlier had been to send enough planes to Vietnam to provide five close air support sorties a day for each battalion, an average of only three were being used by late 1966. Reliance on USAF air support varied from unit to unit, ranging from almost eight daily sorties by battalions of the 25th Infantry Division to none for those of the 196th Light Infantry Brigade.[64] These variations were attributable to a variety of factors—weather, the size and location of the battles, the predilections of the individual ground commanders, and the amount of time it took for the planes to start bombing after the initial ground contact. All of these elements except the latter were beyond the power of the Air Force to alter.

In late 1966, the time from when the troops first closed until the first bombs were dropped or aerial bullets fired was, on the average, still over an hour. This time was consumed by ground commanders deciding to ask for help, by pilots flying to the battle site, and by both the air and ground officers preparing for the strikes once the planes arrived. Since no point in South Vietnam was more than fifteen minutes from the nearest jet planes, part of this response time was attributable to the ground commanders. The first of these factors depended on the Army, and ground commanders were averaging forty minutes before they requested air support.[65] The second element was up to the Air Force. Airborne jets diverted from nearby missions were reaching the scene in an average of seventeen minutes, many sooner. Jets called from ground alert took eighteen minutes longer, and prop planes needed an additional seven minutes to respond.[66] These average figures, based on all responses, make the situation sound worse than it was, however, since only the first flight of fighters had to respond quickly. Too quick an appearance by subsequent flights could, and at times did, result in the stacking of planes over the target and consequent confusion.

Once the fighters arrived, it took time for the forward air controllers to brief the pilots and mark the targets; for the fighter pilots (at times) to burn off fuel; and for the ground commanders to mark friendly troops, set up communications, and clear the strikes.[67] The Army and the Air Force consumed about equal amounts of time during these last–minute preparations.

Most of the Air Force time delays had been eliminated by late 1966 and little room remained for further tightening. One immediate step the Air Force did take as a result of the report was to rely more on air diverts and less on

217

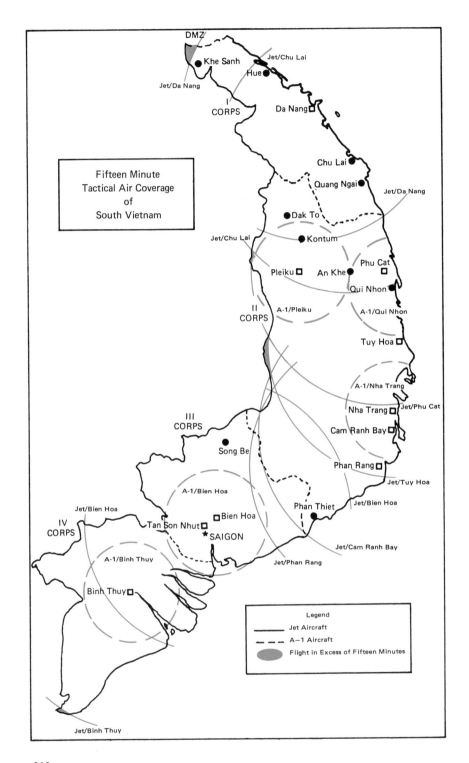

Fifteen Minute
Tactical Air Coverage
of
South Vietnam

DMZ

Jet/Chu Lai

Khe Sanh

Hue

Jet/Da Nang

I
CORPS

Da Nang

Chu Lai

Quang Ngai

Jet/Da Nang

Dak To

Jet/Chu Lai

Kontum

Phu Cat

Pleiku

An Khe

Qui Nhon

II
CORPS

A-1/Pleiku

A-1/Qui Nhon

Tuy Hoa

A-1/Nha Trang

Nha Trang

Jet/Phu Cat

III
CORPS

Cam Ranh Bay

Song Be

Phan Rang

Jet/Tuy Hoa

A-1/Bien Hoa

Phan Thiet

Jet/Bien Hoa

Jet/Bien Hoa

IV
CORPS

Bien Hoa

Tan Son Nhut

SAIGON

Jet/Cam Ranh Bay

A-1/Binh Thuy

Jet/Phan Rang

Binh Thuy

Legend

———— Jet Aircraft

- - - - A—1 Aircraft

⬤ Flight in Excess of Fifteen Minutes

Jet/Binh Thuy

218

USAF Combat Sortie/Loss Rates
WW II, Korea, and Southeast Asia

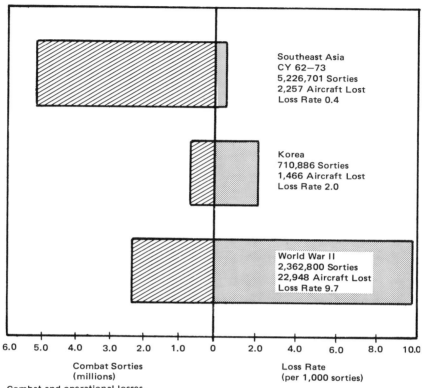

Southeast Asia
CY 62–73
5,226,701 Sorties
2,257 Aircraft Lost
Loss Rate 0.4

Korea
710,886 Sorties
1,466 Aircraft Lost
Loss Rate 2.0

World War II
2,362,800 Sorties
22,948 Aircraft Lost
Loss Rate 9.7

6.0 5.0 4.0 3.0 2.0 1.0 0 2.0 4.0 6.0 8.0 10.0

Combat Sorties Loss Rate
(millions) (per 1,000 sorties)

Combat and operational losses.

Includes 2 B-52s destroyed at Kadena and 2 at Anderson while supporting Arc Light.

Sources: SEADAB
USAF Statistical Digest

ground alerts. In 1966, thirty-six percent of the immediate requests brought planes diverted from other missions in progress; this figure rose to seventy-seven percent air diverts two years later.[68] Longer range proposals for improving response times, such as building a new attack plane that could be kept on continuous airborne alert or employing a vertical takeoff and landing fighter, while frequently discussed, were found to be impractical.

The Army's preoccupation with the speed and accuracy with which Air Force planes responded to their requests tended to play down an equally

Table 8

USAF Aircraft Losses in South Vietnam
1965–1968

Aircraft	Combat Losses				Operational Losses*				Total
	1965	1966	1967	1968	1965	1966	1967	1968	
Fixed Wing									
A–1	12	11	1	5	5	1		2	37
A–37			1	5			1		7
AC–47	1	1	4	5			1	1	13
B–52							1		1
B–57	5	5	4		2				16
C–7			1	2			1		4
C–47						1			1
C–123	3	5		3	2	2	1		16
C–130	4	2	5	7					18
F–4	2	4	15	16		3			40
F–5	1	6				1	1		9
F–100	14	20	28	43			1	1	107
F–102	4	1	1						6
F–104	2								2
F–105				1					1
HC–47					1				1
HU–16		1							1
O–1	19	14	26	30	3	6	3	2	103
O–2			3	20			2		25
OV–10				1			1		2
RB–57	2			1					3
RB–66	1								1
RC–47			1						1
RF–4C		1		7					8
RF–101		1	1	1					3
U–3				1					1
U–10							1		1
UC–123		2	1	1					4
	70	74	92	149	13	14	13	7	432
Helicopters									
CH–3			1	1					2
HH–3				2					2
HH–43	1	1	2	1					5
	1	1	3	4					9

*Other than destroyed by enemy fire—accidents, pilot error, fuel exhaustion, friendly fire, explosion, etc.

Source: Combat Information Center, WPAFB, Ohio.

important benefit of air power, namely, its ability to bring massive firepower to the battlefield. Often ground commanders in Vietnam needed this concentrated firepower more than they needed quick responses.[69]

Although only 20 percent of the Air Force's 355,000 sorties in South Vietnam during 1966 were strikes, more than half of the 88 planes lost that year were fighters carrying out those strikes. Super Sabres headed the casualty list with 20, followed by A–1s (12), F–5s (7), F–4s (7), B–57s (5), and an F–102 (table 8). The loss rate for tactical fighters and bombers that year was 0.63 planes for each 1,000 sorties, or 1 plane lost for each 1,587 sorties. Overall, the loss rate for the war in Southeast Asia (0.4) compares very favorably with the loss rates experienced in Korea (2.0), where air opposition was more formidable, and in World War II, where heavy opposition to air attacks downed 9.7 planes for each 1,000 sorties flown. In addition to the tactical strike planes lost in South Vietnam in 1966, 20 Bird Dogs were destroyed, as were 10 transports, 2 jet reconnaissance planes, an AC–47 gunship, and a search and rescue HU–16.

Armed with bombs and CBUs, three Air Force F–100 Supersabres head for a suspected Viet Cong position in South Vietnam, February 1966.

A highly accurate electro-optical guided bomb on a F–4 Phantom II. Guided bombs were but one class of weapons developed or improved during the war.

Chapter IX

Refinements of Aircraft and Munitions
1967

Although the Air Force had little direct input into the strategy that determined how its forces were being used in South Vietnam, it was responsible for organizing, training, and equipping those forces. More and more, the energies of airmen both in Washington and throughout the stateside commands were being bent toward improving that support. By early 1967, General McConnell's five deputies at the Air Force's Pentagon headquarters were devoting ever-increasing time and attention to programs for Southeast Asia.*

Officers and civilians in the planning half of the Plans and Operations staff grappled with the impact of the conflict on the Air Force's present and future shape around the world. They continually modified strategic plans for America's nuclear forces and the Air Force's structure and strategy in Europe, the Middle East, and the Pacific. One group, working on the worldwide munitions situation, drew up plans for replenishing the war reserve munitions in Europe that had been diverted to Southeast Asia the year before. Another division, concerned with matters of special warfare, spent most of its time on problems rising out of Southeast Asia, particularly escape and evasion, prisoners of war, psychological operations, and civic action programs. The thrust of these projects and studies was to determine the future status of special warfare units within the Air Force.[1]

Other planners prepared studies supporting General McConnell's persistent campaign for stronger bombing measures against North Vietnam. When, for example, the President in February asked for a list of military actions that

---

*Deputy Chiefs of Staff for Plans and Operations, Programs and Resources, Personnel, Research and Development, and Systems and Logistics.

would increase the pressure on Hanoi to end the war, McConnell and his staff succeeded in nudging the Joint Chiefs' reply in the direction of urging a comprehensive, rather than a piecemeal, air campaign.[2] Again, in April, the Plans people provided McConnell a rationale with which he convinced the chiefs to pare down to 80,000 a request from General Westmoreland for 200,000 more soldiers. The Air Force Chief again persuaded the others to adopt his strategy calling for strong air and sea attacks against the north, rather than trying to match the enemy man for man on the ground, a strategy that, in his view, favored the enemy.[3] The matter came up again in May and June when Secretary McNamara proposed sending a memorandum to the President severely modifying the chiefs' proposal for a comprehensive bombing campaign against the north.[4] Air Staff studies supporting the value of such a campaign helped convince the Secretary not to forward this memorandum.[5]

In the Operations half of this staff, officers kept a close eye on developments in Southeast Asia. Although much of their work also focused on the bombing campaign against the north, they monitored developments in the south as well, including B–52 results, sortie requirements, Air Force and Marine close air support, the reliability of the reporting system, the rescuing of downed airmen, accidental strikes against friendly troops and civilians, the details of the airlift operations, and the new radar bombing system. Elsewhere in the office, a director of strike forces supervised programs that included turning the F–5 squadron over to the Vietnamese, activating another psychological warfare squadron at Nha Trang and a defoliation squadron at Bien Hoa, arranging for jets to replace some of the weary A–1s in the Vietnamese Air Force, modifying C–123s by putting auxiliary jet engines on them, finding a suitable replacement for the aging C–47s, transferring helicopters from Thailand to the 20th Helicopter Squadron at Nha Trang, introducing the O–2s into the tactical air control system to complement the Bird Dogs, and arranging for the fourth Skyspot radar station in the delta.[6] At the same time, an evaluation director, whose job it was to plan, direct, and control operational tests, kept abreast of progress in electronic warfare and saw that the schedules were met on projects with such intriguing names as Combat Dragon, Seed Joy, Dancing Falcon, Charging Sparrow, Rapid Roger, Combat Bullseye, and a myriad of other experiments with new equipment and procedures for South Vietnam.[7]

Staff members in another Air Staff office, Programs and Resources, oversaw air base construction, communications, and organizational and manpower issues. Civil engineers there monitored the building of new bases and rehabilitation of older bases in Vietnam and Thailand. Particular attention was given to Tuy Hoa and Phu Cat, which were nearing completion during the first part of 1967, and to U Tapao in Thailand, which had been designated in March for expansion for use by B–52s.[8]

Five Air Force Red Horse engineering squadrons in Vietnam and another in Thailand were working alongside the civilian construction firms building barracks, runways, taxiways, aprons, munitions storage areas, hardstands, and bomb-loading facilities. These permanent squadrons were augmented from time to time by the temporary Prime Beef engineering units. Forty-two of these units had been flown into the area since 1966 to solve emergency engineering problems; and at the beginning of 1967, twenty Prime Beef teams were at work in the two countries.[9] Besides planning the support for these teams, the Pentagon engineers dealt with such problems as providing shelters and revetments for the tactical planes in Southeast Asia and solving earth erosion difficulties.[10]

The fluid tactical situation and continuing deployments led to expansion of the radio and telephone networks the Americans had installed in 1965 and 1966 to link their forces throughout the theater. Many new lines were laid in 1967, six of them underwater cables around the coasts of Vietnam and Thailand. From cable heads at the coastal cities of Da Nang, Nha Trang, Cam Ranh Bay, Qui Nhon, Vung Tau, and Sattahip (U Tapao), communication trunks ran inland. Dozens of existing systems were improved by doubling or tripling the number of channels available between locations. This program was closely supervised by the Air Staff's communications office.[11]

Other members of the Program and Resources staff approved and kept track of the many organizational changes that were occurring with disconcerting rapidity. As squadrons were added or subtracted and names and functions changed, the staff monitored the new configurations. Early in the year, for example, O-2s and additional C-47s were sent to Vietnam for psychological warfare missions. At the same time, the Organizations office approved a new air commando wing, with sixty-three planes, for Thailand. In March, five of the reconnaissance squadrons in Southeast Asia were renamed tactical electronic warfare squadrons to distinguish them from the other more conventional reconnaissance units in the theater. The air headquarters in Hawaii, finding it difficult to keep pace with all the changes, asked the Air Staff's help; and in June the Organizations staff directed all the commands to keep Hawaii informed before changes were made.[12]

Keeping tabs on the manpower vicissitudes that accompanied these organizational shifts fell to the Manpower office, which had to see that the number and types of Air Force people in Southeast Asia did not exceed the ceilings set by Secretary McNamara.[13] At the beginning of 1967, there were 385,000 Americans in South Vietnam, 52,900 of them belonging to the Air Force, with an additional 26,000 Air Force members stationed in Thailand. In November 1966, the manpower ceiling for June 1967 had been set at 439,500, rising in December to 463,500, and to 469,300 by the middle of 1968. Of this number, the Air Force quota was to remain fairly steady at 55,400 airmen in South Vietnam.[14] In January 1967, however, the number

This lighting system mounted on a C–123 would illuminate
a two-mile area with the aircraft flying at 12,000 feet.

was revised upward to allow 471,600 in South Vietnam by June of that year,
the Air Force portion increasing by 575 people.[15] Further changes throughout the year, inspired by the changing tactical situation on the ground in
South Vietnam, kept the office fully occupied making sure that these figures
were honored, while competing demands from other parts of the world were
satisfied.

Setting policies for obtaining, training, evaluating, and assigning military
and civilian members of the Air Force was the province of a third section of
the staff, Personnel.[16] It fell to the training people within this organization to
make sure that the flying, military, survival, and technical training programs
of the Air Training and Tactical Air Commands were providing the
commanders in Southeast Asia and elsewhere with the right numbers and
kinds of people.[17] In trying to keep up with the escalating demands in
Southeast Asia, those responsible for flying and survival training adopted in
1967 such measures as increasing the annual number of new pilots by
fourteen percent, agreeing to train a hundred pilots a year for the Marine
Corps, and supervising the changeover in helicopter pilot training from the
older H–19s to the newer UH–1s, along with making plans to reduce training
time and get people into the theater more rapidly by combining the three
existing survival training programs.[18]

Technical training programs were also being reshaped for the conflict.
Peacetime practices had been shaken up by the large demand for people, the
shift of emphasis from nuclear to conventional munitions, the unfamiliar
nature of many of the enemy's munitions and booby traps, and the insecurity
of bases in Southeast Asia. In 1966, for example, the demand for munitions
specialists rose 240 percent over what it had been the previous year, and the

ordnance disposal people that were needed increased ninefold. By early 1967, the Air Force's technical training schools were running students through combat preparedness courses of all types at a rate of 60,000 a year, most graduates intended, either directly or indirectly, for the war in Asia.[19]

Of the five Deputy Chief of Staff offices, Research and Development devoted the most time to the conflict. Offices in the Air Staff were organized by function rather than by geography, but a special Southeast Asia Division was created in Research and Development to act as the focal point for all war-related matters being worked in the office's other divisions.[20] An Armaments Division supported and supervised the work of the Systems Command in developing new conventional bombs, fuzes, mines, guided weapons, riot control munitions, flares, and air-to-surface missiles.[21] The Aeronautical Division provided technical support to produce and obtain aircraft and weapon systems.[22] By early 1967, this division was at work on dozens of projects for Southeast Asia, including developing a night capability for the new O-2s and the future OV-10 forward air control planes and preparing numerous subsystems for the new C-130 gunship that was about to be introduced into the war.[23]

Since March 1966, the means to destroy the enemy at night—one of the knottiest problems in Southeast Asia—had received a top priority among the Research and Development staff. For almost a year, a special division had been supervising a host of projects, grouped under the name Shed Light, to address the problem. Two decades of emphasis on the requirements for nuclear war and space exploration had resulted in a paucity of research for air power in limited conflicts. By 1967, Shed Light, in attempting to correct that deficiency, was addressing ten aircraft systems; three fighter modifications; and over ninety supporting projects to improve navigation, illumination devices, night sensors, target-marking equipment, and weapon delivery systems. The planners worked simultaneously on two approaches. The first was a self-contained attack system in which an aircraft would have on board all the sensors and weapons needed to navigate, locate the enemy, and destroy him at night without outside assistance from either the ground or other aircraft. The second system, called Hunter/Killer, envisioned a team effort in which one relatively unarmed plane would seek, locate, and mark targets, while heavily armed planes without sensor devices would attack and destroyed the targets.[24]

It was expected that the newly developed, but controversial, F-111 fighter-bomber would eventually fill the role of the self-contained attack system, but since the plane would not be ready until the following year, the research people prepared interim aircraft for night attack missions.[25] The first of these, called Tropic Moon I, was an A-1 fitted with television to view the enemy at night. By the end of the year, four of these planes were on their way to Vietnam for testing. A follow-on plane, Tropic Moon II, was a B-57 equipped with improved television and electronic equipment. Three of these arrived at Phan Rang on Christmas Eve.[26] Even before they touched down, however, the Research and Development staff was well along in planning for Tropic Moon III, also a B–57, carrying even more sophisticated equipment— forward-looking radars with terrain-warning and moving-target indicators, low-light-level television, and forward-looking infrared systems.[27]

For the Hunter/Killer operation, Shed Light planners were examining the possibilities of adapting C–130s (called Hunter), O–2s, OV–10s, C–123s (called Black Spot), Grumman S–2Gs, and A–26s (called Lonesome Tiger) for the night mission. The Air Staff's function in Shed Light was to obtain approval and funding and to oversee the progress of the Systems Command, which was developing the equipment; the progress of the Logistics Command, which was procuring it; and the progress of the Tactical Air Command, which was testing it.

Seeing that all the required weapons systems, services, and materiel got into the hands of those in the field who needed them was the responsibility of the fifth headquarters unit, Systems and Logistics.[28] Coordinating principally with the Systems Command, the Logistics Command, and the Military Airlift Command, this office monitored current stocks of equipment, made up deficiencies, and devised ways to get the materiel to the users. During early 1967, this office undertook, among other things, replacing ground radars in Vietnam and providing aircraft guns, prefabricated shelters, forklifts, pallets, life rafts, and generators.[29] Like all Air Staff offices, it remained responsive to quick changes in the war. After a KC–135 collided with an F–8 over the Gulf of Tonkin, the office instructed the Logistics Command to send more radar air traffic control equipment to Dong Ha. When General Momyer ordered RF–4Cs on day missions over North Vietnam to stay above 12,000 feet, after several were lost to ground fire in January, the Systems and Logistics people provided larger lenses for the planes' cameras to obtain satisfactory pictures.[30] They satisfied an increased requirement for herbicides during the year by sending substitutes, placing priority orders for new supplies, and wheedling industry into voluntary cooperation.[31] The office also participated in the development of new riot control munitions.[32]

The Reports and Analysis Division of Systems and Logistics kept close tabs on the quantities of munitions being used in Southeast Asia, producing a computerized file used as a uniform data base by all government agencies that needed the information.[33] With the alleviation of the munitions shortage early in 1967, the Air Staff, through this division, discontinued the use of the "Special Express" surface vessels and returned to conventional point-to-point shipping by the Military Sea Transport Service.[34]

During this period, the Transportation Division, also of Systems and Logistics, opened up regular MAC flights from various stateside bases to Pleiku, Cam Ranh Bay, Da Nang, and Bien Hoa in Vietnam and to Bangkok,

Korat, and Udorn in Thailand, thereby reducing part of the strain on the intratheater airlift and alleviating some of the congestion at Tan Son Nhut.[35] To reduce intratheater airlift even further and to relieve overcrowding at the Travis AFB, California, hospital, the Air Staff approved in April new MAC medical evacuation flights directly from Da Nang to Travis and from Da Nang and Cam Ranh Bay into Andrews AFB in Maryland.[36] Then in mid-June, it approved direct cargo flights from both Travis and Guam into the newly expanded U Tapao Air Base in Thailand.[37] The division also arranged to use some of MAC's dedicated Special Assignment Airlift Missions for such tasks as bringing Turnkey personnel back from Vietnam between May and July when they finished building the base at Tuy Hoa, delivering sorely needed HH–3 helicopters to Vietnam for search and rescue missions, airlifting Shrike missiles from New Jersey to Thailand, and, in March, evacuating 180 Arc Light personnel and 75 tons of equipment from Guam to Okinawa, out of the path of a typhoon.[38]

As a result of these measures, the face of the air war continued to change throughout 1967. Most noticeable was a substantial shift in the types of munitions and aircraft being used against the enemy. America's preoccupation during the fifties and early sixties with the strategies of nuclear deterrence and massive retaliation had left it ill-prepared in the quality and quantity of air munitions with which to fight the war in Southeast Asia. By 1964, the technological base for other than nuclear weapons was almost nonexistent.

A review that year had revealed that much of the existing nonnuclear ordnance, such as 500-pound and 750-pound general purpose bombs, was rapidly becoming obsolete.[39] Not only did these older munitions have problems with accuracy, fragmentation, and ballistics, but they also had been designed for wars with slower planes and more stationary targets. Faced now with jungle warfare in which targets were spread over wide areas and not easily pinpointed, the older general purpose weapons had to be supplemented by area munitions. New ordnance was needed for the new conditions— penetration of dense foliage to keep the enemy out of large areas or, failing that, to strike light materiel and soldiers. In tailoring its munitions to specific kinds of targets, the Air Force had need of a dozen types of ordnance—high explosive bombs, incendiaries, dispenser munitions, guns and gun pods, missiles, guided bombs, rockets, target markers, flares, mines, riot control bombs, and fragmentation munitions.[40]

Even under the best conditions, however, technical difficulties, test failures, cost ineffectiveness, and funding limitations swelled the amount of time needed to move a weapon system from concept to battlefield. Spurred on by the Southeast Asia emergency, the Air Force took several steps to reduce this lead time. Beginning in 1965, the field commander in Vietnam was allowed to funnel his weapons needs, in the form of a Southeast Asia

Operational Requirement, directly to the Systems Command for action, thereby hastening the process. At the same time, the Systems Command set up a liaison office at Tan Son Nhut to assist the field commander with his munitions problems and to coordinate his needs with the stateside commands that were to fill them. To circumvent the ponderous funding machinery, the Systems Command created a petty cash fund to use at its own discretion for initial research on promising weapons.[41] Finally, the Air Force compressed the traditional step-by-step process for developing munitions, conducting concurrently, whenever possible, the functions of several offices: the Office of Aerospace Research, which managed research on new weapons; the Systems Command, which engineered them and put them into production; the Tactical Air Command, which tested them on its stateside ranges; and the Logistics Command, which handled subsequent production and distribution.[42]

This telescoping of research, engineering, production, and testing quickened the flow of new air munitions into the theater by early 1967. Only two years earlier, the Air Force had been using twice as many older munitions as modern in Southeast Asia; but by May 1967, only fifteen percent of the munitions in the Seventh Air Force's inventory was of the older variety.[43]

This concurrence was a mixed blessing, however. While it sped up the introduction of several weapons, it also slowed the completion of others by creating new problems for procurers, developers, testers, and users.[44] By restricting competition at the procurement stage, it raised costs, which introduced delays. Engineers were plagued by complex requirements that frequently forced redesign and led to further delays. Also, since most of the weapons were self-destructive, developers found it difficult to analyze failures, an essential part of the development process. Further, the accelerated pace of development overwhelmed testing facilities. The resultant brevity of stateside testing periods often made field commanders in Vietnam hesitant to accept munitions.[45] Much ordnance arrived in the theater before it was completely free of defects, and as much by necessity as by design, therefore, the battlefield became the final testing ground for new families of weapons.

If it were ever so, it was no longer true that air weapons could be designed independently of the navigational, guidance, and fire control systems that determined their accuracy. The greater sophistication of aircraft, the wide variety of planes flying, the primitive nature of the enemy, and the terrain in Southeast Asia required weapon systems, not just weapons. Not only were the new types of ordnance (and the means to deliver them efficiently) in demand, but they also had to detonate when and where they would do the most good. Older bombs were often incompatible with the newer delivery systems. The high speed of newer planes, for example, frequently damaged the bombs' fins, causing the aircraft to flutter. Bomb lugs often did not fit the ejector racks. Many fuzes had serious safety and operational limitations. Too many bombs had high dud rates. The 2.75-inch rocket launchers imposed speed restrictions on the planes that carried them, making the aircraft more vulnerable to ground fire.[46]

The Air Force's new measures began to show some dividends. Eleven new munitions were introduced into Vietnam in 1965, 24 the next year, and 7 in 1967 (table 9).[47] One of the most effective of these was a new antipersonnel munition, the cluster bomb unit (CBU), that was on its way early in 1967 to becoming the workhorse of the war. Based on a Navy prototype, this weapon, the CBU–24, had required only 9 months to move from conception to introduction into the theater. It consisted of two elements, a large bomb-like canister, or dispenser, and over 600 bomblets, each the size of a flashlight battery, packed into the dispenser. Once the dispenser cleared the aircraft, a timing fuze opened it like a clamshell, spilling its contents over a wide area. The bomblets were detonated by fuzes. By the beginning of 1967, all jet planes were fitted to use the new ordnance; and by April, tests that allowed A–1Es to carry the CBUs were completed. The Joint Chiefs considered the CBU–24 important enough to assign it the highest priority on their production list.[48] Through the course of the war, 17 varieties of cluster bombs were used, 42 percent of them CBU–24s.

As the year progressed, the cluster bombs were refined and improved. For example, when fighters carrying different mixes of ordnance began employing CBUs with Skyspot, the pilots discovered that they first had to drop the time-fuzed CBUs, which needed higher altitude, on Skyspot targets before they could go on to armed reconnaissance missions, which were flown closer to the ground.[49] This led to the development of a proximity fuze that could be used from any height, giving the pilots greater flexibility between high-level Skyspot and low-level armed reconnaissance attacks.

New fuzes were also developed to get around the problem of the bomblets bursting prematurely in the high jungle foliage. One type of fuze installed in the small jungle bomblets caused them to explode only when their aerial rotation slowed down below 2,000 revolutions per minute. After leaving the dispenser in midair, these bomblets would begin to spin and would become armed when their rotation reached 3,000 revolutions per minute. As they glanced off tree limbs or foliage, their rotation would slow to the speed at which they would detonate.[50]

Other new fuzes developed for general purpose bombs remained in wide use throughout the conflict. One such fuze was designed to set off the bomb only on violent impact. At first there were problems when these bombs struck water or mud, became embedded, and detonated harmlessly below the surface. Eventually these fuzes were modified so that they would fire when fluid entered small openings on the fuze's face, before becoming embedded in the ground.[51]

Table 9

Munitions Provided to Southeast Asia
1965–1967

1965	Napalm "B"	FMU–7A/B Fuze
	SUU–24/A Dispenser	CBU–2A Munition
	BLU–23 Fire Bomb	SUU–11A/A Gun Pod
	CBU–14 Dispenser Munition	CBU–12 Screening Munition
	SUU–16 Gun Pod	GAU–2B/A Gun
	BLU–27/B Firebomb	
1966	WDU–4/A 2.75" Flechette WH	AC–47 Gun Module
	MHU–83 Lift Trucks	FMU–30/B Fuze
	BLU–26/B Bomblets	CBU–24/B Munition
	SUU–23 Gun Pod	CBU–22/A Screening Munition
	MHU–85 Trailers	GAU–4/A Gun
	ADU–282/E TER Adapter	ADU–281/E MER Adapter
	CBU–7/A Dispenser Munition	BLU–32 Fire Bomb
	Westco Mixer Kits	CBU–25A Clustered Jungle
	7.62-mm Machinegun Module	Bomb
	BLU–3/B	SUU–31/B Dispenser
	CBU–29/A	SUU–11/A Dispenser
	MXU–470/A Gun Module	CAROLINA MOON
1967	CBU–19/A Antiriot Control	MER/TER Reloading
	Bomb	Equipment
	FMU–26/B Mutipurpose Fuze	FMU–54/B Retarder Fuze
	FMU–35/B Long Delay Fuze	Armored Flare Box
	MAU–91/B Retarded Bomb	
	Fin Assembly	
1968*	CBU–28/A Dragontooth Mine	CBU–30/A Antiriot Control
	Cluster Bomb	Bomb
	CBU–46/A Improved Jungle	SUU–42/A Dispenser
	Bomb	SUU–41/A Dispenser
	LAU–62/A Flare Launcher	

*January 1 to March 31

In March, the Air Force introduced a new cluster munition, the CBU–19, which had over 500 bomblets packed into a 130-pound canister. On impact, the bomblets released a riot control gas over an area of 6,000 square yards. Since the agent temporarily incapacitated people, it proved valuable in areas where friendly and enemy troops were mixed.[52] It was also used in air

The Pave Way I laser guided bomb.

rescue operations to slow down enemy troops closing in on downed flyers. Research continued throughout the year on an advanced riot control munition that could be carried by both slow and high-speed aircraft. By September of the next year, this new weapon, the CBU–30, was in use in Southeast Asia.

Among the most promising programs under way in 1967 was the research being done by the Systems Command to alter the method of delivering bombs. From the beginning of aerial warfare, falling bombs were guided solely by gravity, and their accuracy depended on calculations made before the ordnance left the airplane. Despite refinements over the years in the equipment and methods for making these calculations and in the aerodynamic characteristics of bombs, a weapon's success or failure was still predetermined by the time it departed an aircraft. In mid-1967, General McConnell gave his staff approval to speed up research on bombs whose direction could be changed along their path toward the target.

Investigation began on three types of guidance methods: one that permitted the falling bomb to correct its downward course in response to a laser reflecting from the target; an electro-optical system, in which the guidance system of the bomb used the light and dark contrast between the target and its background material; and a guidance system in which the infrared energy emanating from the target was used.[53] These projects were labeled, respectively, Pave Way I, II, and III.

Some technology for these guided munitions already existed. The Walleye missile, which the Air Force began to use in Southeast Asia in August,[54] contained television tracking equipment that would form one element of the new electro-optical guided bomb; but the Walleye itself was not fully satisfactory. Being a Navy weapon, it was not available in the numbers the Air Force wished; more important, it performed poorly against low-contrast targets and could not be used at night.[55] Another missile the Air Force was employing in the war, the Bullpup, used a radio-controlled system and would also be incorporated into the research into new guidance systems. The Bullpup missile was limited because the aircraft that launched it had to follow it after release until impact, restricting its use to permissive environments and good weather. Finally, a laser instrument that a forward air controller could use to illuminate ground targets had been tested successfully in 1966.[56] McConnell's instructions in July 1967 to proceed with development of guided weapons would result a year later in the introduction of the first of the "smart" bombs into the conflict.

By the end of the year, the Defense Communications Agency had developed and tested two kinds of electronic sensors to ferret out the enemy and determine his movements. One type, a seismic sensor, was designed to be implanted in the ground to measure vibrations from passing bodies. The second, an acoustic sensor, reacted to sound waves passing through the air. Both types of sensors were dropped from aircraft, either fighters or helicopters, and were designed to relay signals to an orbiting aircraft that passed them to a ground receiving station for interpretation and integration with information from other intelligence sources. This new development in electronic warfare was first used late in the year, with some success, to plot the movement of enemy soldiers down the Ho Chi Minh Trail. At the end of the year, in response to an enemy buildup, sensors were being dropped around the Marine base at Khe Sanh in I Corps.

Of equal import with the munitions and sensors were the new planes that entered the fray. During the summer of 1967, both the Vietnamese and American Air Forces underwent substantial facelifts as some newer types of airplanes replaced their weary and increasingly ineffective predecessors. The program to modernize the Vietnamese Air Force, agreed to the previous summer, moved forward on the 1st of June when Ambassador Bunker turned over twenty F–5s to Premier Ky and the Vietnamese 522d Fighter Squadron at Bien Hoa. This was the first step in the unfolding of the program that would see four of the six Vietnamese fighter squadrons gradually convert from A–1s to jets. Besides the F–5s for the 522d, three of the other squadrons were to receive A–37s as soon as the planes were tested in Vietnam. The two remaining squadrons would continue to fly the A–1s.

Secretary McNamara had been won over to allowing the VNAF to have the F–5s on the grounds that the jets had proved themselves to be good close air support vehicles, that they posed no threat to North Vietnam and therefore did not signal escalation, and that they would permit the VNAF to defend the country against air attacks when the USAF finally withdrew.[57] The impact of the move was as much psychological as it was military. The South Vietnamese were sensitive to taunts from the northerners that the

United States would not trust them with jets, and the activation of the jet squadron was an important status symbol for the southerners.

There was some basis for the claim that the United States did not trust the Vietnamese with jets, but not for the reasons implied above. The VNAF's safety record with conventional aircraft had been poor. Since 1962 they had lost 287 planes, more than half of them (153) to accidents. In 1967, the force suffered 32 major aircraft accidents for every 100,000 hours it flew,[58] compared to the Air Force's accident rate of 7.4.[59] In July alone, the VNAF had 18 mishaps with its conventional planes, 12 the result of pilot mistakes— hitting trees on napalm passes, ground looping on landing, colliding in midair, taxiing into a fence, landing with the gear up, losing control on takeoff, nosing over after stopping an aircraft too quickly, and running off the runway.[60] In August, there were 10 major flight accidents, a single major ground accident, a minor flight accident, and 6 flight incidents, but only a single reported combat loss.[61]

While many of these accidents stemmed from the inexperience of VNAF pilots, the widespread absence of safety awareness and the absence of a program to instill it was making the problem difficult to correct.[62] The Air Force's advisory group, which oversaw the VNAF's development, had been eclipsed since the large-scale USAF arrival began in 1965; and a flying safety program for the VNAF, which had been in the plans, had fallen victim to higher priorities. Some advisory group officials complained that they were not getting top caliber people for so sensitive a mission. Few officers possessed the linguistic and cultural skills needed for the job,[63] and advisor duty was frequently viewed as inferior and undesirable compared to a more glamorous and career-enhancing tour with the Seventh Air Force.[64]

The 33 Vietnamese pilots chosen for the first jet squadron, however, were hand picked by Premier Ky and had trained in the United States and the Philippines. They took over the planes from the deactivated 10th Fighter Squadron and were assisted at Bien Hoa by a mobile team sent by the Air Training Command to teach the squadron to maintain the planes. The Vietnamese lost little time taking to the air, logging 388 combat sorties in June and 436 the following month. In December, they flew 527 sorties, striking enemy supply routes and supporting ground troops in South Vietnam. Their safety record during the first 6 months was excellent, with only one plane lost.[65]

This conversion to jets was the forerunner of the transition the following year of three other fighter squadrons to jets and four of the five helicopter squadrons from H–34s to the newer UH–1D and the transition early in 1969 of many of the three transport squadrons' C–47s into AC–47 gunships.[66]

While these changes within the VNAF were a step toward modernity, the changes that USAF aircraft underwent in 1967 were symptomatic of that service's acceptance, still with reluctance in some quarters, of the realities and

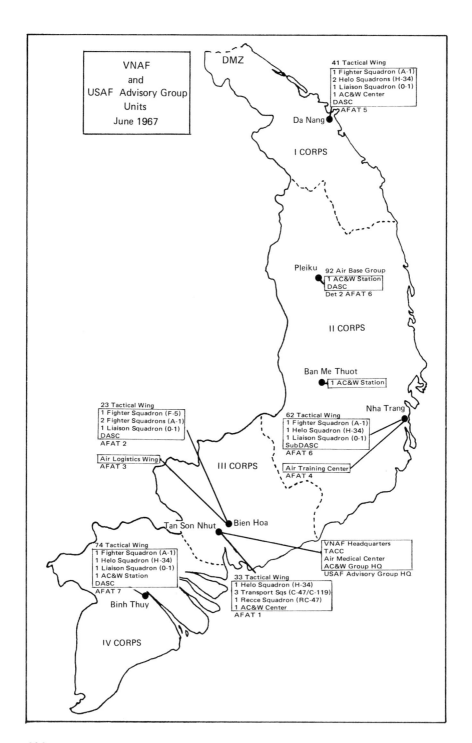

VNAF
and
USAF Advisory Group
Units
June 1967

DMZ

41 Tactical Wing
1 Fighter Squadron (A-1)
2 Helo Squadrons (H-34)
1 Liaison Squadron (0-1)
1 AC&W Center
DASC
AFAT 5

Da Nang

I CORPS

Pleiku
92 Air Base Group
1 AC&W Station
DASC
Det 2 AFAT 6

II CORPS

Ban Me Thuot
1 AC&W Station

Nha Trang

23 Tactical Wing
1 Fighter Squadron (F-5)
2 Fighter Squadrons (A-1)
1 Liaison Squadron (0-1)
DASC
AFAT 2

62 Tactical Wing
1 Fighter Squadron (A-1)
1 Helo Squadron (H-34)
1 Liaison Squadron (0-1)
SubDASC
AFAT 6

Air Logistics Wing
AFAT 3

III CORPS

Air Training Center
AFAT 4

Tan Son Nhut • Bien Hoa

74 Tactical Wing
1 Fighter Squadron (A-1)
1 Helo Squadron (H-34)
1 Liaison Squadron (0-1)
1 AC&W Station
DASC
AFAT 7

VNAF Headquarters
TACC
Air Medical Center
AC&W Group HQ
USAF Advisory Group HQ

33 Tactical Wing
1 Helo Squadron (H-34)
3 Transport Sqs (C-47/C-119)
1 Recce Squadron (RC-47)
1 AC&W Center
AFAT 1

Binh Thuy

IV CORPS

An Air Force C–7 during Operation Junction City.

requirements of a flexible response strategy—a doctrine that the Air Force had eschewed in the 1950s in favor of massive retaliation. Research and development efforts on improved weapon systems, which had been under way for over a year, bore fruit in 1967 with the introduction of several second generation aircraft for this type of war. In addition to taking over the Caribou airlift operation, the Air Force began replacing its AC–47 gunships with AC–130s, its few remaining A–1s with jet A–37s, its Bird Dogs with O–2s, and some of its helicopters with armed models.

By midyear, the metamorphosis of the six former Army Caribou companies into Air Force squadrons had moved along well. Answers to the two questions that had not been settled by the April 1966 agreement between the Army and Air Force Chiefs—should the new airlift planes be integrated into the common service airlift system and could the Air Force match the Army's earlier performance with the planes—were becoming clearer, at least to Air Force leaders.

The first question was resolved by a compromise of sorts, albeit one skewed strongly in the Army's direction. The eighty-nine planes at first continued, as before, to support specific ground units—the Military Assistance Command, Vietnam, and the Military Assistance Command, Thailand; the U.S. Army's I Field Force, II Field Force, 5th Special Forces Group, 1st Cavalry Division, and the U.S. Army, Vietnam, headquarters at Long Binh; the III Marine Amphibious Force in I Corps; and the newly revived pacification program of the Agency for International Development. In fact, one of the squadrons, the 537th at Phu Cat, was set aside solely for the 1st Cavalry Division and worked directly with it through a detachment at An Khe.[67]

237

Momyer reviewed this arrangement after the first month of operation, as agreed, and recommended that the Caribous be brought directly into the common airlift system. A minor advance in that direction was achieved in April when the job of scheduling all the planes was given to the centralized airlift control center (ALCC) at Tan Son Nhut. Requests for the planes were funneled into the ALCC from MACV, and schedules were sent out from there through the airlift wing at Cam Ranh Bay.[68] However, the control center still lacked the power to determine Caribou itineraries and remained essentially a conduit servicing the wishes of the customers. Ground commanders strongly opposed any slackening of their control over the planes, and Westmoreland expressed satisfaction with the existing arrangement. While he did agree to a contingency plan in which the Caribous could be integrated in case of emergency, he opposed further centralization. Since the chiefs' agreement allowed the MACV commander this prerogative, the C–7s remained decentralized. The best that Momyer could do was attempt to have the planes operated more efficiently than they had been, squeezing more sorties out of the same number of planes. The surplus flights could then be used for the common good of the war throughout South Vietnam.

The Air Force's statistics suggested, on the second issue, that the Caribou record in 1967 not only matched but surpassed that of the Army the year before. Averaging 50 missions a day (450 sorties), the planes flew into 188 of the 300 primitive strips in Vietnam. The missions included support to Special Forces camps, medical evacuations, radio relays, emergency resupply, and tactical emergencies, as well as airdrops of paratroopers, ammunition, building supplies, gasoline, rations, and live animals. They delivered livestock and fowl to the Vietnamese Army, which lacked refrigeration in the field.[69] From their main bases at Cam Ranh Bay, Vung Tau, and Phu Cat, some of the squadrons stationed 3 or 4 planes at Da Nang, Pleiku, Nha Trang, An Khe, and at Don Muang in Bangkok, Thailand.

The Caribou was an excellent plane for front line support into short rough surface landing strips. Able to land on a 700-foot field, it could take off in an even shorter distance and could carry 5,000 pounds of cargo, 32 passengers, 28 fully equipped combat troops, or 20 litter patients.[70] Compared to the Army's performance of 1966, Air Force C–7s in 1967 flew 20 percent more hours and 26 percent more sorties and the planes carried a third more passengers and 10 percent more cargo. The flyers had squeezed an additional squadron's payload out of a slightly smaller number of airplanes than the Army had operated.[71]

Impressive as these figures were, they did not prevent the Caribou issue from being interjected into the larger debate between the Army and the Air Force regarding helicopter and tactical airlift support of ground forces. Several points had been left vague in the 1966 agreement between the chiefs. By that pact, the Air Force was allowed to use helicopters for search and rescue and for special warfare operations, but this latter term had not been defined. General Johnson, the Army Chief, was disturbed early in 1967 when several Air Force helicopters of the 20th Helicopter Squadron at Nha Trang fired on the enemy while supporting U.S. Army forces.[72] As a result, the agreement was amended in May to specify that Air Force helicopters would support Air Force units, other government agencies, and indigenous forces "only when operating without U.S. Army advisors or not under Army control."[73]

The helicopter controversy spilled over into the airlift part of the agreement. The matter transcended the Caribous and touched on the larger issue of tactical airlift support of Army units in the field.[74] The Air Force defended the ability of its C–130s, C–123s, and C–7s to support the Army fully; but Johnson, in testimony before the House Armed Services Committee, expressed dissatisfaction with the C–130s and with what he perceived as the Air Force's downgrading of the Caribous and Buffalos (C–8s). This latter plane was seen by the Army as a better plane than the others for the short-range tactical transport role. (The Air Force had received four C–8s from the Army along with the Caribous and had later turned them over to the space program for experimentation.)[75] The issue was exacerbated in May when the Defense Secretary turned down an Air Force request for sixteen more C–7s to make up for losses.[76]

That preconceptions seemed to be carrying more weight than battlefield results was due in part to conflicting reports from the field. Successive Army generals commanding the I Field Force at Nha Trang commended the Air Force airlift commander in Vietnam. The first said, "The Air Force operation of the Caribou has been outstanding. It has been far more effective than when it was under Army control." Similarly, the second stated, "You have done a great job with the C–7A. The Air Force has operated the Caribous far better than they were operated when under Army control."[77] Similar attestations came from the 1st Cavalry Division and other customers. On the other hand, the Army staff in Washington received complaints from the II Field Force at Long Binh that the Air Force's unfamiliarity with ground problems and its stringent rules for crew duty time, flying hours, and flying safety caused cancellation of some Caribou flights. As a result, continued the reports, the Army had to use more of its helicopters to move men to forward areas.[78] The controversy remained unsettled, colored less by the actual Caribou operations than by the larger consideration of roles and missions. At stake was the postwar relationship between the Army and Air Force in the area of airlift support. South Vietnam was providing a laboratory for working out the divergent opinions of the two services.

Meanwhile, the Air Force moved ahead in 1967 in its transition of gunships, attack planes, forward control aircraft, and helicopters to more suitable successors. Replacement of the twenty-five AC–47 gunships was

An AC–130A Gunship II.

foreshadowed in September when an AC–130 landed at Nha Trang to begin an operational testing period. This system, a product of the Shed Light project, contained night observation devices, side-looking radar, and forward-looking infrared equipment that could detect heat from vehicles after they turned off their engines or drove under a canopy. Following preliminary tests at Eglin AFB in Florida, the plane was flown to Vietnam to see how well its sophisticated equipment would perform the roles of close air support, interdiction, and armed reconnaissance. For three months, it supported troops in the delta, struck the Laotian trails in the Tiger Hound area, and flew armed reconnaissance missions in the highlands of II Corps. The plane flew two or three missions a day; and the results, particularly during night interdiction attacks, were encouraging. It spotted ninety-four trucks and destroyed thirty-eight. When the test ended in December, commanders in Saigon were excited about the prospect of the plane, called Gunship II, replacing the AC–47s. General Momyer ordered it returned to the states for a seven-month refurbishment, but Westmoreland did not want to let it go. They compromised by allowing the plane a minimum overhaul. It was back in Southeast Asia by February 1968, when it flew its first official combat mission.[79]

The transition to the second generation of gunships, however, was not to be so uncomplicated. Even though field commanders, citing the existence in Vietnam of maintenance facilities and pilots familiar with the plane, supported the AC–130, Air Force Secretary Brown at first preferred the venerable C–119 as the new gunship. This plane was cheaper, he contended, more available, and its use would not cut into the airlift mission, which

Air Force A–37s on their first combat mission, South Vietnam, August 1967.

depended heavily on C–130s. The outcome was a compromise in which C–119s would be converted for close air support and local base defense roles and C–130s for night interdiction attacks against infiltrators in Laos. The secretary approved the C–119 conversion in June and authorized eight C–130s to undergo the necessary alterations in November, thus laying the groundwork for the introduction of a mixed gunship force into Southeast Asia in 1968.[80]

By the end of 1967, USAF A–1s were no longer based in South Vietnam. During the last 2 months of the year, the 1st Air Commando Squadron, the last vestige of the Farm Gate unit on whose wings the United States had first flown into Vietnam 6 years earlier, transferred its remaining 17 Skyraiders from Pleiku across the Mekong River to Nakhon Phanom in Thailand.[81] The earlier controversy over the relative merits of propeller-driven and jet planes was rapidly being won by those who favored the latter. Even as the A–1s were preparing to leave Vietnam in August, 18 lightweight jet A–37s were flown into Bien Hoa to begin a 3-month combat test. This plane was well known to jet pilots in Vietnam, who had learned to fly in the T–37 trainer version. The 2-seat twin-jet aircraft had been modified to carry 4,800 pounds of ordnance on 8 wing pylons and had a 7.62-mm minigun in its nose. It had a range of 650 miles and could fly as fast as 480 miles per hour.

The A–37 squadron, named the 604th Air Commando, began its tests on the 15th of August, flying 12 combat sorties a day in support of ground troops and against enemy supplies in South Vietnam. By September 5, the daily sortie rate had reached 60. At the end of October, some of the planes were sent to Pleiku to fly armed reconnaissance and visual reconnaissance missions and to perform night interdiction strikes in Tiger Hound. By the time the tests ended in mid-December, the planes had logged 4,300 sorties. Only a single A–37 was lost, the result of an unfavorable maneuver after the aircraft was over its home base. The squadron was then attached to the 14th Air Commando Wing at Nha Trang, although its planes remained at Bien Hoa and continued to fly from there.[82]

Observers both in Vietnam and on the Air Staff were pleased with the plane's performance. It accelerated and decelerated rapidly and maneuvered well. Its compact delivery system was highly accurate. Easy to maintain, it could be turned around in an hour and a half between missions.[83] The Air Force's project manager, with some hyperbole, dubbed the test "the most exciting aviation venture of 1967."[84] Encouraged by the tests, the Air Force sought approval to buy more than the 127 planes that were already being built, but the Tactical Air Command demurred. Responsible for developing a new attack plane, the command's planners were less than enthusiastic about placing emphasis on a subsonic plane that would not meet the requirements of other potential combat theaters around the world.[85]

The need for a new forward air control plane had become apparent in 1966 as the ground environment in northern South Vietnam became increasingly more dangerous for the Bird Dogs. Delays in the development of the OV–10 Bronco, designed specifically for the forward air control role, led to a search for an interim aircraft. In May 1966, the Tactical Air Command decided that the Cessna 337, a twin-engine (one pusher, one tractor) plane, seemed most adaptable to the air controller role. By July 1967, these new O–2As, as the Air Force called them, were beginning to replace the O–1s in some of the tactical air support squadrons. The new planes were seen as a complement to, rather than a replacement of, the countrywide Bird Dog force. Most were assigned to controllers in I Corps, where ground reaction was the heaviest, thereby releasing O–1s for duty in the lower three corps. Citing the same rationale it had used in the case of the Bird Dogs, the Seventh Air Force decided against arming the new observation craft.[86]

By September, the 20th TASS in I Corps had phased out all but a few of its O–1s and was flying forty-two of the new planes over the Demilitarized Zone and the Tally Ho region from operating locations at Da Nang, Quang Ngai, Quang Nam, Tam Ky, Quang Thi, Kon Tun, Hue, Khe Sanh, Kham Duc, and Dong Ha.[87] At year's end, the squadron had seventy-six of them, with sixteen O–1s remaining for special missions into the more primitive fields. The three squadrons in the other corps in South Vietnam maintained a preponderance of Bird Dogs. A fifth squadron, the 23d TASS, which had been created in 1966 across the river in Thailand at Nakhon Phanom, had converted all its thirty-four planes to O–2s, and was flying them in Laos along the Ho Chi Minh Trail. It frequently lent pilots and navigators to the 20th when action picked up in the zone and Tally Ho areas.[88]

The O–2 was not an unalloyed improvement over its predecessor. Pilots who flew it were pleased with the greater range and speed it had over the Bird Dogs. Unlike the O–1, the new plane could cover the entire Tiger Hound area in one flight. Airmen also liked the idea of having two engines, even though the plane's performance on one engine was marginal. The O–2 had better equipment for night missions—transponders, radios, instrument lighting, and more flares. On the other hand, the O–2 needed more room for takeoffs and landings than did the O–1. As one pilot put it, he noticed at his field that the C–130s and C–123s had shorter groundroll time than did his O–2.[89] This meant the new control plane could fly in and out of fewer airfields than the Bird Dog. Most pilots judged the O–2 better than its predecessor for controlling strikes but inferior for visual reconnaissance missions. Forward visibility from inside the plane was poor.[90] The engines were not powerful enough and the plane lacked armor.[91] Although 137 of them were in use by controllers by year's end, commanders and crewmen were looking forward to the advent of the OV–10.

A number of new O–2s in 1967 were being put to a different use in South Vietnam—dropping leaflets and broadcasting messages to both friend and foe from the sky. As the intensity of battle heightened and spread northward late in 1966, the lone psychological warfare squadron (the 5th ACS) of C–47s and U–10s at Nha Trang was unable to give enough attention to the entire country. In March 1967, the squadron was split in two, with a second squadron (the 9th ACS) taking over the two northern corps, while the 5th covered III and IV Corps.[92]

In May, the new squadron began replacing its U–10s with O–2Bs. By the end of the year, it had twenty-five of these new aircraft equipped with loudspeakers and leaflet dispensers, along with six C–47s for flare operations.[93] In April, the squadron's headquarters were moved to Pleiku. The planes there and at Nha Trang were for use with the Army and ARVN ground forces, and those at Da Nang supported the Marines, the Army, and the ARVN in the hostile I Corps. Except for some initial difficulties with loudspeaker drivers and unfamiliar radios, the O–2s adapted quickly to their new role. One of the first assignments for the new plane came during the national and provincial elections in September when the squadron dropped several million leaflets containing instructions on voting procedures for the South Vietnamese.[94] On other missions, they warned people of impending defoliation flights or exhorted enemy troops to lay down their arms and join the southerners. The loudspeaker and leaflet planes assisted in every major Marine and ARVN ground operation during the second half of the year, although the Marines preferred to use their own planes for flare drops.[95]

Another of the Nha Trang squadrons changed some of its equipment early in 1967. At the end of January, fourteen UH–1F Huey helicopters were flown from Thailand to rejoin their parent unit, the 20th Helicopter Squadron, whose headquarters were at Nha Trang. The helicopters had been in Thailand for almost a year training Thais in their fight against insurgents within their own country. Political pressure forced their move back to

An Air Force UH–1F with a 7.62-mm minigun in the doorway.

Vietnam. At Air Force headquarters, interest was high in keeping these aircraft, the only helicopter gunships in the Air Force, engaged in the war.[96]

When the Huey gunships first arrived back in Vietnam, they were without a mission but by mid-February were starting to fly covert missions out of Nha Trang, Tan Son Nhut, and Kontum for MACV's Studies and Observations Group (MACSOG).[97] Four Hueys, called Green Hornets, provided armed protection on some missions for troop-carrying CH–3C helicopters as they deposited or extracted friendly patrols in enemy areas both in Vietnam and Laos. In December, the unit at Kontum moved to Ban Me Thuot. It was missions of this unit that upset the Army staff, and several times during the early months of the year, activities were suspended until the rules were clarified.

Two other units at Nha Trang were supporting MACV's special operations group in 1967. One of these, the First Flight Detachment, flew 6 specially equipped Heavy Hook C–123s to insert, extract, and resupply agents in North Vietnam; deliver psychological warfare material; and provide logistic material for other MACSOG activities. Starting in 1964, the USAF trained 7 Chinese aircrews from Taiwan at the base to fly the planes. The following year, the planes inserted and resupplied 22 teams in the north, flew 30 psychological warfare missions, and delivered 656,000 pounds of MAC-SOG cargo. In 1966, they were joined briefly by some Vietnamese flyers and that year inserted 16 teams, flew 42 psyops missions, and delivered 5 million pounds of supplies. By early 1967, however, American flyers had taken over the operation, which reached a high that year of 23 insertions, 67 psyop flights, 11 million pounds of cargo, and 25,000 passengers.

To complement the C–123s, four C–130s, dubbed Combat Spear, began flying similar missions to support Shining Brass infiltration teams on the trails of Laos in December 1966. These planes formed a detachment of the 15th Special Operations Squadron.[98]

By the close of 1967, the Air Force was well on its way in Southeast Asia to having a new generation of air munitions and planes and to developing, largely through trial and error, successful tactics for using them. The equity the Air Force was building in low-scale, tactical warfare, however, was having an effect on its doctrine, both on the way it was developed and on content.

During the two decades since its creation in 1947, the Air Force had tended to construct its doctrine in a priori fashion, moving like an idealistic youth from general theories of air power to practical applications. Experience had played less a role in the formulation of doctrine than had ideology and conceptual frameworks concerning the nature of air power itself. However, worldwide events of the 1960s, particularly in Southeast Asia and the Middle East, were bringing about a more inductive process. In many ways, doctrine was changing during this decade from a preconceived philosophical expression to one that mirrored recent events.

More important, changes in the substance of doctrine were in the making in 1967, largely as a result of the Southeast Asia conflict. In the fifties, when America's nuclear arsenal was first challenged, the Air Force stressed the deterrent value of threatening a potential enemy with massive nuclear retaliation. This concept was reinforced throughout the decade as ballistic missiles and space vehicles were incorporated into successive revisions of the doctrine.[99] At the same time, confident that preparedness for general war was sufficient to forestall or win lesser forms of conflict, the theoreticians of doctrine minimized the need for air power specifically tailored for limited wars. Even the experience with limited warfare in Korea was dismissed by most as a temporary diversion from the true path of nuclear deterrence.[100] Notwithstanding some notable dissenters, including the tactical air commander Gen. Otto P. Weyland, Air Force doctrine reflected the prediction of former Army Chief of Staff Gen. Matthew B. Ridgway that "the days when wars had limited effects is past. War, if it comes again, will be total in character."[101]

The first break in this solid front of nuclear and general war thinking appeared in the Air Force's 1964 version of its doctrine,[102] inspired by the Soviet attainment of nuclear parity and the emphasis of the Kennedy and Johnson administrations on military forces that could fight at any level. The result was a recognition by the Air Force that it must be ready for combat at whatever level the national leaders decided was needed and that the Army, Navy, and Air Force would have to play more equal roles than they had in the past.[103] While nuclear superiority as an umbrella to deter general war remained the keystone of the doctrine, alongside it now appeared interest in finding ways to deter (or fight) wars of lesser scope. Although the 1964 doctrine recognized this concept of "flexible response" in a general way, it did little to flesh out the implications for air power in conflicts on levels lower than general nuclear war.

By 1967, the war in Vietnam was providing insights into the complexities of warfare on one of these levels—a conflict in which the goal was neither the total destruction of the enemy nor seizure of his territory but rather to discourage him from further adventures. Planners worked through the year to incorporate this new type of warfare into the Air Force's basic doctrine, but events were moving too rapidly and the implications were too pervasive to permit a definitive statement to emerge.

Yet policy pronouncements, those building blocks and mirrors of doctrine, uttered by Air Force leaders in late 1966 and 1967 suggested that a fundamental reexamination of basic concepts was taking place. In some cases, older ideas were brought into sharper focus; in others, they were augmented or even changed. The need to deter wars at every level, from local to nuclear, brought with it a new emphasis on close cooperation between air and ground forces, an air mission that had been muted since the Air Force's creation. In many ways, this development was a return to the thinking prevalent during World War II when, still part of the Army, the air arm looked upon ground and air forces as coequals.[104]

This newly refurbished idea became the common demoninator of statements made by Air Force leaders. "Virtually all military operations," said Secretary Brown, "either to deter or to fight a war, are joint in nature today. They require the special competence of each of the military services."[105] "Ground, naval, and air units are indispensably codependent," wrote the Air Force's Vice Chief of Staff. "At no other time in history have the military services operated so closely together as they are operating today, and in Vietnam there is no meaning to the question of who is supporting whom."[106]

Discussions of tactical air employment, whether for airlift, reconnaissance, interdiction, or close air support, echoed the theme that air assets made it possible for ground forces to fight successfully.[107] Being prepared to go in any one of several directions depended on having the right number and types of airlift planes, with a good system for controlling them, to deliver troops and equipment both worldwide and locally inside a war theater.[108] Recent experience with the Caribous in Vietnam was pushing tactical airlift doctrine in the direction of intimate cooperation with ground forces. This concept of airlift mobility, having little place in the nuclear doctrines of the past, was relatively new and was being forged from the experiences in Vietnam.

Interdiction in Vietnam was proving to be quite different than in earlier wars where the pressure of friendly ground troops contributed to forcing the enemy to consume his supplies and equipment. The absence of defined fronts in Vietnam, plus long amorphous international boundaries, granted the enemy both mobility and sanctuaries for replenishment. As a result, the concept of interdiction for this type of war was changing from one of weakening the enemy so that his subsequent contact with friendly forces would be ineffective to one of attempting to build an air barrier to seal off Vietnam itself from sanctuaries and outside aid.[109]

Likewise, the concept of close air support was changing to one of much closer integration with ground forces. Close air support in former wars had augmented the firepower of surface forces, but the use of the Army's airmobile division with its own aircraft in Vietnam was altering the concept. Instead of being superimposed on ground firepower as in the past, Air Force planes were now becoming an indispensable extension of the Army's own weapons, both air and ground.[110]

So close had become the integration of all these facets of air power with ground operations that General McConnell dismissed as myth the popularly held conception that the war in South Vietnam was a ground war.[111] To him it was an air-ground war in which the two elements of military power had become so closely linked that neither was primary nor either supportive; but these ideas were still in ferment in 1967, and it would be another four years before they would appear in published doctrinal form.

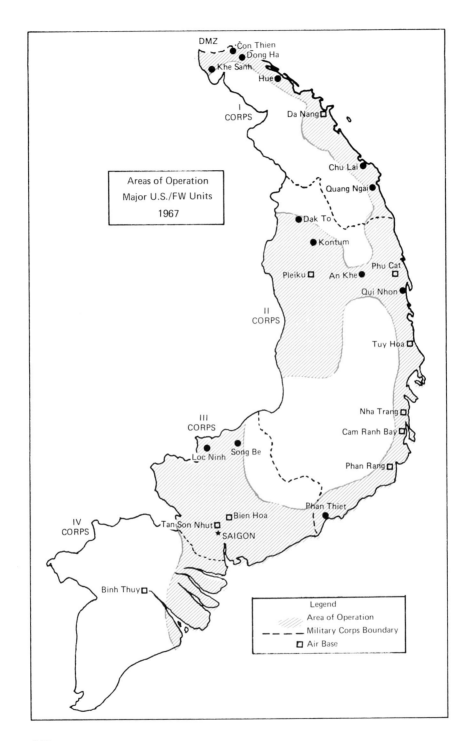

Areas of Operation
Major U.S./FW Units
1967

DMZ
Con Thien
Dong Ha
Khe Sanh
Hue

I
CORPS

Da Nang

Chu Lai
Quang Ngai

Dak To
Kontum
Phu Cat
Pleiku
An Khe
Qui Nhon

II
CORPS

Tuy Hoa

Nha Trang

III
CORPS

Cam Ranh Bay

Loc Ninh
Song Be

Phan Rang

Phan Thiet

IV
CORPS

Tan Son Nhut
Bien Hoa
SAIGON

Binh Thuy

Legend
Area of Operation
Military Corps Boundary
Air Base

Chapter X

Air Operations
January 1967–March 1968

Military operations in South Vietnam during 1967 appeared on the surface as reenactments of those of the previous year. In III Corps, U.S. and South Vietnamese troops continued to search out and destroy the enemy in the huge war zones north of Saigon. In the central highlands of II Corps, light screening forces were positioned along the Cambodian and Laotian borders as trip wires, to be reinforced by larger units when North Vietnamese regiments moved across the borders. A mobile riverine force, composed of a naval task force and elements of the U.S. 9th Infantry Division, was introduced into IV Corps. Two separate strategies were pursued in I Corps. In the southern portion, U.S. and South Vietnamese soldiers continued the expansion begun with Masher/White Wing the year before. In the northern reaches, the objective was to thwart the North Vietnamese invasion through the Demilitarized Zone and Laos and to neutralize enemy base areas in the coastal plain. The other side of the coin, the pacification effort, was centralized under MACV in May with creation of the Civil Operations and Revolutionary Development Support program.

Although the strategy changed little, the year's activities brought substantial refinement to the Air Force's already good working relations with the Army and the ARVN and produced further evidence that more stringent control was needed over the heterogeneous air activities in and around the Demilitarized Zone. In the course of the year, Air Force fighter-bombers and B–52s flew close air support missions in forty major ground operations* and

---

*See Appendix 6, USAF Support of Major Ground Operations, 1965–1967.

hundreds of smaller engagements. At the same time, they accelerated the pace of their interdiction missions to stanch the flow of enemy troops and supplies into the country.

The first major ground campaign of the year was waged against the Viet Cong's 9th Division, which had rebounded from the defeats of 1966 and was back at full strength in War Zone C. The initial phase in January was Cedar Falls, a two-division sweep of the Iron Triangle, 10 miles north of Saigon, which sheltered the enemy's Region IV headquarters and pointed like a dagger at the capital. For 3 weeks, allied forces walked through the area, foot by foot, destroying a huge network of base areas, tunnels, supply complexes, and training camps. The troops were supported by 1,100 tactical sorties and 102 raids by B–52s. Although the enemy chose to flee rather than fight, over 700 of them died, over 200 were captured, and close to a million pages of enemy documents were seized. Once the area was taken, bulldozers carved out landing zones and cleared a strip of land the length of the triangle as a jumping-off point for the next operations.[1]

In reporting on the operation, the air liaison officer with the 1st Infantry Division noted some familiar difficulties. Ground commanders still had too strong a tendency to request more planes than they needed and to call in immediate air strikes on targets that could have been better hit by artillery. In some instances, FACs were "badgered" by brigade personnel to find appropriate targets after the air strikes were approved and allocated.[2] A similar observation was made by the director of the air support center who remarked that "they seem to plan all operations on the amount of air strikes they can get, not the number of targets that are available."[3] This tendency towards excess posed two problems: not only were many sorties wasted, but aircraft often arrived carrying ordnance ill-suited to the targets.

A shortage of radio channels continued to plague the FACs. The three controllers, each working one of the division's brigades, had to share the same FM frequency, and it became overcrowded. In addition, the radio equipment on the Bird Dogs was still not totally compatible with that of the Army.

Once again, the after action reports made no distinction between those who succumbed to ground fire and those "killed by aircraft." All were listed generically as "killed in action." Ground commanders noted informally, however, that about half of those killed in Cedar Falls could be attributed to air action.[4]

These were problems that, theoretically at least, might not have arisen had the same agency controlled both the planes and the ground troops. To do so, however, was unacceptable to the Air Force, which preferred working on these individual problems to weakening the potency of air power by dividing it and attaching it to individual ground units.

Most of February was spent by the troops positioning themselves for the plunge into War Zone C. Three brigades of the 25th Infantry Division swept

Operation Junction City Operational Area

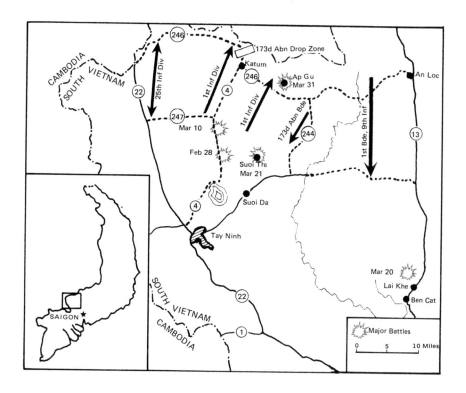

south and west of the zone along the Cambodian border in Operation Gadsden, while elements of the 1st Division, in Operation Tucson, moved along its eastern and northern edges. These movements were backed up by 678 tactical air strikes and 78 B–52 raids.

The main operation, called Junction City, got under way on the 22d of February. The objective of the first phase, scheduled to last until mid-March, was to seal off the northern part of Tay Ninh province along the Cambodian border, while the 1st and 25th Divisions swept northward through the central and western portions of the zone, respectively, squeezing the enemy between them.

At Bien Hoa, 845 troopers of the 173d Airborne Brigade boarded 16 C–130s and were dropped near the border in the first parachute assault of the war.[5] The soldiers moving up from the south made no contact with the enemy until the morning of the 28th, when a company of the 1st Infantry Division stumbled into a Viet Cong staging area east of Route 4. One U.S. platoon was

An F–100 flies through the smoke and debris of a secondary explosion during Operation Junction City, March 1967.

pinned down by several battalions and almost annihilated by a ground assault. The second platoon hastily formed a perimeter and fought back desperately. A forward air controller, diverted to the scene, arrived overhead within minutes and directed a flight of F–100s from Phan Rang against the enemy. Ten minutes later, two B–57s arrived from the same base and, with the Super Sabres, kept the enemy at bay while a relief column was organized. The fighters cleared out a landing zone nearby, and helicopters brought in two companies. At about the same time, three F–100s hit a large concentration of enemy troops attacking the trapped soldiers with napalm and 750-pound bombs.[6] The relief column linked up with the besieged platoon and together they made their way back to the landing zone under the cover of bombs, napalm, and CBUs as the U.S. planes forced the enemy to break contact.[7]

U.S. and South Vietnamese soldiers continued their sweep northward up Route 4. Unopposed by major enemy forces, they unearthed dozens of base areas. On the night of March 10, two enemy battalions, possibly seeking to divert the Americans from attacking their main headquarters elsewhere in the war zone, mortared a U.S. artillery post 18 miles north of Tay Ninh City near Route 4. After 20 minutes of shelling, they attacked from opposite sides. An AC–47 lit up the battlefield with strings of flares, then strafed the tree line along the eastern edge of the post. A FAC was scrambled from the small airstrip at Suoi Da, a nearby Special Forces camp, and was soon directing 4 F–100s as they pummeled the advancing troops with napalm, CBUs, and 20-mm cannon fire. This strong air reaction, coupled with ground artillery, broke the back of the attack, which was reduced to sniper fire by the next morning. Nearly 200 Viet Cong and 3 U.S. soldiers died in the 4-hour engagement.[8]

By the end of the first phase of Junction City on March 17, the Air Force had flown 69 B–52 sorties and made 1,541 preplanned and 453 immediate tactical strikes. During the second phase, which lasted from March 18 through April 14, the troops concentrated on the eastern portion of the zone. The Air Force added another 2,000 fighter-bomber and 7 B–52 sorties. On 3 occasions the enemy chose to stand and fight, and 3 times the combination of air strikes and artillery repulsed him.

In the first of these encounters, just after midnight on March 20, a 1,000-man Viet Cong regiment opened up a mortar attack against a U.S. company of 160 men guarding an artillery fire support base 5 miles north of Lai Khe. The tanks and armored personnel carriers were formed in a circle with their guns pointed outward; and from the hatch of a carrier, the commander radioed for a flare ship and armed helicopters. Guns from the armored vehicles and artillery broke the enemy's first assault, driving them back into a nearby rubber plantation. The fighting remained heavy, and at two in the morning, the commander called for air support. An O–1 from Lai Khe appeared within 5 minutes, and 2 F–100s were quickly scrambled from the alert pad at Bien Hoa. When the enemy attacked the second time, the ground commander played his tanks' searchlights on the soldiers to point out the target to the FAC. The two Super Sabres caught the Viet Cong in the open with napalm and CBUs. They again withdrew into the plantation and began directing heavy fire against the perimeter and the attacking planes. Four more flights arrived at intervals, strafing and bombing the enemy until the battle subsided. At daybreak, 227 enemy bodies were strewn around the perimeter, while 3 U.S. soldiers and a pilot had been killed. During the 5-hour battle, 17 F–100s and 2 F–4s were involved, flareships worked through the night, and three FAC sorties were flown.[9]

On the following day, a spectacular battle erupted near Suoi Tre, a cluster of huts 19 miles north of Tay Ninh, at a U.S. fire support base carved out two days earlier to support the second phase of Junction City. Twenty-five hundred Viet Cong soldiers opened up a mortar attack on the base and its 450 men at half past six on the morning of the 21st. Then they attacked. The 17 artillery pieces slowed down but did not stop the enemy, who broke through the southeastern side of the perimeter. A Bird Dog arrived from Dau Tieng at seven and, within minutes, was directing a flight of F–5s that dropped bombs and napalm on the tree line opposite the perimeter. When the F–5s were finished, the Bird Dog came down to estimate the results. As it descended, the plane flew into a hail of machinegun bullets, its left wing disintegrated, and the plane plummeted to the ground, killing the pilot.

Initially without air support, the U.S. soldiers cranked down their artillery pieces and fired point blank into the advancing enemy's ranks. Still the Viet Cong moved forward. One by one the big guns fell silent, either knocked out by satchel charges or drained of ammunition. A second FAC arrived and concentrated a flight of F–100s in bombing along the edge of the jungle. "There must have been 500 of them coming at me," one of the soldiers later recalled, "and this guy laid napalm right in on top of them and then I didn't see them anymore."[10]

The FAC's job was made more difficult by the overcast with its ragged bottom at 1,000 feet and air congestion over the embattled landing zone. At least 4 O–1s and 9 helicopters were in tight orbit over the base. The FAC flew up above the overcast and brought down 3 F–4s that bombed and strafed the enemy. The Viet Cong drive began to falter. A line of U.S. tanks crashed through the jungle and swept around the perimeter, destroying enemy resistance. The Viet Cong fled back into the jungle, pursued by fighter-bombers dropping napalm on them. By half past one in the afternoon, the battle was over. One-sixth of the 654 Viet Cong bodies discovered on the battlefield were officially credited to air strikes, but once again this figure was arbitrary.

Coordination and cooperation between air strikes and artillery had been superb and saved the day. As the tanks rolled against the fleeing enemy, fighter-bombers paved their way by dropping cluster bombs a hundred yards ahead of the armored vehicles.[11] The battle was a major defeat for the Viet Cong's crack 272d Regiment.

The final major encounter during Junction City began on the last day of March three miles south of the Cambodian border in the northern part of the war zone. During a search and destroy mission near the town of Ap Gu, a U.S. battalion was helilifted, unknowingly, into the midst of the enemy's 271st Regiment. When two of the battalion's companies fanned out from their helicopters, they were met with heavy fire from trenches just inside the nearby woods. Withering machinegun, rifle, and antitank rocket fire pinned them down in serious trouble. Bombs and napalm from two F–100s relieved the pressure enough to allow them to withdraw with their wounded. The enemy pursued, leaving their prepared positions in an attempt to outflank the retreating U.S. soldiers. In doing so, they were drawn into the open where two more flights of F–100s struck them. They fled back into the jungle, prodded by strikes from a third flight of Super Sabres.[12]

Tactical aircraft continued to hit the enemy throughout the day as the U.S. force was augmented with two more companies. During the night, the Viet Cong regrouped and struck the landing zone with mortar fire at five the next morning. An hour later, a large ground assault across the open field between the jungle and the perimeter was met by a flight of F–100s. The forward air controller described what happened:

It was still pretty dark down there. We couldn't see anything except tracers going all over the place. We dove down through it and dropped a smoke grenade right in the middle of the area. Then we began walking the napalm towards the perimeter. We put it in at seventy-five meters, then two more at fifty meters, and finally the fourth went in about twenty-five meters from our troops. Then we strung CBU all across the clearing. We continued to make CBU runs until they ran out. Then we had them give a general hose down with strafe as we slipped in the next flight. This one had napalm and bombs which we put on the same outcropping of woods where the attack was coming from.[13]

The first air strike brought the enemy attack to a halt, the second turned it into a rout. "By 0750," the brigade commander reported, "the VC attackers were in full retreat as the full might of U.S. close air was brought to bear."[14]

Repulsed on the northeast side of the perimeter, the Viet Cong shifted their attack to the other side. Prevented by the direction of the artillery fire from bringing his fighters in from the east, the forward air controller had to fly them over the base into the sun. The combination of napalm, bombs, CBUs, and rockets once again stopped the enemy. Throughout the day, sixty-two F–100s, six B–57s, five F–5s, and four F–4s dropped more than a hundred tons of ordnance around the landing zone.[15]

In the afternoon, three B–52s struck likely withdrawal routes midway between the landing zone and the Cambodian border.[16] The enemy suffered another major defeat, losing over 600 soldiers, while 17 Americans died. Over 15,000 rounds of U.S. artillery melded with 103 tactical air sorties in a well-orchestrated repulse of a determined enemy. When later asked at what time he sensed the see-saw battle had shifted in his favor, the battalion commander, Lt. Col. Alexander M. Haig replied, "With the arrival of the air, tactical air, and especially the ordnance, the CBU ordnance was the main factor."[17]

Junction City was scheduled to end on the 14th of April, but the success of the first 2 phases prolonged it for another month. Until mid-May, U.S. soldiers carried on operations as a mobile brigade force in the lower portions of War Zone C, but contact with the enemy was sporadic. Air Force fighter-bombers flew 5,002 sorties in the operation; and B–52s, for the first time supporting a major ground operation with preplanned sorties, added 126 more. Over 2,000 airlift sorties moved 17,500 passengers and 11,300 tons of cargo into and around War Zone C. Reconnaissance planes photographed 89 targets for strikes.* The Americans suffered 282 killed; the enemy nearly 10 times as many (2,728). After one-third of its men had perished, the 9th VC Division fled eastward into War Zone D, but the 7th VC Division soon took its place.

---

*See Appendix 6, USAF Support of Major Ground Operations, 1965–1967.

B–52s and KC–135s lined up at U Tapao, Thailand, in May 1967.

After completing their Junction City mission on the 10th of April, 3 of the B–52s from Guam landed at U Tapao in Thailand, the forerunners of a contingent of bombers that would use that base until the end of the war. The Thai government had given its approval in March; and by July, 15 of the bombers were in place. U Tapao was a forward operating base from Guam, where the missions were scheduled. Typically, a bomber would depart Guam, fly its mission, land at U Tapao, fly 8 missions from there, launch from Thailand on its next mission, and return to Andersen. By March, the big bombers were flying 800 sorties a month. When 15 of the B–52s were operating from U Tapao, 450 of these sorties originated from Thailand, the remainder from Guam. The decrease in the number of missions from the island base released 11 of the Stratoforts that SAC wanted to return to the states. The Air Force, however, held up the move pending the outcome of a request from General Westmoreland to increase the sortie rate to 1,200 a month.[18]

Secretary McNamara did not approve the new higher sortie rate until November. The decision was delayed by Westmoreland's difficulty in justifying the increase and by the Air Force in determining the best way to implement it. At no time since the Arc Light bombings began in June 1965 did the MACV Commander indicate that a certain level of effort was adequate to do the job. As monthly sortie rates rose from 300 in 1965 to 450 the following August, then to 600 in December and to 800 in March 1967 (table 10), the number of planes increased from 30 to 50 to 61. Unable to be specific about the results of the B–52 strikes,[19] Westmoreland justified each of these increases with the argument that with more sorties, he could attack a greater variety of targets and satisfy a larger number of requests. McNamara had routinely approved the hikes; but by early 1967, SAC was concerned

Table 10

Arc Light Sorties
June 1965–March 1968

		North Vietnam	South Vietnam	Laos	Total
1965	Jun		27		27
	Jul		140		140
	Aug		165		165
	Sep		322		322
	Oct		291		291
	Nov		310		310
	Dec		283	24	307
			1,538	24	1,562
1966	Jan		347	24	371
	Feb		274	39	313
	Mar		332	66	398
	Apr	44	261	112	417
	May		309	102	411
	Jun		330	65	395
	Jul		413	18	431
	Aug		411	39	450
	Sep	93	292	48	433
	Oct	57	286	65	408
	Nov		504	27	531
	Dec	86	531	42	659
		280	4,290	647	5,217
1967	Jan	6	615	112	733
	Feb		630	76	706
	Mar		599	211	810
	Apr	18	485	320	823
	May	26	686	96	808
	Jun		671	161	832
	Jul	30	600	206	836
	Aug	120	596	116	832
	Sep	432	401		833
	Oct	386	424	39	849
	Nov	117	568	131	816
	Dec	229	336	243	808
		1,364	6,611	1,711	9,686
1968	Jan	15	675	231	921
	Feb		1,299	160	1,459
	Mar	35	1,633	184	1,852
		50	3,607	575	4,232
	Total	1,694	16,046	2,957	20,697

Source: JCS STRATOPS, January 1965–December 1966 and
SAC COACT, January 1967–March 1968.

with the impact Arc Light was having on its ability to maintain its full worldwide nuclear alert. The Joint Chiefs scrutinized more carefully the request for 1,200 sorties. Westmoreland pointed to the increased use of B–52s against infiltration routes in northern South Vietnam and Laos and to the additional support he had been able to provide his ground commanders in South Vietnam. He argued that, in Cedar Falls and Junction City, he had been able for the first time to commit the bombers ahead of time to major ground operations.[20]

Several plans to accommodate the new sortie rate were examined by SAC and the Air Force, including placing bombers on Okinawa and Taiwan, in addition to those already on Guam and in Thailand. Political sensitivity scuttled the idea of bombers at the first two sites, and it was decided to rely on Guam and Thailand with a buildup by mid-1968 of fifty-two bombers at the former base and twenty-five at the latter. Tankers would support them from Guam, Thailand, Okinawa, and Taiwan—two, thirty, forty-four, and fifteen respectively.[21]

While Junction City was still in progress, General Momyer sent a strongly worded letter to his wing commanders urging them to double their efforts to prevent accidental attacks (short rounds) on friendly troops or civilians.[22] While errors of this kind are endemic in warfare, the situation in Vietnam contained several factors conducive to bombing errors. The absence of clearly discernible bomb lines created a fluid environment in which it was not always possible to distinguish friendly from enemy forces. From the air, all soldiers looked alike and guerrillas were indistinguishable from noncombatants. Particularly frustrating was the enemy tactic of maneuvering as closely as possible to friendly forces to avoid devastation from the air. The use of jets in such a relatively compact area called for unusually strict attention to detail to avoid hitting friendly Vietnamese. The extraordinary propaganda value to the enemy of even the smallest error added to the pressures for accuracy.

Top leaders in Vietnam were acutely sensitive to the potentialities in this environment for accidental loss of life. General Westmoreland's philosophy that "one mishap, one innocent civilian killed, one civilian wounded or one dwelling needlessly destroyed, is one too many"[23] was embodied in stringent rules of engagement for using artillery, tanks, mortars, naval gunfire, aircraft, and armed helicopters. The voluntary limits that Americans placed on air power in South Vietnam reflected its status as an instrument of the Vietnamese government's policy. Consequently, the approval of a province chief or of a higher Vietnamese authority was the basic requirement for an air strike. Strike aircraft had to be directed either by a forward air controller or by radar. In cases where this was impossible, the commander of a ground unit or the pilot of the plane supporting the unit could designate the target. Exceptions were made for strikes in specified strike zones where there were no friendly forces or populace. In these zones, pilots could use their own judgment in hitting targets.

One set of rules governed attacks on villages and hamlets; a more stringent set controlled strikes in urban areas. Strikes on hamlets and villages always had to receive prior clearance and be controlled by a forward air controller. If the strikes supported a ground action, planes were to warn the inhabitants by either leaflets or loudspeakers in sufficient time to allow them to leave the area, but the ground commander could dispense with this warning if he judged that it would jeopardize the mission. Attacks in urban areas required higher level clearance, and leaflets and loudspeakers had to warn the civilians in all cases. Aircraft could not use incendiaries unless friendly survival was at stake.

Detailed, often constraining, rules were in force to prevent short rounds. Forward air controllers were to have thorough knowledge of the ground scheme of maneuver and had to receive the ground commander's clearance before directing strikes. The ground forces were responsible for marking their own positions before each strike. The forward air controller had to mark the target and receive confirmation from the ground commander that the mark was accurate.

Pilots were enjoined from flying over populated areas when armed, and all armament switches had to be placed in the "safe" position until the plane entered the target area. Aircraft could jettison munitions only in designated areas, except during inflight emergencies, and had to be under positive radar control when jettisoning. Whenever possible, pilots were to jettison ordnance over water within or near the target area. They could fire on religious monuments or public buildings only after a senior brigade or higher commander determined that the enemy was hiding inside. Even then they had to use weapons that would keep damage to a minimum.

Special rules guided air activity near South Vietnam's borders. In the Demilitarized Zone, planes could strike only clearly defined military targets. Pilots could not cross over the Cambodian border without specific authorization from MACV. All strikes within three miles of the border had to be tracked by radar and be closely controlled by either a forward air controller or Skyspot, and all operations planned near the Laotian border had to be reported in advance to MACV.[24]

Despite the greatest of human concern and attempts at prevention, there were some short rounds. The occasion for Momyer's admonition was a particularly unfortunate incident at the small village of Lang Vei near the

Laotian border three miles west of the Marine outpost of Khe Sanh in I Corps. On March 2, 1967, 2 F–4Cs from Da Nang were flying an armed reconnaissance mission in Laos just west of Lang Vei. After determining their position to be 20 miles inside Laos by both radio and visual identification of river, road, and mountain landmarks, the pilots dropped their CBUs, 500-pound bombs, and rockets along a road that seemed a likely sanctuary for enemy trucks.[25] Unfortunately, they had misread the radio bearing and had been misled by ground features almost identical to those in the target area. The ordnance fell in the center of Lang Vei, killing 100 Vietnamese civilians and wounding 250. Civic action teams and American aircraft spent the night evacuating the wounded. Only on the following day, when they were flown over both Lang Vei and the intended target area in Laos, did the pilots realize their error.[26]

Lang Vei was the most serious air short round in the 2 years jets had been used in the country. In 1965, Air Force planes had committed 14 miscues. Since they had flown 45,709 sorties that expended ordnance in South Vietnam and Laos in 1965, the error rate was one for each 3,265 sorties. The following year, as familiarity with the environment increased, the rate dropped to one in 5,035 sorties (21 incidents in 105,745 sorties). The short round at Lang Vei was the third in 1967.

There was no single cause for these incidents. Most resulted from a series of factors, some correctable, others not. Some accidents, such as that at Lang Vei, were due to navigational error. Others occurred when pilots were given the wrong coordinates for their targets. On several occasions, for example, ground commanders in the heat of battle provided pilots their own coordinates rather than those of the enemy.[27] Sometimes target coordinates were inadvertently transposed on the ground and passed erroneously to the flyers. Equipment malfunctions accounted for other short rounds. Occasionally, a faulty bomb-release mechanism would cause ordnance to hang for several seconds after the other bombs were dropped, causing it to fall in populated areas.[28] Unfamiliarity with the characteristics of ordnance by ground commanders at times led to errors. The CBU–2A, for example, was a deadly antipersonnel weapon that dispensed 400 fragmentation bomblets from an external pod. Bomblets occasionally hung in the tube, creating a "dribble factor" that resulted in a longer than normal string of exploding bombs. On several instances where the ground commander was unaware of this trait, friendly troops found themselves in the path of such a string of bomblets.[29] Incomplete communication between the ground and the air, as well as faulty or delayed intelligence as to the exact position of friendly forces, led to a number of short rounds. Very few accidental bombings could be traced to unprofessional performance on the part of the pilots.

In admonishing the flyers, the Seventh Air Force Commander reflected the statement of General McConnell, "When in doubt, don't deliver."[30] The

Air Force experienced 24 more short rounds in the remainder of 1967, which, with 157,000 sorties, amounted to one in each 5,851 sorties.

In the closing days of Junction City, the Army pulled one of its main units, the 196th Light Infantry Brigade, out of the campaign and moved it into the northern I Corps where it gradually joined with two other brigades to form an Army division, the reactivated 23 Infantry (the Americal). In the period between early morning on April 9 and sunset on April 14, Air Force C–130s flew the 196th's 3,500 men and 4,000 tons of equipment the 300 miles from Tay Ninh to Chu Lai, while heavier equipment traveled north in Navy LSTs. The next month, the planes helped move the remaining 2 Army brigades and, in one 48-hour period, airlifted 1,200 Marines and 300 tons of their equipment from Okinawa to Dong Ha, just below the Demilitarized Zone.[31] This was the first step of a gradual move of Army units into the northern provinces, but by early the following year, U.S. Army troops would outnumber the Marines in I Corps by half.

The occasion for this first introduction of Army forces into the northern corps was a resumption early in 1967 of the North Vietnamese threat of invasion through and around the Demilitarized Zone. The battles of 1966 against these enemy divisions were but a prelude to much heavier fighting the following year. Operations Hastings, Prairie, and Tally Ho had temporarily checked the enemy's invasion; but the North Vietnamese, holding to a strategy of attempting to draw U.S. troops from the populated southern regions of the country, had turned the northern half of the DMZ into a vast armed camp by early 1967. Interdiction strikes at the enemy's rear in Tally Ho were reduced during the rainy winter months; and by the time good weather returned in the spring, many of the enemy had filtered back into Quang Tri Province. As many as 58,000 were dug deeply into the province's western jungles. In response, more Marines were rushed from southern to northern I Corps, their place in the southern half of the corps taken by Army units.

The Marines struck first, late in April, against the Communists dug in around their western base at Khe Sanh. As Air Force C–130s and C–123s flew food and ammunition into the isolated outpost, two Marine battalions drove two regiments of the 325th Division off the hills surrounding Khe Sanh, putting them out of action for several months.

Defeated in the west, the North Vietnamese then shifted to the east, with a series of attacks against Con Thien, the Marine post two miles below the DMZ that commanded the main infiltration corridors through the zone.

Operation Hickory Operational Area and the DMZ Area

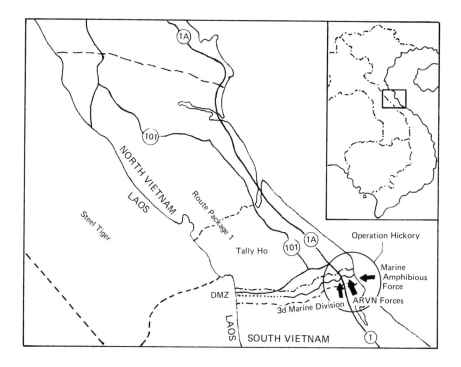

MACV answered with Operation Hickory, the most ambitious assault of the war to that time and the first U.S. ground venture into the Demilitarized Zone.

On the 17th of May, the day before the ground forces entered the zone, B–52s and tactical planes carried out an extensive softening-up operation. The following day, Marine and ARVN units swept through the southern part of the zone, while a Marine amphibious force tried to create a diversionary landing on the zone's eastern coast. Supported by artillery, naval gunfire, tactical fighter-bombers, and large B–52 raids, the ground forces struck at the enemy for 11 days, killing 780 of them and temporarily blunting the offensive.[32]

During the planning for Hickory and in its early stages, coordination was poor between the participating organizations—the III Marine Amphibious Force and its air arm (the I Marine Aircraft Wing), the Seventh Air Force, and MACV. Several months earlier, the Marines had moved their artillery pieces closer to the zone and were lobbing shells across it into the Air

Force's Tally Ho area. Since Marine doctrine endowed the ground commander with control of all supporting artillery and air strikes that affected his troops, the Marine commander on the 13th of May asked for control over all aircraft operating within range of his artillery, including the Tally Ho area. The next day, a team of Seventh Air Force officials traveled to Phu Bai and worked out a verbal agreement with the Marines that allowed the Air Force to keep control in Tally Ho and move its interdiction strikes down to the zone's midline, the Ben Hai River. The Marines would support their own forces, including the landing force, south of the river with their own aircraft.[33] Despite this agreement, the Marine air wing two days later issued an order setting up a Marine air control center to direct all air support, not only in the Demilitarized Zone, but in Tally Ho as well.[34] Neither the air wing's parent organization (III MAF) nor MACV had yet to assign operating areas. That same afternoon MACV did so, nullifying both earlier arrangements by giving the entire zone to the Marines and the area north of the zone to the Seventh Air Force.[35]

Confusion still existed when the operation got under way on the 18th. As the Marines swept into the southern part of the zone, the Marine commander, without coordinating with the Seventh Air Force, directed Air Force FACs to strike the enemy just north of the Ben Hai river. When the Air Force's command and control plane, Hillsboro, arrived on the scene, it invoked MACV's directive and ordered the FACs out of the zone and to its north, withdrawing interdiction support from the Marines who had reached the river. It took three days to clear this matter up so that Air Force units could support the Marines within the zone.

The failure to firm up operational concepts until the day before the operation was launched generated other problems. The Seventh Air Force originally planned to include naval carrier planes with its own fighters in its preparatory strikes on the 17th, but the Marines did not announce a firm date for launching the ground assault until the 16th, too late to coordinate the Navy's strikes. The Seventh Air Force had to take up the slack, requiring major last-minute schedule changes. When the carrier planes joined the fray the next day, they arrived without target information. There had not been time to get the target materials to the carrier, and the Navy pilots had to rely on FACs and Skyspot to find their targets. The delayed announcement also prevented proper integration of the timing of these Navy flights, tied to their carrier launch cycles, with the Air Force fighter bombers. As a result, a deluge of Air Force and Navy planes descended on Hillsboro and the FACs on the 18th, severely taxing their capacity to control them. Many had to be turned away to other areas.[36]

After the initial indecision about whether Navy or Marine aircraft should support the landing operation, it was decided that the Marines should support their own troops. The operation was kept so secret, however, that the

Marine air control agency did not learn of it until after the force had landed and frantically called for emergency air support to get them out of trouble.[37]

The secrecy surrounding the operation also complicated life for the forward air controllers at Dong Ha, who were the key to the air strikes. The 20th TASS at Dong Ha supplied the FACs, intelligence, and the Hillsboro plane; and as late as the 16th, no one there was aware of the impending operation or that one hundred additional sorties were being scheduled into their area the following morning.[38] One of the FACs had heard rumors of the operation while on a trip to Da Nang on the 15th, but critical planning for it was left up to the operational troops. The Air Force and the Marine air control agencies were unable to help, each having learned little of the operation. Representatives of the three units (two Air Force, one Marine) met at Dong Ha late on the 16th and, unaware of what was transpiring at higher headquarters, spent the night working out a plan to control the next day's fighters. At three in the morning, the first word came from MACV informing the FACs that they would be controlled by Hillsboro rather than by the ground control units. The night's work at Dong Ha went for naught.

Operation Hickory pointed up the drawbacks of divided control once again and impressed on many military leaders in Saigon the need for a single control point to manage aircraft flying in a complex military operation. However, the Air Force's interdiction role in South Vietnam and in the extended battlefields around its perimeter had been formally recognized by an important change to the reporting system early in 1967. In February, at the Air Force's urging, the Joint Chiefs relieved the Air Force of the requirement to report direct air support sorties and replaced that category with air interdiction for use in the daily operational reports. The chiefs noted that direct air support was not an official JCS category of air action. In approving the substitution, interdiction was defined as "air operations conducted to destroy, neutralize, or delay the enemy's potential before it can be brought to bear effectively against friendly forces, at such distance from friendly forces that detailed integration of each air mission with the fire and movement of friendly forces is not required."[39] The problem that had kept this important category out of the reporting system up to this point, namely, the idea that all flights in South Vietnam were integrated with ground action, was neatly circumvented by including "detailed" in the new definition. The Air Force began reporting the more familiar and useful categories that reflected what it was doing. By exception, the Marines were allowed to continue to report direct air support sorties. The new system went into effect on the first of

An F–100F and the refueling boom of a KC–135 over Vietnam in June 1967.

April and, after a month of adaptation, direct air support sorties virtually disappeared from the Air Force's reports.*[40]

Even before Hickory, the Air Force had stepped up its interdiction campaign north of the Demilitarized Zone in Tally Ho (table 11). When bad weather arrived the previous October, most of the fighter-bombers were shifted to Steel Tiger, an interdiction area in Laos west of the DMZ; but when the rains ended early in 1967, the planes returned in force to Tally Ho. The most important and heavily defended roads, particularly Route 101, lay in the eastern portion of the Tally Ho area, where the O–1s could no longer safely fly. As the summer bombing campaign gained momentum at the end of May, the Seventh Air Force began to experiment with jet aircraft as FACs in those portions of Tally Ho where the light observation planes could not go.

The two-seat F–100F was chosen for the new program, since it could carry an observer in addition to the pilot. Two squadrons of Super Sabres had just occupied the new base at Phu Cat; and the new unit, called the Misty FACS,* was set up as a detachment of one of them. Since they were not a separate unit, planes and pilots had to be borrowed from those already in the country. Seven F–100Fs were located and flown to the base, while fighter pilots were borrowed for four-month periods from other F–100 units at Phu Cat, Tuy Hoa, and Phan Rang. The planes were modified to carry two

---

*See Appendix 5, USAF Tactical Sorties in South Vietnam, 1965–1967.
*The program's formal name was Commando Sabre. The controllers were universally called Misty FACs, however, from their call sign.

Table 11

Compendium of Strikes in Tally Ho Area
January 26 – August 30, 1967

Week*	Sorties Strike	Sorties VR/FAC	Structs Dest	Structs Dmgd	Bridges Dest	Bridges Dmgd	Watercraft Dest	Watercraft Dmgd	Trucks Dest	Trucks Dmgd	Gun Posns Dest	Gun Posns Dmgd	Secondary Expls	Secondary Fires	Road Cuts	SAMs
1	295	28									4	12	15			
2	373	32	1								6	10			13	
3	262	35						2		(stand down—results not reported)						
4	600	37		33	2	1	10	25		1	9	6	18		12	
5	556	26					15	5	1	3			2		6	
6	517	25		5	1	2	5					8	13		10	
7	531	29	2	1					5	1			18		4	
8	659	39		26					1	3		3	26		19	
9	565	34	29	23	1	1	10	21				1	16		24	
10	577	77	9	14		3		1		1			42		21	
11	400	53	2	17	2	3							17		22	
12	308	40		4	1	3		7	2	4		1			23	
13	370	55		2	1	4	1			7		10	24		22	
14	443	93		58	1	1	2			32		15	59		29	
15	276	69	13	34	2	1		2		11		5	32		39	

Week*	Sorties		Structs		Bridges		Watercraft		Trucks		Gun Posns		Secondary		Road	SAMs
	Strike	VR/FAC	Dest	Dmgd	Dest	Dmgd	Dest	Dmgd	Dest	Dmgd	Dest	Dmgd	Expls	Fires	Cuts	
16	519	84	1	7	1	3	4	17	10	15	2	9	27		11	
17	655	89		17	1				5	12	17	58	48		29	
18	375	79		49	3	1	5	18	3	8	5	21	53		52	
19	370	80	1	10	2	3	8	13	2	9	8	7	39		22	
20	301	74		7		3		3	4	6	3	26	30		29	
21	479	121		19		3		5	1	4	9	9	29		23	
22	268	87	5	18	1	5	3	4	3	14	2	13	68		37	
23	193	140	19	27	2	2			1	5	3	10	54		31	
24	330	180	4	18	1	2	4	6	2	10	3	24	97		31	1
25	241	83		19	3	3	5	22		10	2	6	77		38	
26	191	62		9	7	12	20	42	2	6	4	12	23		59	
27	287	74	1	19	4	2	3	7	28	46	7	26	322	438	29	
28	259	64		15	3	1	5	11	6	8	8	17	83	452	33	
29	276	48		12		2	2	5	15	31	2	8	203	472	15	
30	282	44	13	34	6	4			8			30	70	181	27	
31	389	50	17	21	6	8	5	5	2	8			39	85	56	
Total†	12,147	2,031	117	518	51	49	102	221	101	255	91	342	1,554	1,628	766	1

*Beginning January 26, 1967.
†Totals reported.

external fuel tanks, two internally mounted 20-mm cannon, and two launchers that could fire fourteen rockets. Only the broadest guidance was provided for the program, allowing the pilots to develop procedures as the situation dictated. Because the pilots dealt directly with the scheduling shop in Saigon, they were able to experiment with various schedules to determine which was the most effective.

The first flights took place on June 28, and for a week, the Misty FACs went unopposed. They encountered ground fire for the first time on July 5 and from then on were fired at on half of their missions. During July, the first full month of operations, they flew 82 missions and controlled 126 strikes, mostly by F–105s and F–4s. The jet FACs gradually developed a mission profile that remained basic for the remainder of the war. Each day they flew 2 staggered missions of 2 aircraft each, with the second aircraft arriving an hour after the first. By refueling in midair, each pair of planes could perform visual reconnaissance and control strikes for 4 hours. By July, the Tally Ho area was under surveillance from seven to eleven each morning and from two until six each afternoon. Because of the jet's speed, the FACs could also arrive quickly at the scene of downed airmen and soon added search and rescue operations to their other functions.

As the summer wore on, it became evident that the jet FACs were identifying many more targets than the jet fighter pilots on armed reconnaissance missions had been finding. The latter were limited by the amount of fuel they could carry and their lack of formal training in visual reconnaissance. Soon the strike pilots were taking orientation rides with the Misty FACs and learning how much they had been missing. A later evaluation of the program showed that more than twice as many targets were struck on missions where jet FACs were present as when the strike pilots had to locate their own targets.[41]

One of the important questions about the program when it started was whether jet aircraft could perform visual reconnaissance. These early flights showed that they could. Visibility was excellent from both seats of the F–100F, and the pilot could easily use a hand-held 35-mm camera to supplement his visual sightings. The plane could remain over its area for fifty minutes between refuelings and was highly maneuverable at high speeds and low altitudes.

While these factors assured the continuation of the program, several drawbacks of the Super Sabre led to a search for an even more suitable aircraft. Not enough F–100Fs were available, and they were scheduled to be phased out of the inventory by 1970. The plane's engine was not powerful enough to evade antiaircraft artillery nor for the climb maneuvers required to deliver marking rockets. Pilots frequently were forced to boost their speed by using afterburners. Coupled with a very high use rate of eighty hours a month, this resulted in high maintenance and out-of-commission rates.

The F–4, which was more powerful and available in greater numbers, was considered as a replacement for the F–100F, but experiments early the next year revealed disadvantages. Visibility from the rear seat of the Phantom was poor. Its fuel consumption at the low altitudes was greater than that of the F–100, and it required more rather than less refueling. Its turn radius was greater than that of the Super Sabre, and staying close to the target increased its fuel consumption even more, further reducing the time it could stay in the area. The tests showed that the F–4 was suitable, but not clearly superior to the F–100.

At the same time, many factors favored moving the jet FAC operation to Da Nang, where it would be closer to the operating area. Although Phu Cat had full F–100 maintenance facilities and personnel, this was offset by the many advantages of the northern base. By flying from Da Nang, the planes would have an additional hour over the target and inflight refueling could also be reduced. Most important, the intelligence operation at Da Nang was geared toward the Tally Ho region, whereas at Phu Cat the main mission, and consequently the intelligence program, concentrated on South Vietnam. However, the ultimate decision, made early in 1968, was to keep the Misty FACs at Phu Cat and open a second jet FAC unit, with F–4s, at Da Nang.[42]

By July, the North Vietnamese had set their strategy for the coming year. They and the Viet Cong would filter into the southern cities where, during the coming February Tet holidays, they would incite uprisings aimed at bringing the populace over to their side. To mask the plan, they would continue to draw U.S. and ARVN forces away from the urban areas. They would do this by increasing their shelling of the Marine outposts south of the Demilitarized Zone as long as the weather permitted and then, with the advent of the northeast monsoon in October, shift their attacks to border posts in the drier jungles of II and III Corps. Besides creating diversions, these assaults on the border camps would serve to sharpen their troops and, if successful, remove some of the obstacles to their infiltration from Laos.[43]

The artillery duel that followed Hickory picked up intensity during the late summer. The enemy increased his bombardment of the Marine posts at Con Thien, Dong Ha, and Gio Linh during July and August until, by early September, over 1,000 rounds were hitting these positions each day. The Marines were at a disadvantage with fixed artillery pieces facing the mobile and shifting weapons of the enemy firing at them from within the Demilitarized Zone and the Tally Ho area.

On the 11th of September, the Seventh Air Force mounted a major air bombardment campaign, called Neutralize, to destroy this artillery and its supporting equipment and munitions. The locations of the enemy's artillery and antiaircraft guns were constantly fed to a centralized intelligence task force, with the information coming from high- and low-level air reconnaissance, night infrared flights, Army OV–1 planes with side-looking radar, aircraft with radio direction-finding equipment, and visual reconnaissance by FACs and strike pilots.

Once again, a myriad of air and ground firepower converged on a small area. Air Force strike planes flew out of Phu Cat, Cam Ranh Bay, Da Nang, and Ubon Air Bases. Other strike planes were diverted when needed from northern bombing missions. The Misty FACs did much of the controlling in Tally Ho, some Air Force Covey O–2 FACs from Da Nang patrolled inside the Demilitarized Zone, and Army OV–1s joined the reconnaissance effort along the coast. Marine FACs and strike planes from Da Nang and Chu Lai attacked in and below the zone, while the Marines in I Corps and naval ships offshore poured shells into the Neutralize area.[44] Above all of this flew sixteen daily sorties of B–52s.[45]

During the first two weeks of the operation, some difficulty was encountered in getting these elements to work together. The Marines controlled all air and ground operations in and below the zone, and the Air Force directed strikes above the zone in Tally Ho. The Covey O–2 FACs had the hardest time. Since Tally Ho was too hot for them, they flew visual reconnaissance missions and directed Marine strike planes in the zone under Marine control. Frequently, they could not operate in the zone because of heavy Marine artillery fire. At other times, the Coveys found Marine and Army FACs working the same area and barely avoided midair collisions with them and the strike planes they were directing. On several occasions, the FACs were cleared by the Marines into a specific area only to have a heavy barrage of friendly artillery burst beneath them. In a few instances, the O–2s entered their area only to find themselves in the middle of a bombing assault being controlled by Marine ground radar. The Marines, on the other hand, were forced to hold up their artillery fire for long periods of time while planes struck targets in the Neutralize area. In one period of twenty-four hours, their artillery pieces were voluntarily kept silent for twenty-one hours while the enemy continued to bombard them.[46]

Most of these operational difficulties were cleared up after a late September visit to the control agencies by General Momyer. Shortly thereafter, the Seventh Air Force installed a high-level Air Force liaison team at the Marine control center at Dong Ha. The Coveys ceased to be threatened by artillery fire; and for the remainder of the operation, the longest the Marines had to withhold their fire was four hours.[47] While this arrangement fell short of the Air Force's goal of controlling all aircraft in a joint operation, it proved to be a suitable ad hoc solution to the immediate problem and allowed the units to work together.

During the rest of September and until the operation ended on the last day of October, Air Force tactical planes flew over 1,400 sorties and the Marines close to 1,600. The weather was often poor, and one third of the flights had to rely on ground radar to drop their ordnance. The B–52s added 820 sorties, 335 of them against targets chosen by the Seventh Air Force and 485 against those nominated by other agencies.

Conditions conspired against obtaining an accurate picture of the results. Attempts were made to use two methods: visually and photographically counting the damage (bomb damage assessment) and measuring the change in intensity of the enemy's bombardment.

The first of these evaluation methods was unsatisfactory for many reasons. Poor weather hampered the efforts of reconnaissance planes to assess the damage, and ground followup was impossible. The large proportion of radar-controlled flights prevented the fighter pilots from observing their results. The nature of the targets ruled out reliable assessment, and often the pilots could tell they hit something only when large secondary explosions followed their strikes. Official estimates tell only part of the story. Destroyed were 63 artillery pieces, 55 antiaircraft artillery positions, 308 structures, 74 bunkers, 7 automatic weapon positions, 10 mortars, 19 trucks, 11 rocket positions, 6 watercraft, 10 railroad positions, and a cave. It was estimated that 392 of the enemy died, but the actual figures were probably much higher.

More indicative of the effects of Neutralize was the dramatic decline in the number of incoming artillery rounds. In July, 6,100 rounds had pummeled the three Marine positions. By September, the number had risen to 7,400. After the concentrated air assault in October, the number dropped to 3,600. Finally, at the end of the month, MACV announced that the siege of Con Thien, the most beleaguered of the positions, was over.[48]

Although blocked by Neutralize from infiltrating through the Demilitarized Zone, the North Vietnamese continued to move down the Laotian trails to strengthen their base camps and staging areas for the coming offensive. By late 1967, there were 228,000 North Vietnamese and Viet Cong soldiers poised inside and on the fringes of South Vietnam, half of them combat troops, and 6,000 more were arriving each month. Some 40,000 laborers worked to keep the trails open, while another 25,000 soldiers guarded them from attack.[49] To avoid detection and the massive air strikes that were certain to follow, the enemy staged a series of assaults on border posts.[50]

The first set of attacks came in October along the Cambodian border in the northern part of III Corps, eighty miles north of Saigon. U.S. and ARVN forces had been sweeping the area since late September in a search and destroy operation called Shenandoah II. Contact with the enemy was light; but on the 27th, three North Vietnamese battalions struck an ARVN headquarters near Phuoc Binh (Song Be). Artillery, air strikes, and helicopter light-fire teams drove them away.[51]

Two days later, three regiments of the Viet Cong's 9th Division, which had entered northern III Corps after Junction City, attacked two camps near the town of Loc Ninh in what General Westmoreland later characterized as a prelude to the Tet offensive. For eleven days, air and artillery strikes kept the enemy from overrunning the outposts while reinforcements were flown in. On the first night, the enemy seized the northern half of one of the camps and the Vietnamese irregulars retreated to the southern half. The district chief and an American advisor remained behind and, barricading themselves inside a deep command bunker, maintained contact with the FACs who quickly arrived on the scene. Throughout the night, AC–47 gunships and artillery hit the top of the bunker, keeping the enemy away until reinforcements arrived at daybreak. F–100s from Bien Hoa fired at enemy artillery in rubber trees east of the camp. Repeated attacks by the Super Sabres and gunships drove the Viet Cong out of the camp northward toward the town. The FAC called in A–37s to strafe the retreating soldiers and bomb enemy bunkers along the road. C–130s flew ARVN and U.S. reinforcements to the scene, and helicopters then moved them to positions around the town, completing a ring of protection.

The heaviest action took place on November 2, when 111 strike sorties and a B–52 mission drove back assaults from both the eastern and western flanks of the town.[52] Once again, air strikes were well orchestrated with the ground action. The ground soldiers probed forward until they contacted the enemy, then backed off and called for air strikes. Until the aircraft arrived, the artillery pounded the enemy. Aircraft and artillery then joined, the fighter-bombers moving their strafing runs progressively closer to the friendly troops until the enemy disengaged.[53]

The ring of U.S. troops around Loc Ninh continued to make contact with the Viet Cong until the 7th of November, when the enemy faded away. All told, 452 tactical and 39 B–52 sorties had helped to protect the town, together with 21 gunship and 35 Skyspot attacks. The Viet Cong suffered a resounding defeat, losing at least 852 men, while 50 friendly troops died.[54]

The Viet Cong kept up their diversionary pressure at month's end with a battalion-size attack against nearby Bo Duc, the district headquarters in Phuoc Long Province. They came close to capturing the CIDG camp there, which sat four miles from the Cambodian border. Just after midnight on the 29th, the enemy struck in a well-planned assault, protected by antiaircraft guns and aided by the imaginative use of smoke and signal flares and machineguns positioned around the camp. The VC quickly overran one of the camp's two connected square compounds. At half past one, F–100s arrived from Bien Hoa and soon learned how well the enemy had planned the attack. Since Cambodia lay just north of the camp, the enemy figured correctly that the planes would strike from east to west to avoid the border. They positioned their machineguns two miles east of the camp, away from the attack, and greeted the strafing aircraft with unprecedented barrages of fire and tracers. The fighters were forced to shift the direction of their attack around from the north, constricting their approaches.[55] The Viet Cong used smoke bombs to obscure the target from the planes; and the pilots, since they could not see the targets, could not fire on one of every three passes. Had it not been for a ten-knot ground wind that helped to blow some of the smoke away, the situation would have been worse.[56] The enemy used red flares to signal attacks and to alert gun crews to incoming fighters. They appeared to have a well-organized movement of supplies by truck from the Cambodian border. Fighter-bombers placing ordnance within twenty feet of the besieged troops and a dozen Army light-fire teams held off the enemy for eleven days while U.S. planes flew reinforcements and supplies into the area. Finally, on the 8th of December, the Viet Cong made two final attacks and withdrew, ending the siege.[57]

These assaults in III Corps were accompanied by several similar attacks farther north. As the action was winding down around Loc Ninh, a major battle was shaping up in the central highlands of II Corps. Although the ensuing battle of Dak To fit the pattern of the other attacks as part of the larger pre-Tet preparation, later evidence suggests it was not directly connected. A North Vietnamese colonel who deserted to the allies the following April indicated that the battle was planned by local unit commanders over his opposition. The local commanders wanted a battle to gain combat experience and to build up their troops' morale.[58] Whether intended or not, the battle served the same purpose as the others by drawing American troops to the border and away from populated regions, in this case from Tuy Hoa.

The U.S. 4th Infantry Division had been scouring the triborder area in Kontum Province since the first of October in Operation MacArthur. Late in the month, reconnaissance patrols discovered that the North Vietnamese 1st Division was converging on Dak To and was digging deeply into the dozen jungle-covered hills that surrounded the town. In response, one of the 4th's brigades moved into the Dak To Special Forces camp. A B–57 strike on November 1 produced a gigantic secondary explosion, confirming the enemy's buildup. Nine more battalions of U.S. soldiers were helilifted into the hills to dislodge them.

Beginning on November 3, the Americans, supported by fighter-bombers and B–52s, slowly began pushing the stubborn enemy from the hills. The battle culminated with a successful fight for Hill 875, one of the largest ground actions of the war to that time. Three U.S. battalions were rushed to the aid of a besieged unit that was pinned down on the hill with high casualties. The enemy's capitulation on the 23d, after two days of aerial and artillery bombardment, marked the close of the battle for Dak To.

Air Force fighter-bombers flew 2,096 close air support sorties, half of them immediates. Gunships provided 62 sorties and B–52s an additional 305. Over 300 flights by C–130s delivered 300 tons of provisions into Dak To. Two C–130s were destroyed, another Hercules was damaged on the runway by mortar fire, and an F–4 was downed by ground fire.[59]

Although the actual number killed, as in most battles, was probably much higher, 1,650 of the enemy were known to have died. Attempting to differentiate between those killed by air strikes and those who succumbed to other types of fire again was "an exercise in futility."[60] The problem of judging results was further compounded since some enemy sites were destroyed beyond recognition, the enemy removed bodies and cleaned up the sites before friendly troops arrived, and friendly ground units could not penetrate into the regions hit by the B–52s. Allied losses consisted of 283 U.S. and 61 Vietnamese soldiers.[61] The Army's praise for the tactical air support it received was effusive.

In addition to flying in supplies, the Air Force's principal activity during the battle was strafing and bombing engaged Viet Cong troops, destroying enemy fortifications, and clearing landing zones for helicopter assaults. Most of the aircraft were simultaneously loaded with napalm for the first task and with 500-pound or heavier general purpose bombs for the other tasks.

The thickness of the jungle canopy aided the enemy. At times, the planes had to use their general purpose bombs to clear the dense bamboo and hardwood cover before they could drop their napalm. The Communists resorted to their familiar tactic of hugging the ground troops, making it too dangerous for the aircraft to use cluster bombs, but the accuracy and effectiveness of napalm against troops in contact was proven once again.[62] The scene was repeated on several of the hills—a flight of A–1Es started dropping napalm a hundred meters ahead of the friendly ground troops and worked it down to seventy-five. The ground commander wanted it closer, and the next run hit the enemy at fifty meters. They wanted it still closer, and the succeeding flight placed it at twenty-five meters. The radio voice from the ground then announced: "I think we've moved it close enough. The trees are burning over my head."[63]

These strikes were the turning point. The commander later recounted how, after the napalm hit, he saw many figures in the trees leaping out burning and yelling. Some jumped up and, with their clothes burning, charged the perimeter, firing wildly. Fire from a machinegun nest cut them down.[64]

The need for the planes to carry mixed loads of napalm and iron bombs caused some difficulties. Due to the rapidly shifting nature of the fights, the

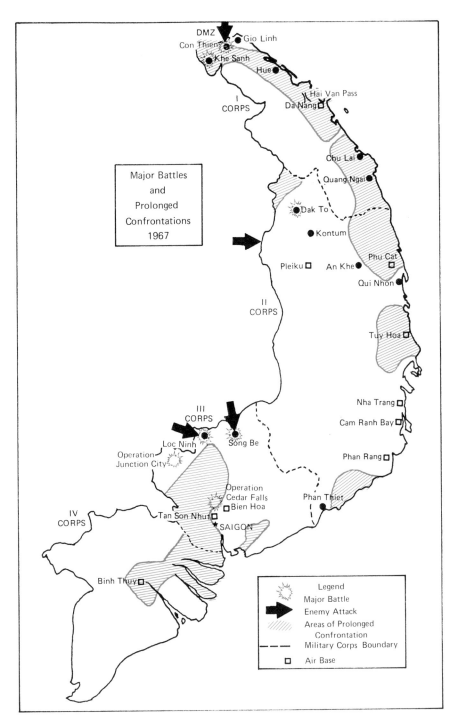

Major Battles
and
Prolonged
Confrontations
1967

DMZ

Con Thien · Gio Linh
Khe Sanh
Hue

Hai Van Pass
Da Nang

I
CORPS

Chu Lai
Quang Ngai

Dak To
Kontum

Phu Cat
Pleiku An Khe
Qui Nhon

II
CORPS

Tuy Hoa

Nha Trang

Cam Ranh Bay

III
CORPS

Loc Ninh Song Be

Phan Rang

Operation
Junction City

Operation
Cedar Falls
Bien Hoa
Phan Thiet

Tan Son Nhut
IV   SAIGON
CORPS

Binh Thuy

Legend
Major Battle
Enemy Attack
Areas of Prolonged
Confrontation
Military Corps Boundary
Air Base

275

ground commanders called in an unusually high ratio (50 percent) of immediate strikes. These often required last-minute reloading of the planes to make sure that they had the appropriate ordnance. The need to reload, at times, delayed the aircraft in arriving at the scene of battle. The FACs and ALOs continued to remind the Army commander that more preplanned strikes would permit more sorties, and would lessen the time it took to get planes to the targets.[65] The obvious inability to anticipate all the enemy's moves, however, put limits on the number of sorties that could be planned ahead of time.

The necessity to carry both napalm and iron bombs also limited the size of the bombs the aircraft could drop. To clear a landing zone big enough for one helicopter took, on the average, 9 sorties with 500-pound and 750-pound bombs.[66] The normal munition used to clear a landing zone in Vietnam was the daisy cutter, a conventional bomb with a pipe extension on its nose that caused it to detonate just above the ground, thereby clearing a larger area. The 8-inch-thick bamboo and the 6-foot-thick ironwood trees encountered in the hills around Dak To, however, made this type of ordnance only marginally effective.

In all their attacks in III and II Corps, the enemy was defeated. Yet, as events were to prove, U.S. troops had been successfully drawn from the cities and training provided for enemy troops. The enemy proved quite willing to exchange men for experience.

The defeat the North Vietnamese suffered at Khe Sanh in April at the hands of the Marines shifted their attacks to the east only temporarily. Late in the year, U.S. intelligence pinpointed a major surge in the number of enemy trucks along the roads around Khe Sanh, from 480 in September to 1,116 in October, 3,823 in November, and 6,315 in December.[67] By the end of the year, 2 North Vietnamese divisions were in the immediate environs of the base. Just north of it was the 325th Division, mauled in April but now back at full strength. Slightly to the southwest of the post was the seasoned 304th Division that had helped to defeat the French at Dien Bien Phu 14 years earlier. A regiment of the 324th Division and the entire 302nd Division were within 15 miles of Khe Sanh, ready to reinforce the closer troops.
Throughout December, the number of contacts between these units and the Marines increased substantially. In Westmoreland's view, the North Vietnamese were not, as in the past, passing through on their way south but were digging in to besiege the base. Since the April battles for the hills around the camp, the Marines had reinforced Khe Sanh with 2 additional battalions and

The U.S. Marine Corps base at Khe Sanh, South Vietnam.

naval engineers had rebuilt the 3,900-foot runway. Hercules aircraft flew in tons of asphalt and pierced steel planking, and by fall, the runway was accommodating C–123s and C–130s that kept its supply links open.

Early in January 1968, there was every indication that the enemy had shifted from the defensive to the offensive in I Corps and that the two North Vietnamese divisions around Khe Sanh intended to seize the base, in a move reminiscent of their victory over the French at Dien Bien Phu in 1954. While the military leaders in Saigon were aware of the threat to the base, they also recognized the opportunity that a concentrated enemy presented as a target for air power. The American strategy was clear: to use its airplanes in a sustained bombing campaign to disrupt the enemy and forestall any offensive that was planned.[68]

The air campaign, called Niagara, involved Air Force, Marine, and Navy planes. Westmoreland, seeking to invoke the emergency powers he had announced in June 1966,[69] attempted to obtain for his air commander, General Momyer, total control over all these aircraft. When Admiral Sharp in Hawaii refused to accede to this arrangement the day before the campaign began, a nebulous compromise was reached empowering Momyer to "direct and coordinate" all the planes—Air Force aircraft from both South Vietnam and Thailand (for the first time), Marine planes from I Corps, naval aircraft from the carriers, and the B–52s. As before, the Marines were to use their planes to support their own ground units, but turn over to Momyer any sorties they did not need for this purpose.[70] Having preserved their air-ground concept intact, the Marines codified the agreement as they interpreted it by establishing six zones around Khe Sanh, with the four closest to the base

Operation Niagra Fire Zones

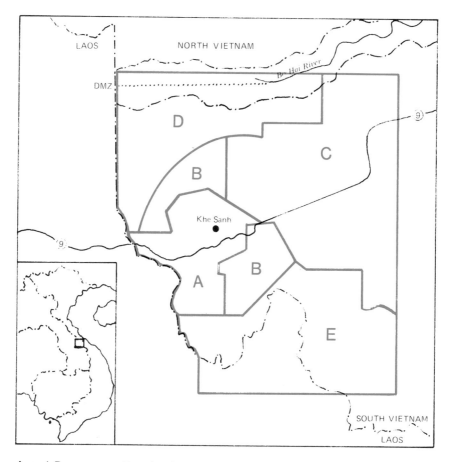

A and B	Restricted fire areas with air and artillery support coordinated and controlled by the Marines at Khe Sanh.
C	Restricted fire area with air and artillery support coordinated and controlled by the Marines at Dong Ha.
D and E	Free strike zones with air strikes controlled by the Seventh Air Force ABCCC

placed under the air control agency inside the base.[71] The areas outside these zones were given to the Seventh Air Force for the weight of its effort. This arrangement, in effect, perpetuated the existence of two air forces operating in a compressed area.

An Air Force F–100 places a strike close to the lines at Khe Sanh.

The Seventh Air Force's effort was orchestrated by a specially configured C–130E airborne command and control plane that orbited over Laos
and controlled all aircraft except the Marine close air support craft. This
control plane also meshed the flights with the Marine's ground artillery as it
fired at the enemy. Fighter-bombers sealed off the Khe Sanh region by
patrolling and bombing the roads leading into the area from Laos. Forward
air controllers directed all strikes in the South Vietnamese portion of the
Niagara zone. Reconnaissance sorties followed the numerous B–52 raids to
gauge the results.

Locating targets that lent themselves to attack from the air was critical
to this interdiction campaign. The Air Force set up an intelligence task force
at Tan Son Nhut, 375 miles to the south, to integrate all incoming
reconnaissance and intelligence information. Intelligence programs for the air
campaigns outside South Vietnam were cut back so that more resources could
be devoted to this special effort. The Air Force's intelligence control center in
Saigon, swollen to over 200 people, quickly developed an overall picture of
the enemy's dispositions that proved valuable, not only for the Niagara
planes, but also for the Marines in both their close air support sorties and
their ground artillery firing.[72]

Information flowed in from many sources. Captured enemy soldiers and
local civilians provided important details on the North Vietnamese plans; the
deployment of men, tanks, and artillery; and the location of bivouac areas,
supply points, and command posts. These data were matched with reconnaissance photos and quickly translated into targets. Other details were supplied

from acoustic and seismic sensors that had been dropped along many of the roads and trails around Khe Sanh. Sensor signals were relayed by an airborne EC–121 to Dong Ha, and the interpreted information went from there to the C–130E directing strike aircraft into the area.

The siege of the Marine camp briefly interrupted the planned beginning of a full-scale sensor-controlled interdiction campaign against the nearby trails in Laos. The system had been successfully tested, however, and a sensor information center was in operation at Nakhon Phanom in Thailand, 140 miles from Khe Sanh. The diversion of these sensors to Khe Sanh proved fortuitous because of the addition of many specific details on the enemy's location and movements throughout the entire area—forty percent of the data used by the Marines inside the camp to coordinate their artillery firing came from sensors.[73] The centralization of intelligence and targeting was an integral aspect of the overall central control of air power.

Bombing began on January 22; and within a week, as many as 300 targets a day were being produced. In addition to unearthing the usual types of targets, intelligence personnel began to identify numerous caves in the limestone mountains they believed housed the headquarters of the enemy. Lucrative ammunition and supply depots were also uncovered and hit by the bombers.

On the 24th, the enemy overran a small outpost eight miles west of Khe Sanh—Ban Houi Sane, just inside Laos—that guarded the main route into South Vietnam. Poor weather prevented the airplanes from stopping the Communists, who penetrated the outpost with armored vehicles, trucks, and tanks—the first indication that the enemy was using tanks. The attack reinforced Saigon's belief that an assault on the main Marine post was imminent. Over 475 Laotian troops and 2,300 civilians fled eastward from Ban Houi Sane to Lang Vei, a Special Forces camp between the Laotian border and Khe Sanh, while B–57s and F–100s protected them from the pursuing enemy by bombing bridges and roads behind them.

The main base at Khe Sanh was effectively pinned down as enemy troops tightened the noose on all sides and poured mortars, rockets, and artillery shells into the enclave. The Marine artillery response had been temporarily weakened by the destruction of the main ammunition dump during an enemy mortar and rocket attack a few days earlier. The base was now totally dependent on air power both for resupply and for defense against an enemy who had begun to tunnel towards the perimeter and appeared on the verge of an all-out assault.

During the first week of the bombing campaign, the fighter-bombers, forced by poor weather to rely on Skyspot radar to find their targets, flew over 3,000 sorties and the B–52s over 200, destroying scores of trucks, gun positions, bunkers, and structures. Under cover of this bombardment, C–130s and C–123s, and briefly a handful of C–7s, landed 158 times through heavy

Airlift at Khe Sanh—supplies
paradropped to Khe Sanh
fall through the clouds after
release by Air Force planes
(top); an arrester cable pulls
supplies from an Air Force
C–130 flying just above the
ground (right); passengers
leaving Khe Sanh run for a
C–123 waiting on the
runway with engines
running (bottom).

ground fire to deliver 1,700 tons of sorely needed ammunition and other supplies to the beleaguered outpost.

On January 30, with the base closely surrounded and Air Force airlift planes keeping it supplied, the enemy launched a nationwide assault on six major cities, thirty-four provincial capitals, and numerous U.S. and Vietnamese installations. All twelve major U.S. bases in the country were hit by rocket and mortar fire, many of them penetrated by enemy patrols. Hoping to catch the allies off guard during the annual Tet holidays and expecting the populace and soldiers of South Vietnam to welcome them as liberators, the North Vietnamese and Viet Cong had infiltrated arms and personnel into the urban areas during the preceding weeks. However, except at the northern city of Hue, where fighting continued until the first week in March, the attacks were put down within days.

The Seventh Air Force dispatched fighters and observation planes to support the ground troops and transports to shuttle supplies between cities while still maintaining its pressure on the enemy around Khe Sanh, and the Tet offensive made little dent in the Niagara operation. During the first three days of the offensive, in fact, Air Force fighter-bombers and B–52s flew more sorties in the environs of Khe Sanh than they had during the three days before the nationwide attacks began.[74] Only once during the offensive was the attention of the Air Force's Saigon intelligence force diverted from the Khe Sanh operation. The enemy began a rocket bombardment of Tan Son Nhut on the 18th of February, and forward air controllers, reconnaissance planes, and the targeting effort were redirected for a few days to root out the assailants in Saigon.[75] The Communists maintained pressure on Khe Sanh throughout the Tet offensive. This nationwide offensive, occurring on top of the Niagara campaign, illustrated again the need for a central point from which to direct fighter-bombers and bombers, forward air controllers, gunships, and helicopters to the areas where they were most needed.

On the 5th of February, the Communists stormed one of the hills near the base and two days later seized the camp at Lang Vei, only three miles from the Marine outpost. Just after midnight on the 7th, an enemy column, spearheaded by nine Soviet PT–76 tanks and backed up by armored vehicles, rolled into the Special Forces camp. A low ceiling, coupled with the swiftness of the move, kept air power from preventing the loss of the Lang Vei. Several thousand refugees moved eastward out of the post toward Khe Sanh, adding to the already overcrowded and confused situation there.

Enemy bombardment of Khe Sanh had now become so accurate and intense that the Air Force transports keeping the base alive were endangered. Early in February, a C–130 was hit by mortar fire as it was landing. The pilot backed the aircraft off the runway as the crew extinguished the fire. Because of continuing enemy fire, the pilot took off with three engines and returned safely to Da Nang.[76]

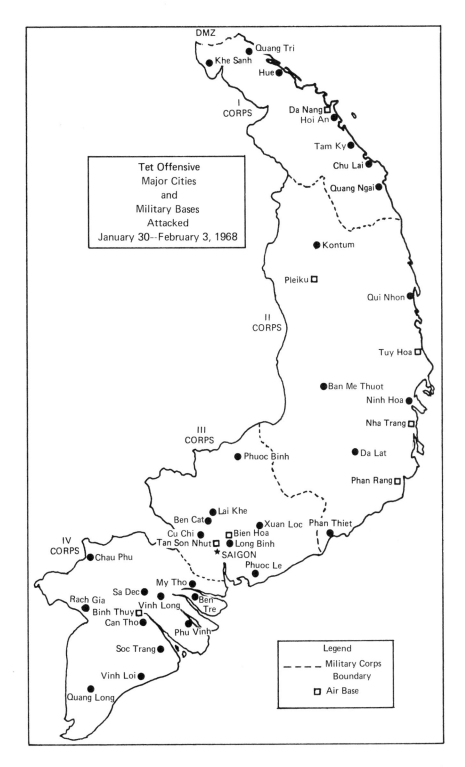

Tet Offensive
Major Cities
and
Military Bases
Attacked
January 30--February 3, 1968

DMZ

Quang Tri

Khe Sanh

Hue

I
CORPS

Da Nang
Hoi An

Tam Ky

Chu Lai

Quang Ngai

Kontum

Pleiku

II
CORPS

Qui Nhon

Tuy Hoa

Ban Me Thuot

Ninh Hoa

Nha Trang

III
CORPS

Phuoc Binh

Da Lat

Phan Rang

Lai Khe

Ben Cat

Xuan Loc   Phan Thiet

Cu Chi   Bien Hoa

IV
CORPS

Tan Son Nhut   Long Binh

SAIGON

Chau Phu

Phuoc Le

My Tho

Sa Dec

Rach Gia   Vinh Long   Ben
Binh Thuy   Tre

Can Tho

Phu Vinh

Soc Trang

Vinh Loi

Quang Long

After a Marine C–130 was destroyed and another damaged while landing on the 10th, Momyer stopped the Hercules from going into the base. The C–123s continued to land but, while landing and taking off, were escorted by O–2s on their wingtips that directed circling fighters against gun positions firing on the transports.[77] The C–130s began to deliver supplies from the air, sometimes parachuting loaded pallets into the camp, at other times sliding them from the rear of their planes as they skimmed 5 feet above the runway. For the first time in airlift history, planes dropped supplies under instrument conditions. After being positioned by radar at a point near the base, the crews took over and released their loads into a 300–foot by 300–foot drop zone. To avoid the intense ground fire, C–123 crews developed a new tactic. Approximately 75 seconds from the drop zone, the aircraft descended at 3,000 feet per minute and leveled off at 800 feet. The plane flew at this altitude for only 15 seconds, dropped its load, and climbed immediately to a safer height.[78] Two-thirds of the material supplied to Khe Sanh throughout the operation was delivered by planes that did not touch down.

While tactical fighters kept the enemy at bay immediately outside the camp, B–52s pounded supply and storage areas beyond 3,000 feet of the perimeter. In mid-February, the Stratofortresses adopted a new method of bombing, called Bugle Note. At first, a cell of 3 bombers arrived at Khe Sanh every 90 minutes around the clock, with one cell taking off from Guam and another from U Tapao every 3 hours at alternate 90-minute intervals. Later, 6 B–52s arrived every 3 hours, providing better target saturation and more time to evaluate results before the next strike. To gain the ability to vary the targets and to some degree the arrival times, the B–52s were assigned targets at the last minute to compensate for changes in the enemy's location and to make it more difficult for the enemy to time the strikes closely enough to alert the MiGs. Throughout February and March, the planes continued to keep the enemy off balance, striking not only in the immediate environs of Khe Sanh, but also along supply routes in Laos and north of the Demilitarized Zone in the Tally Ho region. The concept proved so effective it was expanded to include all the areas hit by the B–52s.[79]

By late February, the North Vietnamese trenches were close to the edge of the camp, but enemy attempts to set up an air defense were inadequate. Fighters destroyed most of the 37-mm antiaircraft weapons, the largest guns mounted; and the greatest threat to the aircraft came from automatic weapons and small arms around the runway.

On the 1st of March, a C–123 was hit by mortar fire while on its takeoff roll, and the six passengers and four crewmen fled to safety as fire consumed the plane. Another C–123, bringing Marine reinforcements from Phu Bai five days later, was waved off final approach because a Vietnamese plane was on the runway. As he circled the field, the pilot called that he was receiving heavy ground fire. His escort observed a fire and then an explosion on the plane's left wing as it was turning into final. The aircraft rolled into a vertical dive, crashed into the jungle, and all forty-eight aboard died. That same day, a tire, punctured by shrapnel on the runway, blew on a landing C–123. While being towed away, it was hit by mortar fire and destroyed.[80] Besides the loss of these three Providers, eight others were damaged during the seventy-day operation. No Air Force C–130s were lost, but eighteen were heavily damaged by enemy fire.

In the defense of Khe Sanh, fighter-bombers and B–52s flew over 24,400 sorties, dropping 100,000 tons of ordnance, and Marine artillery hit the enemy with close to 200,000 shells. Forward air controllers flew over 1,500 sorties and reconnaissance planes close to 1,400.[81] The airlift planes delivered 12,500 tons of supplies into the camp, flying 1,124 sorties to do so. Two hundred Americans died and 1,600 were wounded, compared to an estimated 10,000 enemy casualties—over half the number that began the siege.[82]

A frontal assault was never attempted on Khe Sanh, interpreted by the MACV command as a victory for the air interdiction campaign.[83] By mid-March, the North Vietnamese were pulling back from the base; and by the end of the month, the 325th had left the area, with only the 304th remaining. The Army's 1st Cavalry Division, pushing westward in Operation Pegasus along Route 9 from Ca Lu, linked up with the base on the 8th of April. Four days later, the road was open to friendly traffic.

American military leaders at all levels, including Seventh Air Force, MACV, Hawaii, and the Pentagon, convinced that the enemy had intended to attack the base, proclaimed their failure to do so a telling victory for air power. It was Westmoreland's conclusion that "the key to our success at Khe Sanh was . . . principally aerial firepower."[84] This sentiment was echoed by virtually all others involved in the campaign. No operation of this magnitude, however, is without its costs, and Niagara was no exception. The cost was enormous—roughly half of the air effort in South Vietnam was committed to the campaign for two months.[85] Although there were still sufficient resources to simultaneously quell the Tet offensive, the preoccupation with Khe Sanh during February and March provided the enemy with a permissive environment in which to prepare for a second offensive in May.

The compromise for controlling the air operations arranged at the outset of the campaign, did not work to Momyer's satisfaction. Air space congestion and the lack of aircraft at critical times were common occurrences during the first several weeks of Niagara. Most of these problems were created by the existence of both an Air Force and a Marine agency trying to control airplanes in a tight space. The situation was compounded by the need to integrate Navy and B–52 sorties; and the measures borrowed from Operation Hickory of the previous year, with Air Force liaison officers physically located with the Marine air control agency, were inadequate for an operation of this magnitude.

There was little interference between Marine artillery and Air Force planes, but major problems arose between the planes of the two services. A paucity of information made it difficult for the flying command post to orchestrate the flights. Several times Marine planes hit targets outside their zones without informing the airborne control. There were instances when B–52s dropped their bombs unannounced, endangering unsuspecting forward air controllers below. On several occasions, transport aircraft flew through the Marine zones at the same time as forward air controllers were conducting strikes.

The two separate targeting systems added to the confusion. Sometimes the two air forces hit the same target and other targets went untended. Once, the Marine control agency would not clear Air Force planes to strike in one of its zones until the source of the target information was provided so that it could validate the targets. Despite attempts of the two control agencies to coordinate their strikes, there were times when the Marine control unit became saturated with Marine flights and had to either stack the Air Force planes over the target or turn them away. Some of these aircraft returned to their bases loaded with ordnance but low on fuel.[86]

Early in March, the inefficiency of the operation became evident even to Admiral Sharp. Westmoreland argued that a situation existed that saw Marine planes supporting Marine troops in the same area where Air Force planes were supporting Army soldiers, but the argument transcended the relatively narrow situation around Khe Sanh. The Marines had successfully kept control of their aircraft in I Corps over the years because they had been virtually alone in the northern provinces. The Army began to move into the northern reaches of South Vietnam in April 1967 and now, eleven months later, outnumbered the Marines two to one. Sharp finally acquiesced; and on March 7, Momyer was given "mission direction" over the Marine planes in all of I Corps.[87] Although the term "mission direction" was another of those phrases invented to avoid the emotional overtones of operational control, Momyer interpreted the two as synonymous. While it was a major step toward realization of Air Force doctrine, this decision remained circum-scribed by two modifications. To calm their fear of losing aircraft responsive-ness, the Marines could obtain immediate, emergency strikes without going through the Seventh Air Force. They could also appeal injustices over the head of Westmoreland directly to Sharp.

It took several weeks before the new system was operating.[88] The first mission under the single manager system was flown on March 22. When Niagara ended on the 31st of March, the Marine control agency had barely been integrated into the Air Force's control center in Saigon. Even though the new single manager system had only begun to affect the action around Khe Sanh, that operation acted as a catalyst for the change. Discussions about the value of single management of air resources would continue long after the war was over, and the air operations around Khe Sanh formed a major piece of evidence for such discussions.

However, Khe Sanh was not typical of the conflicts in South Vietnam. For the first time in the war, the enemy presented the type of target for which tactical air forces were best suited. Exaggeration of the importance of this relatively easy success can tend to overshadow the numerous, less publicized instances where air power, day after day, succeeded in supporting ground troops.[89] Nevertheless, the success of the Air Force's effort at Khe Sanh broke the ice and became the model for many Air Force operations in the country during the remaining five years of the war.

The Niagara campaign left as a legacy an effective Seventh Air Force intelligence center and a valuable precedent for intensified interdiction campaigns in South Vietnam. As a result of the Khe Sanh action, MACV became more willing to accept the Air Force's interdiction role in South Vietnam;[90] and in April, the Air Force set up a program within the country. The Seventh Air Force began scheduling a small number of strike sorties, ranging from ten to thirty each day, against the enemy's lines of communications in I Corps, portions of III Corps, and occasionally in the two other corps. This program was managed by the Seventh Air Force's control center in Saigon and was complementary to, but separate from, the continuing close air support requirements of MACV.[91]

The installation of a single manager of air during the Khe Sanh siege, however, did not settle the command and control issue for the future. Since Westmoreland based his case largely on the preponderance of Army over Marine troops in I Corps, the question remained about future arrangements in a unified command in areas where only the Marines were involved.

The events of the first three months of 1968 formed a watershed for the Air Force, as it did for the entire American effort, in Southeast Asia. On the day that the successful Niagara campaign came to a close, President Johnson stopped the bombing of North Vietnam above the 20th parallel. Seven months later, the bombing halt was extended to all of North Vietnam. This led to increased attention to the aerial interdiction campaign along the trails in Laos. At the same time, the American strategy began to change from one of prosecuting the war to one of gradual disengagement. The air effort in South Vietnam took on a whole new complexion as the energies of the Air Force became divided between keeping the enemy at bay militarily and the training and supplying of the South Vietnamese to assume responsibility for their own defense.

B–52 Stratofortresses over the Demilitarized Zone bomb Communist artillery positions inside the zone during November 1967.

Chapter XI

Conclusion

In many respects, a distinct phase of the air war in South Vietnam ended in March 1968. For 3 years, the Air Force had carried out the largest, most sustained ground support campaign in the history of aerial warfare. Although the 58,000 Air Force personnel in South Vietnam at the end of the period represented only 11 percent of the total U.S. military presence, the Air Force, more technologically inclined, contributed much more to the overall war effort than personnel figures alone suggest. One and a quarter million USAF combat and combat support missions had backed up the ground forces inside the country and struck at enemy supplies on its edges, a total that, by the end of the war, would more than double that of World War II. The number of Vietnamese bases from which Air Force jets flew increased from 3 to 7 and the number of aircraft in the country increased from 84 to 1,085. All 424 tactical and reconnaissance planes in South Vietnam by January 1968 were jets. Early in 1965 the Air Force had 1.5 percent of its aircraft in South Vietnam; 3 years later this investment had grown to 19 percent.* The 523 planes in Thailand raised the Air Force total in the two countries to 28 percent. With additional planes in the surrounding areas—the Philippines, Okinawa, Taiwan, Japan, and Guam—the Air Force by early 1968 was devoting approximately one-third of its worldwide aircraft inventory to the conflict.

---

*In December 1964, the Air Force possessed 5,858 aircraft; in December 1967, 5,783. (USAF Statistical Digest, Fiscal Years 1965 and 1968, Table 5.)

How effective were these resources? Part of the answer to this question can be found by examining the results of the Air Force's tactical strike sorties, its system for controlling the aircraft, its command arrangement, its airlift, and its reconnaissance and logistic activities, as well as its impact on the Vietnamese Air Force. The success or lack of success of many of these activities was determined, in turn, by the impact the war was having during these years on the Air Force's structure and methods.

The cutting edge of the USAF's effort in South Vietnam was the tactical fighter force that supported the ground troops. One of the larger disappointments of the war was the inability to measure closely the results of air strikes. Lacking quantifiable data, analysis of the Air Force's effectiveness was extraordinarily difficult. Effectiveness is determined by establishing an objective, devising a set of criteria to measure against, and gathering enough facts to see if these criteria have been satisfied. In South Vietnam, the Air Force possessed neither its own war objective nor enough reliable data to quantify the results.

The military objectives of the war in the south were essentially ground objectives: kill enemy soldiers; neutralize enemy base areas; and open and secure roads, railroads, and waterways. With only a few Air Force officers in decisionmaking positions on the MACV staff, the direct responsibility for attaining these objectives rested with ground commanders. Air strikes, intelligence, and reconnaissance, along with ground artillery and helicopter and naval gun-fire, were officially categorized by MACV as support activities whose purpose was to back up the ground troops.[1] Having no direct responsibility for the United States' war objectives in South Vietnam, the Air Force concentrated on the mission it did have: supporting the U.S. and Vietnamese armies. As a consequence, success came to be measured more by such quantifiable yardsticks as the readiness rates of aircraft, the rapidity of their response to emergency calls for help, sortie rates, and tons of ordnance dropped than by the direct effect these activities had on the enemy. An enormous quantity of data described the Air Force's effort, but little its progress, in South Vietnam.

Besides not having its own objective, the Air Force lacked reliable statistics. Accurate data about the results of air strikes were difficult to acquire, for a variety of reasons. Frequently Air Force strike aircraft were joined by Army helicopters; VNAF, Navy, and Marine planes; and by ground artillery, troops, and armor in assailing the same target. Under such circumstances, no one could tell which of the participating weapons inflicted casualties or persuaded (or failed to persuade) the enemy to disengage.[2] Even had it been possible to sort out the effects of different weapons, there still was no way to relate such information to the overall U.S. war objective. Reports on how many soldiers were killed in a given encounter, how many roads were cut, or how many structures destroyed, for example, shed little light on the long-range effects of these strikes on the enemy's morale, security, recruiting, or intelligence.

The traditional instrument for evaluating the results of air strikes was the bomb damage assessment, which was suspect in South Vietnam. Doubt prevailed about the completeness and accuracy of poststrike reports by pilots. On most missions the jungle canopy obscured results. Often pilots reported "smoliage" (smoke and foliage) as the only observable outcome of their missions. Ground followups were rare. Even those results that were reported seldom lent themselves to fruitful analysis since they were not updated as further information became available.[3]

Periodic changes in the method of reporting air strikes compounded the problem of evaluating the Air Force's performance. Terminology frequently overlapped, and some terms, such as "direct air support" were invented for the occasion. When MACV excluded the use of the term "interdiction" in reporting Air Force sorties in 1966, the Seventh Air Force expanded its definition of close air support to include some traditional types of interdiction strikes. These changes of terminology posed a barrier to establishing trends and to determining the relative emphasis within the overall air effort.[4]

Even though results of the tactical strike effort often eluded quantification, individual instances of its effectiveness emerged from special studies and from the testimony of its consumers. There was widespread agreement among these sources that air power was the decisive factor in frustrating the enemy's determined offensive early in the spring and summer of 1965. The South Vietnamese Army was powerless in the face of the Communists; and until U.S. ground troops were sufficiently in place by late summer, air power kept the Communists from moving into the final phase (conventional combat) of their insurgency.

In May 1965, B–57s and A–1s drove 2,500 Viet Cong attackers from the provincial capital of Song Be with a loss of almost 300 soldiers. At the beginning of June, A–1s, B–57s, F–100s, and Marine F–4s repulsed another major enemy attack against Ba Gia in northern I Corps. Several weeks later, 644 Air Force sorties saved the Special Forces camp at Dong Xoai, north of Saigon. In many of these and similar actions, the South Vietnamese were sustained by USAF airlift of food and supplies into their beleaguered positions. On June 18, the B–52s flew their first mission against enemy forces entrenched in War Zone D. The combination of tactical strikes and B–52 missions cut the heart out of the offensive. Airplanes defeated further attempts against Dak To in June and Duc Co in August.

Frustrated by these air attacks and seeking at least one victory before the U.S. Army could oppose them in force, the Communists in October struck against a Montagnard fort at Plei Mei in II Corps. They were driven off in a fierce 10-day battle. Only air power stood between the garrison and its attackers during the first 3 days, and the United States was able to deploy its ground forces behind this aerial shield. General Westmoreland and other U.S. and South Vietnamese military leaders credited air power with making this deployment possible.

After U.S. ground troops took over the war late in 1965, air power continued to contribute heavily to enemy attrition in South Vietnam at an extremely low cost in U.S. loss of life. During the ensuing 2 years, the Air Force flew about 25 percent of its tactical strike sorties (46,000) and 30 percent of its B–52 sorties (3,300) in supporting 73 successful major U.S. ground offensives against the Viet Cong and North Vietnamese troops. The remaining 150,000 strike sorties and 7,700 Arc Light sorties were consumed in other actions against both enemy soldiers and supplies within the country.* On many of these occasions, the fighters, working in concert with FACs and gunships, destroyed enemy troops that had been fixed in position by allied ground forces. President Johnson's characterization of the air effort in the siege at Khe Sanh as "the most overwhelming, intelligent, and effective use of air power in the history of warfare"[5] was a contemporary recognition of the decisive nature of tactical, B–52, and airlift missions in preserving the Marine base.

Unlike their missions in Laos and North Vietnam, the Air Force's planes in South Vietnam almost exclusively supported ground forces. To do this, the Air Force installed and honed an excellent air support system while fighting the war. The main components of this support operation were the planes and the tactical air control system that guided them.

On the whole, the Air Force was satisfied with the performance of its fighters and bombers and delighted with the accomplishments of its gunships. Some viewed the replacement of propeller fighter planes with jets as ill-advised, pointing to the A–1's longer loiter time, greater accuracy, superior ability to work under low ceilings, and its much lower cost to buy and maintain. Jets, on the other hand, were quicker to respond than were the prop planes and were less vulnerable to ground fire. Fixed-wing gunships proved to be one of the more notable successes of the war. Used in South Vietnam principally at night, their long loiter time and accuracy permitted them to play a major role in defending hamlets and Special Forces camps.

Besides keeping helicopters outside the Air Force's tactical control system, the Army expressed some dissatisfaction with the system's respon-

---

*See Appendix 5, USAF Tactical Sorties in South Vietnam, 1965–1967; Appendix 6, USAF Support of Major U.S. Ground Operations, 1965–1967; and Table 10, Arc Light Sorties, 1965–1968.

siveness, a function of how long it took after fighters were summoned for them to strike the enemy, how compatible their ordnance was with the target, and how well the targets were chosen. Since some of this disagreement predated the Vietnamese conflict and harked back to an ancient family feud between the two services, statistics alone are inadequate to resolve the differences of opinion. They do, however, help to illustrate some of the problems encountered in tactical air warfare.

The time required for fighters to hit the enemy depended, among other things, on the type of sorties flown. Of the two types of close air support sorties, preplanned and immediate, the Air Force in Vietnam preferred the former, which were scheduled the day before the operation. By allocating a given number of sorties to specific Army units in advance, the Air Force could better plan how it would use its other resources. It made for a more rational and efficient application of its aircraft, which had to fill many different requirements. On the other hand, the system of preplanned sorties forced the ground commander to plan far ahead of the operation and at times deprived him of the flexibility to change plans in a constantly shifting combat environment.[6] More to the Army's liking were immediate sorties that were either diverted from their planned missions or scrambled from alert on the runway. However, a drawback to immediate strikes was the frequent loss of ordnance compatibility when aircraft were diverted to new targets. Diverted planes, loaded with ordnance for one target, were often sent to a target for which the ordnance was ill-suited, diminishing both responsiveness and effectiveness.

It took, on the average, twenty minutes after it was called before a diverted aircraft began to expend its ordnance, and a scrambled plane took twice as long. Since no point in South Vietnam was more than fifteen minutes from the nearest jet planes,[7] part of this time was consumed by the ground commanders in marking targets and briefing the forward air controllers before the strikes. While the Air Force was justifiably proud of having cut response time in half since 1965, often it still took too long for the Army. One-third of the fire fights in South Vietnam lasted less than fifteen minutes, half less than thirty minutes. Three-fourths of the battles were over within an hour.[8] Even a twenty-minute response time allowed support for only fifty-five percent of all engagements.

The third gauge of responsiveness is the selection of proper targets. Prohibited in South Vietnam from flying either armed reconnaissance or interdiction missions, in which they could choose their own targets, Air Force flyers relied on the surface forces to identify targets and to request that they be struck. By asking for a maximum number of preplanned sorties each day, in hopes that many of them would later be converted to immediates, ground commanders often did not have enough specific worthwhile targets for all their requests. Air Force and ground control officers complained

The OV–10 Bronco, which became the FACs' first armed aircraft.

frequently that many flights were no more than harassment missions against suspected enemy targets.[9]

A key member of the tactical air control team was the forward air controller. Having disbanded its controller system after the Korean war, when the emphasis returned to strategic planning, the Air Force rebuilt it for Vietnam on a trial and error basis. Although airborne FACs had set a precedent in Korea, the system was dismantled after the war and had to be reconstructed for Vietnam with planes borrowed from the Army and pilots diverted from fighter cockpits.

The rebuilding of the FAC system virtually from scratch had advantages and disadvantages. On the one hand, it provided flexibility to allow the Air Force to tailor its program to the specific requirements of jungle warfare, unencumbered by irrelevant practices derived from the earlier conflict. On the other hand, due to the piecemeal buildup of forces, the controllers looked to one organization, a support group, for their maintenance and supply, while receiving their mission orders from another, the control center. Despite repeated proposals to change it, the divided command arrangement under which the FACs operated was not cleared up by 1968. Inadequate coordination between the suppliers and operators at times jeopardized the controllers' effectiveness. With a fixed amount of resources, ongoing programs often were shelved when the control center levied new missions. Suggestions for change were not adopted out of concern that reorganizing the controllers, who were already working at full tilt, would disrupt operations more than continuing with the less-than-ideal system.[10]

An issue nearing resolution early in 1968 was whether the forward air controllers' planes should be armed. Neither the O–1 Bird Dog nor its successor, the O–2, which entered the theater in 1967, carried armament. A third-generation control plane, the OV–10 Bronco, was still being tested early in 1968. Since forward air controllers arrived at the scene of battle before the fighters, some Air Force officials saw arming the Bronco as a way to decrease response times. The Broncos were armed as they came into use later in the war and served that purpose well.[11]

With the increase of interdiction missions in South Vietnam after Khe Sanh, a new type of air controller emerged—the strike control and reconnaissance (SCAR) pilot. He performed visual reconnaissance and directed fighter strikes, as did the forward air controller, but was not a fighter-qualified pilot and was not tied to the ground commander for selection of his targets. Another innovation of the exigencies of warfare, the SCAR was concerned primarily with Air Force-generated interdiction targets in specific geographic areas.[12]

The Air Force's experience in South Vietnam between 1965 and 1968 provides a further illustration of the obstacles encountered by its traditional, deep-seated conviction that air resources are more efficient and effective when controlled by a single manager, in this case, MACV's Deputy for Air. What set this war apart from its predecessors was the vast number of helicopters and the need to define who controlled them. Although Air Force leaders during the advisory period had sought to acquire management of the helicopters, the issue was settled in fact, if not officially, before 1965 when the Air Force lost its bid for substantive representation at the policymaking levels of MACV. The McConnell-Johnson agreement early in 1966, in which the Air Force abandoned its claim to the helicopters but gained control of fixed-wing transports, was basically a formal recognition of an established fact. By then, the impracticability of the Air Force obtaining control was apparent; and throughout the war, a major portion of air power—helicopters—remained outside the Air Force's control.

Management of the part of air power that was theoretically placed under Air Force control—fixed-wing fighters, reconnaissance, and observation planes—remained fragmented. The Army continued to fly some fixed-wing reconnaissance and observation planes, the Navy's planes were controlled from Hawaii, and the Marines allowed the Air Force to include USMC fighters in the tactical air control system only grudgingly and after prolonged debates. The decision in March 1968 to make the Air Force the single manager of tactical aircraft in Vietnam was quickly modified, returning substantial control to the Marines. This prevented a true test of the single manager concept and opened the door for resumption of the debate after the war.

The war brought important modifications to the Air Force's strategic and tactical airlift operations, the former undergoing some major adjustments between 1965 and 1968. In August 1965, the Air Force introduced the C-141 cargo plane, doubling the airlift system's capacity. New ports were opened within the United States, and the geographic balance shifted between the older ones. Before 1965, the majority of airlift planes and flights were concentrated on the east coast of the United States, looking toward Europe. As requirements for Southeast Asia mounted, the imbalance was evened out by creating new aerial ports on the west coast and pressing the east coast aerial ports into serving Southeast Asia. New support squadrons were placed at Midway Island, at Mactan in the Philippines, and at Cam Ranh Bay and Tan Son Nhut in South Vietnam. As a result of the war's escalation, the number of ton miles* to and from Southeast Asia leapt from 700 million in 1965 to 5.7 billion by 1968. While the earlier figure represented 35 percent of the Military Airlift Command's† total, by 1968 Southeast Asia was using 76 percent of the command's capacity. Two–thirds of this was carried in military planes, the rest by commercial contract carriers.[13] The number of aeromedical evacuations increased from 12 sorties with a handful of patients a month to 158 monthly flights with 8,000 patients.[14] These flights were credited with keeping the rate of wounded that died after reaching a medical facility at approximately 1 percent, a dramatic decrease from the 4.5 percent rate of World War II.[15]

Tactical airlift also underwent revision. The C–123s, C–130s, and C–7s in South Vietnam flew all of the traditional tactical airlift missions in South Vietnam including logistic airlift, airborne operations, aeromedical evacuation, and special air support operations. Between 1965 and 1968, the tons of cargo and the number of passengers increased tenfold from 24,000 and 97,000, during the first quarter of 1965, to 250,000 and 992,000, during the

---

*A ton mile is the accepted measure for strategic airlift, the equivalent of one ton of passengers or cargo moved over a distance of one mile. The total figure is the product of the total tons of passengers/cargo and the total miles moved.

†The Military Air Transport Service (MATS) became the Military Airlift Command (MAC) on January 1, 1966.

An Air Force C–141 medical evacuation aircraft at Tan Son Nhut.

same period of 1968.[16] This was accomplished despite the poor condition of many of the fields, the saturation of air space, and the lack of navigational aids and terminal approach facilities.[17] The extraction and air drop techniques developed at Khe Sanh added a new dimension to airlift operations; but the diversion of airlift planes to special missions, such as dropping flares, dispensing leaflets, and spraying herbicides, cut into the airlift capability.[18] Since the tactical air control system in South Vietnam could not handle fighter, reconnaissance, and airlift operations concurrently, a separate airlift network was established. While this flew in the face of the Air Force's preference to have all its tactical forces centrally managed, it proved necessary under the circumstances and, in fact, worked well, leading to a doctrinal modification.

Initially, tactical airlift was not centralized, but this was largely corrected with the creation of the 834th Air Division late in 1966. However, an analogous consolidation of strategic and tactical airlift planes still eluded the Air Force in 1968. Strategic airlift remained the province of the Military Airlift Command and tactical airlift that of the Tactical Air Command, although they had similiar missions. In Vietnam, this resulted in a frequent overlap of responsibilities and functions throughout the theater at aerial ports, command posts, and support squadrons, as well as during evacuation efforts.[19] At the larger air bases, the planes of both systems vied for ramp space, fuel, loading crews, and scheduling. Failure to integrate the two sets of schedules often resulted in bunching of aircraft and saturation of airfield facilities. At Da Nang, for example, the two control centers were located a mile apart, making coordination virtually impossible.[20] Even where control officers were physically located closer together, resolution of conflicts depended more on the negotiating ability of the duty officers than on the importance of the mission.[21]

These experiences in Southeast Asia, however, added further ammunition to the Defense Department's desire to centralize airlift for all the services in the Air Force. A step toward fulfillment of this single manager concept would take place in 1973, when the Vietnam experience was reinforced during the Middle East war. The following year, the Tactical Air Command relinquished its airlift fleet and mission, which were incorporated into the Military Airlift Command.

Although the Air Force resisted, on doctrinal grounds, dedication of the C–7 Caribous to Army units after obtaining them from the Army, some dedication continued and the system worked to the latter's satisfaction. This practice seemed on the verge of being accepted into Air Force doctrine.

Of all the Air Force's activities in South Vietnam, reconnaissance was the most disappointing. Dissatisfied with both the quality and timeliness of the Air Force's reconnaissance support, the Army by 1968 was relying primarily on its own Mohawk OV–1s and the visual reconnaissance products of the forward air controllers, calling on the Air Force only for those targets it could not uncover itself.[22] This was caused principally by the lack of a joint Army/Air Force doctrine for reconnaissance and the consequent lack of a curb on the Army's quest for its own air reconnaissance capability.

Army ground commanders, largely unaware of the inherent limitations of Air Force reconnaissance, frequently either requested information that was unattainable or did not clearly state their specific requirements. Often, for example, requests from the field simply stipulated the scale or sensor to be used. As with airlift, close air support, and many other Air Force operations, Army officers were not familiar enough with Air Force equipment and procedures to make the best use of them.

On the other hand, the Air Force also contributed to the problem. Its system for assisting the Army in framing its requests was less than perfect. Air liaison officers who were assigned to Army units to help process the requests had to be fighter qualified. Given the increasing complexity of the reconnaissance process, these fighter pilot ALOs seldom were sufficiently versed in reconnaissance to make the requests meaningful to the reconnaissance community. Of the three phases of the reconnaissance and intelligence cycle—collection, interpretation, and dissemination—the Air Force was strong in the first but weak in the latter two. The tremendous volume of reconnaissance imagery it amassed overwhelmed its intelligence equipment, facilities, and personnel.

Delays, both within the Army's request channels and the Air Force's mechanism to respond, hurt the reconnaissance program. Due to repetitious handling, requests often remained in Army channels as long as two weeks before being forwarded. The absence of secure and dependable voice and teletype circuits and the location of most Army units far from the nearest airfield that could accommodate the T–39 courier planes made it difficult to get perishable target information to the consumer in time for it to be useful.[23]

While the Air Force had an extensive reconnaissance capability in airborne radio direction finding, it was normally unable to use the results, which were reported directly to the Army units. The information proved extremely valuable in one major exception—the Air Force intelligence operation created during the siege of Khe Sanh.[24]

The most successful reconnaissance missions were those flown by the forward air controllers performing visual reconnaissance, with about sixty percent of the air-derived targets used by the Army from this source. Visual reconnaissance was valuable because it produced both accurate and timely information and because the forward air controllers' planes were stationed with the users of the information. So successful was the daytime visual reconnaissance program that the enemy began moving at night. The ability of controllers to operate at night was extremely limited, however, due to the lack of suitable equipment and inadequate training and experience.[25] Although originally conceived in 1965 as a coordinated effort between the USAF, the VNAF, and the U.S. Army, the visual reconnaissance program soon split into three uncoordinated efforts. Even within each of these, the products, for the most part, were used locally and not fed into the central intelligence data bank for integration with intelligence from other sources.[26]

Behind the operations, and to a large degree determining their effectiveness, was a logistic system that shared the perturbations of the rapid buildup of 1965–66. Logistic practices, such as aircraft maintenance, supply, civil engineering, and air munitions, underwent important modifications throughout the period.

Before 1965, the Air Force's main bases on the periphery of Vietnam maintained the aircraft and stored supplies that were flown into forward bases inside the country when needed. The sudden and large deployment of tactical units during the buildup, however, taxed these bases to the breaking point. For example, the installation at Clark in the Philippines that repaired F–100s and F–4s became so saturated with demands for maintenance by late

1965 that it could no longer keep up with the flow of engines and other material needed to support the forward bases. Consequently, the Air Force converted several of the forward bases in Vietnam into main bases.

Although there was no alternative, the conversion was slow and inefficient and added to the logistic burden. Partially hindering the process was the worldwide logistic system the Air Force had adopted in 1963, the so-called "maximum base self-sufficiency" concept, with each base building up to the point where it acquired enough personnel, material, and money to do as much of its own maintenance as possible.[27] The effect of this in Vietnam was to place an enormous strain on base supply personnel, who suddenly found themselves with accounts of over 100,000 items; on base engineers, who had to provide almost overnight for a vast influx of additional maintenance men, supply people, cooks, security policemen, warehousemen, and civil engineers; and on other base officials suddenly faced with swollen requirements for facilities and electrical power.

The problem was compounded by the attempt early in 1965 by several Air Force commanders, without regard to Vietnam, to extend this idea of self-sufficient maintenance down to the squadron level. When sent to Vietnam, several of these squadrons ended up on the same base, each requiring its own facilities, equipment, and personnel. In some cases, as many as five separate maintenance complexes grew up on the same base. The resulting duplication overtaxed transportation, communications, and other base support functions. While these multifarious maintenance units achieved an excellent rate of aircraft repair, the costs were much higher than would have been the case had the facilities been consolidated.[28]

The Navy, which supervised construction in Vietnam, and the Army, which was responsible for the actual construction of facilities to support the Air Force, were soon overwhelmed by demands for buildings. As a result, the Air Force undertook some of its own construction. Six engineering units, the Red Horse squadrons, were sent to Vietnam to build housing, hangars, shops, and other needed facilities.[29] In addition, emergency Air Force engineering teams, called Prime Beef, moved into the theater on temporary duty. The first three of these arrived at Tan Son Nhut, Bien Hoa, and Da Nang in mid-1965; and by March 1968, 50 teams, with 1,500 personnel from the major commands, had helped to erect base structures throughout the country. Equally successful in easing the logistic logjam was the experiment under the Turnkey concept, in which the base at Tuy Hoa was built in 275 days from initial approval to completion and within the original cost estimate. The contractor, who operated under Air Force supervision separate from other construction in Vietnam, did the job without interfering with the other important construction projects under way in the country.[30]

The shortage of air munitions during this period resulted from both the character and the suddenness of the air response. Although the amount of

Two F–100s land on the aluminum matting runway at Tuy Hoa, December 1966.

munitions on hand in January 1965 was three times the amount called for by the war plans, average consumption rates more than doubled within the year. Further, since plans did not provide for conventional munitions for the B–52s, the big bombers quickly depleted the supply, causing shortages among the tactical forces.[31]

While America's defense strategy had begun to shift early in the 1960s away from principal reliance on nuclear deterrence and toward a more flexible response, the aircraft and other equipment to accompany the new strategy lagged behind and were not sufficiently developed by 1965 to be immediately useful in South Vietnam. Between 1959 and 1967, for example, the Air Force had concentrated on missiles for its aircraft, spending a total of only $170,000 on research for aircraft gun systems.[32] Deficiencies quickly surfaced in such areas as nonnuclear munitions, electronic warfare equipment, and tactical reconnaissance resources. As a result, the Air Force adapted, where it could, existing aircraft, weapons, avionics, and support equipment to keep pace with the constantly escalating level of conflict. Where experienced logistic personnel and adequate facilities existed, as with the airborne command and control planes and the gunships, the systems were adapted smoothly and quickly. In other cases, such as with nonnuclear munitions, where a capability no longer existed, the Air Force was totally dependent on industry.[33] Besides adapting its own aircraft, the Air Force borrowed and modified planes from the Army, Navy, and civilian fleets.[34]

The war in South Vietnam called for quick development and procurement of small numbers of specialized aircraft and aircraft systems. The task force set up to solve the problems of night operations, Project Shed Light, improved the Air Force's record in strikes at night and during bad weather by identifying and coordinating existing research. By focusing the research, Shed Light brought to the battlefield three new types of weapons systems: a self-contained system, the advanced gunship; a combination system with both air and ground equipment (Tropic Moon); and a hunter/killer system consisting of two or more aircraft. This successful experiment in management proved that it was possible to develop specialized equipment needed urgently in war that ongoing programs could not furnish quickly.[35] At the same time, the Air Force succeeded in cutting much red tape and stepping up development by allowing the field commanders to report their operational needs directly to the commands back home that had to satisfy them.[36]

Not all of the newly developed equipment performed well. Some of it was inadequately tested before being sent to the theater because the emphasis on nuclear weapons had resulted in the abandonment of many of the facilities and procedures for testing conventional equipment. The extensive modification that often had to be made to off-the-shelf equipment compounded the complexity. Frequently changing tactical concepts and requirements further slowed development, with the result that some equipment was not used as originally intended and some was not used at all.

Because American tactical bases had been built and operated without enemy interference for over two decades, research emphasis had been placed on high performance rather than on durability and protection.[37] Equipment designed for nuclear operations was simpler since it was supposed that nuclear strikes would most often be one-time, single-sortie missions with reduced exposure to the enemy's countermeasures. The new, nonnuclear missions in Vietnam, on the other hand, committed the equipment to repeated exposure to enemy defenses. Many of the modifications made for Vietnam, such as armor plating on aircraft, were designed to correct this situation by rendering the equipment less vulnerable to enemy action. Many of these modifications were costly, difficult, and caused a drop in the systems' performance while experimentation proceeded.[38]

Another Air Force experiment, aimed at speeding things up by simultaneously pursuing development and production, met with mixed success. The system worked well in those cases where the planners understood the technical complexities of the system, the engineering changes that could be anticipated during production, and the probability that the user in the field would accept the weapons. The products suffered, however, in cases where these factors could not be sufficiently anticipated.[39]

Even while fighting the war, the Air Force made major strides between 1965 and 1968 in modernizing the Vietnamese Air Force. The instrument for

Two of the C-119 transport aircraft being turned over to the Vietnamese Air Force at Tan Son Nhut in February 1968.

this modernization was the 450-man Air Force Advisory Group headed during the first half of the period by Brig. Gen. Albert W. Schinz and during the second half by Brig. Gen. Donavon F. Smith. Directed from their headquarters at Tan Son Nhut, advisory teams worked to assist the Vietnamese at seven bases in the country. By 1965, the Vietnamese Air Force had completed a 3-year expansion that made it comparable in size to a numbered air force—a size deemed adequate for it to defend South Vietnam after the war. The vast influx of U.S. planes that began in 1965 made it unnecessary, in the view of planners, to increase the Vietnamese air arm further. The USAF could absorb any additional requirements arising from the conflict.[40] Consequently, U.S. efforts between 1965 and 1968 centered on reequipping the VNAF and reforming some of its organizations to make it a self-sufficient and viable postwar defensive force. By March 1968, the Air Force was well along toward realizing this goal. The process illuminated many of the problems of modernizing an air force under combat conditions.

The number of planes in the Vietnamese Air Force remained fairly constant throughout the 3 years, increasing only slightly from 359 to 375; but their composition changed. One of the 6 squadrons of A-1s had been replaced with F-5s by 1968, and 3 of the remaining squadrons were scheduled to receive A-37 jets within a year. One of the 3 C-47 transport squadrons had changed over to C-119s, and a second was within a month of a similar transformation. Plans were well along to change 4 of the 5 H-34 helicopter squadrons into UH-1H units. MACV planned an additional 11 helicopter squadrons for the Vietnamese by 1972.

By early 1968, there were 2,300 officers and 13,000 airmen in the Vietnamese Air Force. Rated officers, who had to be under 25 years of age when they entered, signed up for 8 years; nonrated officers under 30 signed up for 5 years; and enlisted men served for 3 years. Despite the pay, which was low even by Vietnamese standards (first lieutenant, $92 per month; basic airman, $30 per month) the force remained fully manned with few desertions.

Due to the youthfulness of the Vietnamese personnel, training remained the number one priority and the hardest to accomplish. Trying to fight while modernizing, commanders were reluctant to assign their personnel to training, which meant losing them from combat. The VNAF still relied principally on U.S. units in both Vietnam and the United States for advanced flying and technical training. Mobile training teams taught F–5 and C–119 maintenance, logistic management, and the English language inside Vietnam. The U.S. Army was training the H–34 pilots to fly the new UH–1s; and Air Force units in the country taught Vietnamese airmen control tower operations, meteorology, armament maintenance, and missile handling. Between 1965 and 1968, almost 1,000 Vietnamese airmen were trained in the United States.[41]

As depicted by the advisory group's commander in March 1968, the Vietnamese Air Force was a rapidly maturing force, most of whose commanders and key staff officers had integrity and acted responsibly. They were well motivated and carried a proportionate share of the load, flying one-fourth of all the strike sorties in South Vietnam. In sum, the VNAF was on its way to becoming a modern, effective jet age fighting force.[42]

It still had a ways to go, however. Interservice contention between it and the Vietnamese Army had precluded sufficiently close contact between the two to allow the Vietnamese airmen to identify fully the air support needed by their ground forces. As a consequence, the Vietnamese Army was not making full use of the air force's resources. Preoccupied as it was with immediate, day-to-day combat, the VNAF by early 1968 was still unable to develop the concept of long-range force development. For such planning, it was still heavily reliant on the United States.

Major aircraft accidents, which claimed an average of twenty-two planes each month throughout 1966 and 1967, remained the biggest problem. Over sixty percent of these accidents were caused by pilot error on takeoffs and landings. Surprisingly, only eight accidents occurred in February 1968 during the Tet offensive, suggesting a dramatic increase in motivation during the crisis.

The VNAF's maintenance record was improving. Between 1965 and 1968, it integrated six new types of aircraft and showed that it could maintain them. Its maintenance depot, however, was unable to handle all crash and battle damage repairs, much of which was done by U.S. contractors. Maintenance discipline and proficiency were still showing the strains caused by traditional work habits and a shortage of personnel.

The VNAF's supply system early in 1968 was slowly digging its way out of the logistic blitz that had inundated it 2 years earlier. As U.S. aid mounted from $15 million in 1965 to $264 million in 1967, the air force did not have enough personnel to cope with the deluge of supplies. The result was a mountainous backlog in receiving, processing, storing, and recording the new equipment. As is often the case, one problem led to another. While incoming items piled up at the central depot, base supply outfits requisitioned items not received a second time rather than tracing their original requests, thereby compounding the logistic problem.

Several other difficulties remained. The VNAF held its supply personnel accountable for all items; and when they could neither produce nor account for an item, they had to pay for it. This created an understandable reluctance on the part of supply personnel to undertake any inventory that might make them financially liable. Without inventories, however, the system remained chaotic. The central depot had as yet to adopt a satisfactory system for managing, planning, and forecasting future requirements. An absence of coordination between supply agencies resulted in serious duplication and waste of time. At times, the only immediate solution to the frequent munitions resupply problem was costly interbase airlift.

The VNAF's medical services had not improved appreciably over the years; and their dispensaries remained primitive, despite some minor improvements. Under strong prodding, Vietnamese medical officers took a few small steps to initiate programs. A newly established nurse corps began with the training of a dozen students. In one instance, they took measures to prevent an epidemic of paralysis caused by human consumption of lubricating oil that had been stolen from Air Force stocks and sold on the black market as salad oil. In general, however, medical progress was insignificant, with a strong adverse effect on morale.

The most encouraging sign of progress, however, was the VNAF's response to the Tet offensive in 1968. When the enemy struck on January 31, 55 percent of the air force's personnel were on leave, many in rural areas that had been isolated by Viet Cong infiltration. Within 72 hours, 90 percent of the force was back on the job. During the first 12 days of February, they dropped over 14,400 flares, compared to a normal monthly average of 10,000. Helicopters, operating with fewer aircraft, flew more than half their normal monthly number of missions. The overall damage was moderate and casualties were light, with less than 1 percent of the VNAF personnel lost, including deserters. Eighteen planes were destroyed, 11 of them victims of ground attacks.

The impact of the war on the United States Air Force by 1968 was pervasive. Since it was a tactical war, its effects were felt most immediately in the Tactical Air Command. Half of the command's tactical units were lost to it when they were assigned permanently to Southeast Asia in 1965, and most of the remaining stateside squadrons were diverted to train replacements for the war.[43] These two factors, combined with an increasing loss of planes in combat, spurred the TAC Commander to advise Congress early in 1966 that the command's operational capability would largely be gone by July.[44] By midyear, TAC's primary mission had coalesced with that of the Air Training Command. Both organizations were totally committed to training replacements for Southeast Asia. The prevailing evaluation was that TAC would be unable to support a second large-scale war should one erupt at that time.[45]

The long-range impact on TAC, however, appeared bright in early 1968. Congressional and military focus on Southeast Asia brought substantial support for modernizing the tactical forces. The Tactical Air Command embarked on a new program, called TAC Enhancement, to reorganize and prepare the tactical force for postwar contingencies and to avoid a repetition of the disruptive Vietnam deployment experience.

Tactical air leaders, all along less than totally enthusiastic about using their resources in Southeast Asia, had resisted the temptation to structure their forces solely for such limited conflicts. Early in the war, for example, a TAC Commander had opposed the development of gunships on the grounds that his command might be left with too large a contingent of the wrong kind of planes when the war was over. This resistance to putting too many tactical eggs in the limited war basket had been behind the infusion of jets into Southeast Asia, viewed in part as a testing ground for new equipment and concepts.

Wartime experience reinforced the notion that tactical weapons needed specialized vehicles for each of the tactical missions—air superiority, close air support, interdiction, tactical airlift, and reconnaissance.[46] By 1968, many of these new specialized aircraft, including the F–111, the A–7D, the A–37, the F–4E, the OV–10, and the RF–4C, were entering the inventory, some for Southeast Asia and some for TAC's postwar structure.[47] The Air Force gave high priority to developing the Airborne Warning and Control System—a plane that could scan several thousand miles of air space, warn of enemy planes, and control friendly aircraft.[48] Also as a result of Southeast Asia, planners were hard at work on better airlift planes that could take off from very short fields or even vertically. For the first time since the end of World War II, tactical air power was receiving the degree of recognition and support that its advocates had been seeking for over two decades.

The war's impact on the Strategic Air Command was only slightly less pervasive. As the monthly sortie rate of the B–52s increased, the need to send first one, then two, and finally three, bomb wings to the Pacific placed major stress on many SAC personnel policies and aircraft. The shift away from an exclusively nuclear role to one including conventional warfare resulted in a need, not only for additional personnel, but also for different types of people. The command at first resisted shifting personnel from strategic operations, but as the monthly sortie rate escalated through 1966 and 1967 and was projected to go even higher early in 1968, the command was forced to drain crewmembers and highly skilled ground support personnel from its strategic units for use in Southeast Asia. Skill levels fell in the units that remained behind, leading to complaints from SAC's numbered air forces.

An acute shortage of munitions specialists, particularly weapons mechanics, arose in 1966. Security policemen, cooks, and supply and administrative people were taken from nondeployed units, quickly trained, and sent overseas. Training and testing throughout the command shifted strongly toward conventional applications. By midyear, the problem threatened to reduce the commandwide manning to sixty-six percent.[49] Through intensive on-the-job training, cross training, field training, and formal schooling, the problem was alleviated, but the advent of a conventional focus was not without its cost. Overall, there were not enough airmen to go around.

The Strategic Air Command's traditional policy of sending its aircraft and personnel overseas on temporary assignments was revised as a result of the experience in Southeast Asia. When it first entered the war in 1965, the command continued this practice because it gave greater flexibility in maintaining a dual capability for both general war and contingencies and because it was less expensive. By late 1967, however, these advantages had been offset by growing problems occasioned by the escalation of operations. An increasing number of SAC personnel were completing tours in Southeast Asia and were ineligible to return to the theater. As more and more returnees were assigned to SAC, the command's ability to send personnel TDY became progressively restricted. Further militating against the TDY system was the plan in early 1967 to deactivate three SAC wings. This, coupled with the opening of the U Tapao base in April, forced the command to make more and more permanent assignments.

By early 1968, conventional B–52 bombing missions had also changed their character. During the first two years of operation, the bombers attacked enemy base camps and other logistic targets; but most of the missions during 1967 were flown in conjunction with ground operations, with most requests coming from field commanders. In many cases, B–52s were providing close air support.

A considerable amount of money that otherwise would have gone toward upgrading SAC's nuclear posture was spent on the new conventional mission. The commitment of strategic bombers to the nuclear alert posture declined as missiles assumed an increasingly prominent role.[50]

The war also had a marked impact on the training and assignment of the Air Force's personnel. The President's decision not to mobilize the reserves, whose callup formed the backbone of the USAF's plans for expansion in the event of a crisis, caught the Air Force short, forcing it to rely exclusively on the regular force.* In addition, the modest size of the increase of the regular force between 1965 and 1968, from 825,000 to 905,000, placed a heavy burden on the regulars and diverted them from modernizing the Air Force to training airmen for a new kind of war, which in many cases required resurrection of earlier, more primitive, and less efficient practices.

To handle the increased number of enlisted men in basic training, a second school was added and the course shortened. The number of entries into officer training almost doubled by 1967, causing shortages of facilities and instructors. Curricula for the follow-on training schools were quickly revised to reflect the specific skills needed for Southeast Asia, such as photo interpreters for a jungle environment and munitions specialists for conventional ordance. The absence in Southeast Asia of many computerized systems that had become standard throughout the Air Force required reversion to manual methods for pay and personnel procedures. Retraining became necessary in these areas.

The increased demand for pilots placed an additional strain on existing facilities. Requests to open a new base for pilot training were turned down. Through a series of measures—juggling schedules, changing the instructor-to-student ratios, borrowing pilots from allied countries as instructors, and using navigators in the back seat of reconnaissance F–4s—the Air Force was gradually able to increase the number of pilots qualified for combat.

By early 1968, the personnel system had made the transition from peacetime to wartime but not without resort to many innovations and expedients. Some glaring deficiencies in personnel planning were unearthed in the process. While the flow of personnel to and from Southeast Asia had been fairly well established by then, it was done at the expense of non-SEA organizations. Late in 1967, the Air Force personnel planners tackled the problem, not only of short-range, but also of future, long-range deployment and manning. They produced a plan identifying manning needs for the next several decades and needs closely attuned to anticipated technological advances.[51] The war had provided a valuable testing ground for the Air Force's personnel system as well as for its tactics, equipment, and its logistic and advisory programs.

Transcending these immediate effects of the war on the Air Force was the conflict's long-term implications for thinking and doctrine. Since its creation two decades earlier, the Air Force had unswervingly stressed in its doctrinal statements air power's primary role as a nuclear deterrent, at first through the nuclear bomber force and later by a combination of bombers and missiles.[52] In this it reflected national policy. The Korean war, tactical in

---

*Although the President did mobilize several Air Reserve units in 1968, these were neither large nor early enough to figure in the USAF's mobilization plans during the critical years of 1965 and 1966.

nature, was seen by most as a temporary aberration from the path of nuclear deterrence. During and after that conflict, the nuclear deterrent mission continued to dominate the thoughts and resources of the Air Force.

A fundamental shift in national military policy away from primary reliance on nuclear deterrence and toward a program to strengthen those forces that might be used at lower levels of conflict began with the advent of John F. Kennedy in 1961. As late as 1964, however, the Air Force continued to maintain that strategic nuclear forces provided the best instrument to prevent wars at all levels. While conceding the need for some forces to be ready to fight limited and conventional wars, it remained wedded to the primacy of the nuclear arsenal as a deterrent of all kinds of war.[53] America's preparedness for the higher levels of conflict, it argued, put any potential enemy on notice that the United States was in a position to raise the threshold of conflict, should one occur, to a level at which it and its allies would hold the advantage.[54]

By 1968, the Southeast Asian experience had modified this view without changing it completely. America's tactical air arm had become the most experienced and battle tested in the world. The many details that determine the success of a tactical force had been tested, modified, and honed to a fine edge. The Air Force's performance had demonstrated air power's importance and ability at the lower levels of conflict, and no other air force possessed this experience. Air power was militarily successful, and this success had been achieved without having to put the enemy on notice that the United States was prepared to raise the level of conflict. Recognition of this brought the Air Force to a qualified acceptance of flexible response. While still viewing strategic forces and the will to use them as the keystone of deterrence, the Southeast Asian experience had shown that "strategic force (alone) may not be a credible deterrent against hostile acts by small powers." Strategic force should be complemented by enough general purpose forces for deterrence at lower levels.[55] This watershed in Air Force thinking established the agenda for future change and planning.

Appendices

Appendix 1

Major USAF Units and Aircraft in South Vietnam
1962–1968

Sorties vs. Tasks

Although the intensity of air activity is traditionally measured in numbers of sorties, there are drawbacks to using sortie rates when comparing the relative weight of air effort performed by the different armed services in Vietnam. This is because the term was applied differently to flights by fixed-wing aircraft than to flights by helicopters. In Vietnam, a sortie for a fixed-wing aircraft was defined in the traditional way—one aircraft making one takeoff and one landing. However, by specific exception, MACV permitted armed helicopters that escorted troop-carrying helicopters in airmobile assaults to log one sortie into and one out of a landing zone, whether they landed or not (MACV Dir 335–2, 21 Mar 65, p 15).

A task, on the other hand, is a single, definite accomplishment by an individual aircraft. Often, several tasks, such as air cover and interdiction, were performed in the course of one sortie by a fixed-wing plane (principally Air Force, Navy, and VNAF).

The unique rules for armed helicopters, coupled with the fact that the troop-carrying helicopters normally logged two sorties for each task, caused the sortie rates for helicopters (principally Army and Marines) to soar past not only the sortie rates for fixed-wing aircraft but also past their own task rates. This double standard is illustrated by the following samples from the MACV Directive that established the system:

> Two B–26s (fixed-wing) take off for the purpose of escorting a train and then perform one interdiction each and return to home base without any intermediate landings—four tasks and two sorties.

> Five UH–1Bs (helicopters) take off for the purpose of escorting troop-carrying CH–21s to a combat area. The five UH–1Bs are required to provide suppressive air-to-ground fire while troops are offloaded, then return to home base without intermediate landings—ten tasks and ten sorties.

> In the above example, fifteen CH–21s (helicopters) take off with troops, land to offload troops, return to base—fifteen tasks and thirty sorties.

This is no frivolous distinction. While sortie rates are useful to compare operations of aircraft of the same type (either all helicopters or all fixed-wing), they are misleading when comparing the performance of services with different types of aircraft. This is illustrated by statistics for daily air tasks and sorties in Vietnam from March to May 1965:

APPENDIX 2

Daily Average

		USMC	USA	VNAF	USAF
March	Tasks	49	1182	261	369
	Sorties	221	1555	277	327
April	Tasks	43	1244	259	359
	Sorties	202	1621	319	240
May	Tasks	72	937	233	411
	Sorties	258	1481	241	364

The Marines, who employed proportionately the most helicopters, used slightly over four sorties (4.2) for each task. The Army, who at this time had many observation and cargo planes in addition to helicopters, used 1.4 sorties for each task. The VNAF, who had some helicopters, used just over one sortie per task. The Air Force, with only a handful of helicopters, used less than one sortie for each task (or 1.2 tasks per sortie). A more accurate comparative picture of what was accomplished by air power can be gained from looking at the number and type of tasks performed rather than at the number of sorties.

Appendix 3

Planning Factors for The Tactical Air Buildup
April 1966

Planning Factors for the Tactical Air Buildup*
April 1966

To establish the phasing of tactical air capability in Southeast Asia necessary to support the buildup of U.S. and Free World Ground Forces, MACV and CINCPAC have agreed on specific planning factors. For planning purposes, each U.S. and Free World Assistance Force (FWAF) (excluding ARVN) maneuver battalion was allotted 5[†] sorties per day. All ARVN battalions together were allotted 7,840 sorties/month or 261.33/day. Since each USMC and ROK Marine maneuver battalion has 4 companies of men, whereas U.S. Army and other FWAF maneuver battalions have 3 companies, it was also agreed, for planning purposes, that the number of Marine battalions will be multiplied by a $1\frac{1}{3}$ weighting factor, allowing 6.67 sorties per day for Marine battalions.

These factors do not assume that the sorties planned would necessarily be performed in the close air support role, but rather, they include all necessary air strikes required to wage the total campaign effectively. In other words, direct air support, interdiction and escort sorties are to be included, as well as close air support sorties.

This paper examines in gross terms the application of in-country resources in support of the ground forces and the overall application of strike sorties within South Vietnam. The period covered is December 1965 through April 1966.

The table below shows the growth of maneuver battalions in South Vietnam.

Additional Maneuver Battalions in SVN

As of 1 Dec 65	Dec	Jan	Feb	Mar	Apr
22 USA	0	6	0	1	3
13 USMC	0	1	1	1	1
133 ARVN	0	0	6	1	1
3 ROK Marine	0	0	0	0	0
6 ROK Army	0	0	0	0	3
1 Australian	0	0	0	0	0
178	0	7	7	3	8
Accumulated total:	178	185	192	195	203

---

*This study, done at PACAF in 1966, illustrates the planning factors used to determine how many USAF squadrons would be needed to support the ground forces in South Vietnam. (PACAF, *Summary of Air Operations in Southeast Asia*, XXI, April 1966, pp. 3–29 thru 3–35.)

†Reduced from 6 to 5 because of addition of B–52s.

APPENDIX 3

Using the planning factors agreed to, the number of maneuver battalions can be computed to determine the number of sorties which should be flown during any period. Note that the increase in ARVN battalions does not affect the tabulation since, by agreement, their support remains constant.

Total Maneuver Battalions in SVN
(Each U.S. and ROK Marine Bn X 1⅓)

As of 1 Dec 65	Dec	Jan	Feb	Mar	Apr
22 USA	0	6	0	1	3
17⅓ USMC	0	1⅓	1⅓	1⅓	1⅓
133 ARVN	0	0	6	1	1
4 ROK Marine	0	0	0	0	0
6 ROK Army	0	0	0	0	3
1 Australian	0	0	0	0	0
183⅓	0	7⅓	7⅓	3⅓	8⅓
Accumulated total:	183⅓	190⅔	198	201⅓	209⅔

Since 7,840 sorties were allotted to all ARVN maneuver battalions together, the following table (same as above without ARVN battalions) is useful in computing strike sorties required (planned).

Total Maneuver Battalions in SVN (Excluding ARVN)
(Each U.S. and ROK Marine Bn X 1⅓)

As of 1 Dec 65	Dec	Jan	Feb	Mar	Apr
22 USA	0	6	0	1	3
11⅓ USMC	0	1⅓	1⅓	1⅓	1⅓
4 ROK Marine	0	0	0	0	0
6 ROK Army	0	0	0	0	3
1 Australian	0	0	0	0	0
50⅓	0	7⅓	1⅓	2⅓	1⅓
Accumulated total	50⅓	57⅔	59	61⅓	68⅔

PLANNING FACTORS FOR TACTICAL AIR BUILDUP

The following tables depict total strike (CAS, DAS, interdiction, and escort) and close air support sorties flown within South Vietnam by each service during the 5 months being considered.

Total Strike Sorties by Service

Service	Dec	Jan	Feb	Mar	Apr
USAF	5,380	4,257	4,675	6,090	3,446
VNAF	2,595	2,520	2,836	2,920	2,500
USN	3,108	3,521	3,160	3,474	3,184
USMC	2,260	2,671	2,778	3,530	3,093
Total	13,343	12,969	13,449	16,014	12,223

Close Air Support Sorties

Service	Dec	Jan	Feb	Mar	Apr
USAF	856	1,026	1,209	1,707	904
VNAF	223	219	191	126	86
USN	97	153	112	259	261
USMC	24	161	992	524	288
TOTAL:	1,200	1,559	2,504	2,616	1,539

Using figures from the third table (Total Maneuver Battalions) with the planned allotment of strike sorties to maneuver battalions, the number of strike sorties required (planned) per day are computed.

Number of Strike Sorties Required Daily
(Based on Planning Factors)

	Dec	Jan	Feb	Mar	Apr
Total Bns minus ARVN	50.33	57.67	59	61.33	68.67
Planning Factor	5	5	5	5	5
No of Sorties Reqd	251.67	288.33	295.00	306.67	343.33
No of Sorties Reqd for ARVN Bns (7,840/30)	261.33	261.33	261.33	261.33	261.33
Total Strike Sorties Required Daily	513.00	549.66	556.33	568.00	604.66

APPENDIX 3

Strike Sorties Flown to Strike Sorties Required (Planned)
(daily)

	Dec	Jan	Feb	Mar	Apr
Stk Sorties Flown	430.40	418.30	480.30	516.58	407.43
Stk Sorties Planned	513.00	549.66	556.33	568.00	604.66
Flown/Planned (%)	83.9	76.1	86.3	90.9	67.4

CAS Sorties Flown to Strike Sorties Required (Planned)
(daily)

	Dec	Jan	Feb	Mar	Apr
CAS Sorties Flown	38.71	50.29	89.43	84.39	51.30
STK Sorties Planned	513.00	549.66	556.33	568.00	604.66
CAS Flown/Planned (%)	7.5	9.1	16.1	14.9	8.5

Since the USMC for the most part provides its own close air support, an additional factor can be developed by excluding USMC battalions and USMC close air support sorties.

CAS Sorties Flown to Strike Sorties Required (Planned)
(daily—excluding USMC air and ground units)

	Dec	Jan	Feb	Mar	Apr
CAS Sorties Flown	37.94	45.10	54.00	67.48	30.43
Stk Sorties Planned	426.33	456.33	456.33	461.33	491.33
CAS Flown/Planned (%)	8.9	9.9	11.8	14.6	6.2

Except for the month of February, when the USMC reported an unusually high percentage of close air support sorties, the ratio of close air support flown daily to the total strike sorties required (planned) daily is generally maintained in the two previous tables. No logic can be found for the large increase in USMC CAS sorties, and it is probably traceable to a change in reporting procedures.

In examining the results of these two tables, it is evident there were approximately six times as many strike sorties available as were needed to satisfy close air support requirements. When a peak situation arises, direct air support, interdiction, and escort sorties can readily be diverted to close air support sorties. In-country tactical aircraft striking in Laos are also available for additional in-country close air support if needed.

PLANNING FACTORS FOR TACTICAL AIR BUILDUP

Historically, all requirements for close air support have been satisfied except those rare cases when weather precluded a strike. One obvious reason for this record is the residual capability inherent in the force levels available in South Vietnam.

From the information available, it appears that any reasonably predictable acceleration in the use of close air support could be satisfied with the ratio of resources now existing. Further, any unusual peaks in such a requirement up to several hundred sorties per day could also be satisfied for limited periods without seriously detracting from the overall air campaign.

Appendix 4

Psychological Warfare Leaflets

CÁC BẠN TRONG HÀNG NGŨ VIỆT CỘNG

Lực lượng ĐỒNG MINH đang tiếp tục mở những cuộc hành quân dọc theo biên giới VIỆT NAM và CAMBOT, để giải thoát cho đồng bào khỏi ách nô lệ của Cộng Sản. Chánh Phủ VIỆT NAM rất hoan nghênh và sẵn sàng chờ đón các bạn trở về với Chánh Nghiã Quốc Gia. Hiện nay các bạn đang chịu đói rét, sống chui rúc trong rừng sâu nước độc, bị đối xử tàn tệ để rồi phải chọn cuộc đời trong một nấm mồ hoang vô chủ, gia đình và thân quyến không ai biết.

Hãy trở về với chánh nghiã, bạn sẽ được tiếp đón nồng hậu, được cung cấp thức ăn, áo quần thuốc men và được dịp lập lại cuộc đời mới.

Hãy đi về hướng ĐÔNG bạn sẽ gặp các lực lượng Đồng Minh đang chờ đón bạn, hãy vẫy một mảnh vải một cái áo hoặc một tờ truyền đơn. Đeo súng sau lưng, mũi súng chỉ xuống đất, bạn sẽ được tiếp đón trở về để lập lại cuộc đời mới trong tự do thật sự.

46-8-245(P)

GIỜ CHƯA PHẢI LÚC TRỞ VỀ VỚI GIA ĐÌNH SAO ?
ANH CHỌN CẢNH NÀO TRÊN NÀY ?

DEAR COMMUNIST FRIENDS

The strength of our allies is showing itself in operations along the Cambodian/Vietnam border. They are there to help the people liberate Communist slaves. The government will welcome you and is waiting for you to return to the rightful cause of our nation. Now you are hungry and cold. Your life consists of stealing through the forest and living in an unhealthy climate. You were met with a cold welcome and when you die your body will be placed in an unmarked tomb which no one will tend.

Come back to the righteous cause. You will be welcome and will receive enough clothing, food and medicine and can make a new life.

Walk to the East where you will meet our allies. Wave a cloth or a handbill. Place your gun on your back with the barrel pointing to the ground. You will be welcomed for returning to make a new life in freedom and truth.

THE COMMUNISTS ARE LOSING THE WAR

The Republic of Vietnam Armed Forces and its allies are pursuing the Communists on land and water, day and night. They give the Communists no time to rest or hide, the same as animals.

Those soldiers who die will have others to replace them. Everyday they oppress their people who have to serve them.

They lied to their people when they said they take them "to study". Last of all they take them to concentration camps to dig trenches and holes; not to hide the people, but to hide the Communists—the Communists who are enemies of our people.

The Communists are the obstacle in the fight for peace of the Vietnamese people.

Leaflets Without Words were Dropped to Illiterate Groups

Bộ đội các bạn không thể nào chống nổi lực lượng vô cùng hùng hậu của Chính phủ Việt Nam Cộng Hòa và các nước bạn đồng minh.
Chờ gì mà chẳng trở về với Chính phủ và nhân dân để được sống đoàn tụ cùng gia đình ?

Your troops can not oppose the strength of the very strong Government of the Republic of Vietnam and friendly nations of alliance.
Why are you waiting and not coming back to the Government and people to live together with your family?

Dear Cadre of the troops of Communist North Vietnam. Your fate will be the same as this one.

Số phận các bạn cán binh trong bộ đội Cộng Sản Bắc Việt rồi sẽ như người này. 245 (P)
SP-914

CÁC ANH EM TRONG HÀNG NGŨ BINH LÍNH MIỀN BẮC!

Trong năm NGỌ này, các bạn hãy coi chừng những Kỵ-sĩ Ngựa-bay! họ sẽ săn đuổi các bạn không ngừng - các bạn không thể nào trốn thoát! phần thắng chắc chắn sẽ về phía Chính-Phủ Việt-nam, thương-tích hoặc cái chết sẽ đến với các bạn. Khi ấy ai sẽ chôn cất tử-tế cho các bạn? Gia-đình các bạn ư? Lẽ-dĩ-nhiên KHÔNG-Ngay cả cái chết của các bạn họ cũng không hay biết nữa là. Hãy ngừng cuộc xâm lăng tàn-sát người Đồng-Chủng của các bạn. Lượm một tờ giấy thông-hành và trở về với Chính-Nghĩa Quốc-Gia của Chính-Phủ Việt-Nam - Hoặc là cái chết và bị vùi chôn nơi hoang-vu giữa chốn rừng sâu, hoặc là trở về với cuộc sống Vinh-Dự? Chọn bên nào? Hãy quyết-định nhanh lên kẻo trễ.

46-3-245N

DEAR COMMUNIST SOLDIERS IN THE RANKS OF NORTH VIETNAM

Beware the Airborne horsemen who will pursue you hard. You can't escape from them; victory is sure for the Government of Vietnam. Wounds and death will come to you and who will bury you? Your family? Of course not! They won't even know of your death. Stop your aggression and the massacre of your fellow man. Pick up a passport and come back to the righteous Nation and the Government of Vietnam. You will be ill-treated and die deep in the wild forest, or will you come back to your life of honor. Which will you choose?

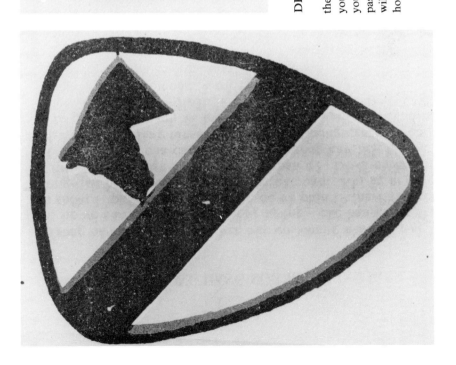

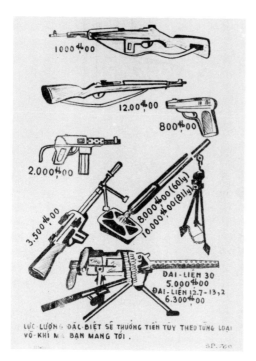

Bring this paper together with your weapon and come to the office of Luc-Luong Dac-Biet.

You will be rewarded with money and you will escape from the Communist's cruel hands.

Luc-Luong of Dac-Biet will reward you according to the kind of weapon that you bring.

Safe Conduct Pass

Front

Reverse

Appendix 5

USAF Tactical Sorties in Vietnam
1965–1967

USAF Tactical Sorties in Vietnam
1965

	Strike[1]	Reconnaissance[2]			Combat Support			Helicopters[2]*	Airlift[2]	Total
		VR	FAC	Other	FL[3]†	DEF[4]	PSY			
Jan	752		1,388	106		55		242	3,623	6,236
Feb	1,204		1,041	98		61		266	3,265	6,005
Mar	1,867		1,157	102		23		243	3,928	7,390
Apr	2,048		1,095	145		21		290	4,057	7,726
May	2,834		1,373	120		75		297	4,743	9,512
Jun	2,492		2,134	133				256	4,958	10,043
Jul	3,414	1,436	1,661	150	92	40		348	5,592	12,711
Aug	3,784	2,245	2,250	190		24		380	5,612	14,577
Sep	3,892	2,377	2,328	214	116	43		447	6,394	15,811
Oct	4,437	2,764	2,712	196	140	64		531	6,864	17,708
Nov	5,265	2,746	2,694	298	221	108	29	611	6,993	18,965
Dec	5,656	2,527	2,479	338	142	182	291	470	5,577	17,662
	37,645	36,407	38,497	2,090	1,201	696	320	4,381	61,606	144,346
						2,217				

*Helicopter missions are measured in tasks.
†January through July FL sorties total 490.

Sources:
1. *USAF Management Summary*, August 6, 1965, p. 16 and January 7, 1966, p. 22
2. PACAF, *Summary of Air Operations in SEA*, Vol. XIV, pp. 4Bi, 4B2-4B4, and 4G1
3. Lawrence J. Hickey, *Night Close Air Support Operations in RVN (1961–1966)*, p. 37
4. Charles V. Collins, Herbicide Operations in SEA, July 1961 – June 1967, p. 71

USAF Tactical Sorties in Vietnam
1966

	Strike					Reconnaissance						Combat Support			Helicopters*				Airlift	Monthly Total
	CAS	DAS	ESC	CAP	ADF	VR	PHO	IR	SLAR	FAC	ARDF	FL	DEF	PSY	PAX	CGO	SAR	EVC	Airlift	Monthly Total
Jan	1,311	2,332	11	370	54	2,638	275	183	13	1,488		83	98	639	300	420	367	64	7,994	18,640
Feb	1,202	3,358	11	376	54	3,503	402	260	10	2,528		112	133	546	329	431	503	86	9,854	23,698
Mar	1,429	3,478	2	384	84	3,873	421	267	4	2,601		100	155	621	249	559	556	165	11,222	26,170
Apr	904	2,535	7	104	11	4,262	413	239		2,423		94	157	760	181	517	542	30	13,583	26,762
May	658	3,631	20	296		4,165	462	222	14	2,125		87	202	775	174	383	606	12	13,693	27,525
Jun	822	4,458	2	347	61	3,841	409	232	1	2,073		289	202	972	121	262	584	42	14,771	29,489
Jul	554	5,741	3	332	80	3,991	343	268		2,176	58	99	137	1,037	159	198	783	32	15,261	31,252
Aug	687	6,557		336	70	4,033	382	241		2,348	73	59	221	1,000	128	147	782	24	15,663	32,751
Sep	613	6,264	5	421	107	4,324	459	285	1	2,322	125	80	229	980	160	136	852	5	15,799	33,167
Oct	776	5,915		501	142	4,236	538	407	2	2,306	186	72	264	901	75	223	698	4	15,714	32,960
Nov	4,651	2,925	16	355	158	4,813	574	318	116	2,683	315	86	398	1,026	99	174	528	20	17,228	36,483
Dec	5,120	2,638	12	388	232	5,707	559	447	97	2,459	389	127	405	825	79	201	592	20	16,710	37,007
	18,727	49,832	89	4,210	1,053	49,386	5,237	3,369	258	27,532	1,146	1,288	2,601	10,082	2,054	3,651	7,393	504	167,492	355,904
	73,911					86,928						13,971			13,602					

*Helicopter missions are measured in tasks.

Source: PACAF, *Summary of Air Operations in SEA* volumes XIV–XXIX.

USAF Tactical Sorties in Vietnam
1967

	Strike						Reconnaissance						Combat Support			Helicopters*				Airlift	Monthly Total
	CAS	DAS	INT	ESC	CAP	ADF	VR	PHO	IR	SLAR	FAC	ARDF	FL	DEF	PSY	PAX	CGO	SAR	EVC		
Jan	5,888	2,548		3	501	158	5,745	503	437	16	3,435	621	136	439	952	91	306	567	13	26,500	48,859
Feb	5,598	2,084		16	564	210	5,957	470	383	11	2,851	479	118	395	1,148	185	204	621	19	28,364	49,677
Mar	6,780	3,006		18	616	153	6,469	535	429	28	3,340	820	176	363	1,194	178	145	769	58	31,619	56,696
Apr	6,502	1,174	1,608	11	462	85	6,190	539	414	31	3,139	905	156	346	1,335	249	94	717	15	33,023	56,995
May	7,050		2,887	22	284	117	6,796	551	433	33	3,480	1,013	54	410	1,603	212	180	492	255	32,972	58,844
Jun	6,744		2,523	27	307	122	6,337	517	409	48	2,742	978	50	525	1,345	145	215	600	62	31,766	55,462
Jul	7,618		2,627	17	386	73	6,670	485	403	42	3,305	962	62	275	1,670	49	114	713	160	31,175	56,806
Aug	7,166	9	2,721	14	372	83	6,733	498	408	25	3,148	970	51	358	1,908	132	222	680	111	31,538	57,147
Sep	7,340	3	3,084		306	46	7,438	615	419	5	3,318	663	47	375	1,556	98	214	663	107	30,903	57,200
Oct	8,060		3,013	14	416	23	7,585	574	381	18	3,428	731	53	495	2,349	224	287	644	105	32,149	60,549
Nov	8,208		2,146	11	264	45	4,213	569	312	10	5,294	600	29	561	2,666	106	207	707	154	29,603	55,705
Dec	8,526		1,710	14	160	95	3,134	683	327	1	6,120	506	39	520	2,715	255	189	711	180	33,110	58,935
	85,480	8,824	22,319	167	4,638	1,210	73,267	6,539	4,755	268	43,600	9,248	971	5,062	20,441	1,924	2,377	7,884	1,239	372,722	672,935
	122,638						137,677						26,474			13,424					

*Helicopter missions are measured in tasks.

Source: PACAF, *Summary of Air Operations in SEA*, volumes XXX–XLI.

APPENDIX 5

Abbreviations:

ADF	–	Air Defense
ARDF	–	Airborne Radio Direction Finding
CAP	–	Combat Air Patrol
CAS	–	Close Air Support
CGO	–	Cargo
DAS	–	Direct Air Support
DEF	–	Defoliation
ESC	–	Escort
EVC	–	Evacuation
FAC	–	Forward Air Controller
FL	–	Flare
INT	–	Interdiction
IR	–	Infrared
PAX	–	Passengers
PHO	–	Photographic
PSY	–	Psychological
SAR	–	Search and Rescue
SLAR	–	Side-Looking Airborne Radar
VR	–	Visual Reconnaissance

Appendix 6

USAF Support of Major U.S. Ground Operations
1965–1967

USAF Support of Major US Ground Operations
November 1, 1965–December 31, 1967
(three or more battalions)

Operation	Dates	Tactical Air Sorties	Tactical Air Mun*	Airlift Sorties†	Airlift Cargo*	Airlift Pax	B-52 Support Sorties	B-52 Support Mun*	Recce Targets
I CORPS									
Harvest Moon	Dec 8–19, 1965								
Hastings	Jul 7–Aug 3, 1966	286	310				40	712	27
Colorado	Aug 6–22, 1966	58	58				51	918	2
Golden Fleece	Sep 17–27, 1966	3	5				27	486	
Macon	Aug 4–Oct 27, 1966	116	105				18	324	10
Prairie	Aug 3, 1966–Jan 31, 1967	154	265				174	3,214	
Stone	Feb 12–22, 1967	4	6						
Union	Apr 21–May 17, 1967	8	14				6	131	
Shawnee	Apr 22–May 21, 1967	14	21				9	195	
Malheur II	May 11–Jun 8, 1967	1,236	1,699	30			26	268	34
Kingfisher	Jul 16–Oct 31, 1967	9	12	61	36	8	176	3,872	
Hood River	Aug 2–13, 1967	202	281	21	1,127	2,961			
Cochise	Aug 11–28, 1967	4	7		5	764			
Benton	Aug 13–Sep 3, 1967	408	574	23	44	623			
Cook	Sep 2–10, 1967	51	68	445	3,631	6,810			
Wheeler	Nov 11–Dec 31, 1967‡	1,304	2,109				88	1,918	36
Kentucky	Nov 1–Dec 31, 1967‡								3
II CORPS									
Silver Bayonet	Nov 1–28, 1965	753			5,040		96		
Masher/White Wing	Jan 24–Mar 4, 1966	600	857		1,100				
Hawthorne	Jun 2–21, 1966	445	338	54	106	195	39	702	
Henry Clay	Jul 2–30, 1966	230	182				21	378	2
John Paul Jones	Jul 21–Sep 5, 1966	388	324	126	671	862	36	648	18

USAF Support of Major US Ground Operations
November 1, 1965–December 31, 1967
(three or more battalions)

Operation	Dates	Tactical Air Sorties	Tactical Air Mun*	Airlift Sorties†	Airlift Cargo*	Airlift Pax	B-52 Support Sorties	B-52 Support Mun*	Recce Targets
II CORPS (continued)									
Paul Revere	May 10–Aug 25, 1966	4,289	4,324	612	2,555	2,880	254	4,619	149
Seward	Aug 5–26, 1966	303	313						1
Thayer/Irving	Sep 8, 1966–Feb 12, 1967	2,951	2,835	349	1,020	4,295	156	3,089	11
Adams	Oct 26, 1966–Apr 2, 1967	239	309	27	227				24
Geronimo	Oct 30–Dec 2, 1966	20	20						14
Pickett	Dec 8, 1966–Jan 19, 1967	50	62	521	2,538	3,459			16
Sam Houston	Jan 1–Apr 5, 1967	2,035	3,008	114	1,182	1,229	93	2,355	36
Pershing	Feb 11–Dec 31, 1967‡	6,159	9,253	16	370	1,932	537	11,449	28
Francis Marion	Apr 5–Oct 12, 1967	3,065	6,467	1	6,095		312	6,552	105
Bolling	Sep 19–Dec 31, 1967‡	712	1,143	471	3,825	6,015	18	1,960	15
MacArthur	Oct 1–Dec 31, 1967‡	3,472	5,176	503	7,312	8,916	376	8,195	81
III and IV CORPS									
Aurora	Jul 1966	48	36	518	1,183	807			
Mokuleia	Jul 15–22, 1966	121	83						11
Cedar Rapids	Jul 17–24, 1966	161	106						
Koko Head	Jul 23–Aug 6, 1966	372	316				27	486	13
Springfield	Aug 1966	253	251				18	324	
Oahu	Aug 1–31, 1966	353	362				51	759	23
Cheyenne	Aug 2–5, 1966	73	45						
Lahaina	Aug 7–Sep 1, 1966	73	78						
Aiea	Aug 8–Sep 1, 1966	262	302				47	801	1
Castine	Aug 1966	37	43						
Amarillo	Aug 23–31, 1966	156	203						
Toledo	Aug 10–Sep 7, 1966	397	449				69	1,242	46

Operation	Dates								
Huntsville	Sep 1966	74	78						26
Sunset Beach	Sep 1966	376	366						14
Kailua	Nov 1966	240	270						2
Shenandoah I	Nov 1966	210	279	3,330	9,684	8,487	225	4,059	26
Attleboro	Sep 14–Nov 24, 1966	1,629	1,757	1,338	3,342	5,212			4
Bismark	Nov 1966	162	217						
Boulder	Dec 1966	45	59						
Silver Lake	Jan 9–19, 1967	43	59						4
Cedar Falls	Jan 8–26, 1967	1,113	1,695	308	1,456	2,701	102	2,219	24
Big Spring	Feb 1–16, 1967	197	255	27	42	214	57	1,411	1
Gadsden	Feb 2–21, 1967	496	757	40	7	1,550	21	493	
Tucson	Feb 14–21, 1967	182	271	66	112	503	18	459	
Farragut	Jan 26–Mar 20, 1967	149	207	236	1,036	2,540	18	392	8
Makalapa	Mar 18–Apr 21, 1967	333	438				6	162	1
Dayton	May 5–18, 1967	61	87						8
Dallas	May 17–25, 1967	190	346	128	580	1,333			
Junction City	Feb 22–May 14, 1967	5,002	7,430	2,057	11,308	17,524	126	4,723	89
Palm Beach	Jan 6–May 31, 1967	159	245						4
Manhattan	Apr 22–Jun 6, 1967	1,002	1,562				24	537	3
Tornado	Jun 5–9, 1967	10	13						2
Blue Field	Jun 5–9, 1967	55	69	60	439	995	12	293	1
Akron	Jun 9–29, 1967	149	200				6	162	
Billings	Jun 12–26, 1967	290	400	599	2,740	2,835			
Concordia	Jun 17–20, 1967	52	63						
Paddington	Jul 10–16, 1967	152	242				42	931	6
Coronado II	Jul 27–Aug 3, 1967	67	80						
Coronado III	Aug 5–17, 1967	101	126	53	33				
Shenandoah II	Sep 29–Nov 19, 1967	1,246	1,852	126	1,330	1,981	97	2,110	14
Fairfax	Nov 30–Dec 14, 1967	988	1,299				6	131	118
Atlanta	Nov 18–Dec 23, 1967	251	412				18	384	17
Yellowstone	Dec 8–Dec 31, 1967‡	506	991	143	1,171	526	15	326	24

*Tons of munitions or cargo

†C-123 and C-130 sorties

‡Figures through December 31, 1967, even though operation continued into 1968.

Compiled from: Seventh Air Force Commander's Operations Command Book, 1967; PACAF, *Summary of Air Operations in SEA*, Vols XI–XLIV; MACV Command Histories, 1965–1967.

Notes

Introduction
The Advisory Years
1955–1964

1. Ronald H. Spector, *The United States Army in Vietnam—Advice and Support: The Early Years, 1941–1960* (Washington, 1983), pp 261–62.
2. Robert F. Futrell, *The United States Air Force in Southeast Asia: The Advisory Years To 1965* (Ofc/AF History, 1981), p 49.
3. Maxwell D. Taylor, *The Uncertain Trumpet* (N.Y.: Harper, 1959), pp 130–164.
4. Futrell, *Advisory Years,* pp 81, 127–34, 157–61, 187–92, 243–56, 418–23; JCS hist, *The JCS and the War in Vietnam, 1960–1968,* Part II, p 24–15 [hereafter cited as *JCS and the War*].
5. Ltr, STRICOM J3 to JCS, May 5, 1965, subj: Policy and Procedure for Assignment of Forces for USSTRICOM.
6. Maj Ralph A. Rowley, *USAF FAC Operations in Southeast Asia, 1961–1965* (Ofc/AF History, 1972).
7. Hist, 2d Air Div, Jul–Dec 1965, III, p 4.
8. Futrell, *Advisory Years,* pp 244–45; ltr, HQ MACV, Nov 26, 1964, subj: Joint Target and Analysis Center; hist, MACV, 1964, p 48.
9. Col Alfred F. Hurley, *The EC-47 in Southeast Asia* (HQ PACAF: Project CHECO, 1968), p 4.
10. Robert F. Futrell, *Ideas, Concepts, Doctrine: A History of Basic Thinking in the United States Air Force, 1907–1964* (Maxwell AFB, Ala, 1974), pp 408–10; MG George S. Eckhardt, USA, *Vietnam Studies: Command and Control 1950–1969* (Washington, 1974), p 37; LTG John T. Tolson, USA, *Vietnam Studies: Airmobility, 1961–1971* (Washington, 1973), pp 4–50.
11. Col Ray L. Bowers, *The Air Force in Southeast Asia: Tactical Airlift* (Ofc/AF History, 1983), pp 103–203.
12. Hist, 405th TFW, Jan 1–Jun 30, 1965, p 245.
13. Intvw, Maj Gen Gilbert L. Meyers, Vice Comdr, 7th AF (Apr 1965–Aug 1966), May 27, 1970, Corona Harvest #0012124, May 22, 1970, pp 50–51, 58; EOTR, Meyers, Jul 31, 1966.
14. An excellent summary of the major issues relating to control and coordination of air resources faced by Gen Hunter Harris, the PACAF commander, is contained in msg, CINCPACAF to CSAF, 110645Z Feb 65; msg, CINCPACAF to 13th AF, 230410Z Jan 65.
15. *JCS and the War,* Part II, pp 17–13.
16. EOTR, Brig Gen Albert W. Schinz, C/AFGP, Nov 22, 1966, p D–10.
17. Maj Oakah L. Jones, Jr, *Organization, Mission and Growth of the Vietnamese Air Force, 1949–1968* (HQ PACAF: Project CHECO, 1968), pp 9–26.

Chapter I
End of the Advisory Period
November 1964–June 1965

1. DIA Bull 135–65, Jul 14, 1965; MACV estimated at this time that there had been 8,250 infiltrators into South Vietnam in 1964, an upward revision of the earlier figure of 7,000; Van Staaveren, "USAF Operations Against Infiltration Through Southern Laos, 1960–January 1968," draft ms (Ofc/AF History, 1978), p 104; *JCS and the War,* Part II, pp 17–23 and footnote.
2. The history of these early military proposals can be traced in the following documents that are either discussed or reprinted, or both, in *The Senator Gravel Edition: The Pentagon Papers* (Boston: Beacon Press, 1971), Vol III:
JCSM 46–64, Vietnam and Southeast Asia, Jan 22, 1964
JCSM 134–64, Feb 18, 1964
JCSM 174–64, Mar 2, 1964
JCSM 222–64, Mar 14, 1964
JCSM 426–64, North Vietnam Operations, May 19, 1964
Memo, Bundy to the President, Next Courses of Action in Southeast Asia, Aug 11, 1964
Memo, CJCS to Sec Def, Recommended Courses of Action, Southeast Asia, Aug 26, 1964
Memo, CJCS to Sec Def, Courses of Action for South Vietnam, Sep 9, 1964
3. *Gravel Pentagon Papers,* III, pp 402, 446.
4. Kenneth Sams, *The Battle of Binh Gia,* (HQ PACAF: Project CHECO, 1965); GEN William Westmoreland, USA, *Report on Oper-*

ations in South Vietnam, January 1964–June 1968, in Sharp and Westmoreland, *Report on the War in Vietnam* (Washington, 1969), p 95 [hereafter cited as Westmoreland, *Report on the War*].

5. Hist, MACV, 1965, p 181; memo, MACV J5, Jan 18, 1965, subj: Increased Air Effort in Vietnam; Kenneth Sams, *Escalation of the War, July–December 1964,* (HQ PACAF: Project CHECO, 1965).

6. Msg, JCS 4213 to CINCPAC, 272333Z Jan 65.

7. Hist, SAC, Jan–Jun 1965, Vol II, pp 240–41.

8. Msg, JCS to CINCPAC, 070010Z Mar 65, subj: Improved Security Measures in the Republic of Vietnam.

9. EOTR, Capt Gary W. Fredericks, DCOP, 3d TFW, Nov 1966, pp 2–4.

10. Msgs, 2d Air Div to 13th AF Command Center, 121555Z, 131420Z, 191951Z, 201815Z, 211915Z, 221935Z Mar 65, subj: Jet Operations in RVN; COMUSMACV to JCS, 191044Z, 201046Z, 211006Z, 211050Z, 261047Z, 271025Z, 281005Z, 291015Z, 301051Z, 311601Z Mar 65, subj: MACV SITREP; COMUSMACV to CINCPAC, 151225Z, 220725Z, 290630Z Mar 65, subj: USMACV Military Report.

11. Hist, 2d Air Div, Jan–Jun 1965, pp 35–36.

12. *Ibid,* p 43.

13. *Ibid,* p 38.

14. Msg, JCS 6692 to CINCPAC, Mar 9, 1965.

15. Hist, 2d Air Div, Jan–Jun 1965, p 11.

16. Hist, MACV, 1964, p 81.

17. Msg, JCS to CINCPAC, 092108Z Mar 65.

18. Msg, MACV to CJCS, 061230Z Mar 65.

19. Msgs, CINCPACAF to CINCPAC, 200315Z Mar 65, subj: Contingency Planning for SEA/Western Pacific; CINCPACAF to CINCPAC, 200316Z Mar 65, subj: PACAF Requirements in SEA.

20. *Gravel Pentagon Papers,* III, p 397.

21. Msg, MACV to CINCPAC, subj: U.S. Troop Deployment to SVN, 07033Z Jun 65.

22. *Gravel Pentagon Papers,* III, p 405.

23. Msg, JCS to CINCPAC, subj: Report of Survey of the Military Situation in RVN, 200019Z Mar 65.

24. McConnell Notebook, Vol I, Item 49, Mar 15, 1965.

25. CSAFM–J–84–65, Mar 19, 1965.

26. Decision on JCS 2343/543, Mar 19, 1965; JCSM–204–65 to SECDEF, Mar 20, 1965.

27. Hist, 2d Air Div, Jan–Jun 1965, pp 39–40.

28. Background Paper, AFXPD to CSAF, subj: USAF O–1 squadrons in RVN.

29. Ltr, STRICOM J3 to JCS, May 5, 1965, subj: Policy and Procedure for Assignment of Forces to USSTRICOM.

30. Hist, 405th TFW, Jan–Jun 1965, pp 246, 260.

31. *Ibid,* p 40; *Southeast Asia Statistical Summary,* DOD/OASD (Comptroller), Jul 1972, Table 2.

32. Hist, 2d Air Div, Jan–Jun 1965, p 37.

33. Lt Col B.A. Whitaker and E.L. Paterson, *Assault Airlift Operations* (HQ PACAF: Project CHECO, 1967), p 43.

34. Msgs, CG, 9th MEB, to COMUSMACV, 131010Z Mar 65 and 151507Z Mar 65.

35. Msg, J.H. Moore, Cmdr 2d Air Div, to Gen Westmoreland, COMUSMACV, Mar 17, 1965, subj: Marine Fighter Squadrons at Da Nang.

36. *A Chronology of Significant Airpower Events in Southeast Asia, 1950–1968* (Project Corona Harvest, 1969) [hereafter cited as Corona Harvest, *Chronology*].

37. Hist, MACV, 1965, p 127.

38. Msg, COMUSMACV to 2d Air Div, 120926Z Apr 65.

39. Msg, CINCPAC to CINCPACFLT, CINCPACAF, and COMUSMACV, 140334Z Apr 65.

40. Msgs, COMUSMACV to CINCPAC, subj: USMACV Military Report, 190630Z Apr 65; CINCPACAF to CINCPAC, subj: Summary of Air Activities, 220632Z Apr 65; COMUSMACV to JCS, subj: USMACV SI-TREP Apr 14–15, 161104Z Apr 65.

41. *Gravel Pentagon Papers,* III, p 336.

42. *Ibid,* p 101.

43. Msg, JCS to CINCPAC, subj: Report of Survey of the Military Situation in RVN, 200019Z Mar 65.

44. Msg, COMUSMACV to CINCPAC and JCS, subj: Commander's Estimate of the Situation, 271339Z Mar 65.

45. National Security Action Memorandum No 328, Apr 6, 1965, in *Gravel Pentagon Papers,* III, pp 453–54, 461, 702–3.

46. As with many decisions taken during the spring of 1965, the one to freeze the level of bombing and experiment with ground forces arose from several factors whose relative importance remains far from certain. Frustration with the lack of quick results from Rolling Thunder played its part, even though the bombing campaign was barely a month

old. This led some advisors, probably sincerely, to conclude that Hanoi's will was more vulnerable to military failure in the south than to destruction caused by bombing in the north. A more bureaucratic, and less charitable, alternative explanation of the shift is suggested in the *Gravel Pentagon Papers* (III, pp 358–59, 410). Gen Johnson's proposal a month earlier to send ground forces to Vietnam, although rejected, had served to focus the attention of the presidential advisors on the considerations of deployment of such forces. This "generated a need to concentrate on issues, arguments, and rationalizations that would serve to promote and justify these new actions." Such diminution of forestal perspective while concentrating on trees is not unknown in committee work. Finally, there were strong forces at work within the Army favoring a test of the relatively new, untried, "flexible response" strategy and force posture that strongly emphasized ground forces.

47. Msg, CINCPAC to CINCPACAF, subj: AF Augmentation, 282311Z Apr 65.

48. JCSM/564–7, Apr 25, 1965.

49. Talking Papers, SECDEF Conf, Apr 19–20, 1965, DOTE, PACAF (Project Corona Harvest #CH0007983).

50. Ltr, CINCPAC #000229, Nov 17, 1960, para 6a.

51. CINCPAC General War Plan (OPlan 1–65).

52. Talking Papers, SECDEF Conf.

53. Msg, CINCPAC to COMUSMACV, 230412Z Apr 65.

Chapter II
Beginning of Direct Involvement
April–June 1965

1. *Gravel Pentagon Papers,* III, p 411.

2. Hist, MACV, 1965, pp 37–40.

3. *Gravel Pentagon Papers,* III, pp 450–52.

4. Msg, MACV to CINCPAC, subj: Introduction of the 173d Abn Bde, 010950Z Apr 65.

5. Msg, HQ 315th Air Div to 6315th Ops Gp, et al, subj: 315th Air Div OpOrd 373–65, 181810Z Apr 65.

6. Melvin Porter, *Air Response to Immediate Air Requests in SVN* (HQ PACAF: Project CHECO, 1969).

7. Corona Harvest, *Chronology.*

8. Sams, *Binh Gia.*

9. Msg, JCS to CINCPAC subj: Rec Actions Concerning SVN, 170222Z Apr 65.

10. Msg, COMUSMACV to CINCPAC, subj: Rec Actions Concerning SVN, 251345Z Apr 65.

11. Msgs, CINCPAC to COMUSMACV, subj: Air Ops in SEA, 230421Z Apr 65; CINCPAC to COMUSMACV, subj: Conduct and Control of CAS Ops, 242345Z Apr 65.

12. Msg, COMUSMACV to 2d Air Div, subj: Air Ops in SEA, 281200Z Apr 65.

13. Msg, CINCPAC to MACV 242345Z Apr 65.

14. Msg, JCS to CINCPAC, subj: Rules of Engagement SEA, 170122Z Apr 65.

15. Msg, COMUSMACV to JCS, subj: USMACV SITREP 118 for the Period 271601 to 281600Z Apr 65, 291100Z Apr 65.

16. Henry F. Graff, *The Tuesday Cabinet: Deliberation and Decision on Peace and War under Lyndon B. Johnson* (Englewood Cliffs, N.J.: Prentice Hall, Inc, 1970), pp 41–43.

17. Msgs, MACV to 2d Air Div, et al, 282100Z Apr 65; MACV to CINCPAC, subj: Air Support in RVN, 031511Z May 65.

18. Msgs, COMUSMACV to CINCPAC, subj: Air Ops in SEA, 010750Z May 65, 020625Z May 65.

19. Msg, ADMINO CINCPAC to Adm Sharp, subj: Navy Augmentation for Air Strikes in RVN, 030055Z May 65.

20. Msg, MACV to CINCPAC, 031511Z May 65.

21. Msg, COMUSMACV to CINCPAC, subj: Air Support Requirements RVN, 310105Z May 65.

22. Msgs, CINCPACAF to CINCPAC, subj: Summary of Air Ops Conducted in SEA, 190755Z May 65; MACV to JCS, subj: MACV Mil Rpt, 170430Z May 65; DIA to AIG 623, 120543 May 65; hist, 2d Air Div, Jan–Jun 1965, pp 220–221.

23. Msg, CINCPACAF Cmmd Post to CINCPAC, 160405Z May 65; hist, 405th TFW, Jan–Jun 1965, pp 265–67.

24. Msg, MACV to CINCPAC, subj: MACV SITREP, 311050Z May 65.

25. Hist, 2d Air Div, Jan–Jun 1965, pp 62–69; hist, MACV, 1965, p 184.

26. Hist, 2d Air Div, Jan–Jun 1965, pp 62–69; msg, 2d Air Div AOC to 13th AF,

130550Z Jun 65; hist, MACV 1965, pp 184–85.

27. Westmoreland, *Report on the War,* p 98.

28. DOA Working Paper, "An Evaluation of the Visual Reconnaissance Program in South Vietnam," HQ 7th AF, Sep 20, 1966.

29. Rpt, Visual Reconnaissance: Concept and Aircraft Support, TACC–WFP, HQ 7th AF, Jun 1966, p 2.

30. Memo, VNAF 02825, subj: Assignment of Observer Aircraft to Sub-Sectors, Jun 17, 1965.

31. *JCS and the War,* Part II, pp 24–1 and 24–2; hist, SAC, 1965.

32. Hist, SAC, 1965 (Hist Study No 101), I, p 199.

33. Msgs, CINCSAC to JCS, subj: SAC OPlan 52–65 Posture, 291745Z Mar 65; JCS to CINCSAC, 142328Z Apr 65.

34. Msg, COMUSMACV to CINCPAC, subj: Use of SAC in RVN (Arc Light), 140805Z May 65.

35. Msgs, JCS to CINCPAC, 292147Z Apr 65; ADMINO CINCPAC to CINCPAC 070236Z May 65.

36. Msg, COMUSMACV to JCS, subj: Utilization of Arc Light B–52s, 190330Z Mar 65.

37. Hist, SAC, Jul–Dec 1965, II, p 267.

38. Msg, COMUSMACV to CINCPAC, subj: Air Support Requirements RVN, 310105Z May 65.

39. Msg, COMUSMACV to CINCPAC, subj: Use of Arc Light Force, 140723Z Jun 65.

40. Msg, COMUSMACV to JCS, subj: Request for Execution of Arc Light Mission, 150305Z Jun 65.

41. Memo, AFXOPJ to CSAF, subj: Changes in Planning and Execution of Arc Light I, Jun 24, 1965.

42. McConnell Notebook, Jun 20 and 22, 1965.

43. Jack Valenti, *A Very Human President* (New York: W.W. Norton and Co, Inc, 1975), p 350.

44. Msg, JCS to DIRNSA, subj: NMCC Opsum 141–65, 181004Z Jun 65.

45. Hist, MACV, 1965, pp 191–92.

46. Memo, AFXOPJ to CSAF, subj: Changes in Planning and Execution of Arc Light I, Jun 24, 1965.

47. McConnell Notebook, Arc Light Briefing, CSAF, Jun 20, 1965.

48. Msg, COMUSMACV to CINCPAC, subj: Constraint on the Use of Thai-Based Aircraft, 291226Z Jun 65.

49. Msg, COMUSMACV to CINCPAC, subj: Arc Light II, 270816Z Jun 65.

50. Msg, JCS to DIRNSA, subj: NMCC Opsum 150–65, 291054Z Jun 65; hist, MACV, 1965, pp 166–67.

51. Hist, 2d AD, Jan–Jun 1965, p 81; msg, PACAF to 13th AF, subj: PACAF OPORD 142–65, 182100Z Jun 65.

Chapter III
U.S. Assumes Major Role
June–October 1965

1. Msg, COMUSMACV to CINCPAC and JCS, subj: U.S. Troop Deployments to SVN, 070335Z Jun 65.

2. *Ibid.*

3. Msg, CSAF to PACAF, Jun 20, 1965, subj: U.S. Army Airmobile Div.

4. Msg, CINCPAC to JCS, subj: Force Requirements and Deployments to RVN, 072325Z Jun 65.

5. JCS 2343/602 JCSM 456–6; msg, CINCPAC to COMUSMACV, subj: Planning for Force Deployments and Commitments in SVN, 130222Z Jun 65.

6. Jones, *Organization,* pp 20–21; hist, 2d Air Div, Jul–Dec 1964, II, pp 34–45; Kenneth Sams, *Nguyen Cao Ky,* (HQ PACAF: Project CHECO, 1965).

7. Sams, *Binh Gia,* p 6.

8. Sams, *Binh Gia;* Jones, *Organization.*

9. *Gravel Pentagon Papers,* III, p 470.

10. JCS 2343/602 (JCSM 456065); msg, CINCPAC to COMUSMACV, subj: Planning for Force Deployments and Commitments in SVN, 130332 Jun 65.

11. Msg, CSAF to PACAF, Jun 20, 1965.

12. Tolson, *Airmobility;* Alfred Goldberg and Lt Col Donald Smith, *Army-Air Force Relations: The Close Air Support Issue* (Santa Monica, Cal: Rand Corp, 1971).

13. Msg, CSAF to PACAF, Jun 20, 1965.

14. *Ibid.*

15. McConnell Notebook, Item 186, Jun 25, 1965.

16. *Ibid,* Item 190, Jul 2, 1965.

17. Memo, AF Plans to CSAF, subj: Reexamination of Concepts for SVN, Jul 10, 1965.

18. Hist, MACV, 1965, pp 41–42; *JCS and the War,* II, pp 22–26.

19. Memo, MACV to SECDEF, Jul 20, 1965, subj: MACV Shopping List for SECDEF.

20. *Ibid,* Item 92.

21. *Ibid.*

22. *Ibid,* Item 30.

23. *Ibid,* Item 20.

24. *Ibid,* Item 18.

25. *Ibid,* Item 81; hist, 13th RTS, Jan–Jun 1965.

26. Msg, MACV to JCS, 041048Z Jul 65, subj: Weekly Strength Report, Vietnam.

27. Memo, MACV to SECDEF, Jul 20, 1965.

28. *Ibid,* Tab D, Item 85.

29. *Ibid,* Item 84.

30. *Ibid,* Tab D, Item 87.

31. *Ibid,* Tab C, Item 40.

32. *Ibid,* Tab C, Item 17.

33. *Ibid,* Tab C, Item 41.

34. McConnell Notebook, Item 217, Jul 22, 1965.

35. *Ibid,* Item 84, Apr 9, 1965.

36. *Ibid,* Item 217, Jul 22, 1965; Valenti, pp 343–45.

37. Valenti, pp 353–54.

38. *Gravel Pentagon Papers,* II, p 477; The President's News Conference of July 28, 1965, in *Public Papers of the President: Lyndon B. Johnson, 1965* (Office of the Federal Register, NARS, 1966), II, p 795.

39. Hist, 405th FW, Jul 1–Dec 31, 1965, pp 84–85; hist, MACV, 1965, p 6; hist, 2d Air Div, Jul–Dec 1965, II, pp 15–16.

40. Hist, 2d Air Div, p 16.

41. McConnell Notebook, Items 76, 97, 113, 117, 121.

42. See note above; HQ PACAF SO G–90, Jul 6, 1965.

43. *Ibid;* Corona Harvest, *Chronology,* pp 107–109.

44. Memo, HQ USAF (AFOCE) for ASD(HL), Oct 9, 1967, subj: Anal of SVN Const Prog.

45. TAC, *The Airborne Forward Air Controller,* Study Guide, n.d.

46. Hist, 2d Air Div, Jul–Dec 1965, II, p 23.

47. PACAF, *Summary of Air Operations in SEA.*

48. McConnell Notebook, Item 246, Hawaii Conference, Aug 12–15, 1965.

49. *Ibid.*

50. Msg, JCS 092159Z May 65.

51. Ltr, COMUSMACV, Aug 25, 1965, subj: Terms of Reference, Deputy Air Operation, HQ MACV.

52. *Ibid.*

53. McConnell Notebook, Item 246, Hawaii Conference, Aug 15, 1965.

54. McConnell Notebook, Item 218, Jul 23, 1965.

55. McConnell Notebook, Item 141, Staff Meet, May 17, 1965.

56. McConnell Notebook, Item 246, Hawaii Conference, Aug 12–15, 1965.

57. *Ibid.*

58. Ltr, MACV, Aug 30, 1965, subj: US-MACV Concept of Operations in Vietnam.

59. Hist, MACV, 1965, pp 72–73.

60. Hist, 2d Air Div, Jul–Dec 1965, II, pp 22–23.

61. Hist, MACV, 1965, pp 167–68; hist 2d Air Div, Jul–Dec 1965, II, p 27.

62. Hist, 2d Air Div, Jul–Dec 65, II, p 26.

63. Corona Harvest, *Chronology,* p 114.

64. McConnell Notebook, Item 273, Sep 8, 1965.

65. Hist, SAC, Jul–Dec 1965, II, pp 270–71.

66. *Ibid.*

67. Talking paper, CSAF, Oct 30, 1965.

Chapter IV
Air Force Deployments and Air Operations
September–December 1965

1. JCSM 721–65 to SECDEF, subj: U.S. Military Posture, Sep 1965.

2. Hist, 12th TFW, Aug 8–Dec 31, 1965.

3. Briefing Book, Gen Smith, Tab I, p 119, AFOCE–H, Dec 21, 1965; Status of Actions, VN, Aug 9, 1965.

4. Memo, Col R.J. Darnell, MACV–J3, subj: Tuy Hoa Airfield Const Implications, n.d.; memo, Brig Gen W.E. DePuy, AC/S, MACV–J3, to C/S MACV, subj: Statement of Nonconcurrence, Nov 4, 1965; rpt, "USAF Airfield Construction in SVN, Jul 65–Mar 67," 7th AF Info Ofc, n.d.

5. Msg, CINCPAC to JCS, 100540Z Jul 65.

6. PACAF, *Summary of Air Operations in SEA,* Vol IV, p 5–A–2.

7. EOTR, Brig Gen Albert W. Schinz, C/AF Adv Gp, Jul 9–Oct 23, 1966; Briefing paper, "Aircraft for VNAF," AFXPOR, Dec 23, 1965.

8. Hist, AF Adv Gp, Jan 1–Dec 31, 1965, p 23.

9. Hist, Skoshi Tiger, Jul 23, 1965–Mar 10, 1966, TAWC, Eglin AFB, Fla, pp 6–8.

10. McConnell Notebook, Item #206, Jul 13, 1965.

11. Hist, 12th TFW, pp 27–9.

12. McConnell Notebook, Pettit rpt, Item #374, Dec 30, 1965; Briefing book, Maj Gen R.N. Smith, Vol II, memo, subj: F–5 Evaluation, Dec 1965.

13. HQ USAF SO 6–110, Aug 4, 1965.

14. Kenneth Sams, *First Test and Combat Use of the AC–47* (HQ PACAF: Project CHECO, 1965), p 2; msg, CINCPACAF to 13th AF, 092142Z Nov 65; Jack S. Ballard, *Development and Employment of Fixed Wing Gunships, 1962–1972,* (Ofc/AF History, 1982), pp 13–14.

15. Final Rpt, "Evaluation of Side Firing Capability in C–47 Type Aircraft," JRATA Project No. 3T–753.0, Aug 2, 1965; Sams, *AC–47.*

16. Smith briefing book, Vol II, memo, subj: Special Air Warfare in SEA, Dec 21, 1965.

17. William A. Buckingham, Jr., *Operation Ranch Hand: The Air Force and Herbicides in SEA, 1961–1971* (Ofc/AF History, 1982), ch III; ltr, MACJ3 to CINCPAC, subj: Defoliation—Operational Evaluation, Dec 27, 1962.

18. Buckingham, *Herbicides,* ch VI.

19. Hist, 6253d CSG, Jul 1–Dec 31, 1965.

20. *Ibid.*

21. Westmoreland, *Report on the War,* p 104.

22. Memo, SECDEF to President, subj: SVN, Mar 16, 1964, in *Gravel Pentagon Papers,* III, p 509.

23. *Ibid.*

24. R.W. Komer, *Bureaucracy Does its Thing: Institutional Constraints on US-GVN Performance in Vietnam* (Santa Monica: Rand Corporation, 1973), pp 100–101.

25. Debriefing Rpt, Schinz, Oct 22, 1965.

26. Ltr, Schinz to MACJ02 thru 2d Air Div, subj: Modernization of VNAF, Oct 15, 1965.

27. Msg, CINCPACAF to CINCPAC, subj: VNAF Modernization, 170436Z Dec 65; Wesley R.C. Melyan, *The War in Vietnam, 1965* (HQ PACAF: Project CHECO, 1967); Jones, *Organization.*

28. Jones, *Organization,* pp 13–14.

29. Schinz, Debriefing Rpt, Annex D, p 11.

30. *Ibid,* Annex G.

31. Melyan, *Vietnam,* p 248.

32. *Ibid,* p 250.

33. *Ibid,* p 252.

34. Schinz, Debriefing Rpt, Annex I.

35. *Ibid,* Annex A.

36. *Ibid,* Annex E.

37. *Ibid,* Annex K.

38. PACAF, *Summary of Air Operations in SEA,* Vol IX, Oct 15–28, 1965.

39. *Ibid,* Nov 12–25, 1965, pp 4–5 thru 4–6.

40. Msg, CINCPACAF to CSAF, 010500Z Dec 65.

41. PACAF Oplan 154–65; msg, CINCPACAF to CSAF, 010500Z Dec 65.

42. Msg, McConnell to Harris and Moore, Nov 24, 1965, subj: Recent Operations in RVN and Command Arrangements.

43. Msg, MACV to CINCPAC, 161115Z Nov 65.

44. Msg, MACV to AIG 7011, 150400Z Nov 65; msg, MACV to JCS, subj: USMACV SITREP 318, 151120Z Nov 65; Melvin F. Porter, *Silver Bayonet* (HQ PACAF: Project CHECO, 1966), p 2.

45. Msg, MACV to CINCPAC, 161115Z Nov 65.

46. Msg, MACV to OASD, subj: Press Trends, 161020Z Nov 65.

47. Hist, SAC, Jul–Dec 1965, II, p 280; msg, AIG 286 to 2d Air Div, 170108Z Nov 65.

48. Msg, MACV to CINCPAC, 160940Z Nov 65.

49. Msg, MACV to OASD, 161020Z Nov 65.

50. Porter, *Silver Bayonet,* p 5.

51. Msgs, JCS to CINCPAC, subj: Use of Arc Light Forces, 161624Z Nov 65; CINCPAC to COMUSMACV, subj: Arc Light, 192304Z Nov 65.

52. Hist, SAC, Jul–Dec 1965, II, p 281.

53. Short Round Summary, 7th AF, TACWFP, Jan 1965–Jun 1967.

54. JCSM 812–65 to SECDEF, Nov 12, 1965.

55. Msg, CINCPAC to JCS, 182321 Nov 65.

56. Msg, JCS to CINCPAC, Nov 21, 1965.

57. Porter, *Silver Bayonet,* p 10.

58. *Ibid,* p 9.

59. Msg, CINCPACAF to CSAF, 010500Z Dec 65.

60. Corona Harvest Intvw with Col Kampe, USA, 1st Cav Div G–4, CH Intvw #101.

61. Msg, CINCPACAF to CSAF, 010500Z Dec 65; msg, 2d Air Div to CINCPACAF, 291200Z Nov 65.

62. Kampe intvw.

63. Msg, CINCPACAF to CSAF, 010500Z Dec 65; rpt, MACV, Monthly Eval for Nov 1965.

64. Ltr, MG H.W.O. Kinnard, USA, Cmdr 1st Cav Div to Lt Gen Joseph H. Moore, 2d Air Div, Nov 21, 1965.

65. Rpt, "Visit to SVN," Maj Gen H.A. Davis, AF Team Chief, Proj New Focus, Nov 19, 1965.

66. Ltr, HQ 1st Cav Div to subcmdrs and staff ofcrs, subj: Lessons Learned, Dec 9, 1965.

67. Ltr, HQ 1st Cav Div to MACV, subj: Lessons Learned, Oct 1–Nov 30, 1965, Jan 10, 1966.

68. Msg, 2d Air Div to CINCPACAF, 291200Z Nov 65.

69. Intvw, Maj R.B. Davis, ALO, 2d Div (ARVN), Feb 15, 1966.

70. Ltr, ALO, 2d Div (ARVN) to I Corps ALO, subj: Combat Operations AAR, Jan 2, 1966.

71. Jack Shulimson and Charles M. Johnson, *US Marines in Vietnam: The Landing and Buildup, 1965,* (Washington, 1978) p. 110.

72. AAR, Lien Kiet 18 (Harvest Moon), ALO, 5th Reg (ARVN), n.d.

73. Intvw, Capt Lewis Keeby, ALO, Quang Tin province, Feb 15, 1966.

74. AAR, Lien Kiet 18; Kenneth Sams, *Operation Harvest Moon* (HQ PACAF: Project CHECO, 1966), p 13.

75. Westmoreland, hist notes, Dec 28, 1965.

76. Rprt, "Operations of the U.S. Marines, Vietnam," Mar 1968, p 59.

77. Robert Burch, *Single Management of Air in SVN* (HQ PACAF: Project CHECO, 1969), p 14, ch VI; Thomas A. Cardwell, *Command Structure for Theater Warfare: The Quest for Unity of Command* (Maxwell AFB, Ala; Air University Press, 1984), pp 111–117.

78. *Ibid.*

79. Westmoreland, hist notes.

Chapter V
Settling in and Sorting Out
January–April 1966

1. PACAF, *Summary of Air Operations in SEA,* Vol XXI, Apr 1966, p 3–30.

2. DIA Bulletins, Feb 1, 10, 26, 1966; Rprt, Senate Committee on Foreign Relations, Jan 6, 1966, 89th Congress, 2d Sess; Westmoreland Briefing, subj: Honolulu Conference, Feb 16, 1966.

3. *Gravel Pentagon Papers,* IV, p 309.

4. Ltr, CINCPAC to JCS, subj: Reprogrammed Phased Force Requirements for FY 1966, Dec 16, 1965.

5. McConnell Notebook, Item 410, SEA Deployments, Feb 23, 1966.

6. *Ibid,* Item 375, Jan 3, 1966; memo, IG to CSAF, Jan 10, 1966.

7. Memo, IG to CSAF, Jan 10, 1966.

8. Memo, CSAF to SAF, Jan 6, 1966.

9. CSAFM–Y–16–66, Jan 5, 1966.

10. Jacob Van Staaveren, *U.S. Deployment Planning for Southeast Asia, 1966* (Ofc/AF History, 1967), p 5.

11. CSAFM-Y–16–66, Jan 5, 1966.

12. Memo, Col E.F. MacDonald to CSAF, subj: Deployment Schedule for SEA and other PACOM Areas, Feb 25, 1966; McConnell Notebook, Item 405, SEA Deployment, Feb 14, 1966.

13. Ltr, CINCPAC to JCS, subj: CY66 Capabilities Program, Feb 12, 1966.

14. Ltr, CINCPACAF to HQ USAF, subj: Phase IIA Eval, Feb 12, 1966.

15. CSAFM Y–32–66, subj: Memo for JCS on Future Air Operations Against NVN; McConnell Notebook, Item 410, SEA Deployments, Feb 23, 1966.

16. JCSM–130–66, Mar 1, 1966.

17. Memo, SAF to SECDEF, subj: SEA Deployment Planning, Mar 3, 1966.

18. Memo, SECDEF to CJCS, subj: Tactical Aircraft Requirements for SEA, Mar 26, 1966.

19. CINCPAC, CY66 Capabilities Program, Feb 1966; hist, MACV, 1966, pp 127–8.

20. Memo, SECDEF to SAF, subj: Deployments to SEA, Mar 31, 1966.

21. Memo, McKee to CSAF, subj: Ammo Situation in SEA, Apr 13, 1966; hist, CINCPAC, Jan–Dec 1966, p 759.

22. Background Paper to memo, Col Germaraad, Dir/Plans to CSAF, subj: Ammo Situation in SEA, Apr 13, 1966.

23. Hist, DCS/P&O, Jan 1–Jun 30, 1966.

24. Meyers intvw, pp 65–66; intvw, General Harris, CH#0018439, Apr 22, 1971, pp 36–37.

25. Msg, CINCPAC to JCS, Apr 24, 1966.

26. McConnell Notebook, Item 440, Debriefing by Maj Gen O'Keefe, Apr 13, 1966.

27. Memo, Dir/Plans to SAF, subj: Background Papers, Jul 4, 1966.

28. NSAM 346, Apr 26, 1966.

29. Hist, Dir/Trans, DCS/S&L, Jan–Jun 1966, pp 51–52.

30. EOTR, Lt Col Allen J. Diefendorfer, 557th TFS, Aug 13, 1966.

31. McConnell Notebook, Item 399, Airfields in SEA, Feb 3, 1966; Item 400, Deployments in SEA, Feb 5, 1966; Item 404, Cmdrs' Conference at Ramey, Feb 11, 1966.

32. Memo, SAF to SECDEF, subj: Feasibility of USAF Contracting with Outside Contractor for AB and Related Const in VN, Feb 5, 1966.

33. Msg, MACV to CINCPAC, subj: USAF Proposal for Additional Cost-plus-fixed-fee Const Contractor in VN, Feb 27, 1966.

34. Msg, CJCS to CINCPAC, et al, subj: AB Const in VN by AF Contractor, Mar 8, 1966; Vernon D. Burke, *AFLC Support of Forces in Southeast Asia: Procurement Support, 1964–1966* (Wright-Patterson AFB, 1968), pp 61–66.

35. McConnell Notebook, Item 483, Turnkey, May 26, 1966.

36. *Ibid,* Item 484, Turnkey, May 27, 1966; Burke, *AFLC Support,* p 5.

37. USAF Management Summary, SEA, Feb 30, 1966, p 70.

38. The text of this agreement is most readily accessible in Tolson, *Airmobility,* p 106.

39. Ltr, McConnell to Bowers, Oct 3, 1972, p 2.

40. Ltr, Yudkin to Bowers, Sep 11, 1972.

41. *Ibid,* p 2.

42. Tolson, *Airmobility,* p 12.

43. McConnell Notebook, Item 426, Disc with Lt Col Stoner, Mar 19, 1966.

44. Ltr, McConnell to Bowers, Oct 3, 1972.

45. Bowers, p 361.

46. Msg, CSAF to ALMAJCOM, 050005Z Mar 66; hist, Skoshi Tiger, Jul 23–Mar 10, 1966; hist, PACAF, Jan–Jun 1966, p 349; msg, PACAF to 2d Air Div, subj: Skoshi Tiger, 062147Z Mar 66.

47. Debriefing rpt, Maj John J. Kerwin, HQ 7th AF, Apr 9, 1966.

48. *Ibid.*

49. Corona Harvest, *Final Report,* Part IIIB, Item 11.

50. EOTR, Col Roy F. Maradin, Cmdr Det 1, 6250 CSG, Dec 1, 1965.

51. ARPA, MR, subj: Aerial Recon in RVN, Sep 17, 1965.

52. Hist, 460 TRW, Jan 1–Jun 30, 1966.

53. EOTR, Capt George W. Baker, OIC Photo Lab, 13th RTS, Dec 1, 1965.

54. Corona Harvest, *Final Report,* Part IIIB, Item 16; Meyers intvw, pp 87–88.

55. Corona Harvest, *Final Report,* Part IIIB, Item 12.

56. Corona Harvest, *Chronology,* p 186.

57. PACAF SO 692, Mar 29, 1966; msg, CSAF, 252211Z Mar 66.

58. Msg, CSAF to CINCPAC, 171547Z Mar 66.

59. EOTR, Brig Gen George B. Simler, DCS P&O, 7th AF, Addendum, Jul 13, 1966.

60. Meyers intvw, p 56.

61. EOTR, Lt Col Virgal E. Sansing, Cmdr 20th TASS, Jul 11, 1967.

62. EOTR, Capt Chris R. Payne, Sect FAC, Pleiku, Mar 13, 1967.

63. EOTR, Lt Col Parker, Dep Dir, DASC, Oct 25, 1966.

64. EOTR, Maj Rustvold, Sect FAC, Phu Bon, Mar 20, 1967.

65. Parker EOTR.

66. EOTR, Capt Rex Miller, FAC and Rgmt Advisor, Kontum Prov, Jun 15, 1966.

67. PACAF, *Summary of Air Operations in SEA,* Vol XXI, Apr 1966, pp 3–12 and 3–14.

68. Miller EOTR.

69. EOTR, Col Scroggin, ALO, II Corps, Jan 11, 1967.

70. EOTR, Capt Gene E. Syarto, FAC II Corps, Mar 27, 1967.

71. Rustvold EOTR; EOTR, Capt Domenick Fanelli, Tay Ninh Province, Apr 11, 1966; Scroggin EOTR.

72. Debriefing rpt, Capt Hugh L. Hunter, Province ALO, May 31, 1966.

73. EOTR, Capt Jonathan Myer, FAC, Kontum Prov, Sep 1966; EOTR, Capt Robert J. Smith, 504 TACC, Apr 1966–Mar 1967.

74. Myer EOTR.

75. *Ibid; In-Country Air Strike Operations, Southeast Asia, 1 January 1965–31 March 1968,* (Project Corona Harvest, 1971), pp 68–80 [hereafter cited as Corona Harvest, *ICAS*].

76. EOTR, Maj Harold Christiansen, Cmdr 510th TFS, Bien Hoa, Oct 10, 1966.

77. Msg, I DASC to 2d Air Div, subj: A Shau Special Forces Camp Attacked, 091015Z Mar 66; WAIS, 2d Air Div, Mar 25, 1966.

78. Christiansen EOTR.

79. EOTR, Lt Col James A. Minish, Cmdr 615 TFS, Jan 15, 1967.

80. EOTR, Maj Eugene Russel, Sep 9, 1966.

81. PACAF, *Summary of Air Operations in SEA,* Data Addendum, Vol XXI, Apr 1966, pp 3–A–2 to 3–A–4.

82. "Concept for improved Joint Air-Ground Coordination," approved by CS/USAF on Mar 19, 1965, and CS/USA on Apr 28, 1965. Text may be found in Corona Harvest, *ICAS,* Vol I, Subtask 1a, pp A–1–1 thru A–1–7.

83. MACV Directive 95–11, Jun 21, 1966, subj: The Joint Air-Ground Operations System.

84. Corona Harvest, *Final Report,* p C–2.

85. Komer, p 71.

Chapter VI
Setbacks for Centralized Airpower
May–December 1966

1. Rpt, "Analysis of Southeast Asia Airlift Operations," Ops Anal, Ofc/Vice CS, USAF, May 66, in hist, 315 ACW, Jan–Jun 1966, p 78.

2. *Ibid,* - 79.

3. Hist, 19th ACS Jul–Dec 1966, pp 26, 36; hist, 309th ACS, Jan–Jun 1966, p 116; hist, 310th ACS, Jan–Jun 1966, p 126.

4. Hist, 311th ACS, Jan–Jun 1966, p 141.

5. Hist, 310th ACS, Jan–Jun 1966, p 130.

6. Hist, 311th ACS, Jan–Jun 1966, pp 142–43.

7. Hist, 19th ACS, Jan–Jun 1966, pp 97–100.

8. *Ibid,* pp 101–3.

9. Hist, 311th ACS, Jan–Jun 1966, p 145.

10. *Ibid,* p 143.

11. Hist, 19th ACS, Jul–Dec 1966, pp 32–34.

12. Hist, 315th ACW, Jan–Jun 1966, p 41.

13. Hist, 315th ACW, Jan–Jun 1966.

14. Hist, 19th ACS, Jan–Jun 1966, pp 105–7.

15. Ltr, 315th ACW to Det 5, 315 Air Div, subj: Airlift System Relationships, May 1, 1966.

16. EOTR, Col Arthur D. Thomas, Oct 1966, p 7.

17. Hist, 315th ACW, Jan–Jun 1966, p 18.

18. Thomas EOTR, p. 7.

19. EOTR, Gen William W. Momyer, n.d., p 12; 483 TCW, OpPlan "Red Leaf," Jun 1966, p 2; 7th AF Command Correspondence Staff Summary Sheet, Oct 28, 1966.

20. Meyers EOTR, p 41.

21. Study, "Analysis of SEA Airlift Operations," AFGOA, Sep 1966, in hist, Dir/Plans, DCS/P&O, Vol 31, pp 94–6; msg, CSAF to PACAF, subj: Theater Airlift Study 24, May 1966.

22. Ltr, Momyer to Harris, subj: Command and Control of In-Country Airlift in SVN, Jul 10, 1966; EOTR, Maj Gen Gordon M. Graham, 7th AF, 1967.

23. MACV Briefing, Nov 5, 1966, in Staff Summary Sheet, DCS/Plans, 7th AF, subj: C–130 Squadron Deployment Plan.

24. Msg, 7th AF to PACAF, personal from Momyer to Harris, subj: Command and Control of C–130 Airlift, Sep 12, 1966.

25. Study, AFGOA, "C–130 Shuttle vs C–130 PCS Operations in SEA," Dec 1966.

26. Momyer EOTR, p 11.

27. Meyers EOTR, p 43.

28. Hist Data Record, 483th TCW, Mar 31, 1967, p 2.

29. Hist Data Record, 537th TCS, Jan–Mar 1967.

30. RMK/BRJ, "Job History of Phu Cat Airbase on Contract BNy–44105."

31. Hist Data Report, 458th TCS, Jan–Mar 1967.

32. Hist Data Report, 457th TCS, Jan–Mar 1967.

33. Momyer EOTR, p 9.

34. EOTR, Brig Gen Rockly Triantafellu, Dir/Int, 7th AF, Jul 1, 1966, pp 24–26.

35. Msg, 7th AF to PACAF, 061234Z Oct 66; William W. Momyer, *Airpower in Three Wars* (Washington, 1978), pp 99–102.

36. Msg, 7th AF to CINCPACAF, Aug 26, 1966; Msg, 7th AF to PACAF, 061234Z Oct 66; Wesley R.C. Melyan, *Arc Light, 1965–1966* (HQ PACAF: Project CHECO, 1967), p 249; Momyer, *Airpower.*

37. Memo, Momyer to Jones, subj: B–52 Concept, Aug 7, 1966; Momyer, *Airpower.*

38. Msg, 7th AF to AFXPD, subj: Control of B–52s, Sep 22, 1966; Momyer, *Airpower,* p 101.

39. Msg, Momyer to McConnell, Nov 11, 1966; msg, 7th AF to PACAF, subj: Arc Light Forces, Sep 22, 1966.

40. Momyer EOTR, p 9.

41. Msg, McConnell to Momyer, subj: B–52 ADVON, Nov 1, 1966.

42. Msg, JCS to CINCPAC, 211713Z Dec 66, subj: SAC B–52 Planning ADVON; Momyer, *Airpower,* pp 102–3.

43. Msg, COMUSMACV to CINCPAC, subj: SAC ADVON for Arc Light Management, 260957Z Dec 66.

44. JCSM 667–66 to SECDEF, Oct 15, 1966.

45. Msg, COMUSMACV to CINCPAC, subj: Arc Light, 230745Z Jul 66.

46. Msg, COMUSMACV to CINCPAC, Aug 12, 1966.

47. Msg, COMUSMACV to CINCPAC, subj: Arc Light, 230745Z Jul 66.

48. JCSM 617–66 to SECDEF, Sep 29, 1966.

49. Hist, SAC, Jan–Jun 1966, p 106; Charles K. Hopkins, *SAC Bomber Operations in the Southeast Asia War* (SAC Hist Study No 204), HQ SAC, 1985, Vol 1, p 168.

50. Memo, Dep SECDEF to CJCA, Sep 1, 1966; *JCS and the War*, Part II, pp 34–39.

51. *JCS and the War*, Part II, pp 34–38.

52. Rprt, *An Appraisal of the Effectiveness of Arc Light Operations in South Vietnam*, HQ CINCPAC (Scient Adv Gp Rpt #1–69), Feb 1969, pp B–33 to B–34.

53. Hist, MACV, 1966, p 400.

54. Rprt, *Review and Appraisal of Arc Light Operations*, Comb Anal Grp and Strat Ops Div, OJCS, J–3, Arc Light Follow-On Study, Nov 18, 1968; rpt, *B–52 Employment in Southeast Asia, 1965–1968* (Project Corona Harvest), p 48.

55. Msg, CINCPACAF to CINCPAC, subj: Flag Pole Rpt for Jul 1966, 200549Z Jul 66; hist, MACV, 1966, p 261.

56. Msg, CINCPAC to JCS, subj: Mk–24 Flares, 262242Z Mar 66; msg, CINCPACAF to CINCPAC, subj: Shortage of Mk–24 Mod 3 Flares to Meet Operational Requirements, 121935Z Mar 1966; hist, MACV, 1966, p 263.

57. Hist, MACV, 1966, p 264.

58. Study, "USAF Airfield Construction in SVN, July 1965–March 1967," 7th AF, Ch 4, on CHECO microfilm S–75; EOTR, Lt Col Allen F. McKay, 35th TFW, Phan Rang, Mar 13, 1967.

59. EOTR, Col Archie S. Mayes, Dir/CE, 7th AF, Jul 1967, p 12.

60. Hist, PACAF, Jan–Dec 1966, pp 433–35; 7th AF, "Airfield Construction."

61. RMK/BRJ, *Job History*.

62. 7th AF, "Airfield Construction."

63. Hist, PACAF, 1966, pp 416–53.

64. *Analysis of Tactical Aircraft Operations in Southeast Asia, 1965–1966* (Center for Naval Analysis, Study 712), II, pp 208–9 [hereafter cited as CNA Study 712].

65. Hist, MACV, 1966, p 394.

66. MACV Dir 95–11, subj: The Joint Air-Ground Ops System, Jun 21, 1966; hist, MACV 1966, p 394.

67. MACV Dir 95–4, Jun 28, 1966.

68. Kenneth Alnwick, *Direct Air Support in I Corps, July 1965–June 1969*, (HQ PACAF: Project CHECO, 1969), pp 11–12.

69. MACV Dir 95–4.

70. James Overton, *FAC Operations in Close Air Support Role in SVN* (HQ PACAF: Project CHECO, 1969), pp 32–33; Rowley, p 9.

71. Msg, CSAF to PACAF, Oct 12, 1965; hist, PACAF, 1966, p 274.

72. Fact Sheet, Replacement Training Unit Program, Maj J.S. Ellard, Ops Dir, PACAF, Jan 25, 1966; hist, PACAF, 1966, p 275.

73. Talking Paper, Recommendation to Air Staff on Expedited Qualified Aircrews, Lt Col F.H. O'Neal, Ops Dir PACAF, Aug 17, 1966; SEA Trends, PACAF, Dec 1966; hist, PACAF, 1966, p 279.

74. Msg, 7th AF to PACAF, Nov 17, 1966; hist, PACAF, 1966, p 280.

75. Msg, 13th AF to PACAF, Nov 4, 1966; ltr, Momyer to Harris, Oct 17, 1966, subj: F–4 Aircrew Manning; msg, 7th AF to PACAF, Nov 4, 1966.

76. Hist, PACAF, 1966, pp 312–13.

77. Hist, 504th TASG, Oct 1–Dec 31, 1966, pp 2–4.

78. *USAF Airlift Activities in Support of Operations in South Vietnam, January 1965–March 1968* [Project Corona Harvest, 1973], pp 3–4 (hereafter cited as Corona Harvest, *Airlift*); TAC, AAC, PACAF, USAFE, *Tact Air Ops: Tact Airlift* (Multicommand Manual 3–4), Vol I, May 30, 1974, p 3–1.

Chapter VII
The "Frontier" Spirit
1966

1. EOTR, Lt Col James A. Minish, Cmdr 615th TFS, Jan 15, 1967.

2. Hist, 7th AF, Jan 1, 1966–Jun 30, 1967, p. 144.

3. EOTR, Col Joseph M. Martin, Cmdr, 3d CSG, Bien Hoa, Mar 23, 1966, p 13.

4. EOTR, Lt Col John F. Rhemann, Cmdr, 612 TFS, Apr 6, 1967.

5. Mayes EOTR.

6. *Ibid.*

7. CNA Study 712, pp 208–9.

8. EOTR, Lt Robert J. Dzur, Ch/Admin Sec, 460th TRW, Jan 10, 1967.

9. EOTR, SMSgt John R. Crawford, NCOIC Prod Brch, Data Auto Div, 377th CSG, May 2, 1967.

10. Hist, 19th ACS, Jan–Jun 1966, pp 92–93.

11. Hist, 19th ACS, Jul–Dec 1966, p 31.

12. Hist, 4th ACS, in hist, 14th ACW, Jan–Jun 66, pp 50–51.

13. CNA Study 712, pp 205–6.

14. EOTR, MSgt Arthur J. Cullinan, 311th ACS, Feb 10, 1967.

15. Hist, 311th ACS, Jan–Jun 1966, in hist, 315th ACW, Jan–Jun 1966, pp 137–38.

16. Hist, 311th ACS, Jul–Dec 1966, pp 56–57.

17. EOTR, MSgt Thomas Livsey, 366th Trans Sq, Da Nang, May 1967.

18. EOTR, Lt Col Robert E. Maggart, Cmdr, 3d CES, Bien Hoa, Sep 13, 1966.

19. EOTR, Lt Col Schauer, Cmdr, 558th TFS, Apr 20, 1967.

20. EOTR, Lt Terrell J. Osborn, 391st TFS, Jan 2, 1967.

21. EOTR, Capt Gene E. Syarto, FAC, I/II Corps, Mar 27, 1967.

22. McKay EOTR.

23. EOTR, Maj Quitman M. Wright, Cmdr, 366th FMS, Nov 12, 1966.

24. Rhemann and Minish EOTRs.

25. Dzur EOTR.

26. Hist, 19th ACS, Jan–Jun 1966, p 93.

27. Dzur EOTR.

28. EOTR, MSgt Thomas H. Mullis, 3d TFW, Mar 31, 1967; EOTR, Capt Burke C. Rogers, 3d CSG, Mar 27, 1967.

29. EOTR, Capt Curtis, 3d HSq, Jan 7, 1967.

30. Martin EOTR.

31. EOTR, MSgt Jodie A. McGuffie, 3d CSG, Dec 10, 1966.

32. Curtis EOTR.

33. EOTR, Maj Harold M. Christiansen, 510st TFS, Oct 10, 1966.

34. Schauer EOTR.

35. Hists, 311th ACS, Jan–Jun 1966, pp 137–38; Jul–Dec 1966, pp 56–57.

36. Cullinan EOTR.

37. Hist, 4th ACS, in hist, 14th ACW, Jan–Jun 1966, p 52.

38. EOTR, MSgt Jerry F. Rutledge, 14th ACS, Nha Trang, Dec 12, 1966.

39. Hist, 310th ACS, Jan–Jun 1966, p 128.

40. Hist, 310th ACS, Jul–Dec 1966, p 52.

41. Ltr, 14th ACW to 1st FFV, subj: ARVN Ammo Storage, May 24, 1966.

42. Ltr, 14th ACW to 7th AF, subj: Real Estate Problem at Nha Trang AB, Sep 23, 1966; hist, 14th ACW, Jul–Dec 1966, p 5.

43. Ltr, 14th ACW to 7th AF, Sep 23, 1966.

44. Minish EOTR.

45. EOTR, MSgt James L. Meacham, 35th TFW, Phan Rang, Jan 15, 1967.

46. EOTR, SMSgt Anthony G. Montera, 39th TFS, Dec 27, 1966.

47. EOTR, Maj Edward D. Casolaro, 633d CSG, Sep 1, 1966.

48. EOTR, Maj William T. Waldrop, 4th ACS, Jan 1967.

49. EOTR, Col Lewis R. Riley, Cmdr, 35th CSG, Phan Rang, written by C.J. Baxter, Base Civ Pers Off, Dec 2, 1967.

50. Maggart EOTR.

51. Rutledge EOTR.

52. Cullinan EOTR.

53. Crawford EOTR.

54. Mullis EOTR.

55. Casolaro EOTR.

56. Cullinan and Dzur EOTRs.

57. Hist, 7th AF, Jan 1966–Jun 1967, pp 275–76; Cullinan, Dzur, Crawford, and Waldrop EOTRs.

58. Waldrop EOTR.

59. Montera EOTR.

60. EOTR, Lt Col Leighton R. Palmeston, 510th TFS/Cmdr 416th TFS, Bien Hoa, Apr 10, 1967.

61. EOTR, Capt Joseph V. Potter, FAC, 1st Inf Div, Bien Hoa, Feb 15, 1968.

62. Minish EOTR, pp 36–41.

63. *Ibid,* pp 30, 36.

64. *Ibid,* pp 27–28.

65. EOTR, Capt Chris R. Payne, FAC, 21st TASS, Mar 13, 1967; Myer and Syarto EOTRs.

66. EOTR, Maj Robert E. Neubauer, FAC, Quang Tri Prov, Feb 8, 1967.

67. EOTR, Capt Rex E. Miller, FAC, Kontum Prov, Jan 15, 1968.

68. Schauer EOTR.

69. Waldrop EOTR.

70. Rutledge EOTR.

71. EOTR, MSgt W.J. Mashburn, 1st Sgt, 14th ACW, Nha Trang, Jan 26, 1967.

72. Wright EOTR.

73. Rhemann EOTR, p 12; McKay EOTR.

74. Mullis EOTR.

75. Wright EOTR, p 2.

76. Mashburn EOTR, p 1.

77. Livsey EOTR, p 1.

78. Curtis EOTR, p 2.

79. McGuffie EOTR.

80. Martin EOTR, pp 4–5.

81. EOTR, Capt John E. Dillon, C/Sec Pol, 633d CSG, Pleiku, May 15, 1967.

82. Crawford EOTR.

83. McKay EOTR.

84. Hist, 7th AF, Jan 1, 1966–Jun 30, 1967, p 165.

85. Rhemann EOTR, Atch 3.

86. These rates surpassed those of the Korean War in which each F–80 flew a daily average of .80 sorties, the F–84s at .66, and the F–86s at .74 (USAF Statistical Digest, Summary, Korean War).

87. PACAF, *Summary of Air Operations in SEA,* Vol XXI, Apr 1966, pp 3–29 to 3–35, Appendix V.

88. Rpt, "USN Liaison Report," Lt Col Paris D. Park, Dec 7, 1965, p 9.

89. Rpt, "TDY to USN," Lt Col M.E. Nelson, Mar 5, 1966. App I, p 9.

90. Rpt, "TDY with USN," Lt Col Charles A. Watry, Jan 1966, to DO, 7th AF.

91. Study, "Ordnance Loadings of Task Force 77 Aircraft," PACFLT Analy Staff Study 12–66, Nov 7, 1966, p 11.

92. Watry rpt; rpt, "AF Liaison Duty with USN," Lt Col Kenneth M. Bowie, Aug 1, 1966.

93. Rpt, "SEA Fleet Air Operations," Lt Col Grant R. Smith, n.d., p 5.

94. Nelson rpt.

95. Rpt, "Liaison with Navy Aircraft Carriers," Lt Col William L. Craig, Apr 23, 1966.

96. Rpt, "AF Liaison Duty with USN," Oct 19, 1966, pp 10, 27, 29; Bowie Rpt, atch, p 2.

97. PACFLT, *Ordnance Loadings,* p 11.

98. CNA Study 712, I, XI.

Chapter VIII
Air Operations
1966

1. Johnson Public Papers, I, pp 9–12.

2. Hist, MACV, 1966, p 339.

3. *Ibid,* p 340.

4. *Ibid,* p 346.

5. DIA, *Southeast Asia Military Fact Book,* 1970, pp A–31 thru A–61.

6. Westmoreland, *Report on the War,* p 117.

7. William Bates and Kenneth Sams, *Operation Masher & White Wing* (HQ PACAF: Project CHECO, 1966), p 2.

8. Combat AAR, "Operation Masher/White Wing, Jan 25–Mar 6 1966," 1st Air Cav Div, Apr 28, 1966.

9. Hist, MACV, 1966, p 372.

10. Bates and Sams, *Masher & White Wing,* p 24.

11. Corona Harvest, *ICAS,* pp 68–80.

12. EOTR, Capt Jon Lucas, Apr 25, 1966.

13. Bates and Sams, *Masher & White Wing.*

14. Kenneth Sams and Bert B. Aton, *USAF Support of Special Forces* (HQ PACAF: Project CHECO, 1969), p 8.

15. WAIS, Apr 16, 1966, p 24.

16. Kenneth Sams, *The Fall of A Shau* (HQ PACAF, Proj CHECO, 1966), p 1.

17. Sams, *A Shau;* PACAF, *Summary of Air Operations in SEA,* Vol XIX, pp 4–7 and 4–8.

18. Westmoreland, *Report on the War,* p 124.

19. Msg, MACV to CINCPAC, 170652Z Mar 66, subj: Intelligence Assessment.

20. Briefing, Brig Gen Carlos M. Talbott, Dep Dir TACC, 7th AF, for SECDEF, Oct 9, 1966.

21. Briefing, Brig Gen Joseph A. McChristian, ACS/J–2 Intel, MACV, Apr 22, 1966.

22. Westmoreland, *Report on the War,* p 116.

23. Msg, MACV to CINCPAC, 171037Z Mar 66.

24. *Ibid.*

25. Momyer, *Airpower,* p 91–92.

26. Melvin F. Porter, *Interdiction in Southeast Asia, 1965–1966* (HQ PACAF, Proj CHECO, 1967), p 62; Warren A. Trest, *Operation Tally Ho* (HQ PACAF, Proj CHECO, 1967), p 1–2; hist, MACV, 1966, p 366.

27. AAR, Lam Son 289/Hastings, Lt Col Marland O. Marshall, ALO, 1st Div (ARVN), Aug 5, 1966.

28. Hist, MACV, 1966, p 366.

29. *Ibid.*

30. AAR, Marshall, p 5.

31. AAR, Marshall.

32. *Ibid.*

33. MR, Momyer, Jul 17, 1966, subj: Concept of Operations for Tally Ho, quoted in Trest, *Tally Ho,* p 5; msg, COMUSMACV to CG III MAF, Jul 18, 1966, subj: Req for Authority for Air Ops in RP I.

34. Msg, COMUSMACV to CINCPAC, 130752Z Jul 66, subj: Laotian Air Ops.

35. Memo, Col Francis R. Cappelletti, C/Tgts Div, 7th AF, Jul 25, 1966, subj: Effectiveness of B–52 Strikes in SEA.

36. Hist, SAC, Jul–Dec 1966, I, p 180.

37. Msg, 7th AF to Tiger Hound Operations, Da Nang, Aug 13, 1966, subj: Tally Ho Divert Aircraft.

38. WAIS, Aug 1, 1966, p 13.

39. Msg, COMUSMACV to CINCPAC, 120308Z Aug 66; msg, CINCPACAF to CSAF, 120341Z Aug 66.

40. Msg, CINCPAC to COMUSMACV, 272336Z Jul 66, subj: Ground Ops in the DMZ.

41. EOTR, Capt W.T. Silva, FAC, 20th TASS, Jul 1966–May 1967, Jun 2, 1967; EOTR, Maj John T. Poirier, FAC Tiger Hound/Tally Ho, Oct 1966–Jul 1967.

42. EOTR, Capt Hugh L. Hunter, ALO/FAC.

43. EOTR, Maj Fred S. Wattinger, FAC, 20th TASS, Tiger Hound/Tally Ho, May 2, 1967; EOTR, Capt Hadley M. Leas, FAC 20th TASS, Jun 14, 1967.

44. Silva and Wattinger EOTRs; EOTR, Capt D.D. Knutson, FAC, 20th TASS Tiger Hound/Tally Ho, Jun 5, 1967; EOTR, Capt Warren S. Livingston, FAC, 20th TASS, May 1967.

45. EOTR, Maj WIlliam J. Cullen, Asst Ops Ofcr, Tiger Hound/Tally Ho, May 1967.

46. EOTR, Robert E. Neubauer, Prov FAC/ALO, 20th TASS, Feb 1967.

47. Warren A. Trest and James G. Bruce, *Operation El Paso* (HQ PACAF: Project CHECO, 1966) pp iv, 1.

48. Rpt, Hqs 1st Inf Div to CG, IIFFV, Jul 3, 1966, subj: Ground Commander's Daily Situation Report; Daily Logs, MSQ 77 Site, Bien Hoa AB, Sep 28, 1966; Trest and Bruce, *El Paso,* p 18.

49. PACAF, *Summary of Air Operations in SEA,* Vol XXVIII, Nov 1966, p 3.

50. USMACV/JOPREP/Daily SITREP 328–66; OPREP 4, 241601Z–251600Z Nov 66; AAR, Operation Attleboro, 1st Inf Div, Apr 6, 1967.

51. Rpt, *Airlift in Operation Attleboro, 18 October–26 November 1966,* CHECO film S–87; Lawrence Hickey and James G. Bruce, *Operation Attleboro* (HQ PACAF: Project CHECO, 1967); Corona Harvest, *ICAS,* p 197.

52. AAR, Maj Donald L. Schmidt, ALO, 2d Bde, 25th Inf Div, Dec 23, 1966, p 1; AAR, Lt Col Thomas W. Carpenter, ALO, 1st Inf Div, Jan 17, 1967.

53. AAR, Lt Col Ulysses J. Howard, ALO, 25th Inf Div, Jan 19, 1967.

54. Schmidt AAR, p 2.

55. Carpenter, Howard, and Schmidt AARs.

56. PACAF, *Summary of Air Operations in SEA,* Vols XIV–XXIX.

57. *Dictionary of US Military Terms for Joint Usage* (JCS Pub 1), Jan 1, 1966, p 39.

58. MACV Dir 95–11, Jun 21, 1966, subj: The Joint Air–Ground System.

59. PACAF, *Summary of Air Operations in SEA,* XVI, p 4–1.

60. Minish EOTR.

61. Msg, 7th AF to AFXOP, Dec 1966, subj: Close Air Support Sorties; PACAF, *Summary of Air Operations in SEA,* Vol XXIX, pp 3–10 and 3–11.

62. Study, "Tact Air Support in SVN, Oct–Nov 1966," AFGOA, n.d., p 13.

63. Corona Harvest, *ICAS,* p 297.

64. AFGOA study, p 6.

65. Corona Harvest, *ICAS,* p 292.

66. *Ibid.*

67. *Ibid,* p 294.

68. *Ibid,* p 293.

69. *Ibid,* p 290.

Chapter IX
Refinements of Aircraft and Munitions
1966

1. Hist, Dir/Plans, DCS/P&O, Jan 1–Jun 30, 1967, p 356.

2. JCS 2339/253, subj: Military Actions for SEA, Feb 20, 1967; hist, Dir/Plans, Jan–Jun 1967, p 164.

3. Msg, COMUSMACV to CINCPAC, 180403Z Mar 67; CSAFM–M–57–67 to JCS, Apr 14, 1967; *JCS and the War,* III, p 43–1 thru 43–3.

4. Draft Presidential Memorandum, subj: Future Actions in Vietnam.

5. JCSM 307–67, Jun 1, 1967, subj: Draft Memo for the President on Future Actions in Vietnam; hist, Dir/Plans, p 165.

6. Hist, Dir/Ops, DCS/P&O, Jan 1–Jun 30, 1967, pp 250–371.

7. *Ibid,* pp 135, 152–173.

8. Hist, Dir/CE, DCS/P&R, Jan 1–Jun 30, 1967, pp 10–11.

9. *Ibid,* pp 82–85.

10. *Ibid,* pp 27, 45–46.

11. Hist, Dir/Command Control and Communications, DCS/P&R, Jan–Jun 1967, pp 192–94.

12. Ltr, HQ USAF (AFOMOBB), Jun 9, 1967, subj: Org Changes in SEA; hist, Dir/Manpower and Org, DCS/P&R, Jan–Jun 1967, pp 69–70.

13. *Ibid,* p 32.

14. Jacob Van Staaveren, *The Search for Military Alternatives, 1967* (Ofc/AF History, 1969), p 4.

15. Memo, Dep SECDEF to JCS, Mar 31, 1967, subj: Program 4 Personnel Strength in SVN; hist, 7th AF, Jan 1966–Jun 1967, p 70.

16. USAF, *Organization and Functions,* Oct 31, 1967, p 99.

17. *Ibid,* p 111.

18. Hist, Dir/Pers Training and Ed, DCS/P, Jan–Jun 1967, pp 98, 107, 115, 117.

19. *Ibid,* pp 131–33.

20. *Organization and Functions,* p 188.

21. Hist, Dir/Dev, DCS/R&D, Jan 1–Jun 30, 1967, pp 4–28.

22. *Organization and Functions,* p 189.

23. Hist, Dir/Dev, Jan–Jun 1967, pp 68–84.

24. Article, Col William H. Fleming, *Sperryscope,* Fourth Quarter, 1967.

25. Hist, Dir/Dev, Jan–Jun 1967, p 176.

26. *Ibid,* p 203.

27. *Ibid,* pp 204–205; Richard A. Pfau and William H. Greenhalgh, *The B–57G—Tropic Moon III, 1967–1972* (Ofc/AF History, 1978), p 13.

28. *Organization and Functions,* p 201.

29. Hist, Dir/Supply and Services, DCS/S&L, Jan–Jun 1967, pp 31–32.

30. *Ibid,* pp 32–33.

31. *Ibid,* p 124.

32. *Ibid,* p 159.

33. *Ibid,* p 161.

34. *Ibid,* p 168.

35. Hist, Dir/Trans, DCS/S&L, Jan–Jun 1967, p. 48.

36. *Ibid,* p 49.

37. *Ibid,* p 54.

38. *Ibid,* pp 56–58.

39. USAF Proj Forecast: Policy and Military Considerations Rpt, Jan 1964, pp viii, III–3, III–4; Futrell, *Ideas,* p 439.

40. PACAF, Input to Corona Harvest, *In-Country and Out-Country Strike Operations in Southeast Asia, 1 January–31 March 1968, Vol II, Hardware,* p i [hereafter cited as Corona Harvest, *Hardware*].

41. AFSC, Activity Input to Corona Harvest, *Acquisition for SEA, 1 January 1965–31 March 1968,* p 19 [hereafter cited as Corona Harvest, *Acquisition*]; *The Development of Nonnuclear Air Munitions for Use in SEA, 1961–1973,* draft ms (Ofc/AF History, 1980), pp I–15–I–18 [hereafter cited as *Nonnuclear Munitions*]; Corona Harvest, *ICAS,* pp 536–38.

42. AFSC, Activity Input for Corona Harvest, *Development for SEA, 1 January 1965–31 March 1968,* p 92 [hereafter cited as Corona Harvest, *Development*].

43. Rpt, "7th AF Inventory," DCS/S&L, Jul 11, 1967; briefing, DCS/S&L, Oct 19, 1967, subj: Overview of USAF Conventional Munitions, cited in Herman S. Wolk, *USAF Plans and Policies: Logistics and Base Construction in Southeast Asia, 1967* (Ofc/AF History, 1968), p 16.

44. Corona Harvest, *Development,* pp 100–102.

45. *Ibid.*

46. Corona Harvest, *ICAS,* p 536.

47. Corona Harvest, *Acquisition,* p 118.

48. JCS 1725/641–1, subj: Military Urgencies: Gravel, Dragontooth, CBU–24/29 and Button; hist, Dir/Plans, Jan–Jun 1967, p 129.

49. *Nonnuclear Munitions,* p II–13.

50. *Ibid,* p II–3.

51. *Ibid.*

52. Corona Harvest, *Development,* p 121.

53. *Ibid,* p 125.

54. Corona Harvest, *Chronology,* p 246; hist, 7th AF, p xiii.

55. *Nonnuclear Munitions,* p V–5.

56. Corona Harvest, *Development,* pp 130–32.

57. Jones, *Organization,* p 29; ltr, USAF to TAC, subj: F–5 Program, Jul 15, 1966; hist, TAC, Jul–Dec 1966, p 369.

58. EOTR, Brig Gen Charles W. Carson, C/AF Adv Gp, Mar 28, 1968–Aug 6, 1969, p 7.

59. Corona Harvest, *ICAS.*

60. AF Adv Gp Summary for Jul 1967 (AFGP–DOI), Aug 23, 1967, pp 318–19.

61. Hist, MACV, 1967, p 213.

62. Corona Harvest, *ICAS,* p 317.

63. EOTRs, Col Delbert L. Light (AFAT 7), Col Harrison H.D. Heiberg, Jr, (AFAT 1), Col Ranald T. Adams (AFAT 6), cited in Corona Harvest, *ICAS,* pp 323–24.

64. Corona Harvest, *ICAS,* p 334.

65. Hist, MACV, 1967, p 213.

66. Jones, *Organization,* p 29.
67. Hist, 537th TCS, Apr 1–Jun 30, 1967.
68. 834th Oplan 500–67, *Airlift Operations,* Apr 12, 1967.
69. Hist, 483d TAW, Jul 1–Sep 30, 1967.
70. Hist, 459th TCS, Jan–Jun 1967, pp 12–13.
71. Corona Harvest, *Airlift,* pp 250–51.
72. Hist, 14th ACW, Jan–Mar 1967, p 35.
73. Msg, AFXDO to TAC, May 26, 1967; "A Solid Agreement," *Army Times,* May 17, 1967; "Change in Army and Air Force Roles Seen Benefiting Huey Cobra Sales," *Aviation Daily,* Jun 5, 1967; "Air Force Wins Extension of Helicopter Role," *Air Force Times,* Jun 12, 1967; supplement to Air Force Policy Letter to Commanders, Jul 1967, p 15.
74. Ltr, Johnson to McConnell, Mar 9, 1968.
75. "Air Force Transfers Last of its C–8s to NASA for Civilian Test Project," *Aviation Daily,* Jul 2, 1967.
76. Ltr, McConnell to Johnson, Feb 24, 1968, p 2; "Air Force-Army Aviation Feud Still Alive," *Aviation Daily,* May 22, 1967, p 23.
77. Ltr, McConnell to Johnson, Feb 24, 1968, p 2.
78. Msg, CG, USARV, to D/Army, USAR-PAC, COMUSMACV, 020748Z May 67.
79. Corona Harvest, *Chronology,* p 269.
80. Ballard, pp 57–65.
81. Hist, 7th AF, Jul–Dec 1967, p xxii.
82. Hists, 3d TFW, Jul–Sep and Oct–Dec 1967.
83. Final rpt, Combat Dragon, Apr 1968, Vol 1, p iv.
84. *Aerospace Daily,* Jan 18, 1968.
85. Hist, TAC, Jan–Jun 1968, I, p 328.
86. Msg, DO, 7th AF to PACAF, Jun 14, 1967; hist, TAC, Jul–Dec 1967, p 695.
87. Hist, 20th TASS, Jul 1–Sep 20, 1967.
88. Hist, 23d TASS, Jul 1–Sep 30, 1967.
89. Hist, 20th TASS, Jul 1–Sep 30, 1967.

90. *Ibid.*
91. Msg, DOTACLO, 7th AF to TAC, Sep 2, 1967; msg, ASD to TAC, 282034Z Nov 67; hist, TAC, Jul–Dec 1967, p 695.
92. Hist, 14th ACW, Jan–Mar 1967.
93. Hist, 14th ACW, Sep–Dec 1967, p 31.
94. Hist, 14th ACW, Jul–Sep 1967, p 30.
95. Hist, 14th ACW, Jan–Dec 1967.
96. Msg, CSAF to CINCPACAF, subj: Helicopter Role in SAW, Jan 20, 1967; msg, CINCPACAF to CSAF, subj: Armed SAW Helicopters, Feb 11, 1967, cited in Donald Nelson, *The USAF Helicopter in SEA* (HQ PACAF: Project CHECO, 1968), pp 25–26.
97. Hist, "E" Flight, 20th Helicopter Squadron, Jan–Mar 1967, p 1.
98. Hists, MACSOG, 1965–1968.
99. *USAF Basic Doctrine,* AFM 1–2, 1953, 1954, 1955, 1959.
100. FEAF, *Final Report on the War,* 1953; AFM 1–2, 1953.
101. Matthew B. Ridgway, "The Army's Role in National Defense," *Army Information Digest,* May 1954, pp 21–30; Futrell, *Ideas,* p 224.
102. *USAF Basic Doctrine,* AFM 1–1, 1964.
103. *Functions and Basic Doctrine of the USAF,* AFM 1–1, Feb 14, 1979, p 6–5.
104. *Command and Employment of Air Power,* FM 100–20, War Dept Field Manual, 1943.
105. Supplement to Policy Ltr for Cmdrs, Jul 1966, p 18.
106. Gen Bruce K. Holloway in Supplement to Pol Ltr for Cmdrs, Oct 1966, pp 4–5.
107. *Ibid,* Jul 66, p 20.
108. Gen Howell M. Estes, Cmdr MAC, in *Ibid,* Sep 1966, pp 11–16.
109. Maj Gen Robert F. Worley, Asst DCS/Operations, Command and Control, TAC, in *Ibid,* Nov 1966, pp 9–10.
110. *Ibid,* pp 10–11.
111. Policy Letter for Commanders, Nov 15, 1966.

Chapter X
Air Operations
January 1967–March 1968

1. Moneval, USMACV, Jan 1967; ltr, Gen DePuy to Every Soldier in the Big Red One, subj: Results of Operation Cedar Falls, Jan 27, 1967; Lawrence J. Hickey, *Operation Junction City* (HQ PACAF: Project CHECO, 1967), p viii.
2. AAR, ALO, 1st Inf Div, n.d.

3. Combat AAR, III DASC, Mar 8, 1967.
4. AAR, ALO, 1st Inf Div, n.d.
5. Bowers, pp 271–78.
6. AAR, Junction City, 3d Bde, 1st Inf Div, Apr 25, 1967.
7. LTG Bernard W. Rogers, USA, *Vietnam*

Studies: Cedar Falls-Junction City: A Turning Point, (Washington, 1974), pp 112–17.

8. Rogers, pp 117–21; Hickey, pp 8–11.

9. Rogers, pp 129–135.

10. Intvw, Maj Bobby J. Meyer, ALO, 3d Bde, 4th Inf Div, Dau Tieng, Mar 29, 1967, in Hickey, p 25.

11. Meyer intvw.

12. Intvw, Capt Geoffrey P. Engels, FAC, 2d Bde, 1st Inf Div, Lai Khe, Apr 12, 1967, in Hickey, pp 34–35.

13. *Ibid.*

14. AAR, 2d Bde, 1st Inf Div.

15. Notes, III DASC Daily Log, Apr 1, 1967.

16. WAIS, 7th AF, Apr 9, 1967.

17. Rogers, p 148.

18. Hist, SAC, Jan–Jun 1967, Vol I, pp 128–38.

19. Hopkins, *SAC Bomber Operations,* pp 166–8.

20. Msg, 7th AF to SAC, subj: Arc Light 1200, 190751Z 67.

21. Hist, SAC, Jul–Dec 67, Vol I, pp 138–48; hist, SAC, 1967, (Hist Study No 111), pp 127–142.

22. Ltr, Momyer to all tact wings and sep op units, subj: Short Rounds, Mar 18, 1967.

23. Melvin F. Porter, *Short Rounds, June 1967–June 1968* (HQ PACAF: Project CHECO, 1968), p 2.

24. MACV Dir 525–13; 7th AF Reg 55–49.

25. Rpt, "The Lang Vei Incident," Formal Rpt of Investigation, HQ 7th AF, Mar 10, 1967.

26. *Ibid*; Melvin F. Porter, *Short Rounds* (HQ PACAF: Project CHECO, 1967), p 35.

27. Short Round Summary, HQ 7th AF, TACWFP, Jan 1965–Jun 1967.

28. Msg, 3d TFW to CSAF, subj: Preliminary Report of Aircraft Accident Not Resulting in Damage to Aircraft, Jul 1, 1966.

29. Porter, *Short Rounds* (1967), p 28.

30. Ltr, Momyer to wings, Mar 18, 1967.

31. Bowers, pp 288–89.

32. Westmoreland, *Report on the War,* p 154.

33. Rpt, "AF Participation in III MAF, Operation Hickory," TACD, May 20, 1967.

34. OpOrd 322–67, I MAW (Hickory), May 16, 1967.

35. Msg, COMUSMACV to 7th AF and III MAF, subj: Air/Artillery Coordination, May 16, 1967.

36. TACD rpt, "AF Participation."

37. Intvw, Maj Allen Getz, USMC, OIC, Det Bravo, May 26, 1967, in Warren A. Trest,

Maj Valentino Castellina, and Lawrence J. Hickey, *Operation Hickory* (HQ PACAF: Project CHECO, 1967), p 3.

38. Intvw, Lt Col Henly, AF Liaison Officer, III MAF, May 24, 1967, in Trest, *Hickory,* p 10.

39. Msg, AFXDC to CINCPAC, subj: In-Country Sortie Reporting, Mar 1967; SM–170–67, JCS to COS, USAF and CINCPAC, Feb 23, 1967.

40. PACAF, *Summary of Air Operations in SEA,* Vol XXXIII, Apr 1967, pp 3–8 to 3–9.

41. Note, 7th AF, DOA, to HQ 7th AF, Dir/Tac Analy, subj: Stormy (F–4) FAC Requirements in RP I, Oct 5, 1968.

42. John Schlight, *Jet Forward Air Controllers in SEAsia* (HQ PACAF: Project CHECO, 1969).

43. Rpt, HQ 7th AF, DIS, Vietnam Intelligence Summary, Mar 9–15, 1968.

44. Intvw, Lt Col Robert P. Halpenny, AC/TACT, HQ 7th AF, TACT, Sep 26, 1967, in Warren A. Trest and Valentino Castellina, *Operation Neutralize* (HQ PACAF: Proj CHECO, 1968), p 11.

45. Hist, SAC, 1967, (Hist Study No 111), pp 152–161.

46. Intvws, Maj Glenn Wasson (Tally Ho Cmdr, Da Nang, Sep 28, 1967), Maj James Beckett (Ops Ofcr, 20th TASS, Sep 29, 1967), Capts James Beltz and Gerald Bouchoux (Covey FACs, Da Nang, Sep 29, 1967), and Maj Robert Armstrong (7th AF Liaison Ofcr with Marine FSCC, Dong Ha, Oct 2, 1967), in Trest and Castellina, pp 12–13.

47. Armstrong intvw.

48. Trest and Castellina, p 35.

49. Hist, MACV, 1967, I, pp 56, 109.

50. Rpt, Vietnam Intelligence Summary, Mar 9–15, 1968, 7th AF DIS; C. William Thorndale, *VC Offensive in III Corps, October–December 1967* (HQ PACAF: Project CHECO, 1968), p 2.

51. Msg, MACV Daily Journal (Command Center Log) 271303Z and 271800Z Oct 67; Thorndale, *Offensive,* p 3.

52. Daily Briefing, 7th AF TACC, Oct 29–Nov 7, 1967.

53. Intvw, Maj P.J. Murphy, ALO, 1 Bde/1st Inf Div, Nov 28, 1967; Thorndale, *Offensive,* p 9.

54. Daily Briefing, 7th AF TACC, Oct 29–Nov 7, 1967.

55. Intvw, Capt R.H. Crooke, ALO, 5th ARVN Div, Binh Long Province, Nov 29, 1967; Thorndale, *Offensive,* p 15.

56. *Ibid.*

57. Thorndale, *Offensive,* p 17.

58. C. William Thorndale, *Battle for Dak To* (HQ PACAF: Project CHECO, 1968), p v.

59. Intvw, Capt Keith Glenn, C–130 Pilot, Nov 20, 1967; Thorndale, *Dak To,* p 8.

60. AAR, "Battle for Dak To, 25 October–1 December 1967," 4th Inf Div, Jan 3, 1968.

61. *Ibid.*

62. *Ibid.*

63. Intvw, Capt Philip Gritten, FAC, 1 Bde, 4th Inf Div, Kontum Prov, Nov 18, 1967; Thorndale, *Dak To,* p 13.

64. *Ibid.*

65. *Ibid.*

66. *Ibid.*

67. Data from HQ 7th AF, DCS/Intel, in Warren Trest, *Khe Sanh (Operation Niagara) 22 January–31 March 1968* (HQ PACAF, Project CHECO, 1968), p 3 [herafter cited as Trest, *Niagara*].

68. Msg, COMUSMACV to CG, III MAF, subj: Priority Arc Light Targeting, Jan 6, 1968, in Trest, *Niagara,* p 4.

69. MACV Directive 95–4, Jun 28, 1966.

70. Msg, COMUSMACV to Cmdr 7th AF, CG III MAF, CJCS, CINCPAC, CMC, CSAF, PACAF, FMFPAC, subj: Air Support of I Corps, Jan 22, 1968, in Trest, *Niagara,* pp 6–7.

71. Msg, CG, III MAF, to Cmdr, 7th AF, subj: Air Support Control, Operation Niagara, Jan 24, 1968, in Trest, *Niagara,* p 79.

72. Material from HQ 7th AF, DCS/Intel, in Trest, *Niagara,* p 47.

73. Hist, Task Force Alpha, Oct 1, 1967–Apr 30, 1968.

74. Sortie Statistical Data, HQ 7th AF, DOSR, and HQ MACV, in Trest, *Niagara,* p 26.

75. Trest, *Niagara,* p 26.

76. Corona Harvest, *Airlift,* p 212.

77. Bernard C. Nalty, *Air Power and the Fight for Khe Sanh* (Ofc/AF Hist, 1986) p 63.

78. Corona Harvest, *Airlift,* p 209.

79. James B. Pralle, *Arc Light, June 1967–December 1968* (HQ PACAF, Project CHECO, 1967), pp 30–31.

80. PACAF, *Summary of Air Operations in SEA,* Vol XLIV, Mar 1968, pp 5–A–1 thru 5–A–4.

81. Sortie Statistical Data, HQ 7th AF, DOSR, and HQ MACV, in Trest, *Niagara,* p 91; Nalty, *Khe Sanh,* p 103.

82. HQ 7th AF, TACC, and HQ MACV rpts, HQ 7th AF DISs, and 834th Air Division ALCC rpts, all in Trest, *Niagara,* pp 112–129; Corona Harvest, *ICAS,* p 41.

83. MACV Quarterly Evaluation, Jan–Mar 1968; Westmoreland, *Report on the War,* p 171.

84. Westmoreland, *Report on the War,* p 171.

85. Rpt, MACV Quarterly Evaluation, Jan–Mar 1968.

86. Trest, *Niagara,* pp 82–83.

87. Ltr, Gen Westmoreland to CG III MAF, subj: Single Management of Strike and Reconnaissance Assets, Mar 7, 1968.

88. Msg, COMUSMACV to CINCPAC, subj: Operation Niagara, Mar 29, 1968.

89. Corona Harvest, *ICAS,* pp 42–43.

90. C. William Thorndale, *Interdiction in SE Asia, November 1966–October 1968,* (HQ PACAF: Proj CHECO, 1969), p 95.

91. Corona Harvest, *ICAS,* p 157.

Chapter XI

Conclusion

1. MACV Dir 95–4, subj: U.S. Air Ops in RVN, Jun 28, 1968; MACV Dir 95–11, subj: Joint Air-Ground Operations System, Jun 21, 1968.

2. Corona Harvest, *ICAS,* p 28.

3. Rpt, *Scenic Harvest,* USAF Academy, Sep 1, 1967; Rpt, *Assessment of the Air Effort in Vietnam and Laos,* Army Strategy and Tactics Analysis Group, 1968; Corona Harvest, *ICAS,* p 28.

4. Corona Harvest, *ICAS,* p 63.

5. Statement made by President Johnson when awarding the Presidential Unit Citation to the 26th Marines, quoted in Nalty, *Khe Sanh,* p 103.

6. EOTR, Brig Gen George W. McLauglin, USAF Dep Dir 7th AF TACC, Jul 25, 1969.

7. Corona Harvest, *ICAS,* p 75.

8. Rpt, *An Examination of Data on Close Air Support of Ground Forces in South Vietnam,* Research Analysis Corp, McLean, Vir, Feb 1968; Corona Harvest, *ICAS,* p 78.

9. EOTR, Maj Billy G. Halbert, 7th AF, TACC, Jun 1966; Corona Harvest, *ICAS,* p 81.

10. Corona Harvest, *ICAS,* p 147.

11. *Ibid*, pp 154–55.

12. Study, *Strike Control and Reconnaissance Analysis*, HQ USAF, Dep Dir/Force Dev, Tact and Airlift Forces Div, Jul 1, 1968, p 1; Corona Harvest, *ICAS*, p 142.

13. Corona Harvest, *Airlift*, p 10.

14. *Ibid*, p 16.

15. *Ibid*, p 32.

16. *Ibid*, p 21.

17. *Ibid*, p 22.

18. *Ibid*, p 25.

19. *Ibid*, p 46.

20. *Evaluation of Airlift in Support of Operations in Southeast Asia, 1 January 1965–31 March 1968* (Project Corona Harvest, 1970), p 293.

21. *Ibid*, p 294.

22. EOTR, Maj Gen Gordon F. Blood, DCS/OPS, 7th AF, Aug 1967–Jan 1969, p 43.

23. *USAF Reconnaissance in Support of Operations in Southeast Asia, 1 January 65–31 March 68* (Project Corona Harvest, Jan 1973), 5–6, 39–40.

24. *Ibid*, p 11.

25. *Ibid*, p 18.

26. *Intelligence Activities in Support of Operations in Southeast Asia, 1 January 65–31 March 68* (Project Corona Harvest, 1972), pp 59–60.

27. AF Regulation 66–27, Apr 18, 1963; AF Manual 66–1; AF Manual 26–2.

28. *USAF Logistics Activities in Support of Operations in Southeast Asia, 1 January 1965–31 December 1969* (Project Corona Harvest, 1973), p 5.

29. *Ibid*, pp 2–3.

30. *Ibid*, pp 166–167.

31. *Ibid*, p 8.

32. *USAF Research and Development and Procurement Activities in Support of Operations in Southeast Asia, 1 January 1965–31 March 1968* (Project Corona Harvest, 1973), p 52.

33. *Ibid*, pp 11, 67.

34. *Ibid*, p 54.

35. *Ibid*, pp 55–56.

36. *Ibid*, p 2.

37. *Ibid*, pp 6–7, 67.

38. *Ibid*, p 30.

39. *Ibid*, p 9.

40. EOTR, Brig Gen Albert W. Schinz, Cmdr, AFAG, Jul 1965–Oct 1966.

41. EOTR, Brig Gen Donavon F. Smith, Cmdr, AFAG, Oct 1966–Mar 1968, pp 3–19.

42. *Ibid*, p 5–3.

43. Hist, TAC, Jul–Dec 1966, pp 2, 333f.

44. Testimony of Gen Gabriel P. Disosway before the Senate Preparedness Investigating Subcommittee of the Armed Services Committee, 89th Cong, 2d sess.

45. Hist, TAC Jul–Dec 1966, p 333.

46. Hist, TAC, Jul–Dec 1967, p ii.

47. Hist, TAC, Jan–Jun 1967, pp 262–63.

48. *Ibid*, p ii.

49. Hist, SAC, 1967, No 111, I, p 20.

50. *Ibid*, III, pp 363–64.

51. Drue L. DeBerry, "The Air Force and the War in Southeast Asia," draft ms (Ofc/AF History, n.d.), pp 226–76.

52. AF Manuals 1–2, *United States Air Force Basic Doctrine*, Apr 1, 1953, 1954, 1955, and Dec 1, 1959.

53. AF Manual 1–1, *United States Air Force Basic Doctrine*, Aug 14, 1964, p 1–3.

54. *Ibid*, p 3–3.

55. AF Manual 1–1, *United States Air Force Basic Doctrine*, Sep 28, 1971, p 1–3.

Glossary

A–1 Skyraider	Single-engine, propeller-driven attack aircraft used by the USAF, Navy, and the VNAF. A–1E had two seats; other models had one. Originally Navy AD–series aircraft. (Douglas)*
A–4 Skyhawk	Single-engine turbojet attack aircraft. Primarily a Navy and Marine aircraft with a single crewmember. (Douglas)
A–6 Intruder	Twin-engine, turbojet, two-place, attack aircraft. Used by the Navy and Marines. (Grumman)
A–26 Invader	Twin-engine, propeller-driven, WW II-era attack aircraft. Version modified for special warfare missions, including photoreconnaissance, designated B–26K. Three crewmembers. See B–26K. (Douglas)
A–37	Twin-engine turbojet attack aircraft modified from the T–37, has three times the power and two times the gross weight of the T–37. See T–37.
AC–47	C–47 transport converted into a gunship by adding side-firing miniguns. The AC–47 had several nicknames: Puff the Magic Dragon, Dragon Ship, and Spooky. See C–47.
AC–130	C–130 transport modified into a gunship through the installation of side-firing guns and night-vision devices. See C–130.
AD–6	Early Navy designation for the A–1H. See A–1.
AA	antiaircraft
AAR	after action report
AB	air base
ABCCC	airborne battlefield command and control center
Able Mable	Limited reconnaissance by Air Force RF–101s over selected areas of Laos and South Vietnam.
ABS	air base squadron
ACS	air commando squadron
ACS/	Assistant Chief of Staff for
actg	acting
ACW	air commando wing
AD	air division
ADVON	advanced echelon
AF	Air Force
AFLC	Air Force Logistics Command
AFSC	Air Force Systems Command
AFB	Air Force Base
AGM	air-to-ground missile
AID	Agency for International Development
Air America	Contract airline that flew for the Central Intelligence Agency in Southeast Asia.
ALCC	airlift control center
ALO	air liaison officer
amb	ambassador
AmEmb	American Embassy
AOC	air operations center
Arc Light	Strategic Air Command B–52 strikes in South and North Vietnam and Laos.
ARDF	airborne radio direction finding
ARVN	Army of the Republic of Vietnam
ASOC	air support operations center
Attleboro	A ground operation in northern Tay Ninh Province, South Vietnam, during September through November 1966.
AWACS	Airborne Warning and Control System

---

*Aircraft manufacturer shown in parenthesis.

B–24 Liberator	Four-engine, propeller-driven, WW II heavy bomber. Eight to ten crewmembers. (Consolidated)
B–26 Invader	See A–26 Invader.
B–26K Counter Invader	Twin-engine, propeller-driven attack aircraft modified from the WW II-era A–26. See A–26.
B–29 Superfortress	Four-engine, propeller-driven, long-range, WW II very heavy bomber. (Boeing)
B–52 Stratofortress	All-weather, intercontinental, strategic heavy bomber powered by eight turbojet engines. Its range is extended by inflight refueling. Flight crew of six. (Boeing)
B–57 Canberra	Twin-engine, turbojet medium bomber developed from English Canberra bomber. Two crewmembers. (Martin)
B–66 Destroyer	Twin-engine, turbojet light bomber developed from Navy A–3 Skywarrior. Modified into RB–66 (reconnaissance) and EB–66 (electronic countermeasures) models. Three to seven crewmembers. (Douglas)
Barrel Roll	Interdiction and close air support operations in eastern Laos (beginning in December 1964). Operations with this name later reduced to only northern Laos (April 1965).
BDA	bomb damage assessment
Big Eye	EC–121D with radar and communications equipment for early warning and control; began in 1965, redesignated College Eye in 1967. See EC–121D.
Birmingham	Joint 1st Infantry Division/25th ARVN Division operation in Tay Ninh Province during April and May 1966.
Black Spot	Modified C–123s with forward-looking radar, low-light-level television, forward-looking infrared detector, laser range finder, advanced navigation system, weapon-release computer, and CBU dispenser. See C–123.
BLU	bomb, live unit
Blue Tree	Photoreconnaissance targets in North Vietnam, begun in 1965
bn	battalion
Brave Bull	Follow-on program to Hilo Hattie, begun in February 1963. The 6091st Reconnaissance Squadron used C–97 aircraft equipped with DRF, IR, and long-range cameras.
Bugle Note	A tactic for providing increased B–52 support during the Communist siege of Khe Sanh that used cyclic launches (first 3 bombers every 90 minutes, later 6 bombers every 180 minutes), with variations to prevent prediction of arrival time. The bombers flew to a predesignated preinitial point and were guided to the targets by Combat Skyspot radar. The concept proved to be so efficient at Khe Sanh that it was expanded to cover all areas hit by the B–52s.
Bullpup	Air-to-surface guided missile, visually guided by launching aircraft command. Used by fighters, light attack aircraft, and helicopters. Intended for close support of ground troops and interdiction and for small targets ashore and afloat.
C–7 Caribou	Twin-engine, propeller-driven, all-weather transport, designed for short-takeoff-and-landing in forward battle areas or unimproved strips. Three crewmembers. As Army transports, designated CV–2. (de Havilland)
C–8 Buffalo	Twin-engine, turboprop, short-takeoff-and-landing transport. Enlarged version of C–7. Three crewmembers. Army designation CV–7. (de Havilland)
C–47 Skytrain	Twin-engine, propeller-driven, WW II-era transport, nicknamed "Gooney Bird." Modified into AC–47 (gunship), EC–47 (elec-

	tronic countermeasures), and RC–47 (reconnaissance). Two to seven crewmembers; used by USAF and VNAF. (Douglas)
C–54 Skymaster	Four-engine, propeller-driven, WW II-era transport adapted from commercial DC–4. (Douglas)
C–97 Stratofreighter	Four-engine, propeller-driven transport variant of the B–29/B–50. Five crewmembers. (Boeing)
C–118 Liftmaster	Four-engine, propeller-driven, long-range transport; military version of commercial DC–6. Five crewmembers. (Douglas)
C–119 Flying Boxcar	Twin-engine, twin-boom, high-wing, propeller-driven transport used by the USAF and VNAF. Modified versions included the AC–119G Shadow and AC–119K Stinger gunships. The K model had auxiliary jets mounted outboard of the piston engines. Four crewmembers in transport; eight to ten in gunships. (Fairchild)
C–123 Provider	Twin-engine, propeller-driven, high-wing transport used by the USAF and VNAF. Four crewmembers. C–123K has two auxiliary turbojet engines. UC–123 was modified for Ranch Hand defoliation missions. (Fairchild)
C–124 Globemaster	Four-engine, propeller-driven, large transport. Five crewmembers. (Douglas)
C–130 Hercules	Four-engine, turboprop, medium-range, high-wing transport. Variants include AC–130 gunship and EC–130 command/electronic warfare aircraft. Four crewmembers; AC–130 had fourteen. (Lockheed)
C–133 Cargomaster	Four-engine, turboprop, high-wing, long-range transport. Four to ten crewmembers. (Douglas)
C–141 Starlifter	Four-engine, turbofan, high-wing, long-range transport, first all-jet strategic transport. Eight crewmembers. (Lockheed)
CH–3 Sea King	Twin-turbine passenger/cargo helicopter with single five-blade main rotor, capable of operating from land or water. Three to four crewmembers. HH–3 variant modified for rescue operations. (Sikorsky)
CH–21 Workhorse	Single-engine (radial piston) passenger/cargo helicopter with twin three-blade rotor. Two crewmembers. (Vertol)
CV–2 Caribou	Army designation of C–7. See C–7.
C/	chief of
Candy Machine	USAF F–102 interceptor air defense teams in Vietnam.
CAP	combat air patrol
CAS	close air support
CBU	Cluster bomb unit; antipersonnel weapon consisting of a dispenser containing smaller explosive devices (bomblets) that contained steel spheres.
Cedar Falls	Ground operation in the Iron Triangle area northwest of Saigon during January 1967.
CG	commanding general
CHECO	Contemporary Historical Evaluation of Counterinsurgency Operations (1962); Contemporary Historical Evaluation of Combat Operations (1965); Contemporary Historical Examination of Current Operations (1970)
CIA	Central Intelligence Agency
CIDG	Civilian Irregular Defense Group
CINCPAC	Commander in Chief, Pacific Command
CINCPACAF	Commander in Chief, Pacific Air Forces
CINCPACFLT	Commander in Chief, Pacific Fleet
cmdr	commander
CNA	Center for Naval Analysis
COIN	counterinsurgency
College Eye	See Big Eye and EC–121D.

Combat Skyspot	MSQ–77 and SST–181 radar-controlled bombing system.
Combat Spear	C–130E support for the Studies and Observations Group.
Commando Sabre	Operations begun in June 1967 to demonstrate the feasibility of using jet aircraft in the FAC role in high-threat areas where O–1s and O–2s were vulnerable.
COMUSMACV	Commander, United States Military Assistance Command, Vietnam
CORDS	Civil Operations and Revolutionary (Rural) Development Support, a joint U.S. civil/military staff that directed U.S. assistance to Vietnam in support of the revolutionary (rural) development program.
Corona Harvest	A USAF project to collect documents on the SEA conflict for historical purposes.
corps areas	The four areas that South Vietnam was divided into for military purposes. Numbered with Roman numerals, from I Corps in the north to IV Corps in south (Mekong River Delta area).
COSVN	Central Office for South Vietnam (Communist headquarters in SVN)
Covey	Call sign of the FACs of the 20th TASS operating in North Vietnam and Laos
CSG	combat support group
CY	calendar year
DAS	direct air support
DASC	direct air support center
DCS/	Deputy Chief of Staff for
Demilitarized Zone	The neutral zone separating the two Vietnams, consisting of demilitarized zones of not more than five kilometers on either side of the demarcation line, the Ben Hai River; located at about the 17th parallel.
dep	deputy
det	detachment
DI	director of intelligence; directorate of intelligence
DIA	Defense Intelligence Agency
Dir/	Director of; Directorate of
div	division
Dixie Station	The location of U.S. naval forces in the South China Sea with strike responsibility for South Vietnam.
DMZ	Demilitarized Zone
doc	document
DRV	Democratic Republic of Vietnam (North Vietnam)
EB–66	B–66 modified to a special electronic configuration. See B–66.
EC–47	A C–47 with radio direction finding equipment. First designated RC–47. See C–47.
EC–121D Constellation	A C–121 (four-engine, propeller-driven transport built by Lockheed) modified as a special search aircraft with bottom and top radar. Sixteen crewmembers. See Big Eye (Official nickname—Warning Star)
EC–130E	C–130E with special electronic configuration. See C–130.
El Paso	A major ground campaign in III Corps during June–July 1966 by the 1st Infantry Division and the III Corps ARVN forces.
encl	enclosure
EOTR	End of Tour Report
F–4 Phantom II	Twin-engine, turbojet, all-weather, supersonic tactical fighter-bomb-

er. Developed from Navy's F–4B (F–4C first USAF model). F–4E had an internal 20-mm Gatling gun; all previous models carried either missiles only or missiles and an external gun pod. Used by USAF, USN, and USMC. Two crewmembers. (McDonnell Douglas)

F–5 Freedom Fighter
Twin-engine, turbojet, supersonic, light tactical fighter. Nicknamed Skoshi (little) Tiger in Vietnam. F–5A has one crewmember, F–5B two crewmembers. Used by USAF and VNAF. (Northrup)

F–8 Crusader
Single-engine, turbojet, supersonic day jet fighter. Used by USN and USMC. One crewmember. (Vought)

F–100 Super Sabre
Single-engine, turbojet, supersonic fighter with a low, thin, swept wing and nose air intake. The F–100F used as a jet FAC had two crewmembers; other models had one. (North American)

F–102 Delta Dagger
Single-engine, turbojet, supersonic, delta-wing fighter-interceptor. TF–102 had two crewmembers; others had one. (Convair)

F–104 Starfighter
Single-engine, turbojet, supersonic, light-weight fighter. One crewmember in A and C models; two in B and D models (trainers). (Lockheed)

F–105 Thunderchief
Single-engine, turbojet, all weather, supersonic fighter-bomber. The two-place F–105G was an F–105F modified for the "Wild Weasel" role for destroying surface-to-air missile sites. (Republic)

F–111
Twin-engine, turbofan, all weather, supersonic, variable-geometry wing fighter-bomber. Most sophisticated USAF aircraft in Vietnam; advanced electronics allowed missions in all conditions. Two crewmembers. (General Dynamics)

FAC
forward air controller

Farm Gate
The detachment of the 4400th Combat Crew Training Squadron deployed to Bien Hoa Air Base, Vietnam with C–47s and T–28s in November 1961.

Flaming Dart
Retaliatory strikes against North Vietnam in early 1965, superseded in March 1965 by Rolling Thunder.

flying crane
The CH–54 helicopter (20,000-pound lifting capacity)

FWAF
free world assistance force

FW
fighter wing

FY
fiscal year

Geneva accords
The agreements of the Geneva Conference of 1954 that led to the withdrawal of French forces from Vietnam and the division of the country into North and South Vietnam.

GCI
ground-controlled intercept

Gooney Bird
Unofficial nickname of the C–47 aircraft.

Gray Eagle
The initial supply packages (for housing, messing, transportation, and operational needs) used to reform expeditionary bases in South Vietnam.

gp
group

GS
general staff

gunship
Any of several modified USAF fixed-wing transport aircraft equipped with side-firing weapons and night-vision devices. (Term also applies to U.S. Army and Marine helicopters equipped with weapons.)

H–19 Chickasaw
Single-engine (piston) transport helicopter with a single three-blade main rotor. Two crewmembers. (Sikorsky)

H–34 Choctaw
Single-engine (piston) transport helicopter with a four-blade main rotor. Two crewmembers. (Sikorsky)

HC–47	C–47 equipped for search and rescue operations with twice the fuel load, stronger landing gear, and jet-assisted takeoff. See C–47.
HH–3 Jolly Green Giant	Search and rescue version of the CH–3, modified with armor plating, jettisonable external fuel tanks, refueling probe, and two 7.62-mm guns. See CH–3.
HH–43 Huskie	Single-engine (turbine) helicopter designed for crash-rescue operations with two contra-rotating, two-blade rotors set at opposing angles above fuselage. F model has armor plating around engine, crew area, and cargo compartment. Two crewmembers. (Kaman)
HU–16 Albatross	Twin-engine, propeller-driven, amphibious, high-wing, search and rescue aircraft with all-metal hull and wing floats. Four crewmembers. (Grumman)
Harvest Moon	A combined USMC/ARVN operation conducted in Quang Tin Province in December 1965.
Hastings	A COMUSMACV-directed operation in July 1966 opposing the NVN 324B Division infiltrating the northern provinces of South Vietnam.
Hawk	U.S. surface-to-air missile capable of destroying supersonic aircraft.
Heavy Hook	C–123 operations in support of the MACV Studies and Observations Group.
Hickory	USMC/ARVN operation in May 1967 against NVN forces infiltrating through the DMZ.
high-drag bomb	A weapon fitted with extra fins to slow its speed and increase the time of fall.
Hillsboro	The C–130 airborne control center in the northern Steel Tiger area during the daylight hours.
Hilo Hattie	An early (1962) evaluation of infrared detection using a C–54 equipped with infrared and radio direction finding equipment and long-range cameras. It was replaced by Brave Bull in 1963.
hist	history
Ho Chi Minh Trail	The NVA logistic supply route of roads and trails through the passes from NVN into Laos and down the eastern side of Laos into South Vietnam and Cambodia.
hootch	A one-story dormitory building (without plumbing) usually housing fewer than twenty personnel.
HS	helicopter squadron
Huey	nickname for the UH–1 helicopter
INT	intelligence
intvw	interview
IR	infrared
iron bomb	a high-explosive bomb
Iron Triangle	A Viet Cong stronghold in an area of dense jungle about twenty miles NNW of Saigon.
JAGOS	Joint Air-Ground Operations System (MACV)
JCS	Joint Chiefs of Staff
JOC	joint operations center
Junction City	The massive two and one-half month (February–April 1967) sweep of War Zone C aimed at opening the area for clearing operations that would eliminate this major enemy sanctuary. The plan was to root out the COSVN and cripple the 9th VC Division.

Jungle Jim	The 4400th Combat Crew training squadron and subsequent USAF air commando activity at Eglin AFB, Florida.
KC–135 Stratotanker	Long-range, high-performance tanker powered by four turbojet engines. Has a flying boom for high-speed, high-altitude, aerial refueling of bombers and fighters. Can be used as a cargo and/or troop transport, carrying up to eighty troops. Four crewmembers. (Boeing)
karst	An irregular limestone region with jagged ridges, sinks, underground streams, and caverns.
KBA	killed by air
KIA	killed in action
km	kilometer
L–19	Previous designation for the O–1. See O–1.
laser	light amplification by stimulated emission of radiation
Lonesome Tiger	Forward-looking infrared detection system in the 1966 A–26 aircraft flight test.
loran	Long-range electronic navigation system that uses a time divergence of pulse-type transmissions from two or more fixed stations. From (LO)ng (RA)nge (N)avigation.
LST	landing ship, tank
M–16 (M–16A–1)	A 5.56-mm, magazine-fed, gas-operated, air-cooled, shoulder weapon designed for either semiautomatic or automatic fire.
MAAG	Military Assistance Advisory Group
MAC	Military Airlift Command
MACSOG	The Studies and Observations Group (SOG) of MACV.
MACV	Military Assistance Command, Vietnam
MAF	Marine amphibious force
Masher/White Wing	An operation conducted in the vicinity of Bong Son in central Binh Dinh Province, a joint U.S./ARVN/ROK effort, including the 1st Air Cavalry.
MATS	Military Air Transport Service
MAW	Marine aircraft wing
mbl	mobile
MiG	Popular designation for certain Russian fighter aircraft designed and developed by the Mikoyan and Gurevich design bureau.
mil	military
Misty	Call sign for the F–100F FACs flying out of Phu Cat and Tuy Hoa Air Bases.
mm	millimeter
monsoon	A seasonal wind in Southeast Asia that blows from the southwest during April to October and from the northeast during the rest of the year.
Montagnard	Mountain tribesmen of Vietnam, Laos, and Cambodia who had a history of antipathy toward the Vietnamese.
MR	memorandum for record
msg	message
mtg	meeting
Mule Train	The nickname of the initial USAF C–123 detachment in Vietnam.
NATO	North Atlantic Treaty Organization
NCO	noncommissioned officer

Neutralize	A concentrated 7th Air Force effort in 1967 to seek out and destroy enemy artillery positions in an area north of the DMZ.
n.d.	no date
Niagara	USAF participation in the battle for Khe Sanh in January–March 1968.
NORM	not operationally ready, maintenance
NORS	not operationally ready, supply
NVA	North Vietnamese Army
NVN	North Vietnam
O–1 Bird Dog	Single-engine, propeller-driven, high-wing, light observation aircraft. One or two crewmembers. Formerly designated L–19. (Cessna)
O–2 Super Skymaster	Twin-engine (one push, one pull), propeller-driven, twin-boom, light observation aircraft. One or two crewmembers. (Cessna)
OV–1 Mohawk	Twin-engine, turboprop, surveillance (day and night) airplane with visual observation and photographic capabilities. Two crewmembers. (Grumman)
OV–10 Bronco	Twin-engine, twin-boom, light-weight, armed reconnaissance aircraft. More versatile than the O–1 or O–2; used in Vietnam after 1968. Two crewmembers. (North American)
One Buck	Tactical Air Command composite air strike force deployment to Southeast Asia in August 1964 in response to the Gulf of Tonkin attack.
OPlan	Operation Plan
ops	operations
PACAF	Pacific Air Forces (USAF)
PACFLT	Pacific Fleet
PACOM	Pacific Command
Pathet Lao	Laotian Communist force or person.
Patricia Lynn	RB–57 infrared reconnaissance aircraft.
Pave Way	Guidance systems for bombs: Paveway I—laser, II—electro-optical, III—infrared. Also used to describe the aircraft delivering the bombs.
Prime Beef	combination of a nickname (Prime) and an acronym (BEEF—Base Engineering Emergency Force).
proj	project
psyop(s)	psychological operation(s)
psywar	psychological warfare
PT–76	Soviet amphibious light tank with 76-mm gun.
RB–57	B–57 modified for reconnaissance. See B–57.
RB–66	B–66 modified for reconnaissance. See B–66.
RC–47	C–47 transport modified for reconnaissance. See C–47.
RF–4C	F–4C modified for photographic and/or electronic reconnaissance missions. See F–4.
RF–101 Voodoo	Reconnaissance version of the F–101. A twin-engine turbojet aircraft, the first supersonic reconnaissance aircraft of the USAF. One crewmember. (McDonnell)
R&D	research and development
R&R	rest and recuperation
Ranch Hand	Nickname of the UC–123 aerial spray detachment deployed to Southeast Asia in 1961–62 and applied to later defoliation and herbicide operations.
rcrd	record

RCS	reconnaissance squadron
Red Horse	Rapid Engineering Deployment and Heavy Operational Repair Squadron, Engineering
RMK/BRJ	Raymond International, Morrison-Knudsen, Brown and Root, and J. A. Jones (engineering and construction firm)
ROK	Republic of Korea
Rolling Thunder	Air strikes against lines of communication and other targets in North Vietnam (March 1965–October 1968).
Route Packages	Numbered geographic areas (I through V, VIA, VIB) in North Vietnam, designated by CINCPAC to permit the assignment of Rolling Thunder responsibilities to CINCPACAF, CINC-PACFLT, and COMUSMACV.
rpt	report
RTS	reconnaissance technical squadron
RVN	Republic of Vietnam
RVNAF	Republic of Vietnam Armed Forces
S–2 Tracker	Twin-engine, propeller-driven, carrier-based, search and attack, antisubmarine aircraft. (Grumman)
SA–2	Soviet-made, surface-to-air, radar-guided missile.
SAAMS	Special Assignment Airlift Missions
SAC	Strategic Air Command
sappers	Individuals who conduct attacks and sabotage using mines, satchel charges, and/or other demolition devices.
SAR	search and rescue
Saw Buck	Tactical Air Command composite air strike force deployments to Vietnam in mid-1962 and afterward. Also the nickname of the C–123 detachment deployed to Vietnam in mid-1962.
SCAR	strike control and reconnaissance
SEA	Southeast Asia
SEATO	Southeast Asia Treaty Organization
Seed Joy	A program to modify the Bullpup for flak suppression.
Shadow	Call sign of the C–119G gunships.
Shed Light	A USAF program to improve night attack/interdiction capability.
Shining Brass	Cross-border reconnaissance into Laos and through the DMZ; ended March 1967.
short rounds	The inadvertent or accidental delivery of ordnance with resultant injury or death to friendly forces or noncombatants. The term originally described rounds or bombs that fell short of the target.
Shrike	A passive homing, antiradar, air-to-surface missile designed for use against hostile radars directing guns or missiles.
Silver Bayonet	The operation in November 1965 near the Cambodian border in Ia Drang Valley of Pleiku Province that was the first test of the Army's airmobile cavalry.
SITREP	commander's situation report
Skoshi Tiger	The test of the F–5 aircraft in Southeast Asia combat situations.
Skyspot	See Combat Skyspot.
SLAR	Side-looking airborne radar; views at right angles to the axis of the aircraft, producing a presentation of terrain or moving targets.
smart bomb	A bomb with a system allowing internal or external guidance after release.
SOIC	sector operational intelligence center
SOS	special operations squadron
Southeast Asia Airlift System	A special, high-priority airlift system to Southeast Asia.

SOW	special operations wing
Special Forces	Military personnel with cross-training in basic and specialized military skills, organized into small multiple-purpose detachments with the mission to train, organize, supply, direct, and control other forces in guerrilla warfare and counterinsurgency operations and conduct unconventional warfare operations.
sqdn	squadron
Steel Tiger	Air Force/Navy interdiction in southern Laos on the Ho Chi Minh Trail, beginning April 3, 1965, after which Barrel Roll was confined to northern Laos.
STOL	short-takeoff-and-landing
STRICOM	Strike Command (U.S.)
SVN	South Vietnam
T–28 Nomad	Single-engine, propeller-driven, 1950-era trainer. The T–28s used in Vietnam had been extensively modified for use as counterinsurgency aircraft. Used by USAF and VNAF; two crewmembers. (North American)
T–37	Twin-engine, turbojet trainer with side-by-side seating for instructor and student. The A–37 was a highly modified version of this aircraft. (Cessna)
TAC	Tactical Air Command
tac	tactical
tacan	tactical air navigation; a radio air navigation system
TACC	tactical air control center
TACS	tactical air control system
Tally Ho	An intensified interdiction campaign in southern route package 1.
TASG	tactical air support group
TASS	tactical air support squadron
TCS	troop carrier squadron
TCW	troop carrier wing
Tet	The Lunar New Year holiday celebrated in Vietnam and other Asian countries during the first seven days of the first month of the lunar calendar; occurs between January 21 and February 19.
TEWS	tactical electronic warfare squadron
TFS	tactical fighter squadron
TFW	tactical fighter wing
Tiger Hound	Nickname of a special Air Force, Navy, Marine, and Army task force that began interdicting southeastern Laos on December 5, 1965.
TRS	tactical reconnaissance squadron
TRW	tactical reconnaissance wing
Turnkey	A USAF base construction concept initiated in 1966 that did not require Army or Navy resources. Construction of a complete base was contracted for as an entire package instead of the piecemeal approach formerly used. The project was operated through the Seventh AF Director of Civil Engineering, who was designated Program Director.
Two Buck	The deployment of fighter, reconnaissance, and airlift forces to SEA beginning April 4, 1965.
U–2	Single-engine, high-altitude, long-range, turbojet reconnaissance aircraft with long, wide, straight wings and a glider-like appearance and characteristics. One crewmember. (Lockheed)

U–3	Twin-engine, propeller-driven utility aircraft. Two crewmembers, three passengers. (Cessna)
U–6 Beaver	Single-engine, propeller-driven utility aircraft. One crewmember, five passengers. (de Havilland)
U–10 Super Courier	Single-engine, propeller-driven, STOL aircraft. Two crewmembers, two passengers. (Helio)
UC–123	C–123 transport modified for spraying. See C–123 and Ranch Hand.
UH–1 Iroquois	Single-engine (turbine) general purpose helicopter with a single two-blade main rotor. Used by U.S. Army. Two crewmembers, five to eleven passengers. (Bell)
UHF	ultra high frequency
UN	United Nations
U.S.	United States (of America)
USA	United States Army
USAF	United States Air Force
USAID	United States Agency for International Development
USARV	United States Army, Vietnam
USMACTHAI	United States Military Assistance Command, Thailand
USMACV	United States Military Assistance Command, Vietnam
USMC	United States Marine Corps
USN	United States Navy
USSTRICOM	United States Strike Command
VC	Viet Cong; Vietnamese Communists
VHF	very high frequency
Viet Cong	Informal name for South Vietnamese Communist forces; ranged from guerrillas to well trained and equipped main forces.
Viet Minh	Short name for a Vietnamese independence group (*Viet Nam Doc Lap Dong Minh Hoi*—League for the Independence of Viet Nam) formed in 1941 that led the struggle for the independence of Vietnam from the French and fought the French in the Indochina War. Viet Minh leaders were absorbed into the Vietnamese Communist Party, the dominant force in North Vietnam, and elements merged with the Viet Cong in South Vietnam.
VNAF	Vietnamese Air Force
vol	volume
VR	visual reconnaissance
VTOL	vertical takeoff and landing
Walleye	A television-guided missile carried by U.S. jets. Guidance was integral to the missile; the aircraft had no control over it after launch.
War Zone C	A VC redoubt NW of Saigon, roughly encompassing NW Tay Ninh Province.
War Zone D	A VC redoubt NNW of Saigon centered on the intersection of the borders of Binh Long, Phuoc Long, and Bin Duong Provinces.
Water Glass	Rotational deployments of USAF F–102 aircraft to Tan Son Nhut AB for air defense.
wg	wing
WIA	wounded in action
Wild Weasel	The name applied to specially configured multiplace fighter aircraft and aircrews used to hunt and kill enemy-controlled surface-to-air missile sites.

THE WAR IN SOUTH VIETNAM

WIS	Weekly Intelligence Summary (Seventh AF)
WRS	weather reconnaissance squadron
Yankee Station	The location of U.S. naval forces in the Gulf of Tonkin that had strike responsibility for North Vietnam.
Yankee Team	A USAF and USN tactical recon program that began in northern and southern Laos on May 19, 1964.
Zulu (or Z)	Zulu Time (Greenwich Mean Time)

Bibliographic Note

Between 1962 and the end of the war, a changing group of military and civilian historians, including the author, microfilmed for Project CHECO (Contemporary Historical Evaluation of Counterinsurgency Operations, later Combat Operations) over 1,000 reels of Air Force documents in Vietnam, Laos, Thailand, and Cambodia and produced in Saigon and Udorn over 200 reports on specific aspects of the war. Four hundred of these reels proved invaluable for this history, as did the following CHECO reports and their supporting documents:

Abbey, Tom G., Capt., USAF. *The Role of USAF in Support of Special Activities in SEA*, July 1, 1976.

Bates, William, and Kenneth Sams. *Operation Masher/WhiteWing*. September 9, 1966.

Burch, Robert, Lt. Col., USAF. *Single Management of Air in SVN*. March 18, 1969.

Hickey, Lawrence J. *Operation Junction City*. November 17, 1967.

Hickey, Lawrence J., and James G. Bruce. *Operation Attleboro*. April 14, 1967.

Hurley, Alfred F., Col., USAF. *The EC–47 in Southeast Asia*. September 20, 1968.

Jones, Oakah L., Maj., USAF. *Organization, Mission and Growth of the Vietnamese Air Arm, 1949–1968*. September 20, 1968.

Melyan, Wesley R. *The War in Vietnam*, 1965. January 25, 1967.

Porter, Melvin F. *Silver Bayonet*. February 28, 1966.

_____. *Short Rounds*. August 23, 1968.

_____. *Air Response to Immediate Air Requests in SVN*. July 15, 1969.

Sams, Kenneth. *First Test and Combat Use of the AC–47*. December 8, 1965.

_____. *Nguyen Cao Ky*. December 14, 1965.

_____. *The Battle of Binh Gia*. December 27, 1965.

_____. *Operation Harvest Moon*. March 3, 1966.

_____. *The Fall of A Shau*. April 18, 1966.

Sams, Kenneth, and Lt. Col. Bert B. Aton, USAF. *USAF Support of Special Forces*. March 10, 1969.

Schlight, John, Maj., USAF. *Jet Forward Air Controllers in SEAsia*. October 15, 1969.

Thorndale, C. William. *VC Offensive in III Corps*. May 15, 1968.

_____. *Battle for Dak To*. June 21, 1968.

_____. *Interdiction in SEASIA, November 1966–October 1968*. June 30, 1969.

Trest, Warren A., *Tally Ho*. November 21, 1966.

_____. *Khe Sanh (Operation Niagara) 22 January–31 March 1968*. September 13, 1968.

Trest, Warren A., and James G. Bruce. *Operation El Paso*. November 30, 1966.

Trest, Warren A., Maj. Valentino Castellina, USAF, and Lawrence J. Hickey. *Operation Hickory*. July 24, 1967.

Trest, Warren A., and Maj. Valentino Castellina, USAF, *Operation Neutralize*. January 5, 1968.

Whitaker, B.A., Lt. Col., USAF, and E.L. Paterson. *Assault Airlift Operations*. February 23, 1967.

In 1968 the Air Force embarked on a comprehensive examination of its performance in Southeast Asia. The project, called Corona Harvest, solicited detailed evaluations from each of the major Air Force commands of its successes and problems. These were combined into a final report. Although historical in neither method nor format, these studies provide valuable insights into the details of fighting the war. The following Corona Harvest reports were particularly useful:

A Chronology of Significant Airpower Events in Southeast Asia, 1950–1968, May 1969.

In-Country Air Strike Operations, Southeast Asia, 1 Jan 1965–31 Mar 1968. May 1971.

USAF Airlift Activities in Support of Operations in South Vietnam, Jan 1965–Mar 1968. January 1973.

USAF Reconnaissance in Support of Operations in Southeast Asia, 1 Jan 1965–31 Mar 1968. January 1973.

Intelligence Activities in Support of Operations in Southeast Asia, 1 Jan 65–31 Mar 68. November 1972.

Evaluation of Command and Control of Southeast Asia Operations, 1 Jan 65–31 Mar 68. n.d.

USAF Logistics Activities in Support of Operations in Southeast Asia, 1 Jan 65–31 Mar 68. n.d.

Evaluation of Personnel Support of Operations in Southeast Asia, 1 Jan 65–31 Mar 68. August 1970.

Pacific Air Forces. *Activities Input for Corona Harvest: In-Country and Out-Country Strike Operations in Southeast Asia, 1 Jan 65–31 Mar 68. Vol II: Hardware.* December 1970.

Air Force Systems Command. *Activities Input to Corona Harvest: Acquisition for SEA, 1 Jan 65–31 Mar 68.* February 1970.

_____. *Activity Input to Corona Harvest: Development for SEA, 1 Jan 65–31 Mar 68.* February 1970.

USAF Directorate of Civil Engineering. *Activity Input to Corona Harvest: Civil Engineering Support in SEA, 1 Jan 65–31 Mar 68.* August 1970.

Analyses of the war took place at other levels of the Air Force. In Hawaii, the annual histories of the Pacific Air Forces traced the war's progress in the context of Air Force activities throughout the Pacific. Studies by Operations Analysis shops at all levels—Seventh Air Force, PACAF, the Air Staff—examined specific facets of the air war. More general historical monographs produced at the Office of Air Force History and useful for this volume include:

Anthony, Victory B., Maj., USAF. *The Air Force in Southeast Asia: Tactics and Techniques of Night Operations. 1961–1970.* 1973.

Nalty, Bernard C. *Air Power and the Fight for Khe Sanh.* 1973.

Rowley, Ralph A., Maj., USAF. *USAF FAC Operations in SEA, 1961–1965.* 1972.

_____. *The Air Force in Southeast Asia: FAC Operations, 1965–1970.* 1975.

_____. *The Air Force in Southeast Asia: Tactics and Techniques of Close Air Support Operations, 1961–1973.* 1976.

Van Staaveren, Jacob. *USAF Plans and Operations in Southeast Asia, 1965.* 1966.

_____. *USAF Deployment Planning for Southeast Asia.* 1967.

_____. *The Air Force in Vietnam: The Search for Military Alternatives, 1967.* 1969.

_____. *History of Task Force Alpha, 1 Oct 67–30 Apr 68.* 1969.

Wolk, Herman. *USAF Logistics Plans and Policies in Southeast Asia, 1965.* 1967.

_____. *USAF Logistics Plans and Policies for Southeast Asia, 1966.* 1967.

_____. *USAF Plans and Policies: Research and Development for Southeast Asia, 1965–1967.* 1969.

_____. *USAF Plans and Policies: Logistics and Base Construction in Southeast Asia, 1967.* 1968.
_____. *USAF Plans and Policies: Research and Development for Southeast Asia, 1968.* 1970.

The Joint Chiefs of Staff's view of the war between 1965–1968 is recorded as Parts II and III of *The Joint Chiefs of Staff and the War in Vietnam, 1960–1968.* In addition to containing a well-written text, in the footnotes of these volumes is a wealth of source references, not only for the JCS, but also for all the agencies working with the Chiefs.

The annual histories produced by the United States Military Assistance Command, Vietnam (MACV) are a rich source, not only for the military, but also for the political, economic, and social aspects of the war. At times prematurely dismissed as "company history," these studies contain analyses of the enemy's strategies, tactics, and orders of battle that are being increasingly corroborated by postwar statements of influential North Vietnamese and former Viet Cong leaders. In a French television interview in 1983, for example, General Vo Nguyen Giap conceded that the north decided to move against the south in 1959, a full year before the foundation of the National Liberation Front, and that in the same year regular North Vietnamese units began crossing the Demilitarized Zone. Strong material and moral support of the Viet Cong by the North Vietnamese government from its very inception in 1960 was attested to in 1982 by Truong Nhu Tang, a minister of justice for the Viet Cong's Provisional Revolutionary Government in the 1960s. These revelations and more, constantly denied by the enemy during the war, constitute the assumptions of the MACV histories that gain increasing credibility as more details become known. These histories are based on the invaluable MACV files that are now in the National Archives, Washington, D.C.

In 1968 the Center for Naval Analysis attempted to measure the relative effectiveness of land-based and sea-based aircraft on the war in 1965–66 in a study titled *Analysis of Tactical Aircraft Operations in Southeast Asia, 1965–1966* (CNA Study 712). By limiting itself to basing systems and dismissing technological differences in aircraft types, this study concluded that sea-based aircraft were more effective because, unlike their land–based counterparts, they were mobile, were deployed more rapidly and were flying within days of deployment, and were unhampered by ground logistics. By omitting as irrelevant technological differences in aircraft and aircraft systems, however, the study overlooked those criteria that would have led to quite different conclusions.

Message traffic transmitted by CINCPAC during the war years exists on several hundred reels of microfilm. Unfortunately, the key to the index code is missing, reducing the usefulness of this source. The messages going both east and west through Hawaii were filmed in chronological order by time–date group as they were received or sent. Over ninety-five percent of those messages dealing with Southeast Asia are routine transmissions and of little value to the researcher. The small percent of useful information is more readily obtained elsewhere. These reels reinforce the impression of CINCPAC as a conduit for the passage of information back and forth between Vietnam and Washington.

The files of the Air Force Headquarters Director of Plans from 1965 to 1968 have been critical to this volume. These files have been retired to the Washington National Records Center at Suitland, Maryland. Oral Histories and End of Tour Reports from Air Force participants in the war helped to fill many of the informational gaps that inevitably exist in official documents.

For an understanding of the doctrinal context of many of the issues surrounding the war in Southeast Asia see:

War Department Field Manual 100–20, Command and Employment of Air Power, 1943.

Air Force Manuals 1–2, United States Air Force Basic Doctrine, 1 April 1953, 1954, 1955, and 1 December 1959.

Air Force Manual 1–1, United States Air Force Basic Doctrine, 14 August 1964.

Air Force Manual 1–1, United States Air Force Basic Doctrine, 28 September 1971.

Books

Ballard, Jack S., Lt. Col., USAF. *The United States Air Force in Southeast Asia: Fixed-Wing Gunships, 1962–1972.* Washington, DC: Office of Air Force History, 1982.

Berger, Carl (ed). *The United States Air Force in Southeast Asia, 1961–1973: An Illustrated Account.* Washington, DC: Office of Air Force History, 1977.

Bowers, Ray L., Col., USAF. *The United States Air Force in Southeast Asia: Tactical Airlift.* Washington, DC: Office of Air Force History, 1983.

Buckingham, William A., Jr, Maj., USAF. *The Air Force and Herbicides in Southeast Asia, 1961–1971.* Office of Air Force History, 1982.

Eckhardt, George S., MG, USA. *Command and Control, 1950–1969,* in *U.S. Army Vietnam Studies.* Washington, DC: Department of the Army, 1974.

Fox, Roger P., Lt. Col., USAF. *Air Base Defense in the Republic of Vietnam, 1961–1973.* Washington, DC: Office of Air Force History, 1979.

Futrell, Robert F. *Ideas, Concepts, Doctrine: A History of Basic Thinking in the United States Air Force, 1907–1964.* Maxwell AFB, Alabama: Air University, 1971.

_____. *The United States Air Force in Southeast Asia: The Advisory Years to 1965.* Washington, DC: Office of Air Force History, 1981.

Goldberg, Alfred, and Lt. Col. Donald Smith, USAF. *Army–Air Force Relations: The Close Air Support Issue.* Santa Monica, Calif: Rand Corp, 1971.

Hooper, Edwin, ADM, USN. *A Story of Naval Operational Logistics in the Vietnam War, 1965–1968.* Washington, DC: Department of the Navy. 1972.

Komer, Robert W. *Bureaucracy Does Its Thing: Institutional Constraints on US–GVN Performance in Vietnam.* Santa Monica, Calif: Rand Corp, 1973.

Lane, John J., Jr, Lt. Col., USAF. *Command and Control and Communications Structures in Southeast Asia.* Maxwell AFB, Alabama: Air University, 1981.

Larsen, Stanley R., LTG, USA, and BG James Lawton Collins, Jr, USA, *Allied Participation in Vietnam*, in *U.S. Army Vietnam Studies.* Washington, DC: Department of the Army, 1975.

Momyer, William W., Gen., USAF. *Air Power in Three Wars.* Washington, DC: Government Printing Office, 1978.

Pearson, Willard, LTG, USA. *The War in the Northern Provinces, 1966–1968,* in *U.S. Army Vietnam Studies.* Washington, DC: Department of the Army, 1975.

Ploger, Robert R., MG, USA. *U.S. Army Engineers, 1965–1980,* in *U.S. Army Vietnam Studies.* Washington, DC: Department of the Army, 1974.

Public Papers of the President: Lyndon B. Johnson. Washington, DC: Government Printing Office, 1966–1970.

Rogers, Bernard W., LTG, USA. *Cedar Falls–Junction City: A Turning Point,* in *U.S. Army Vietnam Studies.* Washington, DC: Department of the Army, 1974.

Shulimson, Jack, and MAJ Charles M. Johnson, USMC. *US Marines in Vietnam: The Landing and Buildup, 1965.* Washington, DC: USMC, 1978.

Tilford, Earl H., Jr, Maj., USAF. *Search and Rescue in Southeast Asia, 1961–1975.* Washington, DC: Office of Air Force History, 1980.

Tolson, John J., LTG, USA. *Airmobility, 1961–1971,* in *U.S. Army Vietnam Studies.* Washington, DC: Department of the Army, 1973.

Tregaskis, Richard. *Southeast Asia: Building the Bases, the History of Construction in Southeast Asia.* Washington, DC: Government Printing Office, 1975.

United States–Vietnam Relations, 1945–1967. 12 vols. Washington, DC: Government Printing Office, 1971.

Westmoreland, William C., GEN, USA, and ADM U.S.G. Sharp, USN. *Report on the War in Vietnam (as of 30 June 1968).* Washington, DC: Government Printing Office, 1968.

Index